D1322627

The State and the Nations

Dedicated to the memory of
Donald Dewar

First Minister of the Scottish Parliament
Who died on October 11th. 2000

The State and the Nations

The First Year of Devolution in the
United Kingdom

Edited by
Professor Robert Hazell

IMPRINT ACADEMIC

Copyright © Robert Hazell and contributors, 2000

The moral rights of the authors have been asserted

No part of any contribution may be reproduced in any form without permission,
except for the quotation of brief passages in criticism and discussion.

Published in the UK by Imprint Academic
PO Box 1, Thorverton EX5 5YX, UK

Published in the USA by Imprint Academic
Philosophy Documentation Center
Bowling Green State University
Bowling Green, OH 43403-0189, USA

ISBN 0 907845 80 0

British Library Cataloguing in Publication Data
A catalogue record for this book is available from the
British Library

Library of Congress Card Number: 00-109674

Contents

List of Contributors

John Curtice is Professor of Politics and Director of the Social Statistics Laboratory at Strathclyde University and is Deputy Director of the ESRC Centre for Research into Elections and Social Trends (CREST). A frequent commentator on both Scottish and British politics in the media, he is co-author of L. Paterson *et al, New Scotland, New Politics?* (Edinburgh University Press, 2001).

Robert Hazell is the Director of the Constitution Unit and Professor of Government and the Constitution in the School of Public Policy, University College London (UCL). Originally a barrister, he spent most of his working life at the Home Office. He left Whitehall to become director of the Nuffield Foundation and founded the Constitution Unit in 1995.

Graham Leicester is a political consultant and Director of the Scottish Council Foundation, an independent think tank based in Edinburgh. He heads a team of academics and others in Scotland monitoring the progress of devolution for the Constitution Unit's 'Nations and Regions' programme.

John Osmond is Director of the Institute of Welsh Affairs, a policy think tank based in Cardiff. He is an author, and a former political journalist and television producer. He has written widely on Welsh politics and devolution. His most recent books are *Welsh Europeans* (Seren, 1997) and *The National Assembly Agenda* (Editor, 1998) published by the Institute with contributions from 46 experts on all aspects of the establishment, operation and policies connected with the new Assembly.

Meg Russell is a Senior Research Fellow at the Constitution Unit, University College London (UCL). She is author of *Reforming the House of Lords: Lessons from Overseas* (Oxford University Press, 2000), and various Constitution Unit Briefings and other articles on parliamentary reform. She is leading a project on the Impact of Devolution on Westminster, as part of the Constitution Unit's 'Nations and Regions' Programme.

John Tomaney works in the Centre for Urban and Regional Development Studies at Newcastle University. His research interests include the political economy of regional development and the politics of devolution in England. Among his recent publications is *A Region in Transition: North East England at the Millennium* (Aldershot, Ashgate), edited with Neil Ward.

Rick Wilford is Reader in Politics, Queen's University Belfast. He has written extensively on both devolution and politics in Northern Ireland. His most recent works include the co-edited 'Politics in Northern Ireland' (Westview Press, 1999) and 'Designing the Northern Ireland Assembly', in *Parliamentary Affairs*, July 2000. He is currently researching devolution and health in Northern Ireland as part of the Constitution Unit's wider research programme in this area.

Robin Wilson is director of the Belfast-based think tank Democratic Dialogue, which he founded in 1995. He has been intimately involved for many years in the debates around UK devolution, as well as the specific issues attaching to the Northern Ireland conflict, on which he has written numerous journal articles and book chapters. He was formerly editor of the current-affairs magazine *Fortnight*. He is a member of the Northern Ireland Community Relations Council.

List of Figures

INTRODUCTION

SCOTLAND

WALES

NORTHERN IRELAND

ENGLAND

INTERGOVERNMENTAL RELATIONS

DEVOLUTION AND WESTMINSTER

THE PEOPLE'S VERDICT

LONDON

Foreword

Like all the Constitution Unit's work, production of this book has been a team effort. But in this case the team goes much wider than any we have previously put together: and the reach goes further. It covers the whole of the UK and is intended to be the first of a series of annual reviews, bringing together the fruits of a major five-year research programme into devolution, funded by the Leverhulme Trust. The programme comprises 11 research projects, underpinned by a regular series of monitoring reports. The quarterly reports on devolution can be viewed on the Constitution Unit's website (http://www.ucl.ac.uk/constitution-unit), on the *Nations and Regions* pages. (They can also be received every quarter by email: if you want to go onto the list of email recipients, please write to us at constitution@ucl.ac.uk.)

The monitoring reports are written by teams of experts in Scotland, Wales, and Northern Ireland. From November 2000, there will be a further monitoring team covering the English regions. The leaders of those teams are the authors of the first part of the book. The four chapters on the Nations are written by Graham Leicester and his team in Scotland, John Osmond in Wales, Robin Wilson and Rick Wilford and their team in Northern Ireland, and John Tomaney from Newcastle University. Their chapters are a pleasure to read, offering real insights alongside the hard facts we asked for to make this a volume of record. And as partners they have been a pleasure to work with, delivering their chapters to very tight deadlines, and producing monitoring reports of consistently high quality.

The second part of the book, on the British state, opens with two long chapters on Whitehall and Westminster by members of the Constitution Unit: Meg Russell and myself, with expert assistance from our researcher Roger Masterman. These constitute our first attempt to record and analyse the impact of devolution on the centre. Next year we hope there will be a similar chapter on devolution and the courts. We also plan to include a regular update on devolution and the centre in the quarterly monitoring reports, in order to cover developments in Whitehall, Westminster, the courts, and intergovernmental relations. The closing chapters include an analysis of public attitudes to devolution by John Curtice, and an account of the new arrangements for the government of London by John Tomaney. They have also been wonderful partners to work with and have delivered their chapters to equally tight deadlines.

The whole book has been edited with exemplary calm and efficiency by our Visiting Research Fellow, Elizabeth Haggett, who returns to Whitehall next month to pursue her career as a barrister. Others in UCL who have helped at crucial steps along the way include our excellent administrators, Rebecca Blackwell and Gareth Lewes, our Devolution Research Fellow,

Dylan Griffiths, Sally Welham in the School of Public Policy, and Tony Fincham and his team in Research Administration. The Leverhulme Trust have supported our work with their usual helpfulness and efficiency: our thanks there go to Barry Supple, Alison Cooper, and Tony Clinch, and to their adviser Lord (Kenneth) Morgan. Thanks are also due to Keith Sutherland at Imprint Academic, for publishing the book in record time.

Lastly, a plea to our readers, to help make this book better and better in the years to come. We are aiming to produce an annual volume of record. What key facts and information about devolution would you like us to capture in subsequent years which we have not managed to include in the first year? If you want additional chapters, or additional coverage of certain topics, or just additional figures and data, write to let us know, and we will do our best to include them.

Robert Hazell   School of Public Policy
September 2000   University College London

1

Introduction: The First Year of Devolution

Robert Hazell

1999–2000 was the first year of devolution in the United Kingdom. It was the year in which the first elections were held in Scotland and Wales, powers were then transferred by Westminster, and half way through the year power was also transferred to the new Executive in Northern Ireland. It was the year in which the devolved assemblies and executives gradually found their feet, and the UK Government began to adjust to the realities of devolution.

The United Kingdom entered the year 2000 with four governments instead of one. It had replaced a unitary system of government with a quasi-federal system. This has led to huge changes not just in Scotland, Wales, and Northern Ireland, but also at the centre. Intergovernmental relations are an important feature of the new system of government, with the new Joint Ministerial Committee on Devolution meeting five times in the first six months of 2000 to bring together Ministers from the UK Government and the devolved administrations. Westminster has been slower to adjust, but 1999–2000 saw the beginnings of a debate on how it too needs to adapt to become a quasi-federal parliament.

This book is the story of that first year: of the growing pains of the new assemblies, of their early successes and failures, and of the changes made at the centre as Westminster and Whitehall themselves embarked on an equally painful process of adjustment. The story begins in May 1999 with the first elections to the Scottish Parliament and National Assembly for Wales, and finishes at the end of July 2000, with the end of the first legislative sessions of the devolved assemblies. That is the timeframe for the book: it is the story of the first year of devolution in 1999–2000. But we have gone back a bit earlier in a few chapters, in order to explain the beginning of the story: so that in Northern Ireland the story begins in 1998, with the Belfast Agreement in April and the first elections to the new Northern Ireland Assembly in June. In the chapter on regional government in England, we have reached back briefly to 1996, in order to explain the development of Labour's policy before the 1997 election. And in the chapter on the Greater London Authority, we have started by describing the fragmented system of governance in London.

In order to set out the key events during the first year, most of the chapters open with a chronology. This introductory chapter does the same, but the opening chronological table in Figure 1.1 (page 2) starts with the election of

**Figure 1.1. Key events during the legislative phase
of devolution 1997–1998**

2 May 1997	New Labour government elected with majority of 179.
11 June 1997	Discussion paper on Regional Development Agencies (RDAs) published by DETR.
July 1997	White Papers published on *Scotland's Parliament* and *A Voice for Wales.*
July 1997	Green Paper *New Leadership for London.*
July 1997	Referendums (Scotland and Wales) Act 1997 receives Royal Assent.
September 1997	Referendums held in Scotland and Wales approve White Paper proposals.
October 1997	Greater London Authority (Referendum) Bill introduced.
26 Nov. 1997	Government of Wales Bill introduced into Parliament.
17 Dec. 1997	Scotland Bill introduced into Parliament.
December 1997	White Paper on RDAs *Building Partnerships for Prosperity* published.
March 1998	Regional Development Agencies Act 1998 receives Royal Assent.
March 1998	White Paper *A Mayor and Assembly for London* published.
10 April 1998	Belfast Agreement signed on Good Friday.
April 1998	Launch of North East Constitutional Convention and of Campaign for Yorkshire.
7 May 1998	Northern Ireland (Elections) Act receives Royal Assent.
7 May 1998	Referendum in London approves plans for new Greater London Authority with directly elected Mayor.
22 May 1998	Belfast Agreement endorsed in referendums in Northern Ireland and Republic of Ireland.
25 June 1998	Northern Ireland Assembly elections.
1 July 1998	David Trimble elected shadow First Minister and Seamus Mallon shadow deputy First Minister in Northern Ireland.
15 July 1998	Northern Ireland Bill introduced into Parliament.
31 July1998	Government of Wales Act 1998 receives Royal Assent.
19 Sept. 1998	Ron Davies elected to lead Wales Labour Party in Welsh elections.
30 October 1998	Ron Davies resigns as Secretary of State and Welsh Labour leader. Alun Michael succeeds him as Secretary of State for Wales.
19 Nov. 1998	Scotland Act 1998 and Northern Ireland Act 1998 receive Royal Assent.

the new Labour government in May 1997. Setting out the full sequence of events completes the record, and also helps to underline the speed at which the devolution story has unfolded. It is an extraordinary achievement — to transform a highly centralised unitary state into a devolved and quasi-federal system of government in the space of only three years.

The chronological table is divided into two parts. Figure 1.1 covers 1997–1998, the period of the 18-month first legislative session of the new government when all three devolution bills (to Scotland, Wales, and Northern Ireland) were passed, together with the Act establishing Regional Development Agencies in England. There is then a brief summary of the devolution legislation before Figure 1.2 is presented, covering the implementation phase. Figure 1.2 sets out the key events covered in this book, during the first year of devolution in 1999–2000.

THE DEVOLUTION SETTLEMENT IN SCOTLAND, WALES AND NORTHERN IRELAND

The legislative scheme for devolution is highly asymmetrical. Each of the assemblies has a different size and composition, a different system of government, and a very different set of powers. There follows a very brief and schematic summary of the devolution settlement in Scotland, Wales and Northern Ireland.

Scotland (population 5.1 million)

- Parliament of 129 members, 73 from single member constituencies and 56 additional members, elected every four years;
- Primary legislative powers and full executive powers, and
- Westminster model of Cabinet government: Parliament nominates First Minister, who appoints Scottish ministers.

Wales (population 2.9 million)

- Assembly of 60 members, 40 from single member constituencies and 20 additional members, elected every four years;
- Secondary legislative powers only (UK Government to consult Assembly on proposed primary legislation immediately after each Queen's Speech);
- All Executive functions of Secretary of State for Wales transferred to Assembly, and
- Legislation allows Assembly to introduce either Cabinet system, with Committees scrutinising Ministerial activities; or Committee-based system, with 'Committee leaders' of subject Committees constituting an Executive Committee. In the event the Cabinet system was chosen: the Assembly First Secretary chairs the Cabinet.

Northern Ireland (population 1.7 million)

- Assembly of 108 elected by Single Transferable Vote, 6 members from each of 18 constituencies;
- Primary legislative powers in two categories ('reserved matters' requiring Secretary of State's consent);
- System of weighted majorities to ensure cross-community consent between unionists and nationalists on all major issues;
- First Minister, deputy First Minister and Executive elected by d'Hondt system to ensure distribution of ministerial portfolios between all major parties. Executive Committee not bound by collective responsibility, and
- Committees and their chairmen appointed in proportion to party strengths, to scrutinise and advise on the work of each Executive Minister.

In terms of executive power, the main functions devolved are as follows:

- **To all three administrations**: health, education and training, local government (including finance), social services, housing, economic development, agriculture, forestry, fisheries, food, transport, tourism, the environment, sport, heritage, and the arts.
- **Scotland only**: the legal system, penal matters and policing (these matters may be transferred to Northern Ireland at a later date if the Secretary of State sees fit).
- **Wales only**: the Welsh language.
- **Northern Ireland only**: social security (but the legislation contains mechanisms to ensure parity of benefit rates), employment, and the civil service.

In Scotland and in Northern Ireland, legislative power is also devolved in the subject areas listed above: a very significant devolution of power (greater, for example, than the legislative power enjoyed by the states in many federations). In Wales, there is no devolution of primary legislative powers. The following functions are reserved to the UK Parliament and Government:

- The constitution;
- Foreign affairs;
- Defence, national security, immigration;
- Macro-economics, fiscal and monetary policy;
- Trade;
- Transport safety and regulation;
- Policing, penal matters, and the legal system (in Wales and Northern Ireland);
- Employment legislation (in Scotland and Wales), and
- The civil service (in Scotland and Wales).

In terms of finance, all three administrations are funded by block grant from Westminster. This is uprated annually by the 'Barnett formula', which adjusts their allocations in line with comparable spending adjustments in England. Within the block grant, they have complete spending discretion. In addition, the Scottish Parliament has power to increase or decrease the basic rate of income tax by up to three pence in the pound.

THE ENGLISH REGIONS AND LONDON

Developments in the English regions and London are not comparable with devolution in Scotland, Wales, and Northern Ireland. London has seen the restoration of a strategic metropolitan authority to replace the Greater London Council which was abolished in 1986. But it is a slimmed down version (400 staff in place of the GLC's 20,000), with direct responsibility only for transport, the police, the fire service and economic development. It has no direct revenue raising power, and in other spheres (planning, the environment, culture, and health) the new GLA has a purely strategic or promotional role. As chapter 9 shows, it is a 'weak mayor' model, which relies heavily on the political clout and profile of the directly elected Mayor to bring other agencies to the table.

The Regional Development Agencies (RDAs) established in April 1999 in the eight English regions outside London are weaker still. Being appointed by Ministers in London, they have none of the legitimacy that comes from election. They are also slimline bodies with mainly strategic functions, centred around preparing an economic strategy for their region. They are wholly dependent on central government for their modest budgets, and in terms of powers, functions, and political authority, the RDAs are light years behind the elected assemblies which have been established in Scotland, Wales, and Northern Ireland.

That concludes the brief summary of the devolution settlement. The next part of the chapter sets out the key events during the implementation phase and the first year of devolution in 1999 and 2000: the period which is the main focus in all the chapters of this book.

A SLOW AND SHAKY START

What are some of the main features of the first year of devolution? From a UK perspective, the first year must be judged a success. It has not led to the break-up of Britain, which had been sternly predicted by Conservative (and some Labour) critics. As chapter 6 on Intergovernmental Relations shows, there have been no major rows with the devolved governments: no ministerial walk-outs, no intergovernmental court battles of the kind which can be a

Figure 1.2. The implementation phase and first year of devolution 1999–2000

20 Feb. 1999	Alun Michael narrowly defeats Rhodri Morgan as Welsh Labour leader.
1 April 1999	Regional Development Agencies established in 8 English regions.
6 May 1999	First elections to Scottish Parliament and National Assembly for Wales.
12 May 1999	Alun Michael elected First Secretary in Wales. Appoints minority Labour Executive of seven Assembly Secretaries.
13 May 1999	Donald Dewar elected First Minister in Scotland.
17 May 1999	Labour-Liberal Democrat Executive elected in Scotland of 11 ministers. John Reid succeeds Donald Dewar as Secretary of State for Scotland.
May-July 1999	Designation of 8 Regional Chambers in England. Launch of North West Constitutional Convention.
1 July 1999	Transfer of powers to Scotland and Wales. Scottish Parliament opened by The Queen. National Assembly for Wales opened.
28 July 1999	Paul Murphy succeeds Alun Michael as Secretary of State for Wales.
11 Oct. 1999	Peter Mandelson succeeds Mo Mowlam as Secretary of State for Northern Ireland.
11 Nov. 1999	Greater London Authority Act receives Royal Assent.
29 Nov. 1999	Election by d'Hondt system of 10 Northern Irish ministers to complete Executive of 12 (with First and deputy First Minister).
2 Dec. 1999	Power transferred to Northern Ireland. Executive holds first meeting.
9 Feb. 2000	Alun Michael forced to resign as First Secretary in Wales.
11 Feb. 2000	Peter Mandelson suspends Northern Ireland Executive after 10 weeks of devolution.
15 Feb. 2000	Rhodri Morgan elected First Secretary in Wales.
20 Feb. 2000	Frank Dobson narrowly defeats Ken Livingstone for Labour nomination for Mayor of London.
4 May 2000	Ken Livingstone wins election as London Mayor, standing as Independent.
8 May 2000	Donald Dewar undergoes heart surgery. Jim Wallace (Lib Dem) deputises as First Minister in Scotland.
30 May 2000	Devolution restored to Northern Ireland. Ministers take their places again in power-sharing Executive.

regular feature of federal–state relations. Seen from Whitehall, the mood is one of quiet assurance. The evolutionary, pragmatic approach has paid off; there have been teething troubles, but the UK Government has not been unduly hampered in the conduct of its business; steady as she goes.

But looking at the individual country chapters in this book, a rather different picture emerges. Here, devolution can at best be described as having got off to a slow and rather shaky start. The new Scottish Parliament should be judged a modest success, on the basis of its achievements in its first year in terms of legislation and the work of its committees; but chapter 2 describes how these have been largely ignored by the Scottish press, which, led by the *Daily Record* and *The Scotsman,* has conducted a campaign of extraordinary ferocity against the new parliament. As a result, most Scots have formed a poor opinion of their new parliament, although they would not want to lose it (see chapter 8 on Public Attitudes).

In Wales and Northern Ireland, the picture is much gloomier. The Welsh Assembly can show few tangible achievements for its first year of operation, apart from ditching its Blairite First Secretary, Alun Michael, after its first six months. In part, this is because it enjoys very limited powers: as chapter 3 records, the Presiding Officer has called for a constitutional convention to expand the Assembly's powers, claiming that there is a majority in the Assembly who would like to see it assume full legislative powers much closer to those of the Scottish Parliament.[1] The Labour administration would not agree to such a radical step,[2] but at the end of the first year, the new Leader, Rhodri Morgan, has commissioned a full review of the Assembly's operation, which will expose the differences. This may lead to calls for changes in the Assembly's statutory framework, and in particular for sharper separation of powers, due to the difficulties caused by the fusion in the Government of Wales Act of the executive within the Assembly in a single body corporate.

In Northern Ireland, the picture is bleaker still. In the Executive and the Assembly, the war of attrition continues between the unionist and nationalist blocs, with far more energy devoted to symbolic issues like flags or the renaming of the Royal Ulster Constabulary than to matters of substance like the programme for government or the budget. Chapter 4 vividly records the roller-coaster negotiations which eventually led to the first formation of the Executive in December 1999, its suspension 10 weeks later in February, and then its second coming in May 2000. The new institutions continue to be extremely fragile. The new Executive is an involuntary coalition boycotted by the two ministers from the Democratic Unionist Party and there are no

---

[1] Lord Elis-Thomas, *Wales — A New Constitution*, lecture to Welsh Governance Centre, Cardiff University, 2 March 2000.

[2] The suggestion was advanced again by Plaid Cymru during the negotiations over Labour's new strategy document *A Better Wales*, published in May 2000.

rules of collective responsibility binding ministers. Its support on the unionist benches in the Assembly hangs by a thread, and could vanish if only a few more UUP members decided to join forces with their anti-Agreement colleagues.

David Trimble's worries do not stop there. The year has seen a growing attrition of support for his position within the party membership as a whole. His internal party support has fallen from 72 per cent of the Ulster Unionist Council after the Belfast Agreement in 1998, to 58 per cent at the Council meeting in November 1999, and to an uncomfortable 53 per cent in May 2000. Equally worrying is the growing polarisation reported in chapter 4, with the erosion of support for the moderate unionists and nationalists (broadly speaking, represented by the UUP and the SDLP respectively), and the rise of their more aggressive challengers in the DUP and the other anti-Agreement unionists, and Sinn Fein. Of particular interest in chapter 4 is the explanation of how this hardening of attitudes can be linked to the legitimisation of the (mutually antagonistic) ethnonationalist definitions inscribed in the Belfast Agreement.

The English regions are at a very different stage of development, but here too there is a serious gap between aspiration and performance. The regions have got off to the slowest start of all. They have yet to see the establishment of regional chambers of the kind promised in Labour's manifesto, which would 'co-ordinate transport, planning, economic development, and bids for European funding, and land use planning'; and they have certainly not seen 'legislation to allow the people, region by region, to decide in a referendum whether they want directly elected regional government.' The main achievement so far has been the creation of eight Regional Development Agencies (RDAs), the other strand of regional policy promised in another part of Labour's 1997 manifesto. But, as chapter 5 explains, the RDAs have not been given the full range of functions and power of John Prescott's vision: they have relatively slender budgets, and have been badly over-sold. Denied responsibility for assistance to industry and skills training, they are little more than re-branded urban and rural regeneration agencies. They have devised regional economic strategies, and launched them in glossy brochures, but have few means of delivering them. As for the regional chambers, they have been conjured into being on a voluntary basis, but they have no statutory powers, functions or budgets, and they operate mainly as a sounding board and secondary line of accountability for the RDAs. Although most have called themselves regional assemblies, they are far from being the precursors to directly elected regional assemblies of the kind envisaged by the constitutional conventions now established in the north-east, north-west and the west midlands, or the Campaign for the English Regions, which was launched in 1999 as their umbrella body. They certainly cannot compare in any way with the devolved assemblies in Scotland, Wales and Northern Ireland.

THE NEW POLITICS

However, the devolution story is not all gloom and doom. It was bound to get off to the slow and uneven start that was implicit in the Government's strategy of an asymmetrical, rolling programme of devolution. It is still early days; and even in the first year, each of the chapters has interesting developments to report. As predicted by its advocates, devolution has brought in its train some innovations in democratic practice in all three devolved assemblies. The most important difference from Westminster is the powerful subject committees in the new assemblies which combine scrutiny and legislative roles: functions which at Westminster are carried out by separate Select and Standing Committees respectively. The new committees have not been an unqualified success, with the Welsh committees in particular struggling to find the right balance between their different roles. Chapter 3 records how they have been marginalised from the legislative process in the first year, have failed to hold the executive to account in a comprehensive way, and have not really engaged in policy making. In Scotland, the committees have been fully engaged in scrutinising legislation, but as a result, some of them have found little or no time for scrutinising the other policies or actions of the executive.

Another innovation has been the committees' involvement in the budget-making process. At Westminster, scrutiny of the Estimates is a charade.[3] In Northern Ireland it was no better, with accelerated passage of the first year Appropriation Bill and acceptance of the Estimates announced by the Finance Minister. But in Scotland and Wales, the assembly committees have made a genuine input into the making of the budget. In Wales, 33 budget recommendations came forward from the subject committees, and the Finance Secretary was able to get the draft budget through by responding to 29 of those points and agreeing to the more generous provision of free eye tests. In Scotland one of the first legislative measures was the Public Finance and Accountability (Scotland) Act 2000, which provides for a much more open and consultative budget-making process. The real test of effectiveness will be whether the parliament's input results in reallocation of resources: in particular reallocation between departments and not merely within each department's proposed allocation.

The other big difference from Westminster is that — thanks to the proportional voting systems — no single party has a majority. In Wales, Labour has chosen to govern as a minority administration. In practice, this requires reaching an accommodation with Plaid Cymru on key issues like the strategy document *A Better Wales*; or the free eye tests conceded in the budget. In

---

[3] House of Commons Procedure Committee, Sixth Report 1998-99, *Procedure for Debate on the Government's Expenditure Plans*, HC 295, 20 July 1999; and the previous critical reports referred to in the Introduction to HC 295.

Scotland, Labour governs in coalition with the Liberal Democrats, and has had to agree a programme for government with them which has led to a compromise over student tuition fees. In Northern Ireland, there is a power-sharing executive of four parties brought together in involuntary coalition, who in their first six months (even allowing for discontinuous operation), could not agree on a programme for government; although an interim agenda appeared towards the end of the year.

Proportional representation was also meant to deliver the 'new politics' which would be part of devolution: more inclusive, consensual, and less adversarial than Westminster. In the heady days after the 1997 referendums, there was a lot of aspirational talk about the new politics which was going to characterise the devolved assemblies. Part of the subsequent disillusionment with their performance may stem from the fact that these aspirations were grossly over-sold and were never going to survive the realities of party politics. But although prey to the usual party rivalries, the assemblies practise a different kind of politics from the single party domination which characterises Westminster. Some of the differences are captured in the following chapters, but the essential difference is what is missing: precisely because no single party is dominant, there is none of the triumphalism which characterised the Conservative Government under Mrs Thatcher, or the arrogance and swagger of New Labour under Blair. The siren voices of old Labour in Scotland and Wales, who long to re-assert their party dominance, show how different it could have been; as would the Northern Ireland Assembly if it were governed simply by the unionist majority.

IMPACT ON THE CENTRE: WHITEHALL RULES, WHILE WESTMINSTER FUMBLES

Most of the interest in devolution lies where the action is: in studying the development of the new institutions in Scotland, Wales, and Northern Ireland. Less visible but of equal importance is the impact on the centre, as the UK Government adjusts to the new demands of governing in a quasi-federal system. Two central chapters of the book look at the adjustments made during the first year of devolution by the two main branches of central government: in Whitehall, and at Westminster.

Chapter 6 describes the machinery and procedures put in place by Whitehall to handle intergovernmental relations with the devolved administrations. In the first year, the machinery seemed to work well: the *Memorandum of Understanding* and Concordats negotiated with the devolved governments seem to be accepted as a useful set of ground rules and, even if advance warning and consultation are still sometimes overlooked, the ethos and expectation are there. Smoothly run initial meetings of all the main intergovernmental bodies were held: the Joint Ministerial Committee (JMC) on Devolution, the British–Irish Intergovernmental Conference, the British–Irish Council and the North–South Ministerial Council. Details of all these meetings are given in chapter 6. So far the UK Government has been the dominant partner, convening the meetings and chairing all meetings of the JMC. In their first year the devolved governments have shown no signs of solidarity with each other, of ganging up together against the UK Government in the way that states do against federal governments.

At Westminster, it is a different story. Despite the efforts of the Scottish Affairs Committee and the Procedure Committee to alert their colleagues in the Commons to some of the consequences of devolution, there was no advance game plan. The underlying difficulty was that the Government did not want to admit to any consequences and, in the absence of any strong lead from the Leader of the House, it was left to the Procedure Committee and individual backbenchers to make the running. Chapter 7 describes the debates during the first year as Westminster grappled with the realities of becoming a quasi-federal parliament. For the time being, going partially against the advice of the Procedure Committee, it has decided to retain all the previous structures which enabled Westminster to operate as a parliament for Scotland, Wales, and Northern Ireland. The separate networks of Scottish, Welsh, and Northern Irish Grand, Select, and Standing Committees are to continue, although their functions are now reduced. What has proved much harder is the question of whether to create equivalent structures for England. The Procedure Committee recommended an English committee for legislation applying only to England, but because this raised the uncomfortable issue of English votes on English laws (the slogan adopted by the Conservatives), the Government preferred to duck the question. Instead, it has persuaded the House to revive the Standing Committee on Regional Affairs, a committee open to English MPs only, which last sat during the 1970s and which provided a forum for debates on regional issues.

The other respect in which Westminster is toying with the idea of becoming a quasi-federal parliament is in the debates about reform of the House of Lords. In recommending a minority of elected members for the new second chamber, the Wakeham Royal Commission proposed that they should be elected to represent the nations and regions of the UK. A House of Lords remodelled on these lines might then fulfil the classic role played by second chambers in federal systems, where the second chamber represents the states or the provinces, while the first chamber represents the people. But the debate on Lords reform has a long way to go before this vision is more widely shared, even at Westminster. And amongst the nations and regions who might be represented in this way in the new second chamber, the debate has barely begun.

PUBLIC ATTITUDES TOWARDS DEVOLUTION

Finally, what do the public think about devolution? The first year experience has left the Scots and the Welsh unimpressed by the performance of the new institutions, but unshaken in their commitment to devolution. Chapter 8 summarises the main findings from all the public opinion polls during the first year. By the end of the year, in summer 2000, 60 to 70 per cent of the people in Wales said devolution had not yet made any difference; while almost 80 per cent of Scots said the new parliament had not made any difference to their lives. But these lukewarm responses did not seem to undermine support for devolution itself; if anything the reverse. 43 per cent of people in Wales said in July 2000 that the Assembly should be given law making power, while in Scotland in April no less than 62 per cent of Scots wanted their parliament to have more powers.

In Northern Ireland, it was a different story. Support for the Belfast Agreement waned during the year amongst the unionists, as it became clear that decommissioning of terrorist weapons was not going to be delivered in advance, and the uncomfortable realities of power sharing with Sinn Fein sank in. Unionist support for devolution had never been strong; by summer 2000 it was evenly balanced, with 50:50 for and against the unionists re-entering the power-sharing executive. The year also saw falling support for the Union, with just 56 per cent of people in Northern Ireland in 1999 thinking that the best thing for Northern Ireland's long term future was to remain part of the UK.

In Scotland and Wales, devolution delivered a boost to the nationalist parties, who both saw significant increases in their share of the vote in 1999 compared with their support in elections at Westminster. This devolution differential looks likely to continue, with 15 to 20 per cent more support for Plaid Cymru, and 5 to 10 per cent more support for the SNP, at elections to the devolved assemblies compared with elections to Westminster. But support for the nationalist parties does not necessarily mean support for nationalism, in the sense of separatism or independence. In Wales, in early 2000, one in ten said they wanted independence, and in Scotland one in four: figures little different from pre-devolution levels.

What is different is the demand for more devolution, for the new institutions to be equipped with extra powers, to ensure that devolution makes a difference. In February, no less than 68 per cent of Scots and 62 per cent of people in Wales said they thought further change to the devolution settlements would be needed. This demand for more devolution and for extra powers is the greatest shift in the light of the first year's experience of devolution, and the greatest challenge facing the UK government as it enters devolution's second year.

2

Scotland

Graham Leicester

THE SCOTTISH ELECTION

There was a palpable sense of relief when the new Scottish Parliament was finally elected in May 1999. The two years since the general election had been consumed by endless agonising over the process and prospect of devolution: the White Paper in July 1997[1], the referendum in September, the Scotland Bill in December, and Royal Assent in November 1998 — and all accompanied by the usual frenzy of media speculation and internal politics. For two years it had seemed that Scotland had been placed on hold in anticipation of a new set of institutions, while Tony Blair forged ahead in London with a raft of policy initiatives and task forces.

Figure 2.1. The first year of the Scottish Parliament (Source: GPC Scotland)	
6 May 1999	First Scottish Parliament Elections.
12 May 1999	David Steel elected Presiding Officer.
13 May 1999	Donald Dewar elected First Minister with 71 votes to Alex Salmond's 35, David McLetchie's 18, Dennis Canavan's 3.
14 May 1999	Labour-Lib Dem Partnership for Scotland signed.
17 May 1999	Labour-Lib Dem Executive announced of 11 ministers; John Reid succeeds Donald Dewar as Secretary of State.
18 May 1999	11 junior ministers announced.
16 June 1999	Donald Dewar presents the Government's first legislative programme containing a total of eight bills.
1 July 1999	Scottish Parliament officially opened by the Queen.
2 July 1999	Parliament sets up Independent Committee of Inquiry into Student Finance by 70-48 votes.
5 July–30 Aug	First Parliamentary Summer Recess.
31 August 1999	Mental Health (Public Safety and Appeals) (Scotland) Bill introduced.
13 Sept. 1999	Mental Health etc Act receives Royal Assent.

[1] Scotland's Parliament, Cm 3658, 24 July 1997.

23 Sept. 1999	Labour win Westminster seat of Hamilton South with majority cut from 15,878 to 556 over the SNP.
29 Oct. 1999	Wendy Alexander, Minister for Communities, announces abolition of Section 28.
1 Dec. 1999	Public Finance and Accountability (Scotland) Bill passes all parliamentary stages.
9 Dec. 1999	John Rafferty, Donald Dewar's Chief of Staff, resigns.
21 Dec. 1999	Cubie Committee Report on Student Finance published.
17 Jan. 2000	Public Finance and Accountability (Scotland) Act receives Royal Assent.
27 Jan. 2000	Scottish Executive proposals on abolishing tuition fees agreed by 68-53 votes.
10 Feb. 2000	Budget (Scotland) Bill passes all parliamentary stages. Scottish Parliament votes 88-17 against a Conservative motion supporting retention of Section 28
17 Feb. 2000	Lord Hardie, Lord Advocate resigns. Colin Boyd, Solicitor General, replaces him.
1 March 2000	Scottish Parliament votes 63-59 to endorse the Executive's local government spending settlement.
10 March 2000	Tony Blair, Prime Minister, addresses the Scottish Parliament.
16 March 2000	Conservatives win the Scottish Parliament by-election at Ayr, turning a Labour majority of 25 into a Tory one of 3,344.
20 March 2000	Budget (Scotland) Act receives Royal Assent.
29 March 2000	Adults with Incapacity Bill passes all parliamentary stages.
27 April 2000	Tommy Sheridan's Abolition of Poindings and Warrant Sales Bill passed 79 to 15 with 30 abstentions; general principle of Ethical Standards in Public Life etc (Scotland) Bill including repeal of Section 28 passed 103 to 16.
3 May 2000	Abolition of Feudal Tenure Bill passes all parliamentary stages.
8 May 2000	Donald Dewar undergoes heart surgery; Jim Wallace deputises as First Minister.
9 May 2000	Adults with Incapacity Act receives Royal Assent.

In this context, the Scottish elections on 6 May 1999 were seen as both an opportunity for a new start and the turning point in Scotland's fortunes. It was the first use of the new electoral system in which each voter had two votes: one for the constituency (under the familiar first past the post arrangement) and one for a party list of additional candidates — additional seats allocated by region in order to bring the overall result closer to proportionality. The results, in terms of votes and seats, were as follows — with the May 1997 election result included for comparison:

Figure 2.2. Votes in General Election 1997 and
Scottish Parliament Election 1999

Party	May 1997 election	May 1999 FPTP	May 1999 2nd vote
Labour	46%	39%	34%
SNP	22%	29%	28%
Liberal Democrats	13%	14%	13%
Conservative	18%	15%	15%

Figure 2.3. Seats won in General Election 1997 and
Scottish Parliament Election 1999

Party	May 1997 election	May 1999 FPTP	May 1999 2nd vote	Total May 1999
Labour	56	53	3	56
SNP	6	7	28	35
Liberal Democrats	10	12	5	17
Conservative	0	0	18	18
Other	0	1	2	3

Some of Labour's support migrated to the SNP, the Lib Dems remained static and the Conservatives fell away even from their abysmal showing in 1997. But the effects of the new proportional voting system and the compensatory effect of the second vote made for a radical change in the political landscape. As Figure 2.3 shows:

- The SNP was transformed from a handful of MPs at Westminster into a serious block of 35 at Holyrood: the official opposition;
- Labour failed to win an overall majority of the 129 seats, as was universally predicted, in spite of winning the same number as in 1997;
- The Lib Dems, on an electoral performance no better than in 1997, won 17 seats and the prospect of a share of power with Labour, and
- The Conservatives returned to the political map in Scotland having been wiped out in 1997, but still without winning a single constituency seat.

Three 'others' entered the Scottish Parliament. Tommy Sheridan won a seat in the Glasgow region for the Scottish Socialist Party, Robin Harper won a seat for the Green Party in the Lothians region and Dennis Canavan stood as an independent constituency candidate in his Westminster seat of Falkirk West, having failed to win a place on the official Labour candidate list. He beat the Labour candidate by a mile.

The apparent mismatch between the results in Figure 2.3 interpreted under the old first past the post voting system and the actual effects of those results in terms of seats and responsibility under the new voting system proved a constant source of tension throughout the year — as will become apparent in what follows. But the most immediate consequence was the opening of coalition talks between Labour leader Donald Dewar and his Lib Dem counterpart Jim Wallace.

CABINET MAKING

There had been intense speculation both before and during the election campaign about the nature of the coalition deal that Jim Wallace would strike with Labour, and indeed, whether Labour would go it alone with a minority administration if he set the price too high. In spite of the inevitability of the negotiation that followed the election, the practicalities of coalition-making still seemed to take many people by surprise. Opponents of proportional representation (PR), including at Westminster, argued that the case for PR was undermined by the absence of government for several days after the election. The Scottish media equally showed little patience with the process. And it appears that the Lib Dems themselves were ill-prepared for the negotiations, with little flexibility in their manifesto and a cast iron commitment to 'abolish' student tuition fees in Scotland.

The latter proved to be the major stumbling block. Wallace had strengthened the commitment during the campaign and was boxed in; Dewar could not concede a fundamental policy of the UK Government with considerable knock-on effects for the rest of the UK as his first act as First Minister and even before a blow had been struck in anger in the Parliament. In the event, this first challenge to the 'new politics' was resolved in the time-honoured manner of remitting the issue to an independent committee,[2] to be chaired by the lawyer, Andrew Cubie, previously a member both of the Consultative Steering Group preparing for the Parliament and the McIntosh Commission on local government. In addition, the talks agreed to an increase in spending on education and to 'make progress' on the proposal to introduce PR for local government elections. This was enough to clinch a deal, and a carefully crafted blend of the two parties' manifestos under the title 'A Partnership for Scotland'[3] was duly issued on 14 May, under Dewar and Wallace's joint signatures.

This cleared the way for Dewar to put together the first Scottish Executive — a cabinet of 11 ministers, supported by 11 junior ministers.

[2] Committee of Inquiry into Student Finance, established 2 July 1999. See: www.studentfinance.org.uk.

[3] 'A Partnership for Scotland: An agreement for the First Scottish Parliament', Scottish Executive, 1999.

Figure 2.4. The Scottish Executive appointed in May 1999

Donald Dewar, First Minister of Scotland
Head of the Scottish Executive. Along with the Deputy First Minister, responsible for the development, implementation and presentation of Scottish Executive policies.

Jim Wallace (Lib Dem), Deputy First Minister and Justice
Along with the First Minister, responsible for the development, implementation and presentation of Scottish Executive policies. Responsible for Home Affairs, including civil law and criminal justice, criminal justice social work services, police, prisons and courts, fire and emergency planning, law reform, land reform policy and freedom of information.

Henry McLeish, Minister for Enterprise and Lifelong Learning
Responsible for the economy, business and industry, including Scottish Enterprise, Highlands and Islands Enterprise, tourism, trade and inward investment, further and higher education, the science base, lifelong learning, training and the New Deal.

Wendy Alexander, Minister for Communities
Responsible for social inclusion, local government and housing. Lead responsibility for Executive policy on equality issues and the voluntary sector.

Sam Galbraith, Minister for Children and Education
Responsible for pre-school and school education, children, culture and the arts, the built heritage, sport and lottery funding.

Sarah Boyack, Minister for Transport and the Environment
Responsible for transport including the development of integrated transport policies for rural areas, the environment, natural heritage, sustainable development, strategic environmental assessments and the land-use planning system.

Ross Finnie (Lib Dem), Minister for Rural Affairs
Responsible for policy in relation to rural development including agriculture, fisheries and forestry.

Jack McConnell, Minister for Finance
Responsible for the Scottish budget, including local government finance, European structural funds and resource allocation and accounting. Assists the First Minister and Deputy on the development and co-ordination of Executive policy.

Susan Deacon, Minister for Health and Community Care
Responsible for health policy, the National Health Service in Scotland and community care.

Tom McCabe, Minister for Parliament
Responsible for Parliamentary Affairs and the management of Executive business in the Parliament. Labour Whip.

Rt Hon Lord Hardie QC, Lord Advocate
Responsible for legal advice to the Scottish Executive; prosecution in the Scottish criminal courts; and tribunals.

Junior Ministers

Nicol Stephen (Lib Dem)	Deputy to the Minister for Enterprise and Lifelong Learning with particular responsibility for training, lifelong learning and the New Deal.
Iain Smith (Lib Dem)	Deputy to the Minister for Parliament with particular responsibility for the Parliamentary handling of the legislative programme. Liberal Democrat Whip.
Frank McAveety	Deputy to the Minister for Communities with particular responsibility for local government.
Jackie Baillie	Deputy to the Minister for Communities with particular responsibility for social inclusion. Responsible for co-ordination of Executive policy on equality and the voluntary sector.
Alasdair Morrison	Deputy to the Minister for Enterprise and Lifelong Learning with particular responsibility for Highlands and Islands Enterprise; the University of the Highlands and Islands; Tourism; and Gaelic.
Angus Mackay	Deputy to the Minister for Justice with particular responsibility for land reform and co-ordination of Executive policy in relation to drugs
Peter Peacock	Deputy to the Minister for Children and Education with particular responsibility for schools, educational standards, children and childcare.
Rhona Brankin	Deputy to the Minister for Children and Education with particular responsibility for culture, the built heritage, architecture, the arts and sport.
Iain Gray	Deputy to the Minister for Health and Community Care with particular responsibility for community care spanning health and social work.
John Home Morrison	Deputy to the Minister for Rural Affairs with particular responsibility for fisheries.
Colin Boyd QC	Solicitor General. Assists the Lord Advocate with particular responsibility for prosecutions.

The cabinet was notable for the blend of youth and experience. It contained four ministers under 40, three of them women. In Westminster, these were people who were filling special adviser roles. In Scotland, they were cabinet ministers. It was a bold step. Balancing this youth were the wise old Westminster hands of McLeish and Galbraith, both ministers in the Scottish Office before devolution. The other ministers either retired to the backbenches (Calum MacDonald, Lord Sewel), or moved on to other departments (Helen Liddell, Lord Macdonald), once the old Scottish Office was finally wound up and replaced by the Scotland Office with its new responsibilities under John Reid (see below). Jim Wallace, the Liberal Democrat leader, was installed as deputy First Minister.

The makeup of the cabinet effectively determined the structure of the Executive in terms of departments. There had been much speculation before the election about the opportunities to organise the Executive on more modern, joined-up lines, with fewer departments and more holistic, cross-cutting portfolios.[4] There were certainly some new titles amongst the cabinet — 'Enterprise and Lifelong Learning', 'Communities' and the splitting of the old 'environment' portfolio into two, to allow an extra Lib Dem into the cabinet as Minister for Rural Affairs. Yet the final departmental structure differed little in substance from what had gone before:

Figure 2.5. The new Executive departments

The Scottish Office Departments	Scottish Executive Departments
Home Department	Justice Department
Department of Health	Health Department
Agriculture, Environment and Fisheries Dept	Rural Affairs Department
Development Department	Development Department
Education Department	Education Department
Business and Industry Department	Enterprise and Lifelong Learning Department
Finance Group	Finance
Corporate Services	Corporate Services
Executive Secretariat	Executive Secretariat

The pattern set by the Executive was then followed by the Parliament — again, in spite of months of agonising over how to depart from the Westminster model. The cross party Consultative Steering Group, chaired by Henry McLeish, had recommended that there should be a number of committees established as mandatory and put in standing orders.[5] These were duly established:

---

[4] For example, *Holistic Government: Options for a devolved Scotland*, (Edinburgh: Scottish Council Foundation, 1998).

[5] *Shaping Scotland's Parliament*, Report of the Consultative Steering Group of the Scottish Parliament, (the Scottish Office, December 1998), '…there are certain Committees whose functions are so fundamental to the running of the Parliament that these should be required to be established', see section 3.2, paragraph 60.

- Standards;
- Finance;
- Audit;
- Procedures;
- European;
- Equal Opportunities;
- Public Petitions, and
- Subordinate Legislation.

In addition, the parliament established a subject committee to match each ministerial portfolio, with an additional committee on local government to follow up specific recommendations in that area:

- Transport and Environment;
- Health and Community Care;
- Justice and Home Affairs;
- Enterprise and Lifelong Learning;
- Rural Affairs;
- Social Inclusion, Housing and the Voluntary Sector;
- Education, Culture and Sport, and
- Local Government.

MAKING IT WORK

With structures in place in the Executive and the Parliament, the next challenge was to make them work. As with any new system, there was a good deal of confusion at the start.

It required an initial vote in the Parliament to settle allowances for office support for the MSPs before they could begin to recruit staff or organise any kind of administrative back up. There was a fierce argument about whether those MSPs elected to represent a constituency (constituency MSPs), and those elected from the regional lists as additional members (list MSPs), should be treated equally for the purposes of allowances. Labour, with only 5 per cent of their MSPs coming from the list, argued for markedly lower payments for list MSPs, on the grounds that they would have fewer constituency duties. Others argued for equality of treatment on the grounds that all had been elected to the Parliament under the same system, that list MSPs would arguably have more constituency business since they represented entire regions, and that any other deal would clearly give Labour an advantage over the other parties. When Labour realised it could not command a majority for its position, a deal was struck between the coalition parties for a sliding allowance scale for list members in the same region (the Lib Dems have no more than one list MSP per region). The media had a field day watching the undignified squabble over allowances take centre stage as the first act of the new Parliament.

Ministers in the Executive were also finding their feet. With the Executive's offices based in two central locations in Edinburgh, and one in Glasgow, many found it easier in the early days to base themselves in the Parliament offices. It took a while for working practices and relationships with the civil service to settle down. Now that they have done, several different practices are evident. Some ministers spend more time in the Parliament than others, and it is clear that the chamber is now a vital arena in which to build or damage a political reputation — much like Westminster. That was never true of the old Scottish Office ministers, and is still a factor not fully appreciated by the media and other commentators who are not in touch with the day to day operation of the Parliament and the distinctive culture and camaraderie of the place that has rapidly developed.

The committees of the Parliament also had to find ways of working. Many met initially over the summer to determine their priorities — and rapidly put the small parliamentary clerking service under strain with their requests for information and briefing. The committees were established with broad powers:

- Scrutiny and amendment of legislation;
- Scrutiny of the activity of the Scottish Executive;
- Conduct of inquiries into matters as required by the Parliament;
- Initiating legislation;
- Scrutiny of financial proposals and the administration of the Scottish Executive, and
- Power to call witnesses.

Each committee has struggled to find a balance between these roles. None has yet found the capacity to initiate legislation, leaving the power of initiative firmly in the hands of the Executive — or of events. Thus the Justice Committee has been swamped with legislation and the Education, Culture and Sport Committee has had to devote a disproportionate amount of time to issues that have commanded public attention: the budgeting issues of Scottish Opera/Scottish Ballet[6] and the financing of the national stadium at Hampden Park.[7]

Most members sit on two committees (six members sit on three), each of which has a potentially wide remit. The system has quickly slipped into overload. There is now a growing concern that there are insufficient staff and resources to service the committees and it is clear that the quality of the clerking is a key factor in determining the effectiveness of some committees

---

[6] Education, Culture, and Sport Committee, 1ˢᵗ Report 2000, Report and Inquiry into the National Arts Companies (Scottish Parliament Paper 65), Session 1, 2000.

[7] No report published as yet.

relative to others. The Parliament's cross-party business bureau has been discussing the possibility of merging some of the committees. The Justice Committee, for example, is clearly over-worked, sitting for 70 hours in the first session compared with the 7.5 hours sat by the Subordinate Legislation Committee. But no change has yet been accepted — notably because of the resistance of the convenors of the committees threatened with merger and their political supporters. We are seeing already that a system involving political patronage is very difficult to shift once established.

At the same time, many MSPs are finding that their workload outside committee business is increasing. Increasingly frustrated by being tied to an Executive agenda in the committees, they are forming numerous cross party groups of their own: there were 20 registered by the end of the session and a further 9 proposed (it is a condition of registration that the group should have members from all four main political parties). Also, as the MSPs' efforts to promote themselves in their constituencies have raised their profile, so their mail bags have expanded (with no increase in secretarial resources to match). This has proved true of list MSPs too: many have made a point of nursing constituencies in their region for the next election and all are anxious to promote themselves and their parties as alternative representatives for all the electors in the region. The result is, as one respondent to an annual panel study of MSPs remarked, that within a year, the role of the MSP has gone from being a calling to being a job, and a pretty hard one at that. Ian Welsh, the Labour backbencher and former leader of South Ayrshire Council, was the first to realise this and take action: he resigned from the Parliament barely six months after the election citing the strain of the lifestyle.

THE EXECUTIVE

The pressure on the Executive has been no less intense. The Parliament has made a tremendous impact on workload over the first session — with nearly 8,500 oral and written questions to answer, over 40 ministerial statements and dozens of ministerial or official evidence sessions before committees. As early as November 1999 Donald Dewar chose to make the strains that devolution had imposed on the system of administration one of the themes of his John P. Mackintosh memorial lecture.[8] He noted that more parliamentary questions were put down in the first four months of the Parliament's existence (including during the recess) than in a whole year at Westminster and that there had been a 35 per cent increase in ministerial correspondence. He also voiced some concern about the way that the Parliament's committees were operating, suggesting that if their performance as the essential engine for delivering the Executive's legislative programme could not be improved,

[8] John P. Mackintosh memorial lecture, 9 November 1999, University of Edinburgh.

'some will argue that reform of the House of Lords gives an opportunity to bind Scotland to the UK by giving the second chamber the power to review Scottish legislation'. This partly reflects a frustration that the committees are less predictable than at Westminster. Party discipline is generally weaker, and can be more easily diluted in a four party system when Labour tries to impose its will.

The expansion in the size of the Executive, with a trebling of the number of ministers, has also added to the workload. Operating in a coalition system and with loose control at the centre, officials are tending to copy papers to all ministers in order to make sure information is shared. This too has contributed to slowing the system down. It is now noticeably creaking, and unable to respond even to the simplest routine inquiry in anything under 2–3 weeks. In consequence, ministers are each developing their own parallel systems for getting information and taking decisions quickly — for example, by using their parliamentary e-mail address. This can alleviate the immediate pressure, but it also exacerbates the dysfunctionality of the formal channels. Finally, the well-intentioned wish to increase public involvement has also led to an increased workload, with every minister initiating consultation exercises. By mid-May 2000, it was calculated the Executive had issued more consultation papers than there had been working days in its life. The machinery of government had clogged up.

As a result of all this, there is a growing and palpable sense of frustration amongst many of the key players in the system — ministers, officials, committees, individual MSPs — that the workload has grown beyond all expectations and is neither adequately resourced, nor effectively managed. The system is failing to realise the potential of the talent or the effort of those within it.

LEGISLATION AND POLICY

The Executive's first major statement of policy following the signing of the coalition 'Partnership for Scotland' was the announcement, on 16 June 1999, of the first legislative programme. It consisted of eight bills — an Education Standards Bill, a Transport Bill, an Ethical Standards in Public Life Bill, a Public Finance and Accountability Bill, an Adults with Incapacity Bill, and three bills relating to land reform.

The programme was immediately criticised for being thin and lacking in vision. Indeed, it appears odd in retrospect that the Executive announced it so early, even before the formal transfer of powers and the opening of the Parliament on 1 July. In September, they launched the much more impressive and comprehensive 'Programme for Government'[9] — a detailed list of all the

[9] *Making it Work together: A Programme for Government*, (Scottish Executive, 9 September 1999).

Executive's commitments, department by department, for the four year term of the Parliament. This looked very much like a relaunch at the time, and is now the yardstick by which the Executive chooses to be measured. A first annual report on progress is due in the autumn.

At the same time, events intervened to ensure that the first item of legislation passed by the new parliament was not in the original programme at all. This was the Mental Health (Public Safety and Appeals) (Scotland) Act 1999. In August 1999, Noel Ruddle was released from the state hospital at Carstairs due to a loophole in the law. The loophole prevented his further detention on the grounds that there was nothing that the hospital could do to treat his condition, which was not the one for which he had originally been committed to Carstairs. There was great public disquiet and the responsible minister, Jim Wallace, the deputy First Minister, was placed under considerable media and political pressure. The Executive responded by enacting emergency legislation to close the loophole, allowing sheriffs in future to take public safety into account in making such decisions. The Act was passed on 8 September 1999 and received Royal Assent five days later.

Since then, the Parliament has steadily progressed a series of bills from the Executive. Most remain in committee at the time of writing. In May 2000, the Abolition of Feudal Tenure etc (Scotland) Act and the Adults with Incapacity (Scotland) Act were the first items on the Executive's programme to receive Royal Assent. Both items had long been on the stocks within the Government and the Scottish Law Commission. Their rapid passage into law was a demonstration of one of the primary purposes of devolution — the ability to pass necessary legislation that was squeezed out of the Westminster timetable. The same ease of passage applies to the Census Amendment (Scotland) Act, which gained Royal Assent on 10 April 2000, allowing the insertion of a question about religious affiliation into the 2001 Scottish Census.

Each MSP is permitted to introduce two Private Member's Bills during the term of the Parliament. Initially, this was an option taken up by very few members. By June 2000 however, one year into the Parliament, over fifteen Bills had been presented. This is perhaps a measure of individual MSPs both finding their feet, and feeling that the business of the parliament in which they are invited to and expected to participate is not actually addressing their prime concerns. The growth of cross-party groups in the Parliament is another indication of members seeking to set up structures through which their true interests may be pursued.

One Member who has caused the Executive some discomfort is the Scottish Socialist, Tommy Sheridan. His Private Member's Bill to abolish warrant sales (the forced sale of the possessions of those in debt) was opposed by the Executive on the grounds that, whilst they agreed with the principle, they would rather look at the issue themselves and propose their own solution. In the critical vote on the Stage 1 debate of principle on 27

April 2000, the Executive's amendment to that effect had to be withdrawn when it became obvious in the debate that they could not command a majority for the amendment in the chamber. This was the first major backbench revolt in the Parliament. Significantly, it was the result of a challenge from the left.

COALITION POLITICS

The circumstances of the withdrawal of the Executive's amendment, a decision taken while Lib Dem leader, Jim Wallace, was on his feet defending it, was a rare public reminder of the strains within the coalition. Since the signing of the partnership agreement, the existence of the coalition has, in general, slipped very much into the background. Members of the Executive, for example, still talk about the 'Labour government' in Scotland.

The two exceptions to the rule are the issues of tuition fees and a change in the electoral system for local government. Labour cannot afford to ignore their coalition partners on either.

The £1,000 payment towards tuition fees, payable by students depending on their circumstances, was introduced by the UK Labour Government. In so doing, it failed to take account of the different structure of higher education in Scotland, where four-year degrees, rather than three-year degrees, are the norm. Scottish universities and their students were thus placed at a potential disadvantage. This provided a perfect example of the kind of anomaly that can arise if UK policy is made without reference to Scottish circumstances. Although in the event the UK Government agreed that students resident in Scotland, attending Scottish universities, should have their fourth year fees waived, its refusal to extend the same concession to students resident elsewhere in the UK enabled the campaign for the abolition of tuition fees to wrap a tartan scarf around itself. By the time of the 1999 Scottish election campaign, only Labour was in favour of the retention of tuition fees; all of the other main parties campaigned for abolition.

The issue proved one of the most difficult to resolve in the talks between Labour and the Liberal Democrats that led to the formation of the coalition. The Lib Dems needed to avoid being seen to make a concession in order to secure office on a topic where there was a majority in the Parliament in favour of abolition. Labour did not want to be committed to a change that might undermine the ability of the UK Labour Government to sustain its policy south of the border — where abolition would naturally be far more costly. In the short term, the issue was resolved by appointing a committee under the chairmanship of Andrew Cubie. It reported just before Christmas 1999, with proposals that meant that Scottish students, attending Scottish universities, would not have to pay tuition fees while they were studying, but would have to pay into a graduate endowment fund once they had started to earn a significant income after graduating. [10]

The other difficult policy issue for the coalition is the question of electoral reform for local government. This was endorsed, in principle, by the McIntosh Commission, set up by UK Government in advance of the Scottish elections to advise on local government reform.

The partnership agreement committed the Executive only to 'make progress' on the issue of proportional representation (PR) for local government elections and the issue was remitted to a committee under the chairmanship of Richard Kerley. The committee reported on 27 June 2000 recommending a move to a single transferable vote system. In the year since the committee's establishment, the backlash against PR in the Parliament and amongst predominantly Labour councillors has grown — yet the Lib Dem commitment remains as strong. It remains to be seen how the Executive will cope with this tension. With the SNP in favour of PR, it would only take a change of heart on the part of the Conservatives to leave Labour in a minority on the issue.

In a way, this is a more difficult issue for the coalition to address — since it is about principle more than money and, in the case of Labour councillors, a call for something akin to asking turkeys to vote for Christmas. The next local elections are due in 2002, although Kerley mooted the possibility that they could be moved to 2003 to coincide from now on with the parliamentary cycle.[11] Nobody expects a change in the voting system in time for that: but the Lib Dems at least want to see legislation on the statute book during this term.

THE UNION

In parallel with these efforts to make the system work in Scotland, there has been a steady flow of initiatives designed to make it work in harmony with the rest of the UK. These initiatives are for the most part described in chapter 6 on intergovernmental relations.

In Scotland, the most interesting manifestation of the Union and Union politics is the Secretary of State for Scotland, John Reid. He took over from Dewar in that role at the time of the Scottish elections. In a post which, it is widely assumed, will wither over time, he immediately raised eyebrows by seeking a large budget to staff the department ('The Scotland Office' — to break with the past and avoid confusion) and new premises in Edinburgh and Glasgow.

There was initially undignified jockeying for position with Dewar to see who was the more important to Scotland, notably in the aftermath of the deal

---

[10] *Student Finance: Fairness for the Future*, Final Report of the Independent Committee of Inquiry into Student Finance, (Scottish Executive, 21 December 1999).

[11] Report of the Renewing Democracy Working Group, (Edinburgh: June 2000), chapter 5.

which granted the Kvaerner shipyard in Govan a reprieve from closure. It soon became apparent that the relationship was getting out of hand and only adding to the sense of disarray in Scotland. The Labour machine in London took note. Reid is now much more likely to appear and speak in support of Dewar. See for example the broadcast at the time of Labour's Scottish conference in March 2000 devoted solely to a conversation between Blair, Dewar and Reid — 'team Scotland'. Labour have thus slowly begun to adjust to the new internal politics of devolution.

The legal system has also begun to adjust. It has been made clear, for example, that the Scottish Parliament is a creature of statute open to challenge in the courts if it is seen as infringing the powers granted it in the Scotland Act. In late autumn 1999, the Countryside Alliance took Labour backbencher Mike Watson MSP to court in order to halt the progress of his Protection of Wild Mammals Bill, a Private Member's Bill introduced to ban hunting.[12] The Alliance claimed that he was, in effect, contravening the Scotland Act because he had breached the Parliament's standing orders by accepting help in drafting the bill without declaring it. The action was rejected in the Court of Session by Lord Johnson at the end of November 1999:

> What I consider is being attempted by the petitioners is to achieve, by a roundabout method, the obstruction of the legitimate presentation of a Bill to the Parliament which must be allowed to regulate its own affairs and determine whether or not, in its opinion, the member is competent to present it.[13]

The Countryside Alliance appealed the judgement and the case was thrown out in the appeal court. However, the judge, Lord Rodger, was at pains to point out that this did not mean that the Parliament, like Westminster, was above the law:

> It is a body which, like any other statutory body, must work within the scope of those powers. If it does not do so, then in an appropriate case the court may be asked to intervene and will require to do so.[14]

The case launched by *The Scotsman* newspaper in September 1999 provides a further example of people being willing to use the courts to exercise some influence over the Parliament and its activities. The newspaper lodged a petition before the Court of Session, seeking to force the Standards Committee to hold its enquiry into the 'lobbygate' affair (see below) in public.[15] In the event, the case was withdrawn by *The Scotsman* after the Committee reversed its decision to meet in private. These cases are the first signs of a

[12] *Whaley v Lord Watson* [2000], Session cases 125, page 133.
[13] *Ibid.*
[14] *Ibid.* page 348.
[15] *Scotsman*, 26 September 1999.

propensity to use the courts to challenge and influence the Parliament and its output — a pattern that was widely predicted and that may well increase once the Parliament starts to produce more legislation and regulation.

There have also been repercussions in Scotland as a result of the fact that the European Convention of Human Rights (ECHR) was incorporated into Scottish law in the areas of devolved powers by the passing of the Scotland Act. Thus it became binding on the Scottish Executive on 1 July 1999, before the rest of the UK. This has already led to two wide-ranging judgements with implications for the rest of the UK. First, the Court of Session in Edinburgh upheld an appeal by a lawyer who argued that temporary sheriffs were not 'independent and impartial' (as required by Article 6 of the ECHR) because their contracts are only for one year and they can be hired or fired by the Lord Advocate, not only a member of the Scottish Executive but also head of the Scottish prosecution service.[16]

Later in the year, Lord Rodger and two other judges decided in the Appeal Court that section 172 of the Road Traffic Act 1988, which gives police powers to demand the identity of the driver of a car from the registered keeper of the vehicle if the driver is not caught at the time of the offence, infringed the right to silence and the right against self-incrimination contained in the ECHR.[17] The decision is being appealed to the Privy Council by the Crown, which fears the potential consequences of the decision, particularly for the use of speed cameras.

Beyond these occasional court cases arising out of devolution and clarifying the position in Scotland, there remains great confusion over who is responsible for what under the Scotland Act. A constant flow of parliamentary questions seeks to explore the devolved/reserved boundary — often with little success. The boundary will be established in practice rather than in theory.

POLITICS AND PERSONALITIES

Finally, we turn to the aspect of the Scottish scene that has changed most considerably over the year since the first elections to the Parliament in May 1999: the daily substance of Scottish politics, the personalities that fill the scene, and the media who report it.

One very clear consequence of devolution in Scotland has been a reinforcement of what some have called 'informational politics'[18] — in which the media is the arena in which politics takes place.

Already by early September 1999, the Presiding Officer of the Parliament, Sir David Steel, felt moved to make a high profile speech defending the new

---

[16] *Starrs and Chalmers v Ruxton* (1999) SCCR 1052.

[17] *Brown v Procurator Fiscal* (2000) SLT 379.

[18] See, for example, Castells, M., *The Power of Identity*, (Oxford: 1997).

institution against the press.[19] He had been upset by the tone and substance of reporting which had dwelled on arguments about the costs of the new system, the debacle over MSPs' allowances, the long summer holiday (they broke a few days after the grand opening), and the fact that MSPs had been given a commemorative medal to mark the 1 July ceremony as if they had already performed great service to the nation. Singling out the tabloids and in particular the *Daily Record,* Scotland's biggest selling daily, Steel hit the headlines with his condemnation of an excessive interest in personalities and non-issues which he described as 'bitch journalism'. Complaints referred by Sir David to the Press Complaints Commission were not upheld and, predictably, his strictures led to several papers accusing him of seeking to gag freedom of expression and cover up the legislature's failings.

The Parliament was also severely tested by the so-called 'Lobbygate' scandal, which hit the fledgling institution shortly after the Steel debacle. At the heart of the row was the allegation, made in an *Observer* story,[20] that a prominent firm of lobbyists, Beattie Media, could improperly influence ministers. Beattie employed Kevin Reid, son of the Secretary of State for Scotland, John Reid, as a lobbyist. The company had previously employed Jack McConnell, Minister of Finance, in a public relations capacity. The alleged relationship between Beattie Media and McConnell occupied centre-stage, although other ministers faced various accusations of possible impropriety. The issue came before the Parliament's Standards Committee. The convenor, Mike Rumbles MSP, initially decided on a private discussion, a position that was quickly changed as the potential damage to the Parliament's reputation became clear, and as the committee decided to pursue a detailed inquiry. Not surprisingly, 'Lobbygate' became a major story, with much reporting and commentary on 'sleaze' and the need to avoid Westminster's failings. In the event, the Committee exonerated all ministers named of any wrongdoing — but the affair certainly knocked the Executive off course and damaged the reputation of McConnell before he found his feet in office.

Worse was to come. In December, just before Christmas, John Rafferty, Dewar's chief of staff, head of the Policy Unit and architect of the Scottish election victory, was forced to resign following allegations that he had falsely briefed journalists that the Health Minister had received death threats due to her pro-abortion stance. This was not only a very public falling out between two old friends (Dewar's reluctance to explain the full details of how such a trusted colleague could forfeit that trust in an apparently minor incident merely fuelled the conspiracy machine), it also left a gaping hole at the heart of the government machine. Just a few weeks later, Philip Chalmers, one of Rafferty's former colleagues in the Policy Unit, also

---

[19] Sir David Steel, *Who speaks for the People of Scotland?,* A Speech to the Church and Nation Committee of the Church of Scotland on 6 September 1999.

[20] 'Exposed: Lobbygate comes to Scotland', *The Observer,* 26 September 1999.

resigned, having been convicted of drink-driving over Christmas. Neither Rafferty nor Chalmers was replaced, leaving a Unit that was already some way short of full strength, struggling to inject any coherence into the Executive as a whole. By the end of January 2000, *The Scotsman's* headline was simply 'Scottish Executive in Disarray.'[21] Shortly thereafter, on the eve of the Lockerbie trial, the Lord Advocate, Lord Hardie, resigned in order to become a judge.

Just as the Executive seemed to be riding out the storm, a new tempest began to rage. In autumn, the Communities Minister, Wendy Alexander, had announced that the Executive proposed to abolish 'Section 28' in Scotland — the clause that prohibits local authorities from 'promoting' homosexuality. Some time later, a similar announcement was made by the UK Government in respect of the law in England and Wales. This was another example of Scottish Labour trying to steal a march on colleagues south of the border. Initially, the proposal caused little trouble, and indeed the Executive's consultations saw more submissions in favour than against. But in the New Year, a potentially powerful coalition began to come together: the *Daily Record* (the largest selling paper in Scotland and usually staunchly pro-Labour), Cardinal Winning (the head of Scottish Catholics, who are more likely to vote Labour), and Brian Souter (one of the owners of the highly successful Stagecoach bus company and a member of the Church of Christ the Nazarene, equipped with the money to fund an anti-abolition campaign).

No less than four polls were published on the subject in the third week of January 2000.[22] Although some of the questions suggested that Scots accepted that children should be taught about homosexuality in schools and that they were prepared to tolerate homosexuality, all found, irrespective of their wording, around a two to one majority against the abolition of a clause that appeared to offer protection against the actual promotion of homosexuality. It was immediately apparent that a body which had been created in order to ensure that public policy was more attuned to the needs and wishes of Scots had, in fact, embarked on a change to which the clear majority of the Scottish public was opposed, including, not least, the many who voted for the parties in the Executive.

Souter then organised his own referendum, distributing voting slips to every person on the electoral roll. He claimed victory when 86.8 per cent of the 34.5 per cent who returned the slips voted to keep the clause. In spite of the result the Executive kept its nerve and, on 21 June 2000, finally passed

---

[21] 27 January 2000.

[22] Section 28 polls:

Publication Date	Pollster/Publication	Support repeal	Oppose repeal
21/1/00	Scottish Opinion/*Mail*	30	50
23/1/00	MORI/*Sunday Herald*	36	60
19/1/00	Scottish Opinion/*Record*	34	66
23/1/00	ICM/*Scotland on Sunday*	31	64

into law the Act repealing the clause. The midwives of a 'new politics' in Scotland and of a more participative, accessible democracy were left with much to contemplate from the whole episode.

In the middle of this turbulence, on 25 April 2000 it was revealed that Donald Dewar had been diagnosed with a leaking aortic heart valve and would have to step down temporarily to have an operation from which he would take six to eight weeks to recuperate. The news merely brought into the open a debate that had been taking place in private since Christmas — about the need for a change of leadership at the top. Enterprise Minister, Henry McLeish, sought to impress upon the media that he had been given special responsibility to mind the shop in Dewar's absence. The prospects of other leading contenders for the succession were aired in a flurry of media profiles. It thus came as something of a shock to all concerned that Jim Wallace, the Lib Dem deputy First Minister, would in fact fill the principal role until Dewar returned. This he did competently, revealing the advantage of long experience in the Commons, and perhaps issuing a sharp reminder to his cabinet colleagues (if not to the public, who have noticed nothing amiss to find a Lib Dem leading the country) that they are members of a coalition. Dewar returned to his role after the summer recess. None of the leadership hopefuls shone in his absence, suggesting to some commentators that his eye may now perhaps fall on someone outside the present cabinet to groom for the succession.

THE PUBLIC

Throughout the year there have been regular opinion polls to test the progress of the parties. There have also been two by-elections. The opinion polls suggest a slight shift over the year away from Labour, its Lib Dem coalition partner and the Conservatives, to the SNP or to the smaller parties.

The full figures from System 3/*Herald* polls, for Holyrood and Westminster, are shown in Figure 2.6. The most significant tests of political opinion have been the two parliamentary by-elections: in Hamilton South caused by the elevation to the peerage of sitting Labour MP George Robertson and, in Ayr, caused by the resignation of sitting Labour MSP Ian Welsh. In the first of these, on 23 September 1999, Labour came close to losing one of the safest Westminster seats in Scotland. On a 41 per cent turnout, Labour beat the SNP by just 556 votes. This was a bad night for all the main parties bar the SNP. The Conservatives were forced into fourth place behind the Scottish Socialist Party candidate. The Lib Dems finished sixth behind a man standing in the name of the local football club.

The second by-election was in a seat that Labour had only just managed to win in the 1999 election, after several recounts, over the sitting Conservative

Figure 2.6. Party fortunes: System 3/*Herald* poll

Holyrood vote intentions

Vote	Con 1	Con 2	Lab 1	Lab 2	LD 1	LD 2	SNP 1	SNP 2	Others 1	Others 2
May election	16	15	39	34	14	12	29	27	3	11
November	9	10	44	33	11	14	30	30	6	13
December	8	9	43	37	9	12	34	33	6	10
January	11	9	42	34	10	14	31	31	6	12
February	12	11	37	32	9	13	36	33	6	11
March	14	11	33	29	11	15	37	34	6	11
April	14	13	34	30	10	14	35	31	8	13
May	13	11	40	31	10	13	30	33	8	13
June	12	11	33	27	12	16	36	35	6	12
July	11	11	37	33	10	12	35	30	6	14

Scottish Socialist Party running at around 5% of 2nd vote

Westminster vote intentions

	Con	Lab	LD	SNP	Others
November	12	50	13	24	2
December	12	50	9	27	2
January	14	49	11	24	2
February	15	45	11	27	3
March	16	40	11	29	3
April	17	44	9	26	3
May	14	48	10	24	4
June	17	39	11	31	3
July	15	46	9	26	4

Polls normally taken at end of month. December = early January

Westminster MP Phil Gallie. Gallie decided not to stand again, since he had, in the event, entered the Scottish Parliament through the list and did not want to create the impression with voters that he felt in any need of 'trading up'.

The poll took place on March 16 2000. John Scott gained the seat for the Conservatives. The SNP came second, beating Labour into third place. The Scottish Socialist Party secured fourth place and the Lib Dems were again squeezed into minor placings with only 800 votes.

Overall, it has been a mixed first year, challenging for all four main political parties. The presence of the SNP as official opposition has been the major consequence of devolution. They have struggled to make the transition. SNP leader Alex Salmond has had to give some of his more able colleagues — like John Swinney and Roseanna Cunningham — their head, at the risk of them outshining the leader. There has also been continued dissent within the ranks

Figure 2.7. Scottish Parliament by-election. Ayr. 16 March 2000

		Votes	%	Ch since 1999	Ch since 1997
Scott	Con	12,580	39.4	+ 1.4	+ 5.6
Mather	SNP	9,236	28.9	+ 9.4	+16.4
Miller	Lab	7,054	22.1	−16.0	−26.3
Stewart	SSP `	1,345	4.2		
Ritchie	LDem	800	2.5	− 1.9	− 2.2
Corbet	Green	460	1.4		
Botcherby	Ind. Vet	186	0.6		
McConnachie	UKIP	113	0.3		
Graham	Pro-Life	111	0.3		
Dillon	Anti-Clone	15	0.0		
Turnout			56.6	− 9.9	−23.6

as the reality of incrementalism sinks in. The general election anticipated in 2001 threatens to be a difficult one for the SNP. The SNP's support is lower for Westminster than for Holyrood (see Chapter 8), and all of its current Westminster MPs will be standing down in seats where the Tories, not Labour, are the main opposition. The coming year looks like one of damage limitation for the SNP — perhaps one of the reasons why Alex Salmond chose to stand down as leader of the party, after ten years at the helm, shortly after the first anniversary of devolution.

In contrast, more Scots seem willing to vote for Labour at Westminster than at Holyrood. Thus, for Labour, the challenge is to increase support for MSPs in Scotland, while at the same time showing enough distinctiveness from new Labour in the south. Labour was slow to realise the damaging effect of allowing personal rivalries in Edinburgh and London to get out of hand. Labour's challenge is internal.

The next general election in Scotland will also test how far the Tories have really travelled since the debacle of 1997. They have played a shrewd game at Holyrood with little reward: their fate still seems linked to Hague and London in a way that many openly acknowledge is 'killing us in Scotland'.

The Lib Dems have struggled to make an impact since the 1999 elections. Power sharing in the Executive has absorbed a lot of the party leadership's energies and has, at times, left backbenchers and grass-root supporters confused about their role. If the Lib Dems are able to concentrate their support in winnable seats at the general election, they could at least hang on to what they have — providing a valuable boost to their credibility as a distinctive voice in Scotland.

PUBLIC PERCEPTIONS

There have been a number of major polls[23] over the course of the first year of devolution that have, in various ways, measured how devolution in principle and/or the new institutions in practice are regarded by the Scottish public. In particular, in February 2000, *The Scotsman* newspaper conducted a major exercise, in which it interviewed 500 people in each of England, Scotland, and Wales in order to examine how the public was reacting to devolution in each of the component parts of Great Britain.

While the Scottish media has been consumed by the alleged failings of the new institutions, the public, it appears, has been underwhelmed by the impact of devolution. Only 5 per cent of Scots believe that the new Parliament has achieved a lot (although around two-thirds are prepared to acknowledge that it has done a little). In the February poll, no less than 41 per cent thought that the Parliament had made no difference. On 29 June, that figure rose to 78 per cent in the System Three poll for the *Herald* on the occasion of the Parliament's anniversary.

The Scotsman poll, in particular, revealed the degree to which Scottish Executive ministers have a lower profile than their UK counterparts. On average, only around two-thirds of Scots have heard of the five Scottish ministers with the highest levels of public recognition. In contrast, well over nine in ten people in England say they have heard of the five UK cabinet ministers with the highest levels of recognition. Amongst Scottish ministers, those who had previously been at Westminster (and had been Scottish Office ministers) all had higher recognition factors than any of the new ministers. It may be that longevity in office will help raise the profile of Scottish ministers. On the other hand, the more limited media opportunities available to Scottish ministers compared with their UK counterparts may mean that the biggest challenge facing the new institutions is to impinge themselves on the public consciousness at all.

Some of the evidence suggests that the perceived performance of the new institutions has helped to undermine support for devolution. Support for devolution, rather than for independence or no parliament, fell from 54 per cent the previous month to 46 per cent in February 2000. But if Scots are beginning to wonder about the effectiveness of the devolution settlement — and no less than two-thirds think that further change will be required — it appears that the reaction is more likely to be to want to make the body more effective, rather than let it wither away. No less than 62 per cent told System Three, in April 2000, that they want the Parliament to have more powers. While in the event it may remain the case that most Scots do not want to leave the UK, it appears that they may well demand that the Parliament is made

---

[23] ICM/The Scotsman, Feb 2000; NOP/Sunday Times May 2000; System 3/Herald, June 2000. For further details, see chapter 8.

more powerful if it is not seen to be meeting their needs. The degree to which this happens may be the real focus of the constitutional debate in Scotland in future years.

CONCLUSION: WHAT NEXT?

At the end of the first year, the impression is of a new system that is steadily settling down into operation. The initial sources of tension are receding. Labour in London and Labour in Scotland seem better co-ordinated than they were a year ago, and more attuned to the fact that they depend on each other for success in both the Westminster and the Holyrood elections to come. The improved relationship has no bearing, of course, on how things might be with governments of different parties either side of the border, but it is at least progress in the right direction. The media have laid off the Parliament itself as the focus of their criticism: the Parliament is now left to get on with its work in peace, with individual issues — rather than the general performance of the institutions — dominating the headlines (as they have always done). And a steady stream of useful, if unexciting, legislation has begun to emerge, along with some insightful committee reports on issues such as economic development. These are pluses that would not have been available without the Parliament.

If there is cause for concern, it lies in two features. The first is the corrosive small-mindedness of the Scottish press and Scottish politics. In a country the size of Scotland the media is a particularly important echo-chamber for political life. This is not least because there has always been an intimate relationship between the media and party politics in Scotland, and also because Scots are avid consumers of their home-grown newspapers. In the broadsheet market, *The Scotsman* is now fighting for its life, not only against the Glasgow *Herald,* but also against the threat of a new broadsheet that is due to be launched in the autumn. In the tabloid market, the competition is even more intense. There are worrying signs of a race to the bottom, which will do nothing to raise the tone of political debate. Although granted the tools to forge a new politics, the press in particular have continued to play the old game, and the politicians have done little to prompt anything different.

The second feature is the general and palpable frustration of many of the principal actors in the system — a sense that the system is consuming so much of their waking lives for so little visible result. The system is 'running on the spot'. That frustration is felt by ministers who cannot force through innovations and who blame their civil servants; by civil servants who cannot find any coherence in fragmented ministerial policy driven by press releases, glossy initiatives, and set piece speeches; by the Parliament's committees either tied down with government legislation or else daunted by the scope of their remit and with an inability to prioritise; by individual MSPs living an itinerant lifestyle based more around the demands of local newspapers and the constituency mailbag than the vision they hold of a better Scotland.

That suggests two scenarios for the future. The first is more of the same. The Executive will continue on its course, implementing the Programme for Government, putting off the difficult choices — PR for local government, genuine change in the education system, effective and timely action to catch up with the digital revolution — until the day after the next Scottish election and a change of faces at the top. The Parliament will fail to establish itself in the public mind, more MSPs will become disillusioned and move on, and the feeling will grow — as local democracy is reinvigorated with the first mayoral elections in England — that perhaps the Parliament was, after all, the wrong institution at the wrong time.

Alternatively, we could see a fresh start. The gear wheels in the machine could finally slip into place. A good many people in the system may be determined to make more effective use of their time when they return for the new term; Dewar will be back with a new enthusiasm and the laptop he learned to use during his convalescence; the purse strings might just loosen a little in the run up to the general election; and as the Executive begins to focus on delivery rather than glossy consultation documents, it could become smaller and more strategic, cohesive, and confident in its dealings with the press.

BIBLIOGRAPHY

Castells, M., *The Power of Identity* (Oxford: 1997).

Education, Culture, and Sport Committee, Report and Inquiry into the National Arts Companies, Scottish Parliament Paper 65, Session 1, 2000.

Harvie, C., and Jones, P., *The Road to Home Rule: Images of Scotland's Cause* (Edinburgh: Polygon, 2000).

Hassan, G., and Warhurst, C., *The New Scottish Politics: the first Year of the Scottish Parliament and beyond* (Edinburgh: The Stationery Office, 2000).

Holistic Government: Options for a Devolved Scotland (Edinburgh: Scottish Council Foundation, 1998).

Making it Work together: A Programme for Government (Scottish Executive, 9 September 1999).

Report of the Renewing Democracy Working Group (Edinburgh: 2000).

Shaping Scotland's Parliament, Report of the Consultative Steering Group of the Scottish Parliament (The Scottish Office, December 1998).

Student Finance: Fairness for the Future, Final Report of the Independent Committee of Inquiry into Student Finance (Scottish Executive, 21/12/1999).

Taylor, B., *The Scottish Parliament* (Edinburgh: Polygon, 1999).

3

A Constitutional Convention by Other Means

The First Year of the National Assembly for Wales

John Osmond

The first year of the National Assembly was experienced around the hinge of Alun Michael's resignation as First Secretary on 9 February 2000. Until then, the Assembly's life was constrained by an imagination that saw devolution operating essentially within a British context, rather than one that sought the freedom to express a Welsh point of view. As the Presiding Officer, Lord Elis-Thomas, graphically put it following the no confidence vote: 'This is the first day of devolution'.[1]

To the surprise of most commentators, Labour had failed to achieve a majority in the first elections to the Assembly in May 1999. What became known as the 'quiet revolution' resulted in Labour losing such strongholds as Islwyn, Rhondda and Llanelli to Plaid Cymru. Labour fell three seats short of the 31 it needed to form a majority government.[2] The outcome provided the platform for the Assembly becoming, in its first year, a constitutional convention by other means. Labour was forced to come to terms with the other parties in a process of negotiation and accommodation that was entirely novel to Welsh politics, though the process had begun informally between the three pro-devolution parties in the 1997 referendum.

A key forum for these discussions was the Assembly's business committee where the business managers of all the parties meet under the chairmanship of the deputy Presiding Officer, Jane Davidson. A pattern of negotiated planning of the Assembly's business was quickly established as soon as Labour was made to realise that it could not automatically command a majority. Indeed there has never been a vote in the business committee, which has generally operated by consensus. It was an important mechanism used by the parties to feel their way through the constitutional complexities of the new institution. The Assembly was established as a corporate body, combining its legislative and executive functions rather than separating them as is normal in parliamentary institutions. Many of the tensions that arose in the first year

---

[1] *Western Mail*, 10 February, 2000.
[2] For a detailed analysis of the result see: John Osmond, *Welsh Politics in the New Millennium*, IWA, August 1999.

Figure 3.1. Key events in the Assembly's first year

6 May 1999	In the Assembly's First General Election Labour wins 28 of the sixty seats but with no overall control. Plaid Cymru comes second with 17 seats, the Conservatives third with nine seats and the Liberal Democrats fourth with six.
11 August 1999	Resignation of Conservative Leader Rod Richards following a charge of serious grievous bodily harm (he was later acquitted). Nick Bourne elected to replace him.
19 October 1999	Motion of censure passed by 30 votes to 27 against Agriculture Secretary Christine Gwyther over her handling of a calf re-processing scheme which had been supported by the Assembly but proved to be illegal under EU regulations.
1 December 1999	Assembly's first budget approved with an agreement to make provisions for extending free eye tests, widely interpreted as Plaid Cymru's price for abstaining.
9 February 2000	Vote of no confidence in First Secretary Alun Michael passed by 31 votes to 27 with one Labour abstention. Cabinet votes in Rhodri Morgan as acting First Secretary.
1 March 2000	Pre-16 Education Committee resolves to take its own legal advice on whether the Assembly has powers over the introduction of Performance Related Pay for teachers.
13 March 2000	Cabinet Minutes published on Assembly's website at www.wales.gov.uk.
10 May 2000	Administration's Strategic Plan *BetterWales.Com* launched, setting out aspirations to be achieved by 2010. Plaid Cymru endorsed a three-page introduction.
24 May 2000	Following the discovery that GM seeds had been sown in field in Flintshire the Assembly declares its wish to limit GM crops growth in Wales as far as possible.
21 June 2000	Majority of Assembly Members, including Labour backbenchers, voted against Cabinet to press ahead with £23m Richard Rogers design for the Assembly Chamber.
4 July 2000	NUT brings successful High Court action against the Secretary for Education and Employment on the legality of DfEE regulations for performance related pay for teachers. The judgement suggests that the Assembly has a right of consultation by the DfEE.
18 July 2000	The Comprehensive Spending Review allocates an extra £421m over three years to match fund for EU Structural Funds for West Wales and the Valleys, breaking the Barnett formula.
23 July 2000	Rhodri Morgan replaces his Agriculture secretary, Christine Gwyther with her deputy, Bridgend AM Carwyn Jones.
3 August 2000	Ieuan Wyn Jones wins Plaid Cymru leadership election following resignation of Dafydd Wigley.

arose as a result of this conundrum. Significant forces, not least emanating from the Presiding Officer himself, sought to prise the executive and the legislature apart. In addition, further tensions arose from Members continually testing the extent of their powers. In practice, these were heavily circumscribed by Westminster continuing to hold not only the purse strings, but primary legislative power as well. In many ways, the first year was about new Members, many of them politically inexperienced, getting to know each other and their way around, and on the whole discovering the limitations rather than the opportunities of their new role.

The result was a good deal of frustration that, from time to time, boiled over, and none more dramatically than in the drama that unfolded in the vote of no confidence in Alun Michael. The immediate cause of his rejection was a long-running argument over the issue of Treasury match funding for EU support for the west Wales and Valleys region. The question had featured prominently in the first elections for the Assembly. Since then, all three opposition leaders had signalled it as the most important issue to face the Assembly in its first term. At stake was securing around £1.2 billion from the EU Objective One Structural Funds to be spent over the seven year period 2000–2006. The funds could only be drawn down, however, if they were matched by roughly an equivalent amount, mainly from the public sector.

To a great extent — which grew larger as the moment for taking the no-confidence vote came nearer — the argument over Objective One, though real enough, was a pretext for an underlying and more fundamental disaffection — that with the style and character of Alun Michael's leadership. The essence of the problem emanated from the Labour leadership contest between him and Rhodri Morgan in early 1999, in which Morgan won the support of the constituencies, but lost on the basis of the trades union block vote. It was noteworthy that a majority of the Labour group in the Assembly, estimated to be as many as 21 of the 28 AMs, had been Morgan supporters. In any event Michael was widely perceived to be the choice of London rather than Wales which, many Labour activists believed, had contributed a great deal to the party failing to win a majority in the Assembly elections.

More fundamentally, however, the position adopted by Alun Michael towards the 'devolution process' was ambivalent. In November 1999 he gave the clearest expression of his views in a keynote lecture at Aberystwyth. He asked the following question: 'What form of government best advances Wales's needs? Centralised power in Westminster? Devolution? or Separatism?' [3]

In response, he said the middle option — devolution — was not some kind of no-man's land between the other two. Rather it was a place in its own right. Further he agreed fundamentally with Paul Murphy, the Secretary of State

---

[3] Alun Michael, *The Dragon on our Doorstep: New Politics for a New Millennium in Wales*, Institute of Welsh Politics, University of Wales, Aberystwyth, November 1999

for Wales, that devolution was a settled matter: 'We have settled the devolution debate. What we have is the settled will of the Welsh people.'

Immediately, however, he contradicted himself: 'While devolution is a place in its own right, this doesn't mean it's static. No I believe in dynamic devolution.'[4]

At every opportunity during his leadership of the Assembly, Michael asserted the 'settled' character of the settlement enshrined in the 1998 Wales Act, emphasising the need for a period of stability and continuity. This was in contradistinction to the emphasis chosen by his predecessor as Secretary of State, Ron Davies, the main architect of the 1997 Act, who said that devolution was a 'process' rather than a settled 'event'.[5] For Alun Michael, however, devolution appeared at one and the same time to be both settled and dynamic. He also had short shrift for Plaid Cymru's notions of Wales achieving greater autonomy within the framework of the European Union:

> Let's not fool ourselves. Self-government within Europe is not an option. The European Union is still a union of member-states. Our European partners do not want to see a proliferation of statelets within the United Kingdom, the Balkanisation of one of their own members. They want to see a United Kingdom — like federalised Germany or regionalised Spain — capable of representing a common position in the Council of Ministers which reconciles the divergent interests of different parts of this idiosyncratic member state. A strong Wales in a strong United Kingdom — that is what devolution is about.'[6]

However merely to describe the United Kingdom as constitutionally 'idiosyncratic' when compared with 'federalised Germany or regionalised Spain' does not address the underlying issue, which is that Germany and Spain are indeed federalised and regionalised, whereas devolution in the United Kingdom has been confined to Wales, Scotland, and Northern Ireland, omitting the 85 per cent of the population that is England. In the omission is the inherent instability, quite apart from the different devolution 'settlements' for Wales, Scotland, and Northern Ireland. Michael's successor, Rhodri Morgan, struck a radically different note on these constitutional questions. In a speech on the eve of his election as First Secretary, he said a devolution process was underway in which Wales, Scotland, and Northern Ireland were progressing at different speeds towards greater self-determination. And he predicted that within a decade or so a written constitution would be needed for the United Kingdom to entrench their powers.[7]

On the question of Wales' place in Europe, he was even more emphatic. This was demonstrated by his response to the repatriation from France of the original Pennal Letter and Seal of Owain Glyndwr to the National Library of

---

[4] *Ibid.*

[5] See Ron Davies, *Devolution: A Process Not an Event*, Institute of Welsh Affairs, February 1999

[6] Alun Michael, *op.cit.*

[7] Rhodri Morgan, *Variable Geometry UK*, Institute of Welsh Affairs, March 2000.

Wales for six months during 2000. Sent from Pennal in north Wales in 1406 by Glyndwr to King Charles VI of France, the Letter is held by the French Ministry of Culture and Archives Nationales in Paris, despite many years of campaigning for its return to Wales. Written in Latin on goatskin parchment, the Letter bears the seal and signature of Glyndwr and urges the French to back his rebellion against Henry IV. At the opening ceremony of an exhibition at the National Library in which the Letter was exhibited, Rhodri Morgan declared:

> The political vision set out in the Pennal Letter is as relevant today as it was 600 years ago. Owain Glyndwr was setting out his vision for Wales as a nation — a nation with a future national existence set in a European context and not solely bound up with its nearest neighbour — England. His vision included a nation with organised institutions including Universities in the North and South where young people could be trained to run the institutions of the State.[8]

In an article in the *Western Mail* a few weeks later, Morgan added a plea that Welsh history should be made more visible, saying that when he had been a boy it had ended with the conquest of Wales by Edward I. Glyndwr, he argued, was the key to understanding Welsh aspirations:

> Owain Glyndwr wanted a country united in a properly organised society with representation from all parts of Wales. He envisaged a Welsh future in a European context ... Six centuries later we are starting to think in those terms again.[9]

Set against the character of Labour leadership in Wales over the previous fifty years, the nationalist sentiment projected by these remarks was startling. It reflected a determination to establish a different identity for what Rhodri Morgan would henceforth describe as *Welsh* rather than *New* or *Old* Labour.

The melodrama surrounding the resignation of Alun Michael and the succession of Rhodri Morgan as First Secretary was quickly recognised as a defining moment in Welsh politics. Certainly it was, as the Presiding Officer so quickly affirmed, an exercise in democracy. But more fundamentally, it registered a shift in the underlying political culture of Wales. A threshold had been crossed. This was not just in terms of opposition against what was seen as imposition of London rule; the no-confidence vote marked a significant change inside Welsh politics as well.

The internal change was most clearly exposed within the Labour Group in the Assembly. In the last resort Alun Michael's position became unsustainable when he lost the confidence of a large majority of his own side. In short, there was a division within the Labour group. How that was experienced and how the aftershock will reverberate through Welsh politics in the period

---

[8] Assembly Press release, 7 April 2000

[9] Rhodri Morgan, 'Time to shed the cloak of political invisibility', *Western Mail*, 17 April 2000.

leading to the next Assembly election, in May 2003, may well determine the course of devolution itself.

THE ADMINISTRATION

The result of the first Assembly elections, in which Labour emerged as the largest party with 28 of the 60 seats but with no overall control, shaped the character of the government that emerged. Labour resolved to govern as a minority administration on the accurate basis that Plaid Cymru (17 seats), the Conservatives (9 seats) and Liberal Democrats (6 seats) would be unable to provide a coherent alternative governing platform (the full constituency and regional list results are shown in Figures 3.2 and 3.3). On the other hand, it was soon to be demonstrated that there were many issues, notably agriculture, where the Opposition would be willing to join forces to vote down the minority administration's policy.

Figure 3.2. National Assembly constituency results May 1999

	% Vote	Seats Won
Labour	37.6	27
Plaid Cymru	28.4	9
Conservative	15.8	1
Lib Dem	13.5	3

Figure 3.3 National Assembly regional list results May 1999

	% Vote	Seats Won
Labour	35.5	1
Plaid Cymru	30.6	8
Conservative	16.5	8
Lib Dem	12.5	3

Nevertheless, for all the rhetoric it deployed about 'open government' and 'inclusivity', Alun Michael's administration still attempted to operate as though it was in the majority. Two examples illustrate this. In October 1999, the opposition parties combined to pass a motion of censure against the Agriculture Secretary, Christine Gwyther, for her failure to effectively negotiate a calf processing support scheme for Welsh farmers with her counterparts in Whitehall and Brussels. Alun Michael simply ignored the vote, which prompted the Conservatives to propose a no-confidence motion in his administration as a whole. As the Conservative leader Nick Bourne declared, it was proposed '...to address how the Assembly is run ...The minority administration acts and fails to react as if it were a majority administration.'[10]

A few weeks earlier, in September, the European Task Force, the main partnership body for EU regional aid in Wales, was unilaterally wound up by Assembly officials, the assumption being that henceforth they would assume control of the Objective One process. One official conceded, off the record:

> We thought that when the Assembly got going we would have 60 Secretaries of State instead of just one. Instead, we haven't got any at all and everything is being run by officials. It's just like the Welsh Office ...[11]

The no-confidence vote in Alun Michael was also a signal that this style of administration was no longer acceptable. It marked the moment when the previous Welsh Office régime was fundamentally challenged for the first time. A new form of accountability and a different political culture was being established. Rhodri Morgan acknowledged this himself, in a speech to the plenary session that confirmed his appointment, when he stated: 'We cannot allow the culling of First Secretaries to become an annual bloodsport of the Assembly.'[12]

The immediate way forward was not to be any kind of formal coalition as, for example, had been hammered out in Scotland between Labour and the Liberal Democrats. Instead there emerged what might be described as a more continental-style informal cohabitation arrangement between Rhodri Morgan's administration and Plaid Cymru. The first fruit was the agreement around Labour's policy document *A Better Wales*, laying out the administration's long-term policies to 2010 across the range of the Assembly's responsibilities. Taken literally, especially in the health and education fields, the document is far reaching, though in the absence of spending and specific timing commitments much of it remains declaratory and aspirational. However, when the final version was published, in May 2000, following a three-month consultation, a new element was the insertion of a three-page *Introduction* setting out 20 specific 'Made in Wales' policies. These have the status of having been negotiated with Plaid Cymru. The main opposition party did not wish to endorse the main body of the document, regarding it essentially as an encapsulation of Labour's philosophy and overall approach. On the other hand, it was content to sign up to the three-page *Introduction*, once some significant concessions to its own aspirations had been made. In the opening 'Vision' statement, there was inserted a commitment to fostering 'the benefits of bilingualism' together with the creation of a Wales 'where young people want to live, work and enjoy a high quality of life'. Among the twenty specific commitments that follow, Plaid claimed authorship of seven,

[10] Assembly *Record*, 2 November 1999.
[11] Martin Shipton, 'Yes Minister, Leave It To Me', *Wales on Sunday*, 5 September 1999.
[12] Assembly *Record*, 15 February 2000.

which although some are not altogether new, should receive a new emphasis and urgency:

- Setting up a Development Fund by December 2000 'to stimulate the creation and growth of small- and medium-sized enterprises';
- By no later than the autumn, to have 'the Rural Development Plan in place and supporting diversification in our rural economies';
- Commissioning 'an early study of the way in which the concept of a Welsh baccalaureate can be developed and aligned with the overall framework of qualifications';
- Developing 'a new national spatial framework for planning, setting a clear context for sustainable development and environmental quality; and a single statement on the opportunities for sustainable development in energy, waste and clean technology';
- Putting in place 'a Wales and the World programme, with a stronger presence in Europe, an awareness programme, new links with the Welsh Diaspora, and fresh opportunities for both business and our young people to engage with the wider world';
- Establishing an 'accelerated programme for reviewing all the Assembly's Sponsored Bodies and the present framework for delivery, to be completed by March 2003', and
- Over the following two years to 'review the present funding formula to ensure fairness and promote greater efficiency and co-operation'.

It is worthy of note that there was no formal debate within the respective party groups on the detail of these commitments. These priorities and their wording were hammered out in negotiations between Labour's Finance Secretary, Edwina Hart, and Plaid Cymru's Director of Policy, Cynog Dafis. It is hard not to conclude that this negotiation, so early on in Rhodri Morgan's administration, was to set a pattern for the survival of his minority government through to 2003. The more substantial and formal 'partnership agreement' or coalition that was later put in place by the administration with the Liberal Democrats in October 2000 was similarly worked through in high-level behind-closed-doors negotiations.

Prior to the onset of democratic devolution, the Welsh Office civil service machine was not primarily concerned with policy development. Rather its main role was administrative, ensuring effective delivery of the services within its responsibilities, and adjusting Whitehall directives here and there to suit local conditions. The coming of the National Assembly changed the civil service role substantially, in three main respects:

- It has to support the Welsh Cabinet in developing a policy programme and driving it forward;

- It has to support the wider Assembly committee structure, in particular the Subject Committees which, under the Government of Wales Act are integrated into the policy-development process, and
- It has to establish links with the Whitehall government, of which it is no longer part, to keep up with policy initiatives and to ensure that proposed relevant new primary legislation gives powers to the Assembly in relation to Wales.

A new form of governance was envisaged by those who designed the National Assembly. The progenitors of the devolution legislation imagined that the executive and backbench members would collaborate on policy development, debate and decision. This is reflected in the Wales Act which established the Subject Committees. In practice, the executive has governed and the backbenchers have been left to exert influence as and when they can.

Meanwhile, the Welsh civil service was developing its new role of supporting policy-making. The main focus was the Policy Unit, established by the former Permanent Secretary, Rachel Lomax, in November 1998, ahead of the first elections to the Assembly. One of the Unit's first tasks was to undertake a *Stocktake of NHS Wales.* This was prompted by a financial deficit of £72 million that had been built up by the Health Authorities and Trusts in Wales by the end of the 1998–99 financial year. As the Assembly got underway, the Policy Unit began to refocus on future issues and on working across the functional areas. As the Assembly's first year drew to a close, plans were put in hand to create a Cabinet Executive which would incorporate the Cabinet Secretariat, the Central Policy and Strategic Planning Unit and the Communication Directorate. At the same time, the size of the Policy Unit was expanded from two to six.

In addition to this mainstream civil service policy resource, the First Secretary has a team of four Labour Party linked advisers in his Private Office. Rhodri Morgan announced the appointment of his four special advisers following an open competition — the first time in the UK that such positions had been filled in this way. This was part of his drive for more open government. Another was the publication of his Cabinet minutes on the Assembly's website[13] six weeks in arrears, starting with the meeting held on 13 March.

THE COMPREHENSIVE SPENDING REVIEW

Chancellor Gordon Brown's statement of 18 July 2000 on the Comprehensive Spending Review (CSR) re-ignited the political debate about Objective One funding in Wales. According to the Secretary of State for Wales, Paul Murphy, the Chancellor's announcement of extra funding for the Assembly's budget represented 'an excellent settlement', a sentiment echoed by the

[13] www.wales.gov.uk

Labour leadership in the National Assembly. In sharp contrast, the Opposition parties were unanimous in claiming that the outcome fell far short of that required to make the most of European funds in West Wales and the Valleys.

As a result of the review, public spending in Wales will be £2 billion higher by the financial year beginning April 2003 than in 2000–2001, due to a 5.4 per cent real terms increase in spending over the next three years. Figure 3.4 gives the National Assembly's block grant for the next three years, together with the extra amounts resulting from the Review and the allocation within these for the Structural Fund Programmes.

Figure 3.4. July 2000 Comprehensive Spending Review settlement for Wales

	2001–2002	2002–2003	2003–2004
Assembly Block	£8.4bn	£9.1bn	£9.8bn
CSR Extra allocation	£480m	£1.173m	£1.821m
Of which Structural Funds	£113m	£148m	£160m

Apart from the amounts, the importance of the settlement was that substantial extra sums were awarded to the Welsh block outside the Barnett Formula (which allocates increased funding to Wales, Scotland and Northern Ireland on a pro rata basis to increases in England). This breaking or, more accurately, by-passing of the Barnett Formula had to occur if significant extra funds were to be found to match the potential European Union Structural Funds that Wales is eligible to draw down over the next six years. As First Secretary, Rhodri Morgan, and Secretary of State, Paul Murphy, put it in an article in *The Western Mail*:

> ...the Government has accepted our special case for funding outside the Barnett Formula. In England the Objective One area only constitutes eight per cent of the population ...In Wales 65 per cent of the population, 1.9 million out of 2.9 million, are in Objective One areas. That is why Wales' case for different treatment was so strong.[14]

Match funding for the Structural Funds will still have to come from within the Welsh block, but the EU funding will henceforth be treated as additional and extra money within the block which has been allowed to cover match funding requirements — an extra £421 million over the next three years. An argument immediately ensued as to whether this amount was enough to enable Wales to draw down all the European money to which it was entitled.

---

[14] 'Once-in-a-generation chance in our hands', *Western Mail*, 19 July 2000.

Labour insisted that it was, with Paul Murphy, for example, insisting that 'no worthwhile scheme' under Objective One would be denied funding.[15] On the other hand, the Opposition parties maintained that there was a significant shortfall in the match funding available. Plaid Cymru's Ieuan Wyn Jones, for example, declared that over the next three years there was a shortfall of at least £357 million.[16] Whilst different interpretations of the settlement were inevitable in the highly charged political context that has characterised Objective One debates in Wales, they also reflected the continuing complexities which surround the treatment of European funds in the Assembly's budget.[17]

THE ASSEMBLY

The Subject Committees were intended to be the 'engine room' of the Assembly's operation, as Alun Michael put it in an exchange on their role with Liberal Democrat Leader Michael German.[18] The architects of the 1998 Wales Act envisaged that the Committees would have a three-pronged role: holding the administration to account, policy-making, and dealing with subordinate or secondary legislation. In practice, what they achieved during the first year was, to a great extent, dependent on circumstances such as the character and range of their brief, the personality of their Chairs, and the attitude of the Cabinet Secretaries themselves. On the whole, none of the Committees held the executive to account in a comprehensive way, except on isolated questions. Furthermore, they certainly did not engage in policy *making*. Rather they were involved in generating a great deal more information about their policy areas and contributing in a general way to policy *development*. Finally, they only sporadically got to grips with considering, let alone improving, secondary legislation.

As far as holding the executive to account is concerned, this was a process most effectively dealt with during plenary sessions of the Assembly, rather than within the Subject Committees. So, for example, the work of the Welsh health service was not effectively scrutinised by the Health and Social Services Committee during the year. It was noteworthy that during its first nine months the Committee found time to consult with a large number of health organisations but did not cross-examine one Health Authority or one Trust. Given the high profile issue of financial deficits amongst the Trusts, this seemed an inappropriate use of time and a strange set of priorities. In

---

[15] *Western Mail* 19 July 2000.

[16] *Western Mail*, 19 July 2000.

[17] For a fuller analysis see Osmond, J., (ed.) *Devolution Looks Ahead, Monitoring the National Assembly May to August 2000*, Institute of Welsh Affairs, September 2000.

[18] Assembly *Record*, 7 December, 1999.

general, the Committee focused on primary, community and social care matters with relatively few debates on acute services. This was remedied later in the year when the Committee set about investigating a number of Trusts and Health Authorities.

One organisational matter that rapidly came to be seen as limiting the Committees' impact was the frequency of their meetings. Except in rare circumstances, they meet just once every two weeks and then only for three to four hours. Committees met during the first year on Tuesdays and Thursday mornings, a time allocation in part determined by the rigid rule that meetings of the Assembly as a whole cannot extend beyond 5.30pm. This is to comply with a pre-condition that Members be allowed to work 'family-friendly' hours. How long this can be sustained is a moot point. Already pre-meeting meetings, for instance for party groups to determine their line in the Subject Committees, are starting early in the mornings, sometimes at 7.30am. It may be the case that 'family friendliness' is proving the enemy of delegated democracy.

However one important impact achieved by the Committees in their first year was to influence the Assembly's budget-making process. The new budget round, in which the administration allocated its £8 billion block grant to the different functions for which it is responsible, from health and education to economic development and agriculture, introduced an entirely new policy process to Wales. Each year, the process begins in June and ends the following February, after ten stages of consultation and debate. Whereas in Welsh Office days, the budget round was conducted behind closed doors, involving just the Secretary of State for Wales, the two junior Welsh Office Ministers and Welsh Office Group Directors, the process is now far more transparent and open to much wider debate. During the first plenary debate on the budget, Edwina Hart noted that of the 33 budget recommendations that had been made formally by the Committees, the Preliminary Draft Budget had met 29 of them, two had been partly met and two had not been met.[19] Although there was disagreement over the extent to which the budget allocations reflected the Committees' degree of priority on certain issues, their views still appear to have been influential in affecting the distribution of resources. An outstanding example was the Cabinet's agreement to make provision available for extending free eye tests — widely interpreted as Plaid Cymru's price for abstaining in the critical vote that allowed the budget through.

Given the political balance within the Assembly — reflected within the Subject Committees — and the potential for more intimate and extensive interrogations and exchanges, there was some potential for the Committee Chairs to emerge as powerful figures. However, during the first year, only two personalities managed to break through in a significant way and this was due largely to the opportunity provided by policy issues. In the first meetings

[19] Assembly *Record*, November 10, 1999.

of the Post-16 Education Committee, for example, there was a determined effort by the civil service to drive through the administration's Education and Training Action Plan. Developed during the previous year under Welsh Office guidance, the Action Plan was far reaching. A new Education and Training Council for Wales was proposed, with the next tier for delivery being at the level of the 22 unitary authorities. Unspoken implications were the abolition of the four Training and Enterprise Councils, a reduced role for sixth forms in secondary schools, and a diminution of the role of the private sector in influencing the content and delivery of training. Critics of the Action Plan also pointed to the lack of consideration of the post-16 curriculum. For these and other reasons, the Post-16 Committee Chair, Plaid Cymru AM Cynog Dafis, proved effective in delaying any change until evidence was heard from all the organisations involved. Thus, in this area of policy at least, the Subject Committee frustrated the intentions of the executive by ensuring a full-scale debate was held well into the autumn.

Another example of a Subject Committee and its Chair dictating events was illustrated by Ron Davies during his short-lived chairmanship of the Economic Development Committee. This was before his resignation in July 1999 as a result of fall-out from his Clapham Common incident the previous October. Under Davies' guidance the Economic Development Committee made the running on the most contentious issue debated by the Assembly in its first year — the question of whether the Treasury would find PES cover to enable the Assembly to match the £1.2 billion European Objective One investment for West Wales and the Valleys over the next seven years.

Davies revealed that, in his former position of Secretary of State, he had made bids to the Treasury the previous year for additional cover for EU receipts for the period 1999 to 2002 to take account of the anticipated extra EU funds. He had asked for £3 million for the first year, rising to £54 million for the second and £263 million for the third. All were turned down, the Treasury saying the Assembly would have to find cover and matched funding for EU receipts from within its existing block grant.

Under close cross-examination from Ron Davies, civil servants revealed where funding cover for EU Objective One spend in the first year of the programme would come from. It was prised out that £19 million was already allocated in the budget; £21 million would come from European Regional Development Fund monies underspent on programmes in Wales over the previous three years; and £35 million would be re-allocated from other parts of the Welsh block compared with the previous year — a total of £75 million. It was also revealed that EU money earmarked for Wales was not added to the baseline defined by the Barnett formula. In other words, the whole spending on EU projects in Wales would come out of the Welsh block, calculated by comparison with English spending departments and without reference to those EU projects. The official explanation was that spending departments in

England used to calculate the Barnett formula have some EU funding themselves. Therefore, spread over the whole of the UK, the sums balance, with
some winners and some losers. Yet Wales is the poorest economic region in
Britain, with the lowest GDP, highest unemployment and highest economic
inactivity rates. Consequently Wales loses all the time under this
dispensation.

Plaid Cymru did some quick calculations and claimed that Wales had lost
out on EU funding by some £50 million a year over the previous five years.
With the extra money that could be drawn down for the Objective One region
between 2000 to 2006 the problem could only get worse. Phil Williams AM,
Plaid Cymru's Economic Development spokesman, paid tribute to the work
of the Committee and its chairman:

> In the first two meetings of the Economic Development Committee, the whole
> matter has been largely cleared up. These two meetings have justified the cost of
> the Assembly many times over. I pay tribute to the Welsh Office civil servants and
> the Chair, Ron Davies. It was due to how those meetings were handled, with a
> judicious mix of informed pugnacity and constructive discussion, that the right
> questions were asked and the right answers given.[20]

Apart from these examples, however, few opportunities emerged for the
Committees to have a decisive impact on the executive in the Assembly's
opening months. The Agricultural Committee was perhaps another example,
although its concerns about beef on the bone followed by the argument on
extending the calf re-processing scheme rapidly got caught up in the
complexities of the Assembly's relationship with Whitehall and Brussels.

Two lessons emerged from the early skirmishes between the Subject
Committees and the executive: it is easier for the Committees to make a mark
when their chairperson is of a different political persuasion to the government, and the Committees also have a better chance when there is a comparatively clear and straightforward policy issue to get to grips with, such as
Objective One funding or the Education and Training Action Plan. In the
case of the Agricultural Committee, the ongoing 'crisis of rural Wales' was a
highly complex question making it difficult to deal with in an easily defined
way, a problem which was exacerbated by the multiple layers of government
and responsibility involved. This is not to say that the Committee should be
inherently unable to come to a strategic view, but rather that the challenge
was greater and therefore likely to take longer.

Committee members were, of course, on a steep learning curve. Most were
taken aback at the workload involved in getting to grips with their brief and at
the amount of paperwork they had to absorb. The Subject Committees meet
on a fortnightly cycle and their agenda is driven by briefing papers submitted

---

[20] Assembly *Record*, 14 July 1999

by the civil service. The papers are voluminous. Moreover, in the early months the papers were first vetted by the Cabinet and often by the First Minister himself. By mid November, each Subject Committee had accumulated more than 50 briefing papers on the Assembly's website. For these two reasons, rather than stimulating debate the briefing papers often inhibited discussion. Three main areas of concern arose among Assembly members as a result:

- Briefing papers to be considered by the Committees sometimes arrived on the same day, even within an hour, of relevant discussions. When complicated issues were being considered there was little time for the Committees to subject the information they were provided with to full analysis. The most notorious example occurred in the Economic Development Committee when a paper giving the executive's view on allocation of Objective One spending between different priorities, such as training and infrastructure, was only tabled when the Committee was already underway;
- Assembly members outside the Cabinet do not have direct lines of communication with officials, despite the fact that, as a body corporate the Assembly as a whole is responsible for decisions. This means that, other than during the Subject Committee meetings, when interrogation is mediated by Cabinet members, information has to be obtained by means of written or oral questions in plenary sessions; and
- Under the Government of Wales Act and the Assembly's Standing Orders, information set out in documents considered by the Assembly Cabinet does not have to be released to Members and neither does advice given by officials to the Assembly Cabinet.

The cumulative result of such practices was that early on the executive utilised its inherent power of information and action to establish a style much closer to the Westminster and Whitehall model than many had envisaged. Ironically, this tendency was assisted by the absorption of a great deal of the time and energy of members in the Subject Committees themselves. Because the Committees are formally about policy development and implementation there is, in effect, no room for a 'backbench' role, in a Westminster sense, for most of the Assembly's 60 members. Excluding the two Presiding Officers, nine full Cabinet members and three Deputy Ministers, the remaining 46 'backbenchers' have, between them, to cover a range of subjects that in Westminster absorbs the attention of around 500 members.

In practice, there are no 'backbenchers' in Cardiff Bay equivalent to those in Westminster. Some in the Assembly are beginning to worry that they are being caught between two competing roles and not fulfilling either adequately. On the one hand, they are supposed to be actively engaged in the policy-making process, but find that role frustrated by the executive. On the

other hand, just because of that frustrated role, they are unable to act as effectively as they should as backbenchers calling the Executive to account.

Such problems facing the Assembly as a debating and deliberative chamber were well summarised by Ron Davies in an address to the Institute of
Wesh Affairs and Welsh Governance Centre in January 2000. In it, he listed
five main areas of concern:

- There is no mechanism for collective discussions on the wide range of
  constitutional issues facing the Assembly. How do we consider whether powers
  and functions are adequate? How do we develop relationships with
  Westminster and Members of Parliament representing Welsh constituencies? Is
  the Assembly of the right size and composition and are the existing electoral
  arrangements satisfactory?
- There is no real process of collective decision making within the Assembly in
  plenary. Too often we're offered a take it or leave it approach from the
  executive and a range of party-political inspired amendments from the
  opposition parties. As a result, the Assembly, as a corporate body, has little
  sense of its own identity. It is to the Assembly as a whole, established by
  legislation and charged collectively with rights and responsibilities to the
  people as a whole, that Parliament has given powers. The Assembly is the
  representative voice of Wales but has failed to develop significant relationships
  or links with the UK Parliament and the other devolved Assemblies.
  Concordats between executives are a second-best substitute;
- There is a clear and growing perception that power is concentrated in fewer and
  fewer hands and that the executive desires to downplay the role of Subject
  Committees both in effective scrutiny of its actions and in discharging their
  policy-making role. Attempts to influence the Office of the Presiding Officer
  and political interference in the circulation of official reports prepared for
  Committees are not hallmarks of an administration at ease with itself and
  confident in its relationship with the Assembly. The National Assembly was
  not designed as a committee or cabinet model or as a committee versus cabinet
  model. It was designed as a hybrid — a cabinet and committee model — and
  will operate most effectively when the rights and responsibilities of all
  concerned are recognised by all concerned;
- There is no effective forum for policy formulation for the Assembly as a whole,
  no process for the engagement of Assembly Members in developing vision or
  strategy and an administration which, in policy making, has yet to develop an
  outgoing and radical approach. It is difficult to identify any policy initiative
  emanating from the Assembly itself. Current policies are those of the UK
  Government or of the Welsh Office pre-devolution. Unfortunately there is no
  effective mechanism in prospect for the Assembly to look outward to engage
  with those in the private or public sector who themselves have a public policy
  research capacity; and
- The administration is surviving day-to-day on the basis of one-off agreements
  with one or other of the minority parties. These agreements, however, are not
  reached on the basis of open and informed debate nor is their existence formally

acknowledged. This does nothing to establish the Assembly's already faltering image.[21]

This intervention provided part of the backdrop for the build-up of pressure that led to the vote of no confidence in Alun Michael a few weeks later. Arguably the criticisms were at least partially addressed, as we have seen, by Rhodri Morgan's new administration developing procedures for open government and seeking an informal accommodation with Plaid Cymru. In the Autumn they were more comprehensively addressed in the coalition deal struck with the Liberal Democrats.

Meanwhile, it was left to the Presiding Officer to champion the rights of the Assembly against pressures exerted by the administration. Matters came to a head in the days leading up to Alun Michael's resignation. At one stage, it seemed that following a no-confidence vote, Michael might simply be renominated as First Secretary by the Labour Group. In turn, this might lead to successive votes of no confidence. In these circumstances, the Presiding Officer might have to intervene to rule one side or other out of order. But which side should he choose? The advice he received from the Office of the Counsel General, Winston Roddick QC, was that he should rule against successive motions of no confidence. However, alternative legal advice the Presiding Officer sought from outside the Assembly was that Standing Orders did not oblige him to make a decision one way or the other. In the event, the issue did not arise since Alun Michael resigned, dramatically, moments before the no-confidence vote was taken.

One consequence of the episode was to place firmly on the agenda the independence of the Office of the Presiding Officer, together with the independence of advice given to backbench AMs. Within days, the Presiding Officer announced that he had appointed David Lambert, on secondment from the Assembly to Cardiff University's Law School, as his legal adviser.[22] Part of his role will be to undertake the task of compiling the Welsh equivalent of the precedents laid down for the House of Commons in *Erskine May*.

The Presiding Officer also proposed to the Cabinet a clearer separation of the 'administrative' and 'parliamentary' functions of the Assembly. This emerged in the first published minutes of the Cabinet, for 13 March. There had been growing unease, especially amongst opposition Assembly Members, that the role of the administration and the Assembly itself was not being clearly delineated, especially in press and media reporting. An outstanding example was the announcement of a decision not to provide a £25 million grant for British Aerospace's superjumbo project at Broughton in Flintshire. This was because the grant, plus the £530 million loan announced by the DTI in mid March, would exceed EU limits on state aid per job created. The issue

---

[21] *Agenda*, Winter 2000, Institute of Welsh Affairs, p. 28.
[22] Assembly *Record*, 29 February 2000.

was widely reported in the press as though the Assembly had decided the matter, when in fact it was an administrative decision (later in the year BAe was awarded £19.5 million).

In his paper to the Cabinet, the Presiding Officer suggested three measures to make the separation of the administration from the Assembly clearer:

- Cabinet members should not have their main offices in Crickhowell House, the Assembly building;
- The Presiding Officer should have control of his own budget; and
- He should also assume responsibility for the Assembly building.

The Cabinet Minutes for 13 March recorded a cautious response:

> The Cabinet agreed that it would be necessary to reach a compromise with the Presiding Officer, but that it did not wish to see the relocation of the Cabinet from the Assembly building, and that careful consideration would need to be given to the composition of the Presiding Officer's budget. It was agreed that Mrs Hart [the Finance Secretary] and Mr Davies [the Business Secretary] would take forward aspects of the paper with the Presiding Officer.

Technically the Assembly as a whole, being a body corporate, is responsible for all decisions made by the administration, through the delegation of powers to the First Secretary, and from him to Cabinet Secretaries. Moreover, Cabinet Secretaries' membership of the Subject Committees also serves to tie the administration and Assembly closely together. However, in practice, the operation of the Cabinet system serves to separate quite clearly the administration and its decisions from the role of the Assembly itself. Towards the end of the Assembly's first year, in an address to the Institute of Welsh Politics in Aberystwyth, the Presiding Officer noted that the minority Labour administration was increasingly referring to itself as the 'Government of Wales':

> This is an important development which means Cabinet Secretaries who form the Cabinet Government within the National Assembly now see themselves as such a corporate entity. However, the other perception is still operating concurrently. That the National Assembly is a body corporate and that all decisions taken by the Government, the Cabinet Secretaries individually or collectively, are in fact decisions of the Assembly, whether the Assembly has voted on them or not ... This issue also goes to the heart of the operation of a democratically elected body. The difficult and complex growth of parliamentary-type government in the National Assembly, from within the body of territorial administrative/executive government in the previous system, has provided the main drama of the first year of powers ... [23]

---

[23] Lord Elis-Thomas AM, *National Assembly: A Year in Power?* Address to the Institute of Welsh Politics, Aberystwyth, 8 July 2000.

THE ASSEMBLY AS A LEGISLATURE

The Assembly's legislative role is not confined to carrying out primary legislation enacted at Westminster. Its activities include not only framing and making Statutory Instruments and other secondary legislation, but also include issuing circulars setting out policy statements to officials at local level, whether in local government, the health service, or the Assembly's non-departmental bodies, the quangos. Often these communications contain guidance on the carrying out of statutory powers and sometimes exercise subordinate legislative powers, as not all such legislation has to be made by formal statutory instruments.

This is an area with which the Assembly, as far as most of its members were concerned, barely came to grips in its first term. How many backbench members, let alone members of the public, were aware for example, that in its first six months, the Assembly enacted more than 20 Statutory Instruments and despatched some 60 circulars, most of them concerned with implementing the School Standards and Framework Act 1998 and the Local Government Act 1999?

What may prove to be a precedent is the way in which the administration has dealt with the Statutory Instruments considered so far which affect Wales as a whole. Under the Wales Act and the Assembly's Standing Order 22 there are three possible routes:

- Full procedure which can involve some 90 stages in which the executive carries out regulatory appraisal which assesses the benefits and costs of the proposed legislation. The draft legislation is passed to the relevant Subject Committee for consideration and possible suggestions to the executive for amendment, and then to the Legislation Scrutiny Committee. Finally it is considered on the floor of the Assembly where further amendments can be moved;
- Fast track procedure in which consideration is confined to the Legislation Scrutiny Committee before being sent to the floor of the Assembly for discussion; or
- Emergency procedure in which the executive has the power to push through secondary legislation without reference to the wider Assembly.

So far much of the secondary legislation considered by the National Assembly has been dealt with through the third, emergency, route. This may be because the Assembly's committees had too much on their plate in the early months to get around to such detailed matters. On the other hand, if the precedent is followed in future, it will mean that one of the purposes of devolution, to make the legislative process more transparent, accountable, and open to amendment, will be lost.

The number of Statutory Instruments dealt with by the Assembly during its first months was, in fact, low when compared with previous Welsh Office activity in any equivalent period. During a typical year, the Secretary of State for Wales at the Welsh Office would have been responsible, either himself or with other government ministers, for making around 600 separate pieces of secondary legislation. But only 100 or so of these would relate solely to Wales. The large majority would apply to both England and Wales, with the driving force being the Whitehall departments. Since devolution, many of the functions previously exercised on an England and Wales basis are exercised solely by the Assembly in relation to Wales.

Consequently, the Whitehall departments make legislation only for England. There has been a significant slowing in the number of Statutory Instruments which relate to Wales. Increasingly, Wales is not participating in secondary legislation made for England nor, as yet, is it making much of its own legislation. Wales is relying on subordinate legislation which is different to that in England where new legislation is being made. The overall result is that the legal systems in England and Wales are beginning to separate in a process that could be described as 'devolution by default.'

In late March, Assembly law-making activity (or lack of it) was the subject of one of the most fractious debates in the post-Alun Michael era. The tone was set by an article in the *Western Mail*[24] signalling an attack by Plaid on the so-called 'legislative deficit' or phenomenon of 'devolution by default'. In Plenary, the Business Secretary, Andrew Davies, mounted a robust defence:

> I read yesterday in the press that almost 600 pieces of legislation are missing. This is arrant nonsense...The evidence so far is insufficient for any sensible conclusions to be drawn about the expected total annual volume of Assembly subordinate legislation in this the first year of law-making.[25]

At the same time, Mr Davies made clear the kinds of problem confronting the organisation in the making of subordinate legislation (which were being compounded by the need to have regulations, for example on rate levels, safely completed in time for the new financial year):

> At this stage of our development, we have originated little legislation of our own. Therefore, we are largely dependent on Whitehall and the European Union, in terms of the timetable for drafting Orders ...The difficulties are caused by the constraint on resources for drafting Orders themselves and the need to comply with our statutory obligations...for such legislation to be bilingual...In our early months of operation, we have largely been constrained by forces outside our control...[26]

---

[24] 20 March, 2000.
[25] Assembly *Record*, 21 March 2000.
[26] *Ibid.*

The debate can also be seen as a pre-emptive strike by the executive against criticism of a heavy use in the making of Assembly laws of urgency procedure or the 'disapplication of procedural requirements.'[27] It was a line of attack developed on behalf of Plaid by Jocelyn Davies AM:

> The potential of the urgency procedure means that it should be used sparingly. The Standing Orders state that it can only be used if it is not reasonably practicable to use the standard procedures. That term is difficult to define and so I have looked at the guidance [which] also outlines the grounds where the Cabinet will not use the urgency procedure. The scenarios cited are a wish to follow a UK Department timetable, a wish to replicate English Orders, or drafting and administrative delays. If we are honest, we have not always followed these guidelines …[28]

The motion put down by the executive effectively called on the Business Committee to seek ways of minimising the use of urgency procedure. The Liberal Democrats voted in favour, while Plaid abstained. The Conservatives were in less forgiving mood. To quote Nick Bourne:

> It is time for us to get our act together and to stop making excuses about the infancy of this body …It is time to say that we need to see these Orders in good time so that we can debate them.[29]

In the event, the scale of the affair was quickly made apparent after the debate. In the period January to 16 March 2000, the Assembly made 12 general orders, the urgency procedure being used on two occasions. In the following fortnight, 31 general orders were made, of which 17 were pushed through with procedural requirements disapplied. This is a long way from the original recommendations of the National Assembly Advisory Group, which heavily emphasised the democratic involvement by Assembly Members in the new modalities of subordinate law making in Wales.

In retrospect, the debate is likely to be seen as marking the low point in terms of Assembly legislative practice and procedure. Soon afterwards, a Subordinate Legislation Working Party was established bringing together representatives from different parts of the administrative and legislative machine, from the Assembly Chamber Secretariat to the Office of the Presiding Officer, and on through the Cabinet Secretariat to the Office of the Counsel General (OCG) and policy divisions, not forgetting the clerk and legal advisers to the Legislation Committee. A project report was produced in May which, in light of the criticism of the use of urgency procedure, laid great emphasis on tighter business processes, for example identification and early warning of forthcoming legislation. One result was the creation of a new Legislation Management Unit within the Office of the Counsel General, with

---

[27] Standing Order 22 paras. 25-28.
[28] *Ibid.*
[29] Assembly *Record*, 21 March 2000.

responsibility for forward planning, progressing Statutory Instruments, Welsh text, managing the publication process, and liaison with subject area drafting lawyers. It is also responsible for identifying devolved issues in primary legislation and communication with policy sections as appropriate. In this way, it is intended that problems such as policy divisions failing to appreciate the rigours of the distinctive Assembly legislative procedures, or the lack of clear 'ownership' or responsibility for a text, shall be bypassed. The Unit will be involved from beginning to end in the making of Assembly legislation, responsible not only for devising individual handling plans, but also for ensuring that Orders are properly signed off and for their registration and publication. It is precisely the kind of nuts and bolts arrangement that is so necessary for the Assembly legislative process to operate efficiently.

At the political level, a striking feature was the reform of the all-party Business Committee which, representing a formalisation of the 'usual channels' at Westminster, is one of the more distinctive parts of the Assembly architecture. Away from the 'theatre' of plenary session, the Committee has effectively supplied the continuing impetus and forum for negotiation of procedural changes, a feature emphasised by various parties to the proceedings.[30] Meanwhile, discussions were held between the Opposition parties and Labour to see if primary legislation for Wales could be expedited in the House of Commons. It was suggested that the Welsh Affairs Committee might be asked to undertake an investigation into the possibilities. These discussions were mediated by the deputy Presiding Officer, Jane Davidson, in her capacity as Chair of the Committee of Chairs of the Subject Committees. An outline agenda for an investigation was tabled by Plaid Cymru's Director of Policy, Cynog Dafis:

- To discover how various government departments respond to devolution and the existence of the Assembly in drafting primary legislation — what principles and guidelines exist;
- To discover to what extent there may be resistance or positive support for allowing maximum discretion to the Assembly;
- To identify (perhaps by considering this year's legislative programme) how variable practice across departments can add to or take away from the Assembly's power;
- To suggest how practice might be made consistent across government departments so as to respond to the Assembly's declared wish to be empowered to the greatest possible degree through secondary legislation, and
- To explore how the Assembly might utilise a fast-track mechanism to achieve its objectives within Westminster primary legislation.[31]

---

[30] See Assembly *Record* 24 May 2000.
[31] Letter from Cynog Dafis AM to Jane Davidson AM, Deputy Presiding Officer, 16 March 2000.

THE SECRETARY OF STATE FOR WALES

The position and role of the Secretary of State for Wales was pushed into the headlines by the Conservative leader, William Hague, during the party's Blackpool conference in October 1999. He told reporters that he would have to be persuaded that the British Cabinet post was justified in the wake of devolution:

> I'm not sure that what the Secretary of State for Wales is now doing justifies his place in Cabinet, his salary, the accompanying flunkies and everything else. I think the case for having a Secretary of State now that we have the Assembly remains to be made.[32]

As it happened, the present incumbent, Paul Murphy, MP for Torfaen, was given an opportunity to defend his position the following day, when he appeared before the Select Committee on Welsh Affairs in the House of Commons. He described his task as having four dimensions. In the first place, he and his junior minister, David Hanson, MP for Delyn, between them sat on more than 20 Cabinet committees. His second role, he said was to deal with the Assembly's block grant and to negotiate with the Treasury, especially in relation to European funding. A third role was to steer primary legislation through the House of Commons where it affected Wales: 'That is a very significant role and one that is different from Scotland.'

However, from his own emphasis, a fourth role came across as the most important. This was a political role — 'to safeguard the devolution settlement':

> ...Devolution is not simply about the creation of the National Assembly in Cardiff but also about how the National Assembly fits into the Government and parliamentary structure of the rest of the United Kingdom. In many ways my presence in the Cabinet is an indicator of the link between the different parts of the United Kingdom in being the United Kingdom itself. By being present as a Member of the Cabinet, as representing Wales, that shows to the world, as it were, that we are still part of the United Kingdom.[33]

However, following a further appearance before the Welsh Affairs Select Committee just seven months later, in June 2000, Murphy was reported as revealing there had been British Cabinet discussions about subsuming the Welsh, Scottish, and Northern Ireland Whitehall Ministries into a single office. The *Western Mail* reported that a senior civil servant had suggested that the Scotland Office's premises, on the other side of Whitehall from the Wales Office Gwydyr House, had been earmarked as the likely office for

---

[32] *Western Mail*, 26 October 1999.
[33] *Western Mail*, 28 October 1999.

what was labelled an Office of the Regions.[34] Meanwhile, in response to a parliamentary question, it was revealed that the number of people working in the Secretary of State's Office had risen from 27.5 to 42.4 full-time equivalents over the previous year.[35]

A protocol on relations between the Secretary of State and the Assembly was debated in February. There are commitments by the Secretary of State to consider all amendments to Bills put forward by the Assembly and to put all of its proposals on the Queen's Speech and proposals relating to future legislation to the UK Cabinet Committee. The Assembly will debate and approve a set of proposals on an annual basis — a kind of shadow Welsh Queen's Speech — a process that will be entrenched in standing orders. The protocol, however, does not address the issue of a possible fast-track procedure at Westminster for distinctively Welsh primary legislation.

THE POLITICAL PARTIES

The Assembly's inaugural session was a turbulent one for all of the political parties. Three of them changed their leaders. The Conservatives were the first, with Rod Richards resigning in August 1999, following a charge of serious bodily harm, made against him by the police as a result of an incident in London. He was later acquitted. Labour's leadership changed the following February as a result of Alun Michael's resignation, and Plaid Cymru elected Anglesey AM, Ieuan Wyn Jones, as leader in August 2000, after Dafydd Wigley resigned because of ill health. More fundamentally, however, all of the parties were faced with the need to adjust to the novel political space opened up by the coming of the Assembly.

Labour was perhaps presented with the greatest challenge, highlighted by the manoeuvrings around the fall of Alun Michael. Divisions within the Labour Group in the Assembly were laid bare in a plenary debate[36] a week before that event, on the Assembly's response to the Westminster Government's legislative programme. The Assembly had twice debated the Queen's Speech in previous plenary sessions. Drawing on contributions from all parties, civil servants had prepared a document purporting to represent a consensus view. Presenting the document, Alun Michael claimed that it was not his, the Cabinet's or the Labour Group's response, but rather that it sought to represent the views of the Assembly as a whole. This claim was bitterly refuted by the Opposition parties. More importantly, however, a

---

[34] *Western Mail*, 28 June 2000.
[35] *Wales on Sunday*, 13 August 2000.
[36] 2 February 2000.

substantial number of Labour members, indeed a majority, were in disagreement as well.

Most anger was directed at the document's suggestion that the Assembly supported the Criminal Justice (Mode of Trial) Bill, which proposed limiting the right of defendants to opt for a jury trial. The Labour Group insisted on a free vote on a Liberal Democrat amendment opposing this and as a result the amendment was passed overwhelmingly. The debate revealed three broad tendencies amongst the Labour Group. First were the Alun Michael loyalists, just five AMs, who shared his caution on striking a distinctive Welsh policy agenda and who were temperamentally inclined to accentuate the unionist, British dimension of Welsh identity. Against these was a larger group of around 14 members — strong devolutionists who wished to see distinctive Welsh policies and greater autonomy for the Assembly. In between was another substantial element in the Group — some eight members, who wavered between the two wings described above. This element swung decisively to the side of Rhodri Morgan following the no-confidence vote.

An Assembly debate on the Westminster Government's annual legislative programme (the Queen's Speech) will be an annual affair. How the Labour Group responds is likely to prove a litmus test on the extent to which there is the emergence of a more distinctively *Welsh* Labour Party. Certainly this proved to be the case in February 2000 and was confirmed by the party's Welsh conference in Llandudno the following month, where a new logo was unveiled — *Welsh Labour — the True Party of Wales* (in contradistinction, of course, to Plaid Cymru). The acid test for this description will be whether the new Labour administration can forge a range of innovative policies in the bread-and-butter areas of health, education and economic development that not only appeal across the Assembly itself but to the wider electorate as well. The coalition arrangement negotiated with the Liberal Democrats later in the year, between August and October, provided a programme. It will be fascinating to see how far Labour remains comfortable with its Liberal Democrat emphasis.

This test simultaneously describes a dilemma for Plaid Cymru. For, as was widely commented in the press and media at the time, by being so instrumental in propelling Rhodri Morgan into the Assembly leadership, the party may have simultaneously blighted its own electoral chances of achieving a majority in 2003. The more successful Labour is in making the Assembly work, the greater its chances of holding on to power. However, Plaid Cymru took the view that the long-term interests of the Assembly in evolving into an effective institution is more important that its own short-term electoral prospects. In reality, there is probably little difference between the two. Plaid Cymru's fortunes are too intimately intertwined with the national project that the Assembly embodies for there to be any other choice.

An on-going dilemma that the Plaid Cymru Group in the Assembly is wrestling with is its attitude to coalition politics. Proportional representation and the electoral arithmetic of Welsh politics suggest that, sooner or later, this will become inevitable (in fact, sooner rather than later). As the second largest party, and potentially in future the largest, it is likely that it will be forced to make real choices in this area. Following the next Assembly election in 2003, the parties may be bunched closer together in terms of the number of seats they hold. If the largest party (Labour or Plaid Cymru) have total seats in the low twenties, a coalition may be forced on unwilling partners to enable the executive to function effectively. That being so, in the wake of Alun Michael's resignation some in the Plaid Group argued that the party should offer a coalition immediately, even in the expectation that it would be rejected, in order to give the party a stronger position in the event of it emerging as the largest Group in the Assembly in the future.

The election of Ieuan Wyn Jones (51), the Anglesey AM and MP, as Plaid Cymru's leader in August 2000, replacing Dafydd Wigley, gave a fresh profile to the party's constitutional objective which had provided the only real hiccup in what had been a remarkably smooth first election to the Assembly in May 1999. Did the party's goal of self-government for Wales mean that it wanted the country to be independent? In the Assembly election, Wigley had eschewed the word 'independence', describing it as an inaccurate description of what was possible in the context of a rapidly integrating European Union. Ieuan Wyn Jones' own formulation seemed to represent the nearest to a consensus in the party, though it still left many in the media mystified as to how it departed from a short-hand description of 'independence':

> I believe that to secure full national status within the European Union would be an accurate description of our aspiration in the modern world. If secured now it would give us the same status as say Ireland or Denmark. In the future, much will depend on how the European Union evolves. In any event, we must aspire to whatever status that will best enable Wales to fully develop our potential as a nation.[37]

For much of the year, the fortunes of the Welsh Conservative Party were overshadowed by the saga of their former leader, Rod Richards, a List AM for North Wales. He resigned in August 1999 for allegedly causing grievous bodily harm to a woman in London. The trial took place at Kingston Crown Court the following June, when he was acquitted. After the result, his solicitor was quoted: 'It is his intention to resume his political career with renewed enthusiasm.'[38]

---

[37] Ieuan Wyn Jones, *A New Leader for a New Era,* Leadership Election Statement, July 2000.
[38] *Western Mail* 24 June 2000.

In subsequent press and media interviews, Richards re-emphasised this ambition, though he continued at arm's length from the Conservative Group in the Assembly after being expelled the previous February for failing to follow the party whip. He had been replaced as Conservative leader in the Assembly by Mid and West Wales AM, Nick Bourne, a more emollient figure whose strategy was to reposition the Conservatives in Wales as a more distinctively Welsh party. This was in contrast to Richards who had sought to highlight the Conservatives' unionist identity.

From the Conservative Group's point of view, the outcome of Alun Michael's resignation in February was wholly positive. From the outset, they had been the most combative of the Opposition parties, wishing to play a classic opposition role. They had resorted, unsuccessfully, to a no-confidence motion against Alun Michael the previous December, following his refusal to acknowledge the censure motion passed against Agriculture Secretary, Christine Gwyther. Now they were seen to be instrumental in bringing a Labour administration down in Wales, at the same time as embarrassing the Labour Government at Westminster. It chimed with their approach of wishing to separate the executive from the legislature, Westminster style, rather than become embroiled in collaborative arrangements, least of all any hint of coalition politics.

As with the Conservatives, the Liberal Democrats — the smallest Group in the Assembly — were faced with creating a profile by a series of specific interventions seeking cross-party consensus, rather than being able to develop a more broad-based project in ways that were open to both Labour, which was running the administration, and to Plaid Cymru which was aspiring to do so. This has placed them in a difficult position in the run-up to the 2003 election. Of all the parties, they are warmest with regard to collaborative politics, indeed in some senses they are ideologically disposed towards it, given their support for proportional representation. They had offered Alun Michael a coalition immediately following the Assembly election, but this had been rejected. In return, they rejected Alun Michael's own desperate offer of a coalition in the hours leading to the no-confidence vote. Due to their small number, however, they remain in a relatively weak position in the Assembly. Rhodri Morgan's administration will be tempted to pursue a more emollient approach, as was demonstrated in the offer of a coalition later in the year. At the same time the Liberal Democrats were wary of having their identity as a distinct party diminished by too close an involvement with a party that is, currently at least, so unpopular in their rural strongholds. In the event the offer of two Cabinet posts and the promise of significant influence on future policy was enough to overcome these fears.

Meanwhile polling data reinforced assessments made at the time of the Assembly elections, that the electorate in Wales is differentiating between the levels of representation now available to them, and that quite distinct patterns of voting are emerging. In January 2000, HTV began a series of opinion polls undertaken by NOP which tracked these responses as follows:

Figure 3.5. How would you vote if a general election for Westminster were held tomorrow? (all figures percentages)

	General Election 1997	July 2000	May 2000	March 2000	January 2000
Conservative	20	25	23	20	21
Labour	55	51	47	50	56
Lib Dem	12	9	12	12	8
Plaid Cymru	10	13	15	16	13
Other party	3	2	2	2	3

Accession to the First Secretaryship by Rhodri Morgan, in February, was assumed to have overcome the lingering resentment of the previous leadership contest and the shadow it cast over the early days of the Assembly. HTV's polling revealed a huge amount of public goodwill for Rhodri Morgan, along with heightened expectations in his leadership of the Assembly. Yet the polls indicated no lift in Labour's support. At the same time, voters in Wales continued to show a clear pattern of differentiation between their voting intentions for a Westminster election and those for the Assembly, as Figure 3.6 demonstrates:

Figure 3.6. How would you vote if an election for the National Assembly for Wales were held tomorrow? (all figures percentages)

	Assembly Election 1999	July 2000	May 2000	March 2000	January 2000
Conservative	16	15	14	14	13
Labour	37	40	41	43	45
Lib Dem	13	8	10	10	6
Plaid Cymru	30	34	32	31	33
Other party	5	3	3	2	3

PUBLIC ATTITUDES

As well as recording voting intention, HTV's regular polls starting in January 2000 also tracked public attitudes to the Assembly more generally, its performance and whether it should acquire more powers. For instance, in March, respondents were asked how they would vote if another referendum were held. This produced a more positive response than the extremely close result achieved in the 1997 referendum.

Figure 3.7. If there were a further referendum on the National Assembly for Wales, would you vote 'Yes' to keep the Assembly or 'No' to abolish it? (all figures percentages)

	ALL	Assembly Vote			
		Con	Lab	Lib D	Plaid
Yes, keep it	53	32	64	45	76
No, abolish it	36	59	26	49	19
Don't know	11	9	10	6	5

Adjusted figures (omitting the don't knows):

	March 2000	Referendum 1997
Yes	59.5%	50.3%
No	40.4%	49.7%

At the same time, answers to a question on how well the Assembly was doing more generally produced a less positive response, stubbornly fixed at just below 50 per cent (see Figure 3.8).

Figure 3.8. Overall, how good a job do you think the National Assembly is doing for Wales? (all figures percentages)

	January 2000	March 2000	May 2000
Good	46	46	46
Poor	41	44	40
Don't Know	13	9	15

The poll also set out to review the public's perception of the Assembly's performance in the key policy areas. Very few of those polled perceived that the Assembly had made a positive difference to the way agriculture was being managed in Wales, nor the economy generally. In the areas of education and the health service, however, where the Assembly has been able to make more resources available and launch new initiatives, public perception of the Assembly having made a positive impact is greater. Whilst a majority of the public still remains to be convinced, the answers to this question are the first signs of the public accepting that the new institutions and procedures of Welsh politics are delivering more than might have previously prevailed.

Figure 3.9. One year on (May 2000), do you believe that the national Assembly has made a positive difference to the running of agriculture, the economy, health or education? (all figures percentages)

	Yes	No difference	Made matters worse	Too soon to say	Don't know
Agriculture	7	42	10	29	11
Economy	11	43	10	29	6
Health	18	43	15	19	5
Education	22	41	7	19	11

HTV's survey in July showed that a significant proportion of the people of Wales wished to see the Assembly given law making powers. Almost one in four, however, remained unconvinced by the constitutional reform and wished to see the Assembly abolished. Of the 43 per cent who wanted law-making powers, support comes from all parties (see Figure 3.10). Whilst one might expect Plaid Cymru supporters to advocate such increased powers, nearly a third of Conservative supporters shared a similar ambition.

Figure 3.10. The National Assembly is one year old. Which of these alternative views comes closest to your own opinion? (all figures are percentages)

The Assembly should continue with its present range of powers and responsibilities				
All	Con	Lab	Lib Dem	Plaid
28	28	34	18	31

The Assembly should have law making powers				
All	Con	Lab	Lib Dem	Plaid
43	31	47	56	59

The Assembly has failed and should be disbanded				
All	Con	Lab	Lib Dem	Plaid
23	39	14	19	8

Don't know / not sure				
All	Con	Lab	Lib Dem	Plaid
6	2	5	7	2

PRESS AND MEDIA

One of the main difficulties that has faced the National Assembly in establishing itself in the minds and affections of the Welsh people has been a sense of its detachment from their everyday concerns. This is largely because in contrast to Scotland, for example, Wales has no national press of quality to report and give a context and explanation to its proceedings.

In terms of an indigenous daily press Wales has only two morning newspapers — The *Western Mail* (weekday circulation 57,035) and the *Daily Post* (weekday circulation in north Wales 46,233).[39] In the capital city, the *Western Mail's* circulation is thought to be no more than 6,000. The overwhelming audience for newspapers in Wales is for the London press, especially the tabloids, which rarely mention Wales at all, and less still the workings of the National Assembly.

The launch of the *Welsh Mirror*, in September 1999, added considerably to the range of indigenous reporting. However, it cannot be said that the Assembly is covered by any newspaper that gives a sense of a 'paper of record.' The *Western Mail* comes closest, often devoting a page a day to proceedings and events at the Assembly. But most stories are given prominence in response to their personality content and human interest. There is little reflective analysis or commentary allowed in the columns, and little evidence of an understanding of the underlying processes at work in the Assembly — processes that might have profound future consequences. So, for example, in November 1999 a joint document on Objective One match funding, signed by the Economic spokesmen of the three Opposition parties flagging up the basis on which they would coalesce around a motion of no confidence in the First Secretary, went unremarked in the Welsh press, apart from a passing reference, some days after the event, in *Wales on Sunday*.

The three television channels in Wales — BBC Wales, S4C, and HTV — have a much larger audience and much greater geographical coverage than the press. This is despite the 40 per cent of north-eastern and south-eastern Wales in the so-called overlap areas where viewers can tune into signals coming from both sides of the border. The Welsh-based television channels have also invested heavily in their coverage of the Assembly. Each has established new studios in the Assembly itself and the news bulletins on radio and television, on all channels, are full of reportage from the Assembly's proceedings. In addition, S4C has digital space for a completely new channel, part of which is being devoted to live coverage of the Assembly's proceedings.

There has certainly been a great deal of space afforded Assembly debates and personalities in the broadcast media. Again, however, the same

[39] Audit Bureau of Circulation, 8 October 1999.

limitation applies to television as to the Welsh press, but for different reasons. However much coverage is provided, it is difficult for the broadcast media to provide the context and understanding of the deeper meaning of issues and events. This remains an advantage of the print media, but in Wales as already stated, there is all too often simply a vacuum here.[40]

The motion of no confidence and resignation of Alun Michael brought the National Assembly under the concentrated gaze of the London press and media for the first time. London journalists descended in large numbers, greatly adding to the sense of drama that built up around the events. Indeed, Welsh radio and television gave coverage to the coverage, so to speak, frequently turning to the visitors from across the border for their impressions, not just of the politics underway, but of the venue itself in Cardiff Bay.

The resignation prompted front-page treatment in the London broadsheets, often accompanied by editorials. However, the main focus of attention was the impact in London itself, and especially at Westminster. Alun Michael's dramatic resignation took place while Tony Blair was on his feet during Prime Minister's Question Time in the House of Commons. Blair was plainly discomforted. The news was relayed to him instantaneously by the Opposition (via mobile phones and bleepers) that 'his man in Wales' had just fallen on his sword. As the headline on Matthew Parris' political sketch in the Times put it, 'Blair wobbles as his party is out-bleeped', while the *Telegraph*'s headline was 'Blair is caught off message as Michael quits'.[41] There was no doubt that the main interest of the London press and media was the backwash Welsh events were having in London, with Blair appearing to lose his grip on devolution. There was also much interest in the precedent Wales might set for the London mayoral contest. As the *Guardian* leader the following day, 'A Lieutenant Departs', put it: '...if London tries to install a puppet, the people will rebel.'[42]

There were, however, some reflections on the impact in Wales itself. An editorial in the *Times* judged that: 'Mr Michael has not only united his opponents against him but inspired the call for further powers to be transferred to Cardiff.'[43]

And, in a leader column headed 'Welsh National Soap Opera', the *Telegraph* reflected:

It may seem strange for a Unionist paper such as this to suggest more power for the Welsh Assembly — to raise its own money, for instance. Since no-one seems

---

[40] For a wider discussion of these issues see Geraint Talfan Davies *Not By Bread Alone: Information Media and the National Assembly*, Wales Media Forum, Centre for Journalism Studies, Cardiff University, 1999.

[41] 10 February 2000.

[42] *Guardian*, 10 February 2000.

[43] *Times*, 9 February 2000.

happy with it in its current, powerless form, that however, would appear to be the only way forward.[44]

However, there was little analysis in the press, whether London or Cardiff-based, to explain what was going on behind the scenes. In particular, no newspaper picked up the full extent of the growing divisions within the Labour Group. For instance, the key debate on the Westminster Government's legislative programme a week before the no confidence vote went virtually unnoticed.

That the Welsh press and media generally did not catch up on such matters, let alone fully understand or interpret them, is a commentary on the current state of Welsh political news coverage and reporting. Television and radio were especially deficient in this regard, given the relatively large resources available to them. The nightly news programmes provided a breathless, and on the whole superficial, coverage of events as the day of the no confidence vote came and went. Reports were invariably reactive. Interviews were generally with the party leaders, with little attempt made to uncover the stresses and strains being placed on all the parties (but especially Labour). The resultant pressure could have been uncovered by interviewing, for example, backbench AMs.

At the same time the no-confidence vote reveale 1 a large appetite amongst the Welsh television audience for political news, certainly when dramatic events were unfolding. On the day of Alun Michael's resignation, BBC Wales' flagship news programme *Wales Today*, broadcasting between 6.30 and 7.00 pm, achieved one of the highest recorded ratings for any Welsh programme. Some 450,000 viewers tuned in to the programme, out of a total Welsh population of just under three million people, about 50 per cent of the available audience at the time.

With the National Assembly a year old in May, the Welsh media invested a good deal of analysis in how much it had achieved in its first year. The *Western Mail* captured the general mood. Alongside a front-page photograph of one-year-old Joshua Harding, born on 6 May 1999 (the day the Assembly was elected), the headline above an editorial put the question:

What's the difference between baby Joshua and the Assembly?
Answer: Joshua has teeth.

The verdict was clear: there had been an expectation that the Assembly could make a real difference to people's lives in Wales, but its progress had not been so good:

It has shown little sign of growing into the institution that had been desired. It is not yet strong; it has no real teeth. When it does walk, it is still with the aid of reins

[44] *Telegraph*, 9 February 2000

held by its mother, Mrs Westminster. It is bad-tempered. Too often it is selfish and self-centred. It is not a happy baby. [45]

The demands of providing pictures to back up the story took BBC *Wales Today* to Baglan Bay (near Swansea), where it reported that the Assembly had approved a new hospital — and to Broughton (in north-east Wales), where local people were resentful at the Assembly's failure (at that stage) to agree a £25 million grant to British Aerospace. This balanced look was matched by a careful conclusion from reporter, Simon Morris:

> The Assembly, with its limited powers, couldn't really be expected to make a big impact in just a year, but if it is to retain the support it has got and persuade the doubters, it has still got a lot of work to do.[46]

HTV's political programme, *Waterfront*, interviewed Kevin Morgan, chairman of the Yes campaign in 1997, for his view of the Assembly's progress. He told the programme that the Assembly was discovering that it did not have the powers it thought it had, but went on to add: 'What is twelve months out of centuries of London government? ... I'm still optimistic.'[47]

Wales on Sunday used the anniversary to pass a verdict on Labour's performance. It published an opinion poll, one year on, which showed that nearly one in four voters were less likely to vote Labour in Wales because of what they called 'the party leadership stitch-up'. Their editorial said:

> It is perhaps surprising that so many people remain angry even after the replacement of Mr Michael by the far more popular Rhodri Morgan. Tony Blair's weasel words of apology last month for his interference in the Welsh Labour leadership contest were too little and too late.[48]

And, indeed, most newspapers confined their analysis of the development of the Assembly to comments on the Labour Party's problems. This was made easier by the fact that the anniversary coincided with the results of the English local elections and the contest for London Mayor. It was a simple task to wrap up Wales and London together with a common charge against the Prime Minister of 'control-freakery'. The *Sunday Times* was typical in asserting that Downing Street had failed to learn the obvious lessons:

> Mr Blair's miscalculation is all the more startling because it follows Labour's near-disaster in the Welsh Assembly elections after No 10's meddling. Downing Street will have to move fast if devolution is not to become the political black hole that the poll tax became for Margaret Thatcher.[49]

[45] *Western Mail*, 6 May 2000.
[46] *BBC Wales Today*, May 5 2000.
[47] *HTV*, May 7 2000.
[48] *Wales on Sunday*, May 7 2000
[49] *Sunday Times*, May 7 2000

Perhaps the outstanding National Assembly media event came at the tail end of the Assembly's first year. This was an angry confrontation on BBC 2's *Newsnight* in August 2000 between the First Secretary, Rhodri Morgan, and presenter, Jeremy Vine. It followed a tendentious short film examining the Assembly's progress that was introduced by Vine in the following terms: 'Don't switch off, there is no easy way to say this. We're about to discuss the Welsh Assembly.' [50]

The comment angered Rhodri Morgan, sitting in the Cardiff studio. The ensuing seven minute video made him angrier still. As he put it, in a newspaper article some days later, under a headline *Why I Blew My Top on Telly* , it was:

> …full of stereotypes like the Gorsedd of Bards walking along and Llew Smith at the Nye Bevan stones above Tredegar. Their choice of politicians to interview was odd, with two die-hard anti-devolutionists like Llew and Helen Mary Jones, who favours independence. People in England would have seen two people, both of whom don't seem happy about devolution. The report implied that most people are fed up with the Welsh Assembly. In fact, as the recent HTV poll showed, the attitude to the Assembly is quite positive. If anything, a lot of people think it should have more powers. Not only was the Newsnight piece a stitch-up, but it was badly stitched …[51]

Although a BBC spokesman claimed the item 'was within the programme's usual humorous style',[52] it provoked an unusually large response, not just in Wales but amongst viewers in England as well. The Welsh Labour Party's headquarters in Cardiff and Morgan's office in the National Assembly were inundated with faxes, emails and calls from people annoyed at what they regarded as an over-patronising tone. One of Morgan's researchers, Annabelle Harle, remarked: 'Because it's August and the silly season, they think it's OK to put Rhodri Morgan in a broom cupboard and have open season on the Welsh.'[53] The *Mail*'s editorial line was also supportive:

> To see him sticking up for Wales and the National Assembly … was an immensely gratifying spectacle. The First Secretary was right to refuse to roll over and let less-than-objective criticism, presented with unnecessary but all too customary arrogance pass unchecked.[54]

---

[50] *Newsnight*, BBC2, 12 August 2000.
[51] *Wales on Sunday*, 13 August 2000.
[52] *Ibid.*
[53] *Western Mail*, 9 August 2000.
[54] *Ibid.*

A CONSTITUTIONAL CONVENTION BY OTHER MEANS

Experience of the first year suggests that greater powers for the Assembly will be driven more by policy demands than by high flown constitutional considerations. This has been demonstrated in all the significant areas of the Assembly's responsibility, from economic development to health, education and agriculture.

In economic policy, there were arguments throughout the year on whether or not the Treasury would meet the Assembly's requirements on providing sufficient match funding to draw down EU Objective One money for West Wales and the Valleys. In February, as we have seen, the issue prompted the resignation of Alun Michael as First Secretary. And, although in July the Comprehensive Spending Review allocation seemed to put the issue to rest, there is little doubt it will return to haunt the administration. The issue provided a classic case of upper and lower tiers of governance joining together to put pressure on a level in between, in this case the British nation-state. The question relates to the most basic matter of all in the devolution process — money. The record of the Assembly in its early years will be judged overwhelmingly on the extent to which it manages to lever extra resources for the more impoverished parts of Wales.

A defining issue in health proved to be the extension of free eye tests to a wider range of groups — ethnic minorities, the hearing impaired, and those with single vision. As we have seen, the matter was regarded as so important by the Plaid Cymru Group in the Assembly that it was the main condition for their decision not to oppose the Labour administration's budget for 2000–01. Without Plaid's support, the minority administration would have had difficulty in getting the budget through. However, once the concession had been made the civil service did its best to claw it back. The Chief Medical Officer for Wales, Ruth Hall, advised that there was no evidence of any health gain by extending free eye tests in the way proposed. Against her, the Opposition parties stressed that:

- At least 50 per cent of glaucoma goes undetected, and
- Since eye test charges had been introduced a decade earlier the number of people undergoing eye tests has fallen by a third.

The arguments persuaded Assembly Health Secretary, Jane Hutt, to support the extension of free tests against the advice of her Chief Medical Officer. The extension was even supported by the Conservatives. The decision added an extra £1.9 million to the forthcoming year's health budget. Opposition AMs took the view this was a case of the civil service being reluctant to contemplate a policy initiative for Wales that was different from England. It proved a rare early instance where the democratic impulse, channelled through the Assembly, won the day.

A major clash over powers arose over the issue of performance-related pay for teachers, in particular linking pay levels with examination results. This provoked the most serious legal test case in the life of the Assembly thus far. The dispute revolved around whether the Assembly possessed the transferred powers to decide the issue for itself, through secondary legislation. The dispute also led to a clash between the Pre-16 Education Committee and the executive over the desirability of Wales being allowed to operate a different system from England. Potentially, two Acts of Parliament allowed competence in the field — the 1986 Education (no 2) Act (under which powers are transferred) and the 1991 School Teachers' Pay and Conditions Act (under which they are not). This was part of the background to a legal test case in which the National Union of Teachers sought judicial review in the Royal Courts of Justice, in July, of regulations issued by the Department for Education and Employment. In his judgement on the case, Mr Justice Jackson found against the DfEE since, he said, it had illegally by-passed both Acts in issuing its regulations on performance-related pay. In relation to the 1986 Act, he added: 'This may be because the Welsh Assembly would not be prepared to make similar regulations governing teachers in Wales ...'.

Meanwhile, agriculture also proved a continual flashpoint for tensions between the Assembly administration and Whitehall throughout the year, from beef on the bone, to frustrations over the Assembly's inability to extend a calf processing scheme in Wales to the issue of GM foods. Constitutionally, the significance of all these debates was that they highlighted policy areas where the Assembly's wishes were being frustrated because it did not have primary legislative power. The examples quoted here represent the kind of issues that are likely to drive the Assembly to seek greater freedom of manoeuvre, greater discretion, more resources, and inevitably more power. The logic is to move first of all in the direction of the Scottish Parliament.

A route forward was defined by the Presiding Officer, Lord Elis-Thomas, in a major speech in March 2000. In it, he responded to calls that had been made by Ron Davies, the Liberal Democrats and Plaid Cymru that he should convene a Presiding Officer's Conference to expand the Assembly's powers. He said he believed there was a majority, possibly a two-thirds majority, in the Assembly who wished to see it assume full legislative powers, with even some of the Conservative Group in favour of extending the Assembly's powers. The 1998 Government of Wales Act which had established the Assembly did not represent a new constitutional settlement, he said. It was too close to the 1978 Wales Act for that. Rather it was merely the best that could be achieved in the circumstances of the time:

> It is not based on a clear legislative principle. It could be said to have elevated piecemeal development to an art form ...We are not at the beginning of a new constitution for Wales. We are at the beginning of the end of the old constitution

...We have the least that could be established at the time. We shouldn't say that a political fix is a national constitution. It is time we looked for more.[55]

He said the parties should come together in a conference under his chairman-ship — equivalent to a Speaker's Conference in the House of Commons — and produce a draft parliamentary Bill granting full legislative powers for the Assembly. This should be presented to the Secretary of State for Wales for him to promote in the Westminster parliament. More than that, the Presiding Officer suggested that the Bill should be presented in the year leading to the next Assembly elections in May 2003, so that it would become a defining issue in that contest.

Labour would not agree to the idea of a 'Speaker's Conference'. However, in July, First Secretary, Rhodri Morgan, announced that there would be a review of how the Assembly was working during the forthcoming year. He stressed that he was anxious that the four parties reach a consensus on any changes and consequently the review should be undertaken within the context of the Government of Wales Act 1998:

> That is, we act within that Act and I am not eager to discuss whether we should amend it ... I do not want to be a piggy in the middle between Plaid Cymru, who may or may not wish to question the Government of Wales Act, and the Conservative Group, who certainly would not.[56]

A Review Group will be chaired by the Presiding Officer and comprise the party leaders and business managers. The review will seek contributions from party groups, individual Assembly members, the Assembly's partners in business, local government, the voluntary sector, academics and others. A spokesman for Rhodri Morgan's office stressed that the review was not Opposition-driven and was not related to the idea of a 'Speaker's Confer-ence'. Nevertheless, it is inevitable that the review will promote debate around the Assembly's status as a body corporate, a need to separate its exec-utive from its legislative function, and its legislative competence. The coali-tion deal reached with the Liberal Democrats in October included the establishment of 'an independent commission into the powers and electoral arrangements of the National Assembly.'[57] However, this would not report until after the next Assembly elections in 2003.

The weekend before Rhodri Morgan's announcement, the Presiding Offi-cer laid down, in a speech to the Institute of Welsh Politics in Aberystwyth, in effect what he interpreted as the parameters of the review. He began by asking a loaded question 'To what extent is the body over which I have the

[55] Lord Elis-Thomas, *Wales — A New Constitution*, Welsh Governance Centre, Cardiff University, 2 March 2000.

[56] Assembly *Record*, 12 July 2000.

[57] *Putting Wales First: The First Partnership Agreement of the National Assembly for Wales*, 6 October 2000.

duty of presiding, really the National Assembly for Wales?' to which he gave the following response:

> Despite the first year of powers, it would be difficult to argue that there is a policy making cycle, in which legislation, in this case secondary legislation, plays its part, from the perception of issues to consultation with interest groups, Assembly debate, the making of legislation, implementation and the monitoring of consequences. There is still no policy-making process for Wales.[58]

The Presiding Officer's assessment of the confusion and uncertainty about the Assembly's powers in relation to Westminster-determined primary legislation was echoed by one of Labour's constitutional experts, Lord Gwilym Prys Davies, in a lecture given to the Law Society some weeks later at the Llanelli National Eisteddfod:

> Under the protocol between the Secretary of State for Wales and the Assembly, and under Section 31 of the Wales Act, the Secretary of State is the link between Cardiff and the department in Whitehall which is responsible for promoting a Bill. However, one cannot be content with the mere existence of a protocol, taking for granted that it will work effectively. It can be difficult to enforce: for example, Cardiff proposals may be contrary to the interests of the UK Government, or low on its list of priorities. Who has the ear of the Prime Minister? And when the Assembly Cabinet wishes to amend a Bill being introduced by a Whitehall department, it is not clear to me what will be the mechanism in place to ensure that the Welsh proposal receives full consideration in the Whitehall department — and in time — as the new Bill is being drawn up and formulated. Where the Bill has substantial implications for Wales, will one of the Assembly's civil servants be a member of the Bill team in Whitehall responsible for preparing the primary legislation? Otherwise, who will be there to scrutinise the Bill and safeguard Welsh interests? If the new primary legislation does not adequately meet the requirements of the Assembly's Cabinet and give it an opportunity to make subordinate legislation to meet our distinctive needs, this may lead eventually to conflict between Cardiff and Westminster and instability. It is here that I see the main threat to the Welsh devolution model.[59]

However, during the first year the central question of how the Assembly might influence primary legislation at Westminster did not feature a great deal, except as a matter of principle. Rather, the major preoccupation was the character of the Assembly itself and differing views about its future direction. A key source of disagreement, and to some extent confusion, was the way a Cabinet system had been grafted on to the Assembly's legal status as a corporate body during the passage of the Wales Act. The corporate nature of the institution means that legally, the Assembly as a whole (that is, all elected

---

[58] Lord Elis-Thomas AM, *National Assembly: A Year in Power?* Address to the Institute of Welsh Politics, Aberystwyth, 8 July 2000.

[59] Lord Gwilym Prys Davies, *The National Assembly: A Year of Laying the Foundations*, The Law Society, 9 August.

Members, whether government or opposition) is responsible for its actions, making it comparable to local government. In practice, however, the Cabinet system makes the Assembly more of a parliamentary body where the executive and legislative functions are separated.

This constitutional confusion was the basis for at least two views about the way the Assembly should work and its potential for development. The first saw the new institution essentially as an addition to the previous Welsh Office arrangements, with the administration continuing to act to a large extent as an outpost of Whitehall with the Assembly Members operating in a kind of advisory capacity. Certainly, in the Assembly's opening months Alun Michael, who had seamlessly moved from his role of Secretary of State for Wales within the Welsh Office to First Secretary within the Assembly, operated in executive terms as if little had changed.

This outlook rapidly became unsustainable, however, as the eventual vote of no confidence asserted. The injection of 60 elected politicians into the previous system of Welsh governance was no mere evolution in which business could carry on as though little of substance had altered. In practice, it was to revolutionise the old territorial pattern of Whitehall-dominated administration. The future was not to be more of the same but, instead, the acquisition of a parliamentary process for Welsh democratic governance. This was the central constitutional debate that animated the Assembly's first year, which crystallised in the motion of no confidence in Alun Michael and was resolved in favour of the parliamentary approach with the coalition deal between Labour and the Liberal Democrats in October.

In a lecture on the eve of his confirmation as First Secretary, Rhodri Morgan referred to the eight years experience that Scots politicians of different parties had had in their Convention leading to the establishment of the Scottish Parliament. This, he said, had built the confidence and trust that was an essential background to the Scottish coalition arrangements. Then he added: 'But in Wales we had nothing like that. We had no constitutional convention. We had no platform for being able to build sufficient trust to enter a coalition.' [60]

Looking back on the National Assembly's first year, it is hard not to conclude that what took place was, in effect, a Welsh alternative to the Scottish Convention — a Welsh convention by other means. It was a time when a relatively powerless institution began the process of feeling its way, testing its powers, and defining the issues which were to be most important for the future. During the first year, a debate was clarified between those who saw the Assembly evolving relatively quickly in a parliamentary direction, with a clearer separation of its executive and legislative functions, and those who felt that the priority should be to make the existing, albeit imperfect, structures work more effectively. Above all however the Assembly provided, for

[60] Rhodri Morgan, *Variable Geometry UK*, Institute of Welsh Affairs, March 2000.

the first time in Wales, a forum where the political parties could get to know each other on an ongoing basis, and start building the confidence and trust necessary to take the devolution process forward.

BIBLIOGRAPHY

Davies, R., *Devolution: A Process not an Event* (Cardiff: Institute of Welsh Affairs, 1999).

Jones, J. and Balsom, D. *The Road to the National Assembly for Wales* (University of Wales Press, May 2000).

Morgan, K. and Mungham, G., *Redesigning Democracy: The Making of the Welsh Assembly* (Bridgend: Seren, May 2000).

Morgan, R., *Variable Geometry UK* (Cardiff: Institute of Welsh Affairs, 2000).

Osmond, J., (ed.), *Devolution Looks Ahead: Monitoring the National Assembly May to August 2000* (Cardiff: Institute of Welsh Affairs, 2000).

Osmond, J., *Welsh Politics in the New Millennium* (Cardiff: Institute of Welsh Affairs, 1999).

Osmond, J., *Adrift but Afloat: The Civil Service and the National Assembly* (IWA, May 1999).

Osmond, J. (ed.), *Devolution: 'A Dynamic, Settled Process?' Monitoring the National Assembly July to December 1999* (IWA, December 1999).

Osmond, J. (Ed.), *Devolution in Transition: Monitoring the National Assembly February to May 2000* (IWA, May 2000).

Talfan Davies, G., *Not by Bread Alone: Information Media and the National Assembly* (Wales Media Forum, Centre for Journalism Studies, Cardiff University, 1999).

4

A 'Bare Knuckle Ride': Northern Ireland

Rick Wilford and Robin Wilson[1]

BACKGROUND: WAR BY OTHER MEANS

At a private conference in September 1998 the Northern Ireland First Minister (designate), the Ulster Unionist leader David Trimble, echoed a fellow unionist's description of recent political developments in the region as a 'bare-knuckle ride'. It might have seemed at that time, five months on from the Belfast Agreement,[2] endorsed by referendum in May[3] and followed by elections to the Northern Ireland Assembly in June,[4] that Mr Trimble could

[1] This chapter draws throughout upon the work of the whole Northern Ireland monitoring team—variously including Lizanne Dowds, Liz Fawcett, Paul Gorecki, Elizabeth Meehan, Paul Mitchell, Duncan Morrow and Graham Walker. For that reason, and since responsibility for its content rests entirely with the authors, we have not separately referenced their contributions. But we are very appreciative of them.

[2] *The Belfast Agreement: An Agreement reached at the Multi-Party Talks on Northern Ireland*, Cm 3883, April 1998.

[3] There were concurrent referendums on 22 May in Northern Ireland and the Republic of Ireland. In the former, on an unprecedentedly high turnout for the UK of 81.1 per cent, the pro-agreement vote was 71.12 per cent (676,966 votes) with 28.88 per cent (274,879 votes) against. In the republic, on a turnout of 56.3 per cent, the pro-agreement vote was even more emphatic: 94.4 per cent (1,442,583) balloted in favour, with just 5.6 per cent (85,748) against.

[4] On the face of it, the election produced a massive pro-agreement majority in the assembly of 80 to 28. The 80 comprised the UUP, SDLP, SF, Alliance, Progressive Unionists and the Women's Coalition. However, within the ranks of the UUP were a number of members who had voted 'no' in the referendum, including Peter Weir (who subsequently resigned the party whip to sit with anti-agreement unionists), Roy Beggs Jnr and Pauline Armitage.

The share of first-preference votes and the number of seats won at the PR-STV assembly election, on 25 June 1998, for each of the successful parties were as follows:

Party	first preferences (%)	seats (no)
SDLP	22.0	24
UUP	21.3	28
DUP	18.1	20
SF	17.6	18
Alliance	6.5	6
* UK Unionists	4.5	5
Progressive Unionists	2.5	2
Women's Coalition	1.6	2
** Independent Unionists	1.3	3

* Four of the five UK Unionists resigned from the party over a dispute with its leader, Robert McCartney MP, to form the 'Northern Ireland Unionist Party' with effect from 15 January 1999. One of the four, Roger Hutchinson, was expelled from the NIUP on 2 December 1999 when, against party policy, he decided to take a seat on an assembly statutory committee. He now sits as an Independent Unionist.

** The three Independent Unionists formed themselves into the 'United Unionist Assembly Party' with effect from 21 September 1998.

afford to unclench his fingers in anticipation of more comfortable progress. Not so.

The Northern Ireland timescale, set by the concession to Sinn Féin (SF) of the principle of talks without IRA arms decommissioning in the event of a renewed ceasefire just after Labour's election, and by Tony Blair's urgency thereafter, ran ahead of the synchronous devolution process for Scotland and Wales. But if the unspoken theory was that the ramshackle Northern Ireland political vehicle had constantly to be pushed for fear it might stall, the sickening jolts and near-disasters, as well as the moments of apparent freewheeling, made for an interesting if tortuous journey. On 1 July 1998, at its first plenary session, the shadow Assembly elected Mr Trimble as First Minister and his nationalist counterpart, Séamus Mallon, deputy leader of the Social Democratic and Labour Party, as deputy First Minister.[5] But on 1 July 1999, when power was devolved to Cardiff and Edinburgh, Northern Ireland was stuck in a sectarian jam, despite the efforts of London and Dublin, discussed below, to clear a path for the transfer of powers.

Decommissioning, as the republican leader, Gerry Adams, once said unguardedly of the IRA, hadn't gone away — unsurprisingly, because disarmament means the IRA, and the other paramilitaries, in effect *would*. If republicans persistently refused to say, as Mr Blair beseeched them, that the 'war' was 'over', it was because it wasn't — not just for them, but for any of the Northern Ireland protagonists. With its provisions for communal registration[6] in the Assembly, and for formation of the latter's Executive Committee by an automatic, d'Hondt mechanism[7] requiring no inter-party

[5] The joint election (defined by the agreement as a 'key decision') of the only nominees, Messrs Trimble and Mallon, as First and deputy First Minister (designate) respectively required the application of one of the cross-community voting procedures stipulated by the agreement. There are two: 'parallel consent', which requires a majority of those present and voting, including a majority of both nationalists and unionists (see note 6); or, 'weighted majority', which requires 60 per cent of members present and voting, including at least 40 per cent of both unionists and nationalists. The nominees were elected on the first of these procedures, although SF members abstained.

[6] In signing the Assembly roll, members were required to designate themselves as 'unionist', 'nationalist' or other. This yielded 58 unionists, 42 nationalists and 8 others. Besides the symbolic value of these badges of communal identity, such self-designations were necessary to enable the tests of cross-community consent within the Assembly to be applied, notably to 'key decisions' as defined by the Agreement. The latter included voting on budgetary procedures, the election of the First and deputy First Ministers (designate) and the adoption of the Programme for Government. The standing orders adopted by the assembly provide that any party may alter its self-designation once during the life of an assembly.

[7] Named after its Belgian inventor, Viktor d'Hondt, the rule operated thus: the total number of seats won by each of the parties was divided initially by 1 so that the party with the largest number of seats (the UUP) won the first executive seat. In the second round, the UUP's total was divided by 2, while the remaining parties had their totals again divided by 1 — this yielded the first 'cabinet' seat for the SDLP since it now had the highest average. In short, each time a party won a seat, its divisor increased by one. This mechanistic process continued until all 10 seats were filled: 3 UUP, 3 SDLP, 2 DUP, 2 SF. D'Hondt favours larger parties in most circumstances: in this case, the UUP and SDLP were allocated 60 per cent of executive seats, based on a combined share of 48 per cent of Assembly members and an even lower combined share (43.3 per cent) of first-preference votes.

agreement,[8] the drafters of the Agreement implicitly accepted its consequences: that post-agreement politics, to borrow from Clausewitz, would be
the pursuit of war by other means.

As with the preceding three decades, the conflict was over the constitutional future of Northern Ireland. Had the Agreement, as 'yes' unionists
claimed (and republican fundamentalists feared), copper-fastened partition?
Or had it set in train, as republican leaders asserted (and unreconstructed
unionists worried) an irreversible political momentum towards a united
Ireland? A week after the Agreement, Mr Trimble secured a 72 per cent
majority in his party's ruling Ulster Unionist Council meeting in Belfast,
reassuring his supporters thus: 'We are not on a road to a united Ireland.'

Mr Adams, meanwhile, insisted to the *ard fheis* (conference) of his party,
meeting in Dublin the same weekend, that the process was indeed transitional towards Irish unity.[9] The SDLP view, as bizarrely expressed by the
future minister Bríd Rodgers,[10] was that the Agreement was not even a settlement: it was 'more fundamental', she said — 'an agreement to disagree'!

The outworking of this sustained constitutional conflict was not difficult
to anticipate. Not only would Northern Ireland be cut off from the modernising dynamic characteristic of the wider UK constitutional reform project
(this chapter is noticeably lacking in references to Scotland and Wales):
devolution would be involution. Worse still, the questions on which politics
would focus would be eminently predictable. Which state apparatus was to
be legitimised and which disbanded, that of the Royal Ulster Constabulary
(and the army) or the IRA? Which standard was to be officially flown aloft,
the Union flag or the Irish Tricolour? Should 'political prisoners' be released
quickly, or should they remain behind bars unless their weapons were
destroyed? And who would control the streets, 'loyal orders' or 'nationalist
residents'? All the conflicts of the post-agreement years were to be inscribed
in those bellwether issues.

Successive efforts to reproduce the pressure-cooker atmosphere of the
week leading up to Good Friday 1998 failed to crack the decommissioning
conundrum. Mr Blair and his Dublin partner, the *Taoiseach*, Bertie Ahern,
were rebuffed at Hillsborough when they tried to shoehorn the republicans
into accepting some — any — decommissioning before the devolved executive was established. That was on April Fool's Day, 1999. As time ticked
away to the now annual 'Drumcree standoff' in Co Armagh in early July over
a contested Orange parade, the two premiers, plus the world's media, heaved
again. At last Mr Blair detected a 'seismic shift' by the republican

---

[8] There was not even any carve-up in the corridors as to which party would get which department;
indeed, even the number of departments was not determined until the December 1998 agreement
between the First and deputy First Ministers Designate, when nationalists successfully held out for 10 to
ensure SF received two.

[9] *Observer*, 19 April 1998.

[10] *Irish Times*, 24 April 1998.

Figure 4.1. Key events in Northern Ireland since 1998

10 April 1998	Promulgation of Belfast Agreement; 'letter of comfort' from prime minister, Tony Blair, on paramilitary arms decommissioning to David Trimble fails to avoid split in his UUP team.
22 May 1998	Agreement supported in referendum by 71 per cent in Northern Ireland — Catholic support almost total but Protestants divided — and 94 per cent in the Republic of Ireland.
25 June 1998	In PR-STV elections to 108-member New Northern Ireland Assembly DUP and SF do well at expense of centre parties — each with 18 per cent of first-preference votes, as against 21 per cent for UUP and 22 per cent for SDLP.
1 July 1998	David Trimble (UUP) and Séamus Mallon (SDLP) elected as, respectively, First and deputy First Ministers (designate) at first meeting of assembly at Stormont.
15 August 1998	In worst ever single attack in the 'troubles', 29 people killed by bomb planted in Omagh, Co Tyrone, by 'Real IRA' splinter group.
31 October 1998	Deadline for establishment of north–south bodies expires in absence of agreement on formation of Executive Committee, owing to impasse over paramilitary weapons.
18 Dec. 1998	Messrs Trimble and Mallon agree on structure of 10 departments for devolved administration, six north-south 'implementation bodies' and six areas for cross-border co-operation.
1 April 1999	Tony Blair, and Taoiseach, Bertie Ahern, agree statement at Hillsborough to resolve impasse on arms decommissioning, but republicans (and others) opposed.
15 July 1999	Abortive attempt to run d'Hondt rule to establish Executive Committee, boycotted by UUP, following prolonged talks on weapons at Stormont; Séamus Mallon resigns as deputy first minister designate.
9 Sept. 1999	Former Hong Kong Governor, Chris Patten, publishes report of his independent commission on policing, to unionist outrage.
18 Nov. 1999	Talks chair, George Mitchell, concludes, apparently successfully, review of implementation of agreement begun 11 weeks earlier.
27 Nov. 1999	David Trimble secures 58 per cent support for entry into government from his party's Ulster Unionist Council, on basis of threat to resign as leader if no decommissioning by January.

29 Nov. 1999	Assembly meets for running of d'Hondt rule to establish ministers for 10 departments — assigned three UUP, three SDLP, two DUP and two SF.
2 Dec. 1999	Powers transferred to assembly; North/South Ministerial Council (NSMC) and British–Irish Council (BIC) formally instigated; Republic's government signs away territorial claim over north; Executive Committee (minus DUP ministers) meets for first time.
13 Dec. 1999	NSMC meets in Armagh.
17 Dec. 1999	BIC meets in London.
31 January 2000	Gen John de Chastelain releases his initial report on arms decommissioning to London and Dublin governments but not to the public.
11 February 2000	Northern Ireland secretary, Peter Mandelson, suspends Assembly to stave off resignation of David Trimble following day; Gen. de Chastelain's initial and second decommissioning reports are published simultaneously.
25 March 2000	David Trimble survives leadership challenge by Rev. Martin Smyth MP at UUP AGM, with 57 per cent support.
5 May 2000	Prime Minister and Taoiseach, after prolonged talks with parties, agree statement on putting arms 'beyond use' and re-establishment of devolution.
6 May 2000	IRA statement holds out eventual placement of weapons 'beyond use' and an interim 'confidence-building' measure, i.e. opening of some dumps for inspection; governments announce arms inspectors to be former ANC Secretary-General, Cyril Ramaphosa, and former Finnish President, Martti Ahtisaari.
27 May 2000	David Trimble wins 53 per cent backing for re-entry into government from UUC, though anticipating concessions on flying of Union flag over government buildings (resisted by SF ministers) and policing reforms.
29 May 2000	Powers restored to Assembly.
31 May 2000	DUP says will not only boycott Executive Committee but will periodically rotate its ministers.
26 June 2000	Arms inspectors say have seen a 'substantial' amount of IRA weaponry, which could not be used without their detection.
29 June 2000	Executive Committee announces interim 'Agenda for Government'.
4 July 2000	DUP motion to have SF excluded from executive attracts support of four UUP assembly members, leaving David Trimble in minority of 26-32 in unionist bloc.
7 July 2000	Assembly rises for summer recess.

27 July 2000	DUP engages in first ministerial rotation, replacing Peter Robinson and Nigel Dodds with, respectively, Gregory Campbell and Maurice Morrow.
28 July 2000	Last major batch of paramilitary prisoners released in line with agreement timescale, amid triumphalist scenes.
19 August 2000	Clashes at Ulster Defence Association parade in Belfast lead to eruption of loyalist feud with Ulster Volunteer Force.
22 August 2000	Johnny 'Mad Dog' Adair, leader of the UDA in west Belfast, re-imprisoned for alleged breach of his licence.

movement. But BBC Northern Ireland's political editor, Dennis Murray, delighted the assembled journalistic throng by commenting that for unionists 'the earth didn't move'.

This attempt to constrain unionists into 'triggering' the d'Hondt procedure proved abortive. On 15 July, while the Assembly went through the motions of constituting an Executive Committee,[11] the UUP's Assembly members remained sequestered in party headquarters in central Belfast, rendering the whole exercise redundant. An exasperated Mr Mallon resigned as deputy First Minister (designate), intensifying the gloom hanging over the devolution process.

BACK TO YOU, MR MITCHELL

In desperation, the two governments twisted the arm of the talks chair, George Mitchell, to have another go at knocking the Northern Ireland politicians' (and paramilitaries') heads together. He was not enthusiastic. Amid the mood of euphoria prevailing in the aftermath of the Agreement, Mr

---

[11] Shortly before the Assembly convened, the Secretary of State had laid a standing order which stipulated that the Executive must include at least three designated unionists and three designated nationalists. Against that stipulation, the process of constituting an executive was utterly idle. Nevertheless, and in the absence of the UUP, d'Hondt was applied. Both the DUP and the UKUP refused to nominate. Ian Paisley rose in his seat to state (New Northern Ireland Assembly Report, 15 July 1999): 'In order to oust Sinn Féin from office, in keeping with the wishes of a majority of Unionist people, I refuse to nominate.' Speaking on behalf of his then intact UKUP, the party's leader Robert McCartney was even more blunt (NNIAR, 15 July 1999): 'As a democrat, under no circumstances would I consider for a second nominating either myself or anyone else in my party to sit in an Executive with two members of the IRA Army Council, Martin McGuinness and Pat Doherty.' The Alliance Party also refused to nominate in protest at the Secretary of State's standing order. For the record, the only nominating parties — SDLP and SF — came up with an 'executive' comprising: Mark Durkan (Finance and Personnel), Sean Farren (Regional Development), Brid Rodgers (Higher and Further Education, Training and Employment), Joe Hendron (Health, Personal Social Services and Public Safety), Denis Haughey (Social Development) and Alban Maginness (Environment) (all SDLP); Bairbre de Brún (Enterprise, Trade and Investment), Martin McGuinness (Agriculture and Rural Development), Pat Doherty (Education) and Mary Nelis (Culture, Arts and Leisure). The procedure gave no clue to the composition of the actual Executive, save for Mr Durkan's subsequent nomination to Finance and Personnel on 29 November 1999; on each occasion, the SDLP plumped for that department as its first choice. Interestingly, in the abortive July nomination process, Eddie McGrady (SDLP) refused to accept the nomination as health minister: Dr Hendron was his party's second choice.

Mitchell had voiced a prescient if little-noticed comment. Three days after Good Friday, the *Times*[12] carried a report under the headline 'Mitchell fears collapse of deal within 18 months', in which the former US Senate majority leader was quoted as bemoaning the 'presumption of bad faith' between unionists and republicans.

The 11-week Mitchell review of the (non-)implementation of the Agreement concluded, apparently successfully, on 18 November 1999. But the sequence of subsequent, choreographed statements by the protagonists proved no substitute for an agreed single text. Inevitably, argument soon developed as to what had, or had not, been 'understood' between the parties. Mr Trimble consented, finally, to the establishment of the devolved executive which, on any objective reading of the Agreement, should have been in existence before 31 October 1998, the due date for the consequent establishment of the North/South Ministerial Council (NSMC). Mr Adams said decommissioning was 'essential' — though, oddly, he did not personally read his statement in the choreographed series to that effect.

Mr Trimble interpreted, perhaps over-interpreted, the IRA's commitment to appoint an interlocutor to the Independent International Commission on Decommissioning headed by the Canadian former general John de Chastelain, plus the pencilling in of a report from Gen de Chastelain in January, as implying decommissioning would have to have begun by 31 January. The UUP leader was under growing pressure from the 'no' camp in his party to draw a line in the sand.

Unionist opinion had grown restive as the 'yes' case looked increasingly vulnerable. Essentially, unionists did not like the Belfast Agreement and two schools of thought joined battle over it. The 'no' campaign represented it as 'appeasement', a 'one-way street' of British concessions to republicans to stop renewed IRA bombs in London. The unionist 'yes' campaign (such as it was) was not so much that the Agreement was positive; rather that its unpalatable aspects — IRA representatives in government, paramilitary prisoner releases and radical reform of the RUC — were bitter pills worth swallowing. Mr Trimble presented the appeal of the agreement in abridged and downbeat terms: it was, he said, 'as good as it gets'. To sugar the pills, it was argued that unionists had shored up Northern Ireland's constitutional position through the reaffirmation of the 'consent principle' and the removal of the republic's territorial claim on the north; and the concessions to the IRA would, crucially, be offset by its disarmament and eventual disbandment.

The difficulty of the 'yes' position was that only the most tenuous linkage connected the decommissioning section of the Agreement — *via* another paragraph to the Agreement's ministerial 'pledge of office' — with SF's presence in government. Yet, even that was effectively severed by the (disingenuous) claim by the Adams/McGuinness republican leadership that its

[12] 13 April 1998.

writ did not extend from the political to the military wing. And, as Mr Mitchell perceived, trust was not going to fill the gap: unionist rejectionists could exploit the fear that, once their feet were under the political table, republicans would stonewall on decommissioning. The security of Mr Trimble's position thus came to depend on unilateral pledges by the Prime Minister.

Notably, in a side letter to Mr Trimble on Good Friday 1998, Mr Blair had said that paramilitary decommissioning should begin by June that year. And, as support for the Agreement was wavering in the Protestant community in the run-up to the referendum, the Prime Minister made three trips to Northern Ireland, suggesting in a speech in Belfast rather stronger links between decommissioning, prisoner releases and paramilitary places in government than were warranted by the Agreement.[13]

But nationalists simply did not accept that the constitutional provisions of the Agreement, or the reaffirmation of Westminster parliamentary sovereignty in the Northern Ireland Act 1998, meant that the Prime Minister could issue such directions. For nationalists, the Agreement was a multi-party contract, not only involving the British Government but also the Northern Ireland parties, the republic's government and (tacitly) the US administration. Unilateralism, therefore, whatever the constitutional niceties, was politically unacceptable. The conflict over the suspension of the institutions in February 2000 and the subsequent crisis over the Police (Northern Ireland) Bill were to reflect these contradictory perspectives.

So Mr Trimble made his own linkage at the conclusion of the Mitchell review. Yes he was, finally, going to accept the formation of the Executive, but he would offer a post-dated resignation letter so that his party could be reassured that, were Gen de Chastelain to issue a negative report on decommissioning in January, the Executive would be collapsed by its unionist members. Republicans immediately cried foul. Even so, the UUP leader's internal party support fell from 72 per cent post-agreement to 58 per cent at the UUC meeting in late November, ratifying his version of the deal. And there was worse to come.

SHADOW BOXING IN THE ASSEMBLY

Following the Assembly elections of 25 June 1998, Northern Ireland experienced a long shadow — or, as one commentator put it, 'shadowy' — period. Yet the breadth and magnitude of overall popular support for the Agreement, in both Northern Ireland and the republic, expressed in the referendums of 22 May 1998, remained remarkably resilient throughout the 19 months of on-off inter-party negotiations. Indeed, the period devoted to the implementation of the Agreement outstripped the period of serious multi-party negotiations that led to Good Friday 1998.

[13] *Irish Times*, 15 May 1998.

There were some positive indications of serious intent among the key political players during the shadow period, notably the contrived reconfiguration of Northern Ireland departments, agreed on 18 December 1998, that yielded 'parity of ministerial esteem': six unionist/loyalist ministers and six nationalist/republican ones. Together — or rather, apart, as it turned out — these dozen individuals would constitute the new Executive Committee, headed by the co-equal First and deputy First Ministers (designate), Messrs Trimble and Mallon.

The complex intricacy of the Agreement entailed that its three 'strands' — within Northern Ireland, North–South in Ireland and 'east-west' — be concurrently effected: none could stand alone. If one strand unravelled, the wider fabric would fall apart. In that respect, it was an all-or-nothing bargain — one that certainly betrayed its consociational lineage, but with ostensibly confederal arrangements knitted into the pattern. This deliberate design, however, extended only to the political institutions crafted by the Agreement's negotiators: the Assembly and the Executive ('strand one'), the North/South implementation bodies and co-operation arrangements ('strand two') and the British–Irish Council (BIC) and the British–Irish Intergovernmental Conference ('strand three'). Indeed, the fate of the BIC — embracing the UK, the republic, and the quainter jurisdictions of the Channel Islands and the Isle of Man — was, and remains, entirely dependent upon the successful implementation of the Agreement.

But the Agreement also lent new impetus to the continuing process of Northern Ireland's social transformation, the outcomes of which are not inextricably tied to the institutions themselves. This process embraced the requirement of 'a new beginning to policing', a reformed criminal justice system, the establishment of a new régime of human rights, and a renewed emphasis on equality of opportunity. It also meant the accelerated release, on licence, of 'scheduled' offenders — provided the paramilitary ceasefires were deemed by the Secretary of State to have remained intact (though this tended happily to correspond with paramilitary groups' claims to that effect).

During the shadow period, the Assembly met on 19 occasions in plenary session. Besides the joint election of Messrs Trimble and Mallon and the endorsement of their reports on the new administrative arrangements and North–South and 'east-west' matters, its major business concerned the devising of standing orders. The all-party, 19-strong Committee on Standing Orders, chaired jointly by a nationalist and a unionist, produced its report in March 1999 — one of ten Assembly reports produced in the pre-devolution period. A revealing indicator of the pull of the past was that the committee resolved not to start with a *tabula rasa*, but rather used the standing orders drawn up by the previous (and ill-fated) 1973–74 Assembly as a basis on which to build, complemented by initial standing orders drawn up by the then Northern Ireland Secretary, Ms Mowlam.

In its report, the committee highlighted an issue that was to assume considerable significance, *viz* the accountability of the Office of the First Minister and Deputy First Minister (OFMDFM). Unlike the other ten devolved departments, there was no provision in the Agreement or the Northern Ireland Act 1998 for a statutory committee to monitor the activities of the office. As such, the Standing Orders Committee expressed its 'concern that important discrete functions of the Office of First Minister and Deputy First Minister would not ... be subject to the scrutiny of a statutory committee' and recommended that the Assembly should address the matter 'as soon as possible'. In the event, it was not until powers were devolved that the opportunity arose to revisit the issue (see below).

POWER DEVOLVED ...

It was only on 27 November 1999, when the UUC endorsed the 'understanding' reached at the conclusion of the Mitchell review nine days earlier, that it became apparent devolution could proceed. On 30 November, Westminster, by 318 votes to 10, approved the devolution order and, after a flurry of necessary formalities, devolution day became 2 December.

In anticipation of the transfer of powers, the Assembly met on 29 November to trigger the d'Hondt rule, thereby enabling the (four) parties to the Executive to nominate their ministerial choices and select their chosen departments. It was a bizarre occasion. The 108 Assembly members (MLAs), especially those outside the ranks of the four major parties, watched with some bemusement as the process unfolded. The nominating officers of the UUP, SDLP, DUP and SF, in that d'Hondt-governed order, stood to nominate their preferred members to the departments. This was clearly a tactical exercise, the outcome of which was unknown. The only certainty was that at the end of the process the coalition would comprise ten ministers who, together with Mr Trimble and a rehabilitated Mr Mallon,[14] would constitute the 12-member Executive Committee.

Everyone knew that d'Hondt would deliver three ministers each for the UUP and SDLP, and two each for the DUP and SF. But, blinded by the communalist fear that republicans might get their hands on the culture ministry — and thereby control public symbolism — the UUP passed up the opportunity to take the education portfolio. To a very sharp intake of breath on the unionist Assembly benches, a former butcher's apprentice and

---

[14] To avoid a vote to re-elect Messrs Trimble and Mallon as First and deputy First Minister, a vote by no means certain given that the 'parallel consent' method would have been required, an extraordinary expedient was adopted. On 29 November, the Northern Ireland Secretary, Mr Mandelson, introduced a special standing order allowing the assembly to vote to reject the deputy First Minister's July resignation. As this was a simple-majority decision, the Assembly was able, retrospectively, to 're-resign' Mr Mallon (*Irish Times*, 30 November 1999).

member of the IRA army council, Martin McGuinness, thus took control of the educational future of the region's children, some of whom, with the encouragement of the DUP, walked out of their schools in protest. When to that was allied Bairbre de Brún's nomination as health minister, it was evident that, as so often, SF had outwitted the plodding unionists and grabbed the big spending departments.

The Executive thus formed was as follows:

- David Trimble (UUP): First Minister;
- Seámus Mallon (SDLP): deputy First Minister;
- Michael McGimpsey (UUP): Minister of Culture, Arts and Leisure;
- Reg Empey (UUP): Minister of Enterprise, Trade and Investment;
- Sam Foster (UUP): Minister of Environment;
- Sean Farren (SDLP): Minister of Higher and Further Education, Training and Employment;
- Mark Durkan (SDLP): Minister of Finance and Personnel;
- Bríd Rodgers (SDLP): Minister of Agriculture and Rural Development;
- Peter Robinson (DUP): Minister for Regional Development;
- Nigel Dodds (DUP): Minister for Social Development;
- Martin McGuinness (SF): Minister of Education, and
- Bairbre de Brún (SF): Minister of Health, Social Services and Public Safety.

After this process, the Assembly turned to nominating the chairs and deputy chairs of the statutory committees, again by means of d'Hondt.[15] This protracted affair completed — there were 20 seats to fill — the parties nominated their MLAs to sit on each of the committees on the following day. The 11-member statutory committees, their composition broadly reflecting party strengths in the Assembly, then began setting their agendas, a task accomplished largely *in camera* — unlike the committees of the Scottish Parliament and the Welsh National Assembly. The alacrity with which the institutions of each of the three strands was put in place was, after the interminable delay of 19 months, impressive.

On the morning of 2 December, the republic's government changed Articles 2 and 3 of its 1937 Constitution, replacing the irredentist claim to

---

[15] The original chairs and deputy chairs, respectively, of each of the ten departmental statutory committees were: agriculture and rural development, Rev Ian Paisley (DUP) and George Savage (UUP); culture, arts and leisure, Eamon O'Neill (SDLP) and Mary Nelis (SF); education, Danny Kennedy (UUP) and Sammy Wilson (DUP); enterprise, trade and investment, Pat Doherty (SF) and Sean Neeson (Alliance); environment, William McCrea (DUP) and Carmel Hanna (SDLP); finance and personnel, Francie Molloy (SF) and James Leslie (UUP); health, social services and public safety, Joe Hendron (SDLP) and Tommy Gallagher (SDLP); higher and further education, training and employment, Esmond Birnie (UUP) and Mervyn Carrick (DUP); regional development, Denis Haughey (SDLP) — who, upon his appointment as a junior minister in OFMDFM, was replaced on 21 December 1999 by his party colleague Alban Maginness — and Alan McFarland (UUP); social development, Fred Cobain (UUP) and Michelle Gildernew (SF).

Northern Ireland with the aspiration to unite the peoples of the island, thereby copper-fastening the 'consent principle'. Shortly afterwards, the two governments exchanged papers formally establishing the NSMC and the BIC. On 13 December, the NSMC held its inaugural session in Armagh, at which the six all-Ireland implementation bodies and the six areas for North–South co-operation were set in train.[16] Four days later, the BIC held its first meeting in London.

At Parliament Buildings on the Stormont estate, the Executive Committee met for the first time on the morning of 2 December, minus its two DUP members. Throughout the initial 10 weeks of devolution, the latter — Nigel Dodds and Peter Robinson — maintained their abstentionist posture, necessitating improvisation to ensure some *modus vivendi* among ministers. They were supplied with Executive papers and engaged in negotiations with their cabinet colleagues — save, of course, the two SF ministers — but they were denied their demand to brief the First and deputy First Minister before Executive meetings and to be debriefed afterwards. The DUP's aloofness did not, though, extend to the statutory committees, nor — with the exception of the 'Committee of the Centre' — to the standing committees established by the Assembly, where they sat and worked alongside SF members.[17]

The initial plenary sessions of the Assembly — held on Mondays and Tuesdays — tended to concentrate on housekeeping, punctuated by the failed attempt by anti-agreement parties to exclude SF by means of a 'petition of concern'.[18] The delay in implementing devolution had had a number of effects, including the absence of any productive work by the Executive Committee on its statutory duty to devise the 'Programme for Government'. It also meant that the initial budget statement by the Finance and Personnel Minister, Mr Durkan, rolled forward the expenditure plans inherited from the direct-rule administration. The £8.9 billion budget for public services, over which the Assembly had full discretion for approximately £5 billion, did however, enable the Executive to engage in some reallocation of funds to the 11 departments. Interviews with some Executive members suggest that the greatest casualties of the reallocation were the two departments headed by the DUP's ministers. As one minister put it: 'The fact that they weren't at the

---

[16] The six implementation bodies were: Inland Waterways, Food Safety, Trade and Business Development, Special EU Programmes, Language, and Aquaculture and Marine Matters. The six areas identified for co-operation were: transport, agriculture, education, health, environment, and tourism.

[17] The six standing committees and their respective chairs and deputy chairs are: Audit, John Dallatt (SDLP) and Billy Hutchinson (Progressive Unionist Party); Committee of the Centre, Edwin Poots (DUP) — who replaced his party colleague Gregory Campbell upon his rotation into the ministerial chair at Regional Development on 27 July 2000 — and Oliver Gibson (DUP); Procedure, Conor Murphy (SF) and Duncan Shipley-Dalton (UUP); Public Accounts, Billy Bell (UUP) and Sue Ramsey (SF); Standards and Privilege, Donovan McClelland (SDLP) and Roy Beggs Jnr (UUP).

[18] To secure a debate (and a subsequent vote, itself subject to the tests of cross-community support) a petition of concern has to bear the signatures of 30 MLAs. Until July 2000, two undated motions by the DUP and the Northern Ireland Unionist Party, originally laid during the shadow period, had failed narrowly to reach this threshold.

table to argue their departmental corners meant that millions were allocated elsewhere.'[19]

Given the continuing impasse over decommissioning, the future of the devolution project remained uncertain. In that context the anti-agreement parties used every opportunity to embarrass the pro-agreement unionists in the Assembly, tabling a successful motion demanding decommissioning by the paramilitaries,[20] and another condemning the report on reform of the RUC by the commission chaired by Chris Patten.[21]

The activities of the two SF ministers provided an obvious target for the anti-agreement unionists. In particular, Ms de Brún became an object of scorn because of her practice of speaking at length in Irish on the floor of the chamber and her early decision to pulp departmental stationery and replace it with a bilingual version. Matters came to a head in the wake of her decision to close a maternity hospital in south Belfast and relocate the service in her neighbouring constituency of west Belfast, a decision taken against the majority (7–4) view of the health committee and, subsequently, a majority (essentially sectarian) in the Assembly.

Further difficulties were raised by the issue of what flag would fly over government buildings. Against a backdrop of incidents of republican intimidation, SF ministers refused to accept any flying of the Union flag over their departments on the 20 or so days of official (usually monarchical) relevance — a situation which SDLP ministers were, by contrast, prepared to countenance in the short term until a long-term solution was found. SF said the remedy, in line with the Agreement's provisions on 'parity of esteem', was either no flags or both flags — the Union flag and Tricolour flying together. Unionists claimed this last would imply joint, London-Dublin authority over Northern Ireland, whereas the Agreement[22] had reaffirmed Northern Ireland's constitutional status within the UK, subject to the consent principle. Inevitably, no meeting of minds took place.

Policing was to exacerbate the rising tensions. In mid-January, Mr Mandelson indicated his broad acceptance of the Patten recommendations.[23] These had inflamed unionists when the former Hong Kong Governor's report was published the previous September — an incandescent Mr Trimble had dismissed it as 'shoddy' and the proposal to remove all reference to the RUC from the name of the new service caused widespread Protestant offence.[24] The Police Federation mobilised more than 300,000 signatures on

---

[19] Interview with a current minister, March 2000.

[20] Northern Ireland Assembly Report, 17 January 2000.

[21] *A New Beginning: Policing in Northern Ireland*, September 1999; NIAR, 24 January 2000.

[22] 'Constitutional Issues', §1.

[23] *Irish Times*, 20 January 2000.

[24] The UUP established a working party to produce an alternative to Patten, including two future ministers and the wife of the former RUC chief constable: Ken Maginnis, Michael McGimpsey, Sir Reg Empey, Trevor Wilson, Arlene Foster and Lady Sylvia Hermon.

an anti-Patten petition (the whole Protestant population of Northern Ireland — man, woman, and child — is only about one million).

But it was the failure of the IRA to deliver any cold steel to the de Chastelain Commission which rendered Mr Trimble's position in the Executive untenable, albeit temporarily. Mounting uncertainty about the durability of devolution meant that activity in the Assembly during early February had a desultory air. Its final plenary session of the initial devolved period, on 8 February, took place amid acrimony epitomised by a failed attempt by the DUP to exclude SF on a petition of concern.[25]

... IS POWER RETAINED

The Northern Ireland Secretary, Peter Mandelson — who had replaced Ms Mowlam in the September reshuffle as part of his political rehabilitation — privately endorsed Mr Trimble's understanding of the 'understanding' reached at the outcome of the Mitchell review. But, partly for the reasons outlined above, and partly because the IRA — under pressure from US opinion-formers — delivered increasingly warm words to the general, the SDLP and, particularly, the Dublin Government rejected the suspension of the new political institutions at the behest of the Northern Ireland Secretary on the eve of the critical UUC meeting on 12 February, at which the party leader's resignation would have been effected.

Had the latter gone ahead, not only would the Executive have collapsed but it would have been very difficult to re-establish it, because the fraying of his support in the Assembly could have prevented Mr Trimble securing the required majority in the unionist bloc to be re-elected as First Minister.[26] At that stage, no one could be certain that the show could be put back on the road.

The two Governments, however, immediately set about securing still warmer words from the IRA. The requirement in the Northern Ireland Decommissioning Act 1997[27] that weapons be handed over or made *permanently* inaccessible or unusable was tacitly watered down to arms being rendered 'beyond use'. The implicit link between devolution and decommissioning at the heart of the Mitchell review was now pejoratively referred to

[25] The DUP attracted support from 29 MLAs, one short of the number necessary to trigger a debate.

[26] The UUP was rocked by its worst-ever electoral performance in the Assembly elections, which left Mr Trimble in command of only 28 of the unionist seats (himself included). While there were 30 other unionists elected, two of these were from the Ulster Volunteer Force-linked Progressive Unionist Party and so were 'yes' supporters. But two subsequent defections left Mr Trimble facing an effective 30-28 'no' majority on the unionist benches, jeopardising the parallel-consent vote required for his re-election, were he to resign. The arithmetic still allowed weighted-majority votes to pass, as these require only 40 per cent of the unionist bloc to go through, given sufficient support from nationalists and 'others'. Two more defections on the June 4th Assembly vote on the exclusion of SF from government represented a further erosion of the First Minister's position.

[27] Similar legislation was passed in the republic.

(by Mr Mandelson) as a 'devolution–decommissioning stalemate' which had delivered neither *desideratum*. In Washington for the annual St Patrick's Day (rather, week) jamboree, the Secretary of State announced further troop withdrawals and hinted at more to come. There, too, Mr Trimble spoke of the possibility of re-entering government without arms being delivered 'up front'.

The latter remark, ill-judged in place and timing, threatened Mr Trimble's leadership of the UUP at the UUC annual general meeting a week later. Challenged by Rev Martin Smyth — described by the *Economist*[28] as 'strikingly inarticulate' — his support still fell again, to 57 per cent. Moreover, Mr Trimble was defeated on a motion proposed by a former ally, David Burnside, linking re-entry into power-sharing to retention of the name of the RUC; an amendment, in the leader's name, instructing the party's MPs to contest the issue 'vigorously' at Westminster, was lost, albeit narrowly. In June, Mr Burnside was to secure a further victory, when he defeated Mr Trimble's chief of staff, David Campbell, in the contest to choose a prospective parliamentary candidate for the by-election (caused by the death of the anti-agreement incumbent, Clifford Forsythe) in the safe UUP seat of South Antrim. Worryingly for the leadership, Mr Burnside, a public-relations professional, was carefully positioning himself not as a rebel but as someone who sought to unite a bitterly divided party.

A further round of intergovernmental manoeuvring nevertheless followed, including discussions with the northern parties. This led, eventually, to a late-night statement on 5 May by the two governments, sufficient to elicit an IRA statement the following morning on foot of which the renewal of the institutions would take place. The IRA's statement duly committed the organisation to initiating a process of putting arms 'beyond use', in the context of the full and 'irreversible' implementation of the Agreement. It would re-engage with the de Chastelain commission and, 'within weeks', allow 'a number' of its arms dumps to be inspected by third parties as a 'confidence-building measure'.[29]

The two governments quickly announced that the inspectors would be the former African National Congress Secretary-General, Cyril Ramaphosa, chosen because of his close republican connections,[30] and the former Finnish President, Martti Ahtisaari; the two were on the scene within days for an initial visit. The RUC Chief Constable, Ronnie Flanagan, was shortly on hand to promise the demolition of two army bases and the dismantling of a

---

[28] 1 April 2000.

[29] *Sunday Tribune*, 7 May 2000.

[30] The republican movement has sought, throughout the 'peace process', to shed the tag of 'terrorist' and acquire the 'democratic' image of the ANC. The latter, conversely, has tended to view the Northern Ireland conflict as 'anti-colonial' and so has built close relationships with republican leaders. Mr Ramaphosa embraced Mr Adams at an SF rally in Belfast in the run-up to the referendum on the Belfast Agreement.

few observation posts. Civil-society figures, including the 'G7' business, trade-union and voluntary-sector grouping, rowed in behind the developments, bolstered by a BBC Northern Ireland poll[31] which suggested that two-thirds of Ulster Unionist supporters backed the re-establishment of the Executive in the wake of the IRA statement.

The old problems, however, remained. On closer scrutiny, the IRA had not been forced into a strategic concession: 'the disposal of arms by those in possession of them' was what republicans had volunteered in the SF submission to the *original* Mitchell review on decommissioning in 1995–96.

The IRA described its 1994 ceasefire as 'complete', refusing the attribution 'permanent'. The choice was deliberate, as the 1996 decision to end the 'complete' ceasefire indicated; it was deliberate also in 2000 with regard to putting arms 'completely and verifiably beyond use'. The big fear of the republican movement is being 'locked in' irreversibly to a democratic path from which it cannot resile, but whose outcome is uncertain. This is critical to its presentation of the Belfast Agreement, especially to those 'volunteers' attracted to the siren voices of the dissident Real IRA, as inevitably transitional in the medium-term to a united Ireland. It is also crucial to sustaining the political leverage that a credible threat establishes — the flavour of which was captured in the headline 'Patten or else says the IRA' in the nationalist *Ireland on Sunday* newspaper.[32]

Mr Trimble, from the other side, shares similar concerns. As he took to the airwaves to persuade delegates the weekend before another critical UUC meeting, he acknowledged concern within the party [33] that if it went back into government with republicans 'we are then locked into a situation'. He said: 'That is simply not the case. We retain complete freedom of action ourselves.'

In another interview, [34] he said of the IRA: 'If it is not permanent for them, it is not permanent for us either.'

DEVOLUTION, ONCE AGAIN

Once more Mr Trimble faced his detractors within the UUC. Despite hints by the British Government of concessions on policing (namely that the RUC name would be incorporated into the 'title deeds' of the new service), indications that the Northern Ireland Secretary would arbitrate on flags and a week's postponement of the council meeting (to 27 May) to garner backing, his support fell still further — this time to an uncomfortably low 53 per cent. Leading the challenge was Jeffrey Donaldson MP, who proposed that unless

---

[31] 10 May 2000.
[32] 4 June 2000.
[33] *Irish Times*, 22 May 2000.
[34] *Irish Times*, 23 May 2000.

and until the onset of IRA decommissioning allowed an executive to be formed including SF, the Assembly should assume only a scrutiny role. Embarrassingly for Mr Trimble, this was just what he had proposed a year earlier — to 'park' the process — but he was able to argue (from experience) that no nationalist party was remotely interested.

Hours of discussion between Mr Blair, Mr Ahern and the parties on the night of 5 May, after their statement had been agreed, failed to secure agreement on the policing impasse. Demonstrating that the RUC has been confined to history is critical to the republican narrative of seamless advance towards the ultimate goal. The issue remained unresolved when the Commons rose.

At the conclusion of the committee stage of the policing bill on 6 July, the Government accepted a UUP amendment which would refer to the new Police Service of Northern Ireland as 'incorporating the Royal Ulster Constabulary', though only the PSNI term would be used for 'operational purposes.'[35] Nationalists — including the SDLP — were outraged, and there was a very real prospect that neither nationalist party would encourage Catholics to join the new service. Discussions between officials in London and Dublin led to a further amendment, defining 'operational purposes' so comprehensively as to lead the UUP deputy leader, John Taylor, to warn that unionists were to be 'betrayed'. At the 11th hour, on 11 July, Mr Mandelson withdrew the amendment[36] — apparently at the behest of the Prime Minister, concerned for Mr Trimble's future.

The UUP leader did (just) gain enough support to win through on 27 May. But he lost two further supporters in the Assembly — Pauline Armitage and Derek Hussey — who made clear in advance of the vote[37] that, along with fellow UUP Assembly members Peter Weir and Roy Beggs, they would not be supporting him. As was to be borne out in the 4 July vote to exclude SF from the Executive, this left Mr Trimble exposed — with just 26 votes (including his own) to count on in the unionist bloc, as against 32 for the 'no' camp.

This would make any 'parallel consent' vote (requiring 50 per cent of the bloc) impossible and three more defections would mean no 'weighted majority' votes (requiring 40 per cent) could be passed either. With the anti-agreement faction now well clear of the 30-member threshold required to turn every vote into a 'key decision', requiring a weighted majority to pass, the margin for Mr Trimble in the Assembly was just as tight as in the party.

It was also notable — as indicated by the 4 July vote — that this arithmetic was unaffected by the fact that the IRA did deliver on its 'confidence-

[35] *Irish Times*, 7 July 2000.
[36] *Irish Times*, 13 July 2000.
[37] *Irish Times*, 25 May 2000.

building' promise, opening up a number of arms dumps to the satisfaction of the international inspectors, who reported on 26 June.[38] It might have been thought this would have seen one or two defectors return, but the report of the inspectors met a divided response in London and Dublin, though welcomed in both capitals. For the Prime Minister, Mr Blair (as for Mr Trimble), it was 'a first step' towards decommissioning. For the Taoiseach, Mr Ahern (and undoubtedly for Mr Adams), it was 'a successful end' to the issue.[39]

One threat to the Agreement was however effectively seen off. The 'Drumcree stand-off' represented a strategic defeat for the Orange Order, now a vehicle for an anti-agreement leadership. The sheer ineptitude of its Grand Lodge, in refusing to talk to the Parades Commission, was surpassed only by the self-destructive willingness of the Portadown 'brethren' to accept on Drumcree Hill the released UDA paramilitary leader Johnny 'Mad Dog' Adair — subsequently to be re-imprisoned for his involvement in the developing loyalist feud. The latter association managed to alienate most Catholics and most Protestants in one go, and wholly undermined the Orangemen's stance that they could not talk to Catholic residents led by a one-time IRA prisoner. Some spoke excitedly of an Orange 'Alamo' — and so it proved to be.

TRIMBLE TREMBLES

Another destabilising event was provided by the extraordinary scenes of triumphalism accompanying the last big batch of prisoner releases on 28 July. Fulfilling the terms of the Agreement, 86 were released, nearly all from the Maze (shortly to be closed) on that one day. They included some of the most notorious killers (on both sides) — the last to be released out of deference to public sensitivity and the bereaved.

While the loyalists rather skulked away, some with faces covered, the IRA prisoners were greeted with champagne, party streamers and confetti.[40] The IRA 'officer commanding' among the prisoners said they were 'unbowed and unbroken'. And the leading SF figure Gerry Kelly was on hand to declare that the prisoners had been victims too. It was, sa d the veteran commentator Mary Holland, 'a breathtakingly insensitive display'.[41]

As the respected *Guardian* correspondent in Ireland, John Mullin, put it:

To many Unionists, including supporters of the Good Friday Agreement, such absolute republican confidence fuelled their jitters, particularly as Sinn Fein was

[38] *Irish Times*, 27 June 2000.
[39] *Sunday Tribune*, 2 July 2000.
[40] *Irish Times*, 29 July 2000.
[41] *Irish Times*, 3 August 2000.

to the fore. They fear less that IRA prisoners will re-offend, than republicans are winning the long game.[42]

Mr Trimble admitted to his 'worries' too. On a BBC *News 24* interview on the day of the last major releases, he said he did not trust his fellow minister Mr McGuinness, and he wasn't sure republicans were committed to peaceful means. 'I do not know for certain that it is all going to work in the way that we want it to,' he said. This inevitably allowed the DUP deputy leader, and by then former ministerial colleague, Peter Robinson, to claim: 'The basis on which David Trimble remains in partnership with IRA-Sinn Féin becomes all the more unreal.'[43]

During the suspension, the DUP had conducted its own review of its strategy pending the return of devolution. Amid much speculation, which centred on the prospect of the party resigning its two ministerial seats and adopting the role of 'loyal' opposition in the Assembly, a statement on 31 May took observers by surprise. The party expressed its intention to resume its full role in the strand-one institutions, including retaking ministerial control of the Regional Development and Social Development departments, but on a rotating basis among its MLAs.[44] It reaffirmed that DUP ministers would continue boycotting Executive meetings but added that they could not 'be regarded as being bound in any way by the ministerial code of conduct' as set out in the Agreement. This renunciation of the code — a *prima facie* breach of the pledge of office and ground for exclusion — would, the party argued, enable its ministers to 'uncover and reveal what is going on in the heart of government'.[45]

This threat elicited a reaction from the Executive at its meeting on 8 June, following the lifting of suspension on 29 May. This included: assumption of responsibility by the First and deputy First Ministers for representing the Executive on transport matters (the responsibility of the Regional Development department) at meetings of the BIC; refusal to nominate the two DUP ministers to attend meetings of the Joint Ministerial Committee; and, pending satisfactory assurances about the integrity and confidentiality of Executive business, an end to the routine distribution of Executive papers to them. In response, the two ministers instructed their officials to stop sending departmental papers to the Executive.

This was, of course, bizarre and unprecedented, and underlined the difficulties in achieving collective responsibility in the Executive committee. One immediate effect was that the long-overdue Programme for Government, the statement of strategic aims and objectives for the Assembly's first

[42] 29 July 2000.

[43] *Irish News*, 29 July 2000.

[44] The first rotation occurred on 27 July when Gregory Campbell replaced Peter Robinson and Maurice Morrow replaced Nigel Dodds.

[45] *Irish Times*, 31 May 2000.

term, was further delayed. Nevertheless, at the 8 June meeting of the Executive it was agreed by ministers — including, albeit at one remove, the two DUP incumbents — that an interim 'Agenda for Government', setting out priorities for action until April 2001, would be produced. While neither a statutory duty on the devolved bodies nor a 'key decision'[46] as defined by the Agreement, the agenda was intended as a bridging measure, designed to restore momentum to the flagging process of agreeing the programme and to indicate that devolution could bring tangible benefits to the population — purposes made clear when the agenda was unveiled at the end of June (see below).

FINANCE: THROUGH ON THE NOD

The restoration of devolution meant MLAs had to play 'catch-up' in relation to two events during suspension: Gordon Brown's fourth budget and the negotiations on the second Comprehensive Spending Review, concluded in July. In effect, members, including ministers, had had little opportunity to contribute to either process and were confronted with *faits accomplis* — or so it appeared.

The first major items of business for the Assembly when it reconvened on 5 June were to approve spending estimates, by way of a supply resolution, and to agree the accelerated passage of an Appropriation Bill conferring the necessary authority on the devolved departments to spend public money. The urgency of these measures, especially the bill, was pressed on MLAs by Mr Durkan: 'The need for urgent approval of the Estimates and the passing of an Appropriation Bill is very clearly exceptional in current circumstances.'[47]

Accelerated passage, provided for in standing orders, meant that legislation was spared a committee stage; however, its adoption required that it be approved *nem con* by the Assembly.

This procedure provided a clear opportunity for anti-agreement unionists to delay devolution, if not halt it in its tracks. Yet it was an opportunity foregone — as Mr Trimble pointed out during the debate on the exclusion of SF from ministerial office, much to the discomfort of the anti-agreement unionists. During his contribution — opposing the motion — the First Minister observed:

---

[46] The key decisions pre-determined by the agreement include the joint election of the First and deputy First Ministers, Assembly standing orders, budgetary procedures and the Programme for Government. They also include the election of the Presiding Officer (speaker) of the Assembly. However, the incumbent, Lord (John) Alderdice, has not yet been confirmed in office by means of a cross-community vote, unlike the three deputy speakers: Jane Morrice (Women's Coalition), Donovan McClelland (SDLP) and Sir John Gorman (UUP). The DUP's nominee for a deputy speakership — Will Hay — did not secure cross-community support.

[47] Northern Ireland Assembly Report, 5 June 2000.

[I]f the DUP really wanted to stop the Assembly it could have done so. There was a moment a few weeks ago when we had before us the matter of the accelerated procedure for the Appropriation Bill. If that had been objected to, the Northern Ireland Administration, the Assembly and all associated bodies … could have been brought to a complete halt by just one person saying one word … 'No'.[48]

While members were decidedly unhappy that the time to scrutinise the estimates was woefully inadequate, they nevertheless approved them and endorsed the accelerated passage of the Appropriation Bill.

The main estimates for the financial year 2000–01 covered a total of £7.8 billion of public expenditure in Northern Ireland, of which £4.3 billion required Assembly approval in the Appropriation Bill. During the suspension, a vote on account at Westminster had provided interim funding, anticipated otherwise to run out at the end of August.

The big spenders, inevitably, were to be health and social services (£1.9 billion) and education (£1.2 billion) — the two spending departments astutely secured by SF — and (outwith the Executive's control) social security benefits (£1.8 billion). A much smaller but notable amount was the £27 million allocated to the OFMDFM — almost as much as the budget for the Assembly (£31.5 million). The sprawling office is to have, when fully recruited, 300 staff, according to a senior civil servant.

In June, the Executive announced the allocation of the first tranche of some £90 million which had become available from a variety of savings and underspends. This was rolled up in what it described as an Agenda for Government. Five headings were set out to define the agenda:

• A step change in economic development;
• A firm basis for better education and health;
• A better and safer environment;
• Practical steps to tackle disadvantage and exclusion, and
• Improved, modern, accessible services.

Each of these was subdivided into measures. The two biggest initial allocations were for improving school buildings (£6.2 million) and reducing hospital waiting lists (£5 million). On the day before the Assembly rose, Mr Durkan announced how the remaining £63 million would be allocated.[49] The principal departmental beneficiaries were Health, Social Services and Public Safety (£11.9 million), Regional Development (£10.9 million) and Agriculture (£9.5 million).

These figures were of course dwarfed by the impact of the Comprehensive Spending Review, which signalled that spending would rise over the three-year period of the review such that £1 billion more would be spent in

---

[48] Northern Ireland Assembly Report, 4 July 2000.
[49] *Irish Times*, 4 July 2000.

2003–04 than had been planned to be expended in 2001–02. Some of the dodgy, double and triple counting characteristic of New Labour's hyping of the first review was belatedly replicated this time around in Northern Ireland — though not by the Secretary of State himself.[50] The £1 billion became £2 billion when accumulated over the period by Mr Durkan, of New Labour's 'sister' SDLP.[51] The Department of Finance and Personnel was obliged to issue a subsequent press release to explain the conflicting accounts.[52]

The First and deputy First Ministers also welcomed the increased public expenditure allocation to Northern Ireland arising from the review.[53] The tone of their statements was notably different, however. While they both emphasised that the additional money would be spent taking forward the devolved administration's Programme for Government, Mr Mallon alone explicitly affirmed: 'We will not necessarily follow the pattern of allocations announced today for England.'

ABORTIVE DEBATES

There was no shortage of controversy on the floor of the reconvened Assembly during the month or so before the summer recess on 7 July. Among the items debated was a motion on the flying of the Union flag on departmental offices and Parliament Buildings on all designated days, moved by Ian Paisley (DUP) on a petition of concern on 6 June, supported by all unionist parties but opposed by the SDLP, SF, Alliance and the Women's Coalition. The motion failed for lack of cross-community consent.

Two debates on equality issues — on 6 June and 27 June — were heated affairs, especially the latter. Moved by Gregory Campbell (DUP), the motion criticised the alleged 'worsening under-representation of the Protestant community', especially in the public sector, and called on the new Equality Commission to 'address the problem as a matter of urgency'. This was opposed by, among others, Dermot Nesbitt (UUP), a junior minister in the OFMDFM, an act anti-agreement unionists regarded as little short of treachery.

Inter-unionist feuding also surfaced during a take-note debate on 5 June concerning the *Memorandum of Understanding* and Supplementary Agreements between the UK Government and the Executive Committee. These matters had been agreed by the Scottish Parliament and Welsh National Assembly on 1 October 1999 but, as for the Northern Ireland Assembly, they had been delayed by the postponed transfer of power and the subsequent suspension. Anti-agreement unionists took particular exception to the one

50 Northern Ireland Information Service, 18 July 2000.
51 *Irish News*, 19 July 2000.
52 Executive Information Service, 20 July 2000.
53 Executive Information Service, 18 July 2000.

additional measure affecting Northern Ireland, namely that the documents recognised its distinctive position within the UK because of its relationship with the republic. The agreements extended the terms of the *concordat* to cover the NSMC and the EU dimension of the cross-border bodies, institutions boycotted by the DUP since their creation. Despite the objections voiced by Mr Paisley and others, the motion was agreed.

Other set-piece debates included the underfunding of public transport and arts policy — the latter quickly descending into acrimony over the resources variously allocated to Irish and Ulster-Scots speakers in the region. A week earlier, on 20 June, the Assembly devoted four hours to a debate on an undated motion laid by Jim Wells (DUP) which sought to prevent the extension of the 1967 Abortion Act to Northern Ireland. None spoke in favour of its extension and the motion was carried.

Because of suspension, the legislative activities of the Assembly were modest. During the first phase of devolution, Mr Trimble had outlined the initial legislative programme, much of it concerned to achieve parity with British legislation.[54] Only three measures had secured Royal Assent by the summer recess, including the Appropriation Bill.[55]

Oral questions to ministers — held on Mondays when three ministers appear on the floor for 30 minutes each — resumed on 19 June. As before, question time enabled anti-agreement unionists to renew their verbal assaults on the two SF ministers, especially Ms de Brún, in part because of her practice of answering questions in both Irish and English. With no translation facilities, this invariably causes some disruption in the chamber and effectively reduces the time available to members in holding the minister to account.

The antipathy of anti-agreement unionists towards SF was given full vent on 4 July, the last sitting day before the recess, when the DUP's petition of concern seeking to exclude SF ministers from office succeeded in attracting the 30 signatures required to trigger a debate and vote when one UUP member, Pauline Armitage, added her name to the existing signatories. There was never any doubt that the exclusion motion would fail since it had to meet the test of cross-community support within the Assembly. But the debate did give rise to considerable concern within the UUP as to whether any other of its members would join the anti-agreement unionists in the division lobby, not least because its official position was to abstain from the vote.

---

[54] The initial legislative programme included: an Equality (Disability etc) Bill, which had reached its second assembly stage on 7 February 2000, but because of suspension an order in council was made under paragraph 1 of the schedule to the Northern Ireland Act 2000; a Ground Rents Bill, which completed its second stage on 19 June 2000; a Dogs (Amendment) Bill, which completed its second stage on 3 July 2000; and a Weights and Measures (Amendment) Bill, which had its second stage on 26 June 2000. A Fisheries (Amendment) Bill had only reached the first stage on 26 June 2000.

[55] The only other two measures to receive Royal Assent were the Assembly Members Pensions Bill and the Financial Assistance for Parties Bill.

In the event, a further two UUP MLAs — Derek Hussey, a former whip, and Roy Beggs Jnr — added their votes to those who had signed the petition. Thus, at the final plenary session it emerged that there were 32 unionists (out of a total of 58) prepared to decant SF ministers from the Executive for a period of at least 12 months. Thus, the already delicate parliamentary arithmetic was even more precariously poised when the Assembly broke up for the summer.

IN COMMITTEE

The Assembly's statutory committees resumed their meetings on 5 June and spent most of their time catching up on departmental developments that had occurred during the suspension. Two of the committees — Higher and Further Education, Training and Employment; and Culture, Arts and Leisure — began their first inquiries, into student finance and inland fisheries respectively, while the Agriculture and Rural Development Committee published its first report just before the end of the session.[56] To date, this is the only report produced by a statutory committee.

The statutory committees had their agendas skewed by the arrested development of devolution. Each was invited by the relevant minister to express initial views on the principles and structure of the draft Programme for Government, and to do so by 7 July, a little over a month after the Assembly had reconvened. Inevitably, this prompted complaints of lack of time, echoed by the new Liaison Committee — comprising the chairs of the statutory committees — created on 21 June. Each committee was also invited to respond to the draft 'equality scheme' devised by the appropriate department in compliance with section 75 of the Northern Ireland Act 1998. This statutory duty to show due regard for equality of opportunity, applying to all designated public bodies in Northern Ireland, derived from the direct rule administration's White Paper, 'Partnership for Equality',[57] published in March 1998.

The workload was added to by the chair of the Finance and Personnel Committee who invited each committee to identify two spending priorities for allocation of end-of-year-flexibility monies and the additional £18 million unallocated from the March budget. Further, each was invited by the chair of the Regional Development Committee to reflect on the implications of the regional development strategy — launched by a pre-devolution consultation paper issued by the Department of the Environment (1998) — for their areas of responsibility. And, finally, each was invited by the relevant

---

[56] *Retailing in Northern Ireland: A Fair Deal for the Farmer?* (Report 1/99/R [Committee of Agriculture and Rural Development], First Report, Session 1999–2000, vols 1 and 2). This was produced as part of its inquiry into debt in agriculture and fisheries.

[57] Cm 3890.

minister to comment on the implications for each department of 'New Targeting Social Need',[58] another pre-devolution commitment embodied in the equality white paper.

In addition to these demands, a number of the committees were readying themselves to take the committee stage of the initial rash of bills. In short, the volume of work confronting the statutory committees mounted considerably during the second phase of devolution, so much so that one — enterprise, trade and investment — decided to meet throughout the summer recess.

The members of the standing committees were, by contrast, rather less exercised and, in the case of the Committee of the Centre, they were not exercised at all. This committee had a decidedly chequered provenance. During the shadow phase, the Committee on Standing Orders had proposed one such body, a 'committee on conformity with equality requirements', to monitor the equality brief of the OFMDFM. With devolution, the issue was revisited and the committee proposed two new standing committees — Equality, Human Rights and Community Relations; and European affairs — responsible for scrutinising a wider range of the responsibilities of the Trimble/Mallon office. On 8 December 1999, the recommendation was endorsed by the Assembly which, a week later, was poised to create a third standing committee — its remit to scrutinise all remaining functions of the OFMDFM.

A motion in the names of Messrs Trimble and Mallon, however, sought to replace the two committees, agreed a week earlier, and instead create a single 'Committee of the Centre' to scrutinise approximately half of the functions of the office, excluding all those relating to its external roles, (North–South, 'east–west' and European matters). The view of the First and deputy First Ministers was that such matters were better dealt with on the floor of the Assembly, rather than in a committee room, and a combined SDLP/UUP vote was sufficient for their motion to succeed.[59] This evoked widespread concern among all other parties — not just the limited accountability but also about the bully-boy tactics of the two major parties. It confirmed a view among many members that the efficient, and open, secret of the Executive was this duopoly — a view reinforced by the appointment of two junior ministers to OFMDFM (see below).

Thus, where there had been two — and potentially three — committees to scrutinise the First and deputy First Ministers' office, now there was one, 17-strong body, enjoying only limited scope. Worse, the Committee of the Centre has failed to get off the ground. The chair and vice-chair — both DUP members — refuse to acknowledge the legitimacy of its SF members and each meeting has broken up in disarray after just a few minutes. This was brought to the floor of the Assembly by Michelle Gildernew, one of the SF

[58] CCRU, 1998, 1999.
[59] Northern Ireland Assembly Report, 15 December 2000.

members, during oral questions to the First and deputy First Ministers: 'The work of the Committee has yet to begin due to the inability of the Chair [Gregory Campbell] to treat all members in a spirit of equality.'[60]

To date, the Committee has not even produced a press release. Besides exhibiting some of the most vituperative exchanges between the DUP and SF, its inaction has prevented even the limited scrutiny of the OFMDFM envisaged. When the Assembly rose for the summer, this matter showed no sign of being resolved.

WIDER HORIZONS

The remarkable thing about activity on the all-Ireland front during renewed devolution was how little notice anyone took of it. There are plenty of things that could still bring the Belfast Agreement down, but the North–South agenda — so critical in 1974 — is not one of them.

The reasons for this have been explored in detail elsewhere.[61] But a key factor has been that the executive all-Ireland structures consist of a limited set (six) of discrete bodies: Waterways Ireland, Food Safety, Trade and Business Development, Special EU Programmes, Language, and Agriculture and Marine Matters. And the NSMC mainly works in 'sectoral format', monitoring the work of these bodies (as well as the six other designated areas for policy co-operation). In other words, the unionist fears which attached to the Council of Ireland in 1974 — echoed in 1998 when the then Minister for Foreign Affairs in the republic, David Andrews, spoke of the desirability of a structure 'not unlike a government' — have not been borne out. The NSMC is not a Trojan Horse for a united Ireland by stealth.

After devolution was restored, a rash of sectoral-format NSMC meetings took place. Characteristically, while only one minister attended from the republic, two attended from the north — the obvious ministerial counterpart, plus a minister from the 'other side' to keep an eye on them. Nationalist ministers, however, also met their counterparts bilaterally, outside of the Agreement's six-plus-six definition of domains of North–South integration.

The suspension of the Executive in February resulted in the postponement of the second summit meeting of the British–Irish Council, which had been scheduled for June in Dublin. The meeting was rescheduled for the autumn, with the main topic — as agreed at the inaugural meeting in London in December 1999 — being drug trafficking and abuse. The republic's government was to take the lead on this issue. According to the UK and Irish joint secretaries, interim reports on all five areas of work specified at the inaugural

---

[60] Northern Ireland Assembly Report, 19 June 2000.
[61] Wilson, 1999

meeting would be produced for the Dublin meeting, and a communiqué issued afterwards.

Notwithstanding speculation about the siting of the BIC secretariat elsewhere, it now appears that this will function jointly between the Cabinet Office in London and the Department of Foreign Affairs in Dublin — underscoring concerns that what was meant to be a multipolar broadening of the (misnamed) 'Anglo-Irish' relationship will remain a constrained, bipolar affair. In the context of the political focus on issues such as decommissioning and policing, and on the restoration of the Executive, scant attention has however been paid in Northern Ireland to the BIC and its future development.

COLLECTIVE RESPONSIBILITY?

Opinion polls in Scotland may suggest the jury is still out on the performance of the Lib-Lab Government in Edinburgh, and the forced resignation of Alun Michael as First Minister in Cardiff was a cathartic experience for the minority Labour administration there. But nothing else in the devolution project — indeed no other administration in the world except, in a much more benign political culture, the Swiss — compares to the government at Stormont. The mechanistic UUP-DUP-SDLP-SF coalition, its ministers allocated to departments by the lottery of d'Hondt, is an extraordinary construction.

There are no rules requiring collective responsibility, over and above the stipulation that ministers should work within the framework of the Programme for Government and the other terms (notably adhesion to non-violence) of the ministerial pledge of office. Even these constraints have been undermined by the failure effectively to sanction SF over continued IRA killings, or the DUP for its refusal to attend Executive Committee meetings.

An instance of the problems to which this can give rise was probably the greatest controversy faced by the administration outside of what passes for the 'normal' stuff of politics in Northern Ireland (policing, flags, parades, decommissioning, prisoner releases) — the SF Health Minister's long-delayed decision on the location of regional maternity services. Yet unionist ministers were sanguine about the outcome. One confided that, because Ms de Brún had not secured the support of the Minister of Finance, Mr Durkan, to meet the cost of her decision, they would 'ambush her in the long grass'. With four parties in government distributed across ten departments, plus the OFMDFM, the potential for 'turf wars' between and among ministers is evident. Another fissiparous matter is the future of the '11+' selection system in Northern Ireland. When the SF Minister of Education, Mr McGuinness, suggested in early June that perhaps it should be scrapped, Mr Trimble was immediately into the lists to insist, as First Minister, that it wouldn't be.[62]

The mutual veto underlying the 'key decision' procedure and the supporting 'petition of concern' epitomise the Agreement's consociational design. These locking — or blocking — devices do embody 'joined-up' government, both within the Executive and between the Executive and the Assembly, but they may also be a source of gridlock. An administrative answer to the problem of the centrifugal tendencies in the Executive has begun to emerge over time. The OFMDFM would be the hub, co-ordinating the work of the ministerial 'team' in pursuit of wider strategic policy objectives. Under the joint control of the UUP and SDLP — and to the chagrin of the other Assembly parties — it would grow like Topsy.

In their agreed statement of December 1998, setting out the departmental and North–South structures, the First and deputy First Minister had rebuffed SF demands for an Equality Department in favour of equality being assigned to their joint office — basically so that neither SF nor, from a more hostile perspective, the DUP would control it. And, under devolution, as the DUP became increasingly semi-detached, its ministers were first to be denied the right to brief Messrs Trimble and Mallon before Executive meetings and, later, to be denied regular access to Executive papers.

The December 1998 statement had assigned 11 functions to the OFMDFM. By the time the First and deputy First Minister reported to the Assembly in February 1999, however, this list had mushroomed to 26.[63] On 6 December 1999, with power transferred, they decided, unsurprisingly, that they now needed two junior ministers in the office. Equally unsurprisingly, they chose colleagues from their two parties (Dermot Nesbitt of the UUP and Denis Haughey of the SDLP) to fill the posts, ignoring the outcry from the other two governing parties. The action was widely condemned as 'jobs for the boys', breaching the Agreement's underpinning philosophy of inclusivity by turning the office into a 'closed shop'[64] for the UUP and SDLP.

In other words, the abnormal arrangements for devolution spatchcocked together in the frenetic final days of the negotiations of the Belfast Agreement are being *de facto* supplanted by a more conventional government-within-a-government. In effect, a working coalition of the UUP and SDLP, whose interrelationships are good (though personal relations between the First and deputy First Minister are non-existent), allied to the centralisation of power all governments now betray (and all democrats bemoan), is overlaying (arguably unworkable) provisions which were inscribed in the Agreement as political fixes to end a conflict rather than as vehicles for effective future governance.

[62] *Sunday Life*, 11 June 2000.
[63] New Northern Ireland Assembly Report 7
[64] Mitchel McLaughlin, SF

POLICY DEFICIT

Direct rule did not only establish a 'democratic deficit' in Northern Ireland, but also what a former Public Health Director of the Eastern Health and Social Services Board diagnosed as a *policy* deficit.[65] Policy portfolios were a luxury for the parties under direct rule, as they had no prospect of moving from opposition to assuming the responsibilities of government, and they did not compete on policy terms. It is extraordinary how durable such attitudes have proved to be.

While the Agreement clearly set down that ministers, as part of their pledge of office, had to agree a Programme for Government, progress was desultory. This was despite the wholly unanticipated (and of course paid) free time Assembly members were to enjoy from their election in June 1998 to December 1999, when power was finally transferred: the hiatus over decommissioning meant that the Assembly only met for about one day a month. It was also despite (or perhaps because of) the complete absence of any debate before the Agreement about the policy consequences of devolution comparable, say, to Wales.[66]

Until the final days before Good Friday 1998 it remained quite unclear what political arrangements the talks might bring forth — if, indeed, they would bring forth any at all. So when powers were transferred the initial legislative programme announced by Mr Trimble on 31 January 2000 was little more than a series of measures designed to achieve parity with relevant British legislation, much of it uncontroversial.

The Agreement bequeathed the requirement that, once in power, the Programme for Government would have to be agreed unanimously by the Executive (as well as being endorsed by the Assembly on a cross-community basis). Given the inclusion of the emphatically anti-agreement DUP within the four-party coalition, the prospect of achieving unanimity was uncertain at the time of writing. The programme could, however, in more benign circumstances, play a vital role as the 'glue' which holds the Executive together—in a political fashion, rather than by administrative *fiat*.

In October 1998, the political advisers to the First and deputy First Ministers asked a senior civil servant attached to their joint office to prepare an outline of a possible programme and to request information from the existing six departments on the main issues to be addressed and policy options. These were generated by the following month — just over one page of headings on the first, and just a few pages each from the Permanent Secretaries on the second. The dependence on officialdom, rather than political leadership, and the assumed continuity with the direct-rule past is noteworthy.

[65] Pollak, 1993: 319-320.
[66] Osmond, 1998.

The following January, a 'brainstorming session' took place at Stormont, for which a rather more substantial document was prepared. Anticipating future difficulties, it was brutally frank — and all too accurate. It warned:

> The Executive itself will be an involuntary coalition with internal political tensions that could degenerate into continual attrition between and within unionist and nationalist blocs.

Of the Assembly, it cautioned:

> Assembly members have up to now been in a 'permanent opposition' mode. They have not had to confront the hard decisions associated with priority-setting and resource allocation. The primary motivation of Assembly members will be to seek advantage for their particular constituencies rather than advancing the interests of the region as a whole.

Not even the electorate was spared:

> The community is imbued with a culture of dependency ('blame them') and inevitably there will be unrealistic expectations about the degree to which the Assembly can solve the region's economic and social challenges.

The document suggested the next steps should be:

- The establishment of the Economic Policy Unit signalled in the December 1998 agreement between the First and deputy First Ministers designate;
- The commissioning of a comprehensive review of public administration;
- The scheduling of debates in the Assembly on the major policy processes already in train, and
- The publication by the FM and DFM of a joint outline programme.

Nothing happened on the first two of these during 1999. Aside from a one-day debate in the Assembly on government proposals for acute-hospital rationalisation, nothing happened on the third. And, on the fourth, nothing emerged except one remarkably aspirational paragraph in the 18 January report from the First Minister and deputy First Minister to the Assembly.[67] The report promised that the programme would:

> ...succeed in delivering efficient, accountable, transparent government and enable us to achieve economic growth and development, the benefits of which will be shared throughout the entire community.

The two chief ministers pledged to:

> ...address the needs of the most vulnerable and disadvantaged ... imbue the community with a sense of enterprise and self-reliance ... tackle educational

---

[67] New Northern Ireland Assembly Report 6.

disadvantage and fully utilise the human capital of our people ... put behind us the tragic years of trauma and separation ...

It was the political equivalent of Motherhood and Apple Pie.

PREPARING THE PROGRAMME

Around the turn of the year, a senior civil servant was appointed to head the Economic Policy Unit in the OFMDFM and he was assigned to begin work on the programme. The Executive agreed in January that the unit would, in conjunction with ministers, determine the administration's 'detailed strategic goals' — but there was still no political direction as to what these might be. A memo to the Executive set out an 'illustrative model' of the programme, much of it borrowed from a Democratic Dialogue paper on the subject.[68]

The second paper defined the Programme for Government as 'a strategic policy statement of the Executive Committee's agreed aims and policy objectives, including ... cross-cutting themes'. It called for 'early agreement at least of the initial draft of the strategic aims, objectives and priorities of the Executive Committee'. This would 'demonstrate publicly the direction of the Executive Committee's work and that devolution will make a difference to government in Northern Ireland', and provide a basis for consultation with the Assembly and more generally 'which otherwise will lack focus'.

The paper also stressed the importance of 'joined up' government, and starting from 'citizens' needs' rather than the 'organisational ease' of departments. It was 'essential' that these considerations were incorporated into the draft programme and the mechanisms for taking it forward.

As to the structure of the programme, the paper spoke of offering a vision with 'at least a ten year time-span', though the main focus would be on the 'strategic reforms' to be enacted in the remaining period of the Executive (the next Assembly elections are slated for 2003). It would thus be written up as:

- A statement of the Executive's integrated strategic aims;
- A list of supportive integrated strategic objectives;
- A list of supporting key departmental objectives;
- A statement of budgetary priorities, and
- A statement of cross-cutting arrangements.

The paper envisaged drafts being presented to the Executive in February and March. Sadly, it was dated 11 February. Within hours, there was no Executive to consider it.

---

[68] Wilson, 2000.

The ensuing hiatus militated against further progress. When the Executive resumed its work in June, the statement after its first meeting made no reference to the programme (though ministers had discussed, *inter alia*, flags). At its next meeting on 8 June, it indicated that an Agenda for Government would be set out before the end of the month for action in the succeeding 12 months. The Programme for Government was described as 'longer term'.

On 29 June, the Executive Committee announced the Agenda for Government, following its weekly meeting. This would be operational until April 2001, when the programme would begin to be effected. Speaking afterwards, Mr Trimble said that the package was very significant but was more important as a representation of the collective will of ministers:

> We can make a real difference for the people of Northern Ireland, when we all work together. Many policies we have described today require Ministers and Departments to co-operate together, to pool their energy. That is what we in the Executive Committee are showing we will do. We want to work as a team, for the benefit of all. We — and we believe the Northern Ireland public — expect that of all Ministers.[69]

Despite the DUP boycott, it was clear that the agenda had been agreed by all ministers — a point noted by the deputy First Minister, Mr Mallon, when, four days later, he and the First Minister fleshed out the details. They told the Assembly: 'The Agenda demonstrates that the Executive Committee can agree, and has agreed, a package of measures targeting specific needs.'[70] (DUP participation had been *via* bilaterals with the OFMDFM.)

The degree of unanimity reached on the agenda augured more hopefully for the preparation of the programme. Mr Mallon said:

> The actions indicate our determination to work together for the benefit of all. We know that we can make real improvements to people's lives when we move forward effectively together.

On 20 July, the two junior ministers in the OFMDFM launched 'a major consultation exercise' on the programme, inviting the views of the unions, business and the voluntary sector.[71] The odd timing — in the depth of the summer break — reflected how the process of devolution, de-devolution and re-devolution had left the Executive Committee in a race against time.

The Minister of Finance and Personnel, under section 64 of the Northern Ireland Act 1998, must lay before the Assembly a draft budget before the beginning of each financial year. The section refers to the paragraph[72] of the Belfast Agreement requiring the Executive to agree a programme, incorporating an agreed budget, the programme to be scrutinised by Assembly

---

[69] Executive Information Service, 29 June 2000.
[70] Northern Ireland Assembly Report, 3 July 2000
[71] Executive Information Service, 20 July 2000
[72] Strand one, §20

committees and passed by a cross-communal majority. Working backwards from April 2001, and allowing for the time it takes for officials to attach financial numbers to agreed projects and policies, this imposes a tight schedule.

Officials in the OFMDFM hoped, at time of writing, to have something prepared for the Executive to agree in September, with a view to scrutiny by the committees in October. Hence the tight pressure on the committees themselves, before the summer, to come up with their own suggestions.

A SMALL REGION BALKANISED

During his review of the implementation of the Agreement, Mr Mitchell confided that from a US perspective he found two things baffling about Northern Ireland. First, politics in the region always gravitated towards the extremes, whereas — in presidential campaigns particularly — US elections were dominated by the pursuit of the centre. Secondly, he said, while US politicians were constantly being pressurised by civic advocates, their Northern Ireland counterparts were comparatively insulated from them.

In essence, both of these complaints can be explained by the victory of ethnonationalism (in both its unionist and nationalist variants) over democracy and civil society in Northern Ireland. As Keane[73] argues, democracy is premised on uncertainty and unpredictability (privileging dialogue and deliberation), whereas nationalism insists on certitude (favouring confrontation and adversarialism); the former similarly requires the clear (horizontal) separation of civil society and state, a separation the latter tends to conflate (as society is divided into vertical blocs).

In recent years, the increasing willingness of the business community to place its head above the political parapet — recognising the nexus between economic prosperity and political stability — has been a positive trend in an otherwise disturbing process of evacuation of the space for civil exchange and a widening partisan polarisation. Rippling way beyond the clashes occasioned by the parades controversy, there has been a proliferation in Northern Ireland of flag- and bunting-flying and kerbstone-painting, clearly assigning geographical areas to one or other ethnic group, defined in nationalist terms. Indeed, huge numbers of loyalist paramilitary flags were erected in predominantly Protestant areas in the wake of the refusal of SF ministers at Stormont to countenance the flying of the Union flag over their departments in the second period of devolution.

Intercommunal tensions have been greatly stoked by a rising wave of low-level, but terrifying, attacks. Principally perpetrated by loyalists — the finger of suspicion particularly attaching to the largest paramilitary

[73] 1998.

organisation, the Ulster Defence Association, ostensibly maintaining a ceasefire — the victims have inevitably been principally Catholic. Particularly at risk have been Catholic and mixed households living in predominantly Protestant areas. But there have also been many arson attacks on Orange halls, as well as on Catholic Church and Gaelic Athletic Association premises.

The attacks have gone largely unreported outside the region's media but they have become a daily feature of news bulletins there — alongside continuing 'punishment' attacks by paramilitaries. On 14 August, for example, a litany of attacks in north and west Belfast, Ballymena, Carrickfergus, Rathcoole and Newtownabbey were reported, under the headline 'Sectarian attacks reach new level of hatred'.[74] Essentially, what has happened is that the organised, selective and high-level violence of the 'pre-ceasefire' period has been replaced, 'post-ceasefire', by disorganised, diffuse and low-level violence.[75]

In August 2000, the process of cultural Balkanisation took a further twist, as a long-simmering feud erupted between the two main loyalist organisations in Protestant west Belfast. Now it was not enough for a ghetto to be labelled 'loyalist'; it had to be defined as 'UDA' or 'UVF'. Counterintuitively, after two killings by the Ulster Volunteer Force, the Northern Ireland Secretary declared the loyalist ceasefires intact.[76]

CAN THE CENTRE HOLD?

Analysing recent opinion survey evidence, Hayes and McAllister[77] detect the hardening out of 'strong pro-state' and 'strong counter-state' positions in the aftermath of the Agreement. On the Protestant side, they note the extremely high support for decommissioning and the extremely high opposition to prisoner releases. They also note how Catholic poll respondents, almost evenly split pre-agreement between 'nationalist' and 'non-nationalist' self-ascriptions (unionists were always more susceptible to ethnonationalist tags) now break down three to one in favour of the 'nationalist' label. The authors link this to the legitimisation of (the mutually antagonistic) ethnonationalist definitions inscribed in the Agreement; to that extent the paradox that the Agreement has been associated with widened communal divisions turns out not to be a paradox at all. The result has been the erosion of the 'weak pro-state' (broadly speaking, UUP) and 'weak counter-state'

---

[74] *Belfast Telegraph*, 14 August 2000.

[75] There have also been increasing incidences of domestic and racially-motivated attacks, though it is unclear how much this is an artifact of greater reporting and RUC sensitivity.

[76] *Irish Times*, 24 August 2000.

[77] 1999.

(broadly, SDLP) constituencies by comparison with their more aggressive political challengers (the DUP and other 'no' unionists, and SF).

The irony of this is thus that the parties of the 'democratic centre' in Northern Ireland, principally the SDLP and the liberal Alliance — for whom political accommodation was always the desired outcome, rather than a wrenching compromise — have benefited least politically from the accord. Alliance endured an embarrassing change of leadership as John Alderdice was elevated to the Lords. The subsequent leader, Sean Neeson, has still to make his mark, and senior figures convey gloom about the party's future viability in a climate so defined by communalist politics. And the SDLP does not feel easy — or, at least, its senior figures do not feel easy — about being defined in nationalist terms. The party chair, for example, happily describes himself as 'Irish', but not 'nationalist'.

Yet, in such a fraught climate, the vulnerability of more moderate 'communal contenders' to outbidding by 'ethnonationalist' parties — to use the distinction of Eide[78]— is very real. Election returns since the Agreement have borne out this ethnic outbidding trend — indeed, on both sides — not only in the Assembly elections in 1998 but especially in more recent council by-elections. A remarkably pugilistic republican MLA won a by-election in Omagh in April 2000 and doubled the party's vote in the process. The republican movement is able to raise huge sums from the more fundamentalist Irish-American diaspora, and an SDLP internal review was embarrassingly leaked in April 2000, warning that the party's 'pre-eminent position within constitutional nationalism has been eroded to the point where it is now a thing of the past'.

The anticipated local government and Westminster elections in 2001 could offer rich pickings for SF, and for the DUP. Both parties suspect that the SDLP and UUP would like the former to be postponed, under the guise of a review of local government. And within the UUP, the selection of the leading anti-agreement figure Peter Weir for the North Down Westminster constituency, followed by the Burnside nomination, were disturbing signals for the leadership of the trend of grassroots party opinion.

There is, however, something of a prisoner's-dilemma scenario here, driven by fear in an atmosphere of mutual mistrust. For there is also evidence of a popular yearning for a less communally-driven, less constitutionally-focused politics. Thus, in answer to the question as to what priorities should engage the new assembly, the Northern Ireland Life and Times Survey,[79] in summer and late autumn 1998, found a clear pattern of two-fifths of respondents saying 'improving the health service' and around one-third suggesting 'increasing employment opportunities.' By contrast, ethnonationalist demands which are the alpha and omega of politics for the protagonists —

---

[78] 1993.
[79] See http://www.qub.ac.uk/nilts.

'making it more likely that Northern Ireland will eventually leave the UK' and 'giving Northern Ireland a stronger voice in the UK' — were felt to be a priority by only one in ten respondents altogether.

In April 1999, Democratic Dialogue commissioned Ulster Marketing Surveys to run eight focus groups across Northern Ireland, to assay public opinion more qualitatively as to what the priorities of the incoming devolved administration should be. The report of these groups[80] detected:

> ...a widespread desire to see politicians take a lead in defusing this oppressive atmosphere of partisan belligerence, by adopting more open, constructive, and less emotional terminology and debate. For example, there was a desire to see practical co-operation on 'non-constitutional' matters and increasing focus on economic and social issues. This aspiration stood out as the most consistently identified first priority for the Assembly.

It is thus all the more unfortunate that the major health issue which the Assembly addressed during the period was the issue of location of regional maternity services, highly overdetermined as the latter was by sectarian considerations. All the more unfortunate, too, that such slow progress was made on the Programme for Government.

CONCLUSION

The hapless Ron Davies once famously remarked that 'devolution is a process, not an event'. On 11 February 2000, cynical observers might have been forgiven for adding 'except in Northern Ireland'. The suspension of devolution after 72 days inclined many to the view that the Belfast Agreement was to prove to be yet another failed attempt to effect a political 'settlement'. Its restoration three months later, amid mounting problems for Mr Trimble, meant that the first phase of the devolution process suffered from arrested development.

At the time of writing, the stability of the new Northern Ireland political institutions was still not guaranteed. Two scenarios were however clear, indicating what needed to be done to ensure the success of this latest in a very long line of Northern Ireland political initiatives.

The malign scenario is not hard to outline. Continuing battles over proxy-sovereignty issues — policing, flags, decommissioning — bedevil the Executive Committee and fuel popular cynicism and support for 'no' unionists, against a background of continuing paramilitary violence. Meanwhile, the self-presentation of SF as not just nationalists but nationalists 'with attitude' favours its growth as against the SDLP in this mistrustful context. Eventually, Mr Trimble's enemies secure 50 per cent plus one and that is that.

---

[80] UMS, 1999: 2

The benign scenario is also clear enough — if highly dependent on responsible political leadership. The cohesion of the 'government-within-a-government' described above beds down to strengthen the political centre and stem the electoral threats from the ethnonationalist outriders. SF moderates its acerbic rhetoric and behaviour over time and the IRA remains quiescent. The DUP finds it has nowhere else to go but inexorably into respectability. The Executive, as well as the other institutions, delivers tangible benefits and the climate of stability fosters confidence-building investment.

Like the conclusion to *Sliding Doors*, either of these scenarios seemed possible at the time of writing. Which one prevails is in the hands of politicians and paramilitaries, not political analysts.

BIBLIOGRAPHY

New TSN: An Agenda for Targeting Social Need and Promoting Social Inclusion in Northern Ireland, Central Community Relations Unit (Stationery Office, 1998)

Vision into Practice: The First New TSN Annual Report, Central Community Relations Unit (Leeds: Corporate Document Services, 1999)

Shaping Our Future: Draft Regional Strategic Framework for Northern Ireland, Department of the Environment for Northern Ireland (Stationery Office, 1998)

Eide, A., *New Approaches to Minority Protection,* (London: Minority Rights Group 1993)

Hayes, B., and McAllister, I., 'Ethnonationalism, public opinion and the Good Friday Agreement', in Ruane, J and Todd, J (eds.) *After the Good Friday Agreement: Analysing Political Change in Northern Ireland* (Dublin: University College Dublin Press, 1999), 30-48

Keane, J., *Civil Society: Old Images, New Visions* (Cambridge: Polity Press, 1998)

Osmond, J., (ed.), *The National Assembly Agenda: A Handbook for the First Four Years* (Cardiff: Institute of Welsh Affairs, 1998)

Pollak, A., (ed.), *A Citizens' Inquiry: The Opsahl Report on Northern Ireland* (Dublin: Lilliput Press, 1993)

Goals and Priorities for the Northern Ireland Assembly, Belfast Ulster Marketing Surveys (UMS, 1999)

Wilson, R., 'Conclusions', in Wilson R., (ed.), *No Frontiers: North–South Integration in Ireland* (Belfast: Democratic Dialogue, 1999)

Making a Difference: Preparing the Programme for Government (Belfast: Democratic Dialogue, 2000)

5

The Regional Governance of England

John Tomaney[1]

INTRODUCTION

Vernon Bogdanor has noted that: 'England is hardly mentioned in the devolution legislation, and yet England is, in many respects, the key to the success of devolution.'[2] The English Question — how England is to be governed in a devolved UK — is beginning to be raised even at the heart of the Government. In early 2000 the Home Secretary, Jack Straw, reported that he detected 'a rising sense of Englishness.'[3] Although careful to stay clear of any specific constitutional proposals to accommodate this new identity, Straw was clear that this sense of Englishness was a response to Scottish and Welsh devolution. Debates about the regional governance of England must be situated in this context.

Broadly speaking, two answers are offered to the question of how to govern England in a devolved UK. The first raises the prospect of an English parliament[4] and the second conceives of England as being governed in the future by regional assemblies. Historically, the notion of a federation based on the constituent nations of the UK has been regarded as unworkable, because an English parliament would represent another form of English domination of the Union. To date, the appeal of the regional government solution has been mainly in the English periphery. Here, an English parliament looks like another form of London dominance. England is a large country and one that contains significant and multifaceted geographical inequalities. These facts, and the perceived threats arising from Scottish and Welsh devolution, have generated an interest in regional government within England. The Labour Party's historical roots in those regions that feel most

---

[1] This chapter contains a lot of references and acronyms. References in the footnotes are listed in the bibliography at pp. 145–7. A glossary of acronyms is at p. 148. I would like to acknowledge the helpful comments of Robert Hazell, Andy Pike, Neil Ward, Ian Jones, John Adams, Phil Alker and Paul Benneworth on an earlier draft of this chapter.

[2] (1999: 265).

[3] *Guardian*, 11th January 2000.

[4] This proposal comes in two forms: *de jure* and *de facto*. Some inside the Conservative Party (and beyond) advocate the constitution of an English parliament to mirror that of Scotland. Others, including William Hague and some inside the Labour Party (such as Frank Field MP) have advocated excluding Scottish MPs from the conduct of English (and Welsh) business, thus using Westminster as a proxy English parliament (see pp. 197–8 and 202–7).

Figure 5.1. Chronology of main events in England	
June 1996	Regional Policy Commission publishes *Renewing the Regions.*
September 1996	Labour Party publishes *New Voice for England's Regions.*
June 1997	Queen's Speech announces legislation on RDAs. Ministers rule out elected assemblies in first term of a Labour Government.
November 1997	Publication of 'Declaration for the North.'
December 1997	Publication of White Paper on RDAs.
March 1998	Regional Development Agencies Act receives Royal Assent.
April 1998	Establishment of North-East Constitutional Convention.
	Establishment of Campaign for Yorkshire.
October 1998	Launch of Campaign for an English Parliament.
March 1999	Launch of Campaign for the English Regions.
April 1999	RDAs vested with powers.
May-July 1999	'Designation' of Chambers (or 'Assemblies').
July 1999	Establishment of North-West Constitutional Convention.
September 1999	Production of Regional Economic Strategies.
November 1999	North-East Constitutional Convention publishes report.
February 2000	Cabinet Office PIU report *Reaching Out.*
May 2000	LGA report *Regional Variations.*

exposed to the consequences of Scottish and Welsh devolution, together with an increasing desire within the regions for a loosening of Whitehall domination, largely accounts for the party's need to address 'the regional question'.

Compared to its proposals for Northern Ireland, Scotland, Wales, and even London, the Labour Party's proposals for the English regions were modest; and in government, its achievements have been more modest still. Nevertheless, the Government has not been inactive in this field. Its major achievement was the establishment of Regional Development Agencies (RDAs) in April 1999, but other significant developments occurred alongside this. Perhaps the most notable of these was the publication, in 2000, of a report from the Cabinet Office's Performance and Innovation Unit (PIU) on the role of central government at the regional and local level. The recommendations of the report, which were accepted in full by the Government, have a number of important implications for the activities of the Government's own regional offices and for structures and practice within and across Whitehall. Another significant development was the establishment, in every part of England, of 'regional chambers' — voluntary gatherings of local councillors and others, primarily intended to monitor the activities of RDAs. The growing importance of the regional agenda in England was also highlighted by the decision of the Local Government Association (LGA) to hold a 'hearing on the regions'. This was designed to gather information and opinion as a prelude to the LGA developing a clear policy on the question of regional government.[5] Finally, the period also saw the creation or consolidation of a number of civic movements within some English regions with the explicit aim of making the case for elected regional government. In some regions, this is linked to growing media attention on the question of devolution.

The main focus of this chapter is events since April 1999, but it is necessary first to clarify some of the background. The chapter begins by examining the position of the Labour Government on the question of English regional government and some of the debates, divisions and controversies that surround it. The chapter then assesses the first year of operation of the RDAs, before turning to an examination of the emerging role of 'regional chambers'. Next, the chapter pays particular attention to the analysis of the problem of regional governance in the PIU report. It looks specifically at the operation of regional Government Offices (GOs) and the changes that are proposed for them. A number of other related developments in the English regions are also explained, including the growth in the number of regional campaigns, along with their consolidation into a national umbrella organisation, the Campaign for the English Regions. Finally, the chapter identifies a series of unresolved issues and conflicts that are likely to have a bearing on the evolution of English regionalism. A glossary of the main acronyms used within the chapter can be found in the Appendix at the end of this chapter.

GOVERNMENT POLICY FOR THE ENGLISH REGIONS

The Government's position on English regional government was developed in opposition by Jack Straw, in response to Conservative attacks on Labour's devolution proposals.[6] Straw, at the time, was a noted sceptic on the subject of devolution and his authorship of the policy was seen as an attempt by Tony Blair to bat the issue into the long grass. Nevertheless, the Straw document made a number of arguments that have since gathered force. Straw pointed out that a tier of regional government existed in England, but that it lacked integration and democratic accountability. Too much of English regional life was governed by quangos. England needed more accountable, better co-ordinated regional government. Centralisation, he maintained, is inefficient. Decentralisation would promote a 'competition of ideas' leading to policy innovation; it would better equip the regions to participate in EU regional initiatives and promote a more focused concern with economic

---

[5] The hearing was chaired by Lord Dearing and its findings were published in a report (LGA, 2000).
[6] Labour Party, 1995, 1996; see Tomaney 1999, for an account of this episode.

development. However, Labour would not impose regional assemblies where they were not wanted. It would encourage the formation of 'regional chambers', drawn from local councillors and other regional interests. Any move to elected regional assemblies would require a region to have 'predominantly' unitary local government. Three hurdles would then need to be crossed:

- The regional chamber would need to approve a plan for a directly elected assembly;
- Parliament would then need to approve the plan, then
- Public assent would be sought through a referendum.

This policy was summarised in Labour's 1997 manifesto as follows:

> The Conservatives have created a tier of regional government in England through quangos and government regional offices. Meanwhile local authorities have come together to create a more co-ordinated regional voice. Labour will build on these developments through the establishment of regional chambers to co-ordinate transport, planning, economic development, bids for European funding and land use planning. Demand for directly elected regional government so varies across England that it would be wrong to impose a uniform system. In time we will introduce legislation to allow the people, region by region, to decide in a referendum whether they want directly elected regional government. Only where clear popular consent is established will arrangements be made for elected regional assemblies.

The manifesto also stipulated than any move in the direction of elected regional government 'would require a predominantly unitary system of local government' and 'no additional public expenditure'. These stipulations were widely regarded as presenting very high hurdles to the achievement of regional government.[7]

In government, Labour has moved slowly in the direction set out by Straw and in its manifesto. In his introduction to the White Paper on RDAs, *Building Partnerships for Prosperity*, the Deputy Prime Minister, John Prescott states that:

> The Government is committed to move to directly-elected regional government in England, where there is a demand for it, alongside devolution in Scotland and Wales and the creation of the Greater London Authority. But we are not in the business of imposing it.[8]

The Government quickly made clear that there would be no move to elected assemblies in its first term and this has been reiterated since. For instance, Hilary Armstrong stated in February 2000 that:

[7] See Tomaney, 1999; Harding, 2000.
[8] DETR, 1997: 7.

It is not realistic to expect significant further progress in relation to the English regions before the next parliament. Finding the right solutions will take time, as was the case with other parts of the United Kingdom. It is therefore too early to speculate on what, if any, structural changes in local government might in practice be needed, and if so, when they might best be made. The Government does not presume that the same single approach will be right for every region. There are already different arrangements in Scotland, Wales and London. But the implications of asymmetric arrangements and the extent of variation, would need to be considered.[9]

Ministers indicated that more evidence of demand would be required before they acted and that the regions themselves needed to bring forward their own workable proposals for regional government. Given this context, the central focus of the Government's approach to the English regions is the creation of RDAs as a means of addressing the economic deficits between the prosperous South East/London and the rest of England. Questions of the democratic accountability of the governance of English regions have received less attention, although the Conservatives attacked RDAs as 'super-quangos' (see below). There has, therefore, been a central ambiguity in New Labour's approach to English regions from the outset. Although officially RDAs are charged with tackling the economic problems facing the English regions, in reality they were also regarded, not least in the regions themselves, as part of a package of constitutional reforms that included Scottish and Welsh devolution and the creation of a London Assembly.

The media frequently assumes that the essential fault line inside the Government is between Tony Blair and John Prescott. Without doubt, Prescott is the most consistent champion of regional government, first giving vent to his thinking on the issue as far back as the early 1980s. He reiterated his commitment in the House of Commons on 24 May 2000, in reply to a question by Jim Cousins MP. However, a close examination of Blair's statements on the subject shows him to be, publicly at least, studiously open-minded, sticking closely to the formulation presented in *Building Partnerships for Prosperity*. Whatever Blair's personal scepticism — or lack of natural sympathy with questions of regionalism — in all his public statements he has left the door open to the possibility of elected assemblies. Were he to come out strongly in favour of regional government — say perhaps in a referendum campaign in his own region of the North East — there is little in previous statements to allow his detractors to present his actions as a reversal of opinion.

Nevertheless, despite the commitment in the manifesto and the White Paper, and notwithstanding the creation of RDAs, progress toward the creation of elected regional assemblies on the part of the Government has been non-existent. The Prime Minister's decision in July 1999 to shift

[9] UNISON, 2000.

**Figure 5.2. Environment, Transport and the Regions
Final policy statement, July 2000**

Labour recognises the legitimate aspirations of the English regions and believes
that the essential next step for those regions which wish to do so should be
facilitated towards fully fledged directly elected regional authorities which could
help renew democracy, modernise the constitution and empower citizens.

Those with reservations about regional assemblies have stated that careful
consideration will need to be given to ensuring that elected assemblies do not
create additional tiers of bureaucracy; to the responsibilities, powers, size and type
of assembly; to the appropriate test of public consent; to the type of voting system;
and to the relationship between assemblies and the other democratic institutions,
including local government and Westminster.

Labour intends, as soon as practicable, to move to directly elected regional
government where and when there is a clear demand for it. The way forward will
include proposals to:

> request that the existing regional assemblies and chambers, working closely
> with the regional partners, develop detailed proposals for elected assemblies in
> their respective regions; and / or publish a Government Green or White Paper
> on regional governance.

> Development of regional governance structures should not result in adding a
> new tier of government to the English system and would require a move to a
> predominantly unitary system of local government as presently exists in
> Scotland and Wales.

Richard Caborn from his job as minister for the regions to a job in the Department of Trade and Industry (DTI) was widely regarded as diminishing the
status of the issue in the view of New Labour. Caborn is a close ally of
Prescott and a long-standing supporter of regional assemblies. His replacement was Hilary Armstrong. Her appointment was seen as signalling Blair's
alleged preference for elected mayors over regional assemblies (see below).

THE POLITICAL PARTIES

Beyond the Government, within the policy-making machinery of the Labour
Party, rank and file members inside the Environment, Transport and Regions
(ETR) policy forum called on the Government to bring forward a White or
Green Paper on the subject of regional government, thus raising the internal
party profile of the issue in the run-up to the preparation of the new Party
manifesto. This development occurred at the same time as some regional
parties (notably in the North East, where a survey showed a big majority of
Labour MPs in favour) submitted strong statements in support of elected
regional government for consideration by the Party's national policy forum.
During early 2000 some prominent MPs, mainly from the North, but also

including ministers, made their own support for regional government clear.[10] The broad thrust of the ETR policy forum's position was adopted by the Labour Party's National Policy Forum in July 2000 (see Figure 5.2), although amendments aimed at committing the Party to a timetable were rejected.

A statement of the Conservative position on the English regions (albeit very brief) is provided in the Party's written evidence to the LGA hearing on the regions, prepared by Nigel Waterson MP. Here, regionalism is described as part of the Government's 'centralising agenda for local governance.'[11] The Conservative Party's policy is summarised as:

> ...abolishing regional development agencies, regional government offices and regional assemblies. Their powers and budgets should be given back to local authorities.[12]

However in February 2000 it was reported that Archie Norman, the Party's spokesperson on the regions, favoured the retention of the RDAs on the grounds that they had secured the involvement of business in regional policy.[13] But in September the Tories confirmed that they would abolish RDAs and Regional Assemblies in their mini-manifesto *Believing in Britain*.

The Liberal Democrats, on the other hand, largely welcome the Government's initiatives to date, but stress the lack of democratic accountability in the current arrangements. The position of the Liberal Democrats is set out in evidence given to the LGA regions hearing by their shadow minister, Don Foster:

> The current degree of devolution should not be overstated as RDAs are responsible to Ministers in London, RDAs must work to central government targets and policies and Government Offices for the Regions must administer central government policies. Since the RDAs are appointed by central government they are naturally inclined to carry out the national agenda rather than be truly responsive to regional priorities. The regions do not have the flexibility and independence to decide policies according to regional need and are more directly responsible to the Secretary of State than to the local electorate in their own area.[14]

The Liberal Democrats sketch out a model of regional government with an extensive range of powers which 'would include some tax varying powers and the ability to enact secondary legislation'. Any such assemblies, in order

---

[10] *Guardian*, 26 May 2000.

[11] Unpublished written testimony submitted to the inquiry is available in two volumes from the LGA.

[12] The Conservative submission does not consider the fact that local authorities have never had control over the budgets which RDAs and GOs now operate; nor the historical origins of the Government Offices which were created by the Major government in 1993.

[13] *The Times*, 8 February 2000.

[14] See note 5.

to receive the support of the Liberal Democrats, would have to be elected by proportional representation. A more recent contribution from the Liberal Democrats describes a model of functions and powers for regional government that draws on the work of the North East Constitutional Convention (see below). It also calls for the creation of a Finance Commission for the Nations and Regions to assign resources to the regions. Overall, its proposals see the English regions as actors in an evolving 'federal' Britain.[15]

Whatever the nominal positions of the parties on the question of regional government, in practice none of them have developed a clear set of proposals — or, arguably, a convincing analysis of the problem — as far as regional government is concerned. Despite this, it is possible to identify a growing regionalism in the shape of a number of central government initiatives and initiatives within the regions themselves.

REGIONAL DEVELOPMENT AGENCIES

The eight new Regional Development Agencies were vested with powers on April 1st 1999 (see Figure 5.1). They represent the centrepiece of the Government's approach to the English regions, and are widely regarded as the product of John Prescott. Prescott made a strong case for creating RDAs in all the English regions as far back as 1982, when he was a front bench Labour spokesperson. Later, in the mid-1990s, he sponsored the Millan Inquiry into regional policy which, among other things, advocated the creation of powerful RDAs (Regional Policy Commission 1996).[16] Their establishment was fraught with inter-departmental conflict, as different parts of the Whitehall machinery sought to prevent functions over which they had jurisdiction being incorporated into RDAs. This meant that RDAs began with a smaller range of powers than had been anticipated by Millan (and Prescott). Moreover, as a result of these Whitehall battles, most of the functions undertaken by RDAs are drawn from DETR. One effect of this is that a large part of the activities (and income streams) of RDAs is concerned with local area-based initiatives (notably Single Regeneration Budget) rather than the strategic regional development goals originally anticipated. The fact that the resources available to RDAs are tied to the delivery of specific (national) programmes, means that they face similar problems to Government Offices (GOs) in terms of delivering genuinely regionalised strategies. According to one RDA chair:

> The way that resources enter the English regions is critical to the ability of RDAs
> to achieve truly integrated public investment; it is already clear that

---

[15] Liberal Democrats, 2000.

[16] The Commission was chaired by Bruce Millan, former Scottish Secretary in the last Labour government and former EU regional policy commissioner.

Figure 5.3. RDA boundaries

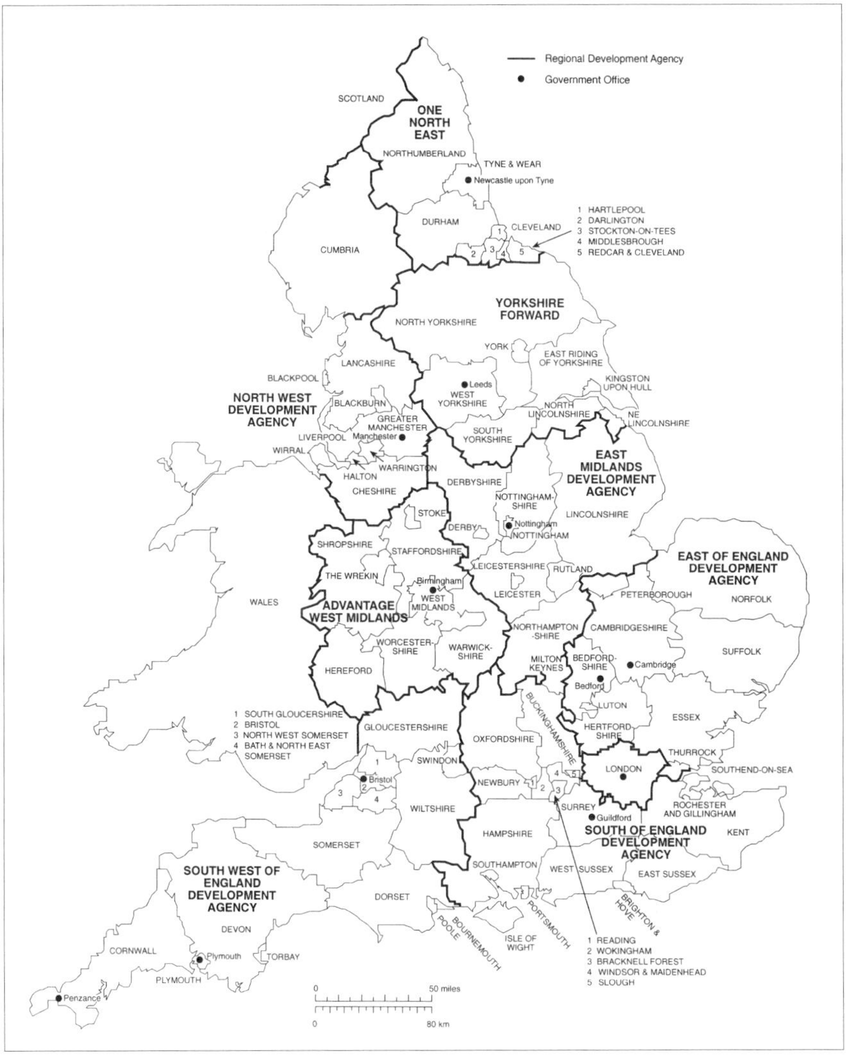

"Departmentalitis" — the way resources and policies are channelled through vertical silos from Whitehall — is the biggest barrier to effective joined-up government.'[17]

The budgets of RDAs are both small and constrained, relative to their Scottish and Welsh counterparts and, arguably, relative to the scale of the problems that many of them face (see Figure 5.4 for the initial budgets of the

---

[17] PIU, 2000: p76.

RDAs, excluding London). The initial budgets of RDAs represented less than 1 per cent of government expenditure in their regions. The financial capacity of RDAs is highly restricted insofar as most of their budgets are specifically drawn from ring-fenced regeneration funds. RDAs can currently switch funds between four of their six principal programme expenditure headings without prior agreement of central government, provided that such transfers do not lead to the size of any programme increasing or decreasing by more than 10 per cent. RDAs cannot alter the balance between capital and current expenditure allocated to them without agreement of the Government. All projects where an RDA's financial contribution exceeds £20 million require Treasury approval.[18] Together, these stipulations tightly restrict the financial flexibility available to RDAs.

Figure 5.4. RDA budget allocations 1999/2000
Source: DETR cited in LGA (2000)

Region	Gross total budget (£000s)	Less receipts (£000s)	Net total budget (£000s)
East	33,760	2,563	31,197
East Midlands	67,348	12,563	54,785
North East	148,810	39,840	108,970
North West	224,726	37,528	187,198
South East	88,336	12,642	75,694
South West	53,997	20,591	33,406
West Midlands	122,442	17,397	105,045
Yorkshire and the Humber	160,239	19,788	140,451

The Select Committee on Environment, Transport and Regional Affairs recommended that from 2001/2002, RDA budgets should be allocated as a single block grant with agencies having 'total freedom to vire between programmes'.[19] Governments have generally resisted devolving this level of financial autonomy to non-departmental public bodies, as long as political accountability for the bodies remains with Parliament. The financial limits surrounding RDAs have begun to receive a high degree of attention in the regions themselves. For instance, the North East RDA and its corresponding Regional Chamber presented a list of projects (valued at £850m) for

---

[18] PIU 2000, para 3.59, 3.60.
[19] House of Commons, 1999: para 47.

consideration in the 2000 Spending Review. Other RDAs were expected do the same. The Spending Review resulted in an increase in the overall RDA budgets from £1.2 billion in 2000/2001 to £1.7 billion in 2003/4. The Spending Review also increases the financial flexibility available to RDAs insofar as RDA funding will be brought together in a single cross-Departmental budget to which DETR, DTI and DfEE will commit funds for a three year period. The RDAs will, however, continue to have to meet nationally defined performance targets.[20]

The intention of RDAs is to develop better policy co-ordination and a space for new approaches to regenerating the economy. The White Paper on RDAs[21] stressed their boards should be 'business-led'. The boards of RDAs are accountable to the Secretary of State. Two parliamentary select committee reports questioned the Government's approach to the creation of RDAs, prior to their establishment. The concerns raised included: a lack of clarity about the relationships between RDAs and existing regional Government Offices[22]; a lack of clarity about how RDAs would be accountable to any future regional Chambers[23] and doubts about the limited range of powers the agencies would have in practice. In particular, it was noted that RDAs would lack a unified budget with the power to raise funds and this would limit their autonomy and flexibility. In key areas such as skills and training — which are critical to economic development — the RDAs will have no direct powers;[24] for a more recent parliamentary investigation of RDAs which reprised some of these arguments see Robinson (2000).[25]

The boards of RDAs generally comprise around thirteen members drawn from those already active in a range of regional organisations and quangos. Of the thirteen, around three or four tend be drawn from local authorities and the private sector, one from higher or further education and one from trade unions. Others variously have backgrounds in rural affairs, the voluntary sector, or other regional quangos. The RDAs themselves are constructed from pre-existing regional quangos, comprising principally English Partnerships, the Rural Development Commission, and various promotional agencies within the regions, as well as taking some staff from GOs. The RDAs

[20] DETR, News Release, 489, 21 July 2000.

[21] DETR, 1997.

[22] Since reiterated in PIU (2000), and LGA (2000).

[23] Also reiterated in LGA (2000).

[24] House of Commons, 1997c, 1998; see also Constitution Unit, 1996.

[25] See House of Commons, 1999. Robinson (2000) has identified what he regards as a more fundamental flaw in the strategy of RDAs. All are seeking to raise the growth in GDP per head in their region to a level above the national average, which as Robinson points out is a mathematical impossibility. I would suggest that this contradiction should be traced back to the ambiguities about the purpose of RDAs. RDAs are generally conceived as a mechanism for raising the economic performance of lagging regions (e.g. Danson, et al. 1992). However, their establishment in England — in all regions simultaneously — was partially conceived, although never really admitted as such, as a constitutional counterweight to Scottish and Welsh devolution.

confronted a major administrative challenge to weld these separate bodies and their staffs into a single organisation in their first year.

The primary task of the RDAs was to produce Regional Economic Strategies (RESs) to guide their actions over the coming ten years. A coincidence of pressing national and EU funding deadlines meant that the time available for the design of these strategies — and consultation upon them — was very limited. Indeed, the extent to which notice was taken of consultation submissions and the reflection of the RESs appears to have been patchy. The Statutory Guidance accompanying the 1998 Act that established RDAs, required them to consult widely in the preparation of their strategies. RDAs were officially vested with their powers on 1ˢᵗ April 1999, with their consultations to be completed by the following September. In practice, the strategies produced by the RDAs corresponded closely to the directions set out in the Act and related Statutory Guidance, leading to some concerns about the level of flexibility RDAs actually possess to devise regional strategies that reflect different sub-national priorities. Indeed, it has been noted that there is a remarkable degree of similarity between each of the Regional Economic Strategies (RESs). This suggests that the specific weaknesses and potentials of the individual regions have not been sufficiently explored to date or, perhaps more likely, that the hand of the centre has lain heavily over the process of strategy making.[26]

The most public difficulty faced by a RDA to date was the resignation, in July 2000, of the chief executive of the West Midland RDA, 'Advantage West Midlands' (AWM). The resignation came after the threat of a motion of censure at a meeting of the West Midlands Regional Chamber. The Chamber had already rejected the RES as too vague at a previous meeting. The background to the resignation was a complaint on the part of elements of the business community that they had not been properly consulted in the preparation of AWM's RES.[27] Whether the West Midlands episode represents a little local difficulty, or the shape of things to come, remains to be seen.

On balance, the major achievement of the RDAs was to create a new organisation in each of the regions and to prepare their RESs in the context of a very tight timetable and with a degree of consultation. In many cases, RDAs were also able to establish sub-regional partnerships for the purposes of delivering their policies. RDAs are already significant actors in each of their respective regions. However, some of the structural handicaps facing the RDAs in the achievement of their goals are becoming apparent. The recent experience in the West Midlands may also suggest the willingness of Regional Chambers to exercise a veto over the strategies of RDAs in the future.

[26] Benneworth, 2000; Nathan, *et. al*, 1999; Robson *et. al.*, 2000.
[27] *Financial Times*, 6 July 2000.

REGIONAL CHAMBERS

Regional Chambers are voluntary associations comprising local councillors in the majority but with additional representation from business, trade unions, voluntary organisations and other interests. Their primary role (although not necessarily their only one) is to provide an element of 'democratic' scrutiny of the RDAs from the regions. As Non-Departmental Public Bodies, RDAs are accountable to parliament, but the Regional Development Agencies Act 1998 requires that an RDA: '...have regard to the view of the Regional Chamber in formulating its economic strategy and to give an account of itself to the Chamber.'

Beyond this, the Government has been reluctant to prescribe a formal relationship between the chambers and the RDAs. However, the Act gives the Secretary of State the power to 'designate' regional chambers. 'Designation' assigns them a quasi-official role as 'mechanisms through which RDAs can take account of regional views and give an account of themselves and their activities'.[28]

Although Chambers are voluntary organisations, the Government has specified some characteristics they must exhibit in order to be 'designated'. The White Paper on RDAs required Chambers to achieve appropriate gender and ethnic balance. It is also expected that local authority representation in the Chamber should reflect regional, local and political balance, and type of authority, and that the main regional 'stakeholders' should be included in the non-local authority element. Figure 5.5 shows that regional chambers have been established in all eight of the English regions, although some have chosen to refer to themselves as 'regional assemblies'.

The Select Committee on Environment, Transport and the Regions regarded the progress in establishing the Chambers as 'quite remarkable'. It described as 'especially noteworthy', developments in areas such as the South West, the East of England and the East Midlands, which had little tradition of partnership working at a regional level.[29] But the Committee also noted widespread concerns that chambers had not been given a statutory footing and that this would limit their effectiveness in holding RDAs to account. In this context, the LGA expressed its concern that:

> RDAs will operate less as genuine "champions" for their regions, open and accountable to their regions, and more as a regional arm of central government.[30]

---

[28] DETR, 1997: 52.
[29] House of Commons, 1999: para 30.
[30] House of Commons, 1999: para 31.

Figure 5.5. English Regional Chambers
Source: While (2000)

	Date of formation or inaugural meeting	Designation	Size and membership balance (Local authority: non local authority)
East Midlands Regional Assembly	December 1998	19 May 1999	105 members (70:35)
East of England Regional Assembly	12 March 1999	21 July 1999	40 members (27:13)
North East Regional Assembly	4 March 1999	23 June 1999	63 members (42:21)
North West Regional Assembly	3 April 1998	19 March 1999	80 members (56:24)
South East Regional Assembly	20 January 1999	21 July 1999	111 members (74:37)
South West Regional Assembly	24 April 1998 (inaugural meeting)	21 July 1999	113 members (81:32)
West Midlands Regional Assembly	January 1999	19 March 1999	60 members (42:18)
Regional Chamber for Yorks and Humberside	March 1998	27 July 1999	35 members (22:13

In its own report on the regions, the LGA went further, stating:

> The regional agenda of the last three years has promoted more systematic consultation and wider partnership working. It has brought regional needs into better focus. This could provide the basis for more decentralisation and devolution in the future. But the [inquiry] panel was struck by an inverse relationship between power and accountability of regional bodies. RDAs are the powerful centrepiece of the regional agenda in England; their accountability is

widely seen as being more to Whitehall than to the region. The Government Offices are the regional arm, directly accountable to Whitehall. Regional chambers are weak bodies, with few means to secure adoption of their views; but they are the most accountable players at regional level.[31]

Aidan While (2000) has undertaken a study of the formation of the Yorkshire and West Midlands chambers (see Figure 5.6). He notes that both built on longer-standing traditions of political 'region-building' that meant that the formation of the chambers was relatively straightforward. The variations in the size of the chambers reflect efforts to respond to differing local political and institutional contexts. In Yorkshire the Chamber has sought to position itself as the custodian of the region's development strategy and has set about creating an operational structure to support this ambition. In the West Midlands the chamber has limited itself to the task of responding to the RDA's agenda. Business has been best equipped to play its role as a 'stake-holder' in the new arrangements. In the West Midlands various business representative organisations formed the relatively well-resourced West Midlands Business Policy Group in 1997 to ensure their collective voice would be heard. While (2000) reports that it had formed better relationships with the Chamber than with the RDA (perhaps foretelling the events of mid 2000). Voluntary organisations have found it more difficult to gain access to the new arrangements, lacking the resources and the experience of the private sector in regional activity.[32] While concludes from his study that 'there is sufficient political will to ensure that the Chambers can become a potent political force'.[33] Events in the West Midlands in mid 2000 reported earlier, may provide a preliminary confirmation of this prognostication.

In a number of regions, in the absence of a statutory recognition of their role, 'Concordats' have been signed to define the relationships between RDAs, Regional Chambers and GOs. The first Concordat was signed in Yorkshire between the RDA and the Regional Chamber. This practice has spread to other regions and has also spread beyond the principal actors. For instance, in Yorkshire the RDA has signed a Concordat with the regional TUC, which assigns the TUC a role in 'delivering' the RDA's strategy. An agreement has also been signed between the trade union workforce develop-ment project and ONE, the North East's development agency[34].

---

[31] LGA, (2000):13. In assessing the relative weakness of Chambers the inquiry panel concludes: '...if they are to work effectively and gain confidence across a full range of sectors, regional chambers need central funding' LGA, (2000): 27. A further dimension of this issue is that groups within the regions are unevenly equipped to participate in the processes established by the RDAs. While business is relatively well equipped, the voluntary sector, for instance, is less well endowed with the resources and skills necessary to contribute to policy making.

[32] See also House of Commons, 1999.

[33] 2000: 344.

[34] I am grateful to my colleague Peter O'Brien for bringing these developments to my attention.

**Figure 5.6. Regional Chamber membership in Yorkshire and
Humberside and the West Midlands (August 1999)
Source: While (2000)**

Regional Chamber for Yorkshire and Humberside	West Midlands Regional Chamber
35 Chamber members Formally designated July 1999	60 Chamber members Formally designated March 1999
Fulltime chamber secretary plus additional support from the regional local government association and other partners.	Secretariat provided by West Midlands Local Government Association (WMLGA)
22 local authority representatives: Leaders of the 22 local authorities in the region.	*42 local authority representatives*: Selected by WMLGA on the basis of the political balance of the region

13 regional stakeholders:
Regional TUC
CBI
Regional Training and Enterprise
  Councils
Regional Universities Association
Regional Chamber of Commerce
  Association
Environment Agency
Rural Community Council
Churches Regional Commission
Regional Forum for Voluntary and
  Community Organisations
NHS Executive
Further Education Association
Cultural Forum
Ethnic minority representation
	9 business 'stakeholders':
	Business leaders selected by Business Policy Group from nominations by member groups (TECs, Chambers of Commerce, Engineering Employers Federation, CBI, Tourist Board, Institute of Directors, Federation of Small Businesses)

	9 other stakeholders: TUC Environmental organisations Voluntary organisations Health authorities Further education Higher education Parish councils Cultural organisations Social housing
Associate members: Police	*5 co-opted seats (no voting rights)*
Observers: GO for Yorkshire RDA	

THE ROLE OF CENTRAL GOVERNMENT IN THE REGIONS

The role of central government in the regions is significant. Leaving aside the functions which, under the devolution arrangements for Scotland and Wales, are reserved for Westminster (e.g. social security), it is evident that a tier of regional government already exists in England. Work undertaken for the North East Constitutional Convention by the Centre for Urban and

Regional Development Studies at Newcastle University illustrates the situation in the North East (see Figure 5.7). It shows an extensive and influential range of activities, albeit one that is fractured and, in the words of the LGA hearing report, frequently 'invisible' to the ordinary citizen. At the centre of the regional tier of government are the Government Offices (GOs). Ironically, given the current position of that party, these were established by the last Conservative Government in 1994 in order to bring a measure of co-ordination to the delivery of government policy in the regions. The Labour Government's position, recently outlined, is to strengthen the role of GOs as a mechanism for 'joining up' government policy in the regions. This position was set out in a report from the Cabinet Office's Performance and Innovation Unit (PIU).[35]

Figure 5.7. The Governance of North East England

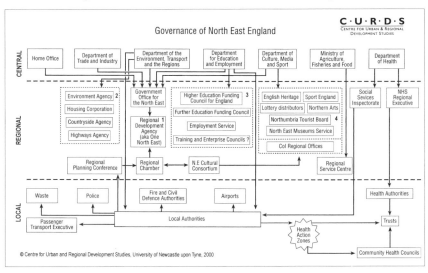

CABINET OFFICE REPORT

Two related issues form the background to the PIU study. The first is the Government's concern to achieve 'joined-up' government, that is to improve the capacity of Government to address strategic, cross-cutting issues and promote innovation in the development of policy and in the delivery of the Government's objectives. Secondly and more specifically, as far as the role of central government in the regions is concerned, a particular issue arises as a result of the proliferation of area based initiatives (ABIs). These are generally concerned with the renewal of disadvantaged neighbourhoods (or combating 'social exclusion'), but cover a range of inter-related policy areas

[35] PIU, 2000.

including employment, health and education.[36] Underlying the PIU report is the assumption that greater effort needs to be made to integrate these different policy initiatives in the name of 'joined-up' government.

The PIU report paints a rather damning picture of how the plethora of ABIs are poorly integrated with each other, leading to the waste of local efforts. At the same time, ABIs are not co-ordinated with mainstream government programmes.[37] The planning requirements of mainstream programmes themselves are problematic because they specify detailed action in accordance with the separately conceived interests of central government departments. These interests are tightly specified in Public Service Agreements regulated by the Treasury.[38] These problems are compounded by the fact that the Government tends to demand short-term 'outputs' from its initiatives rather than long-term 'outcomes'. In addition, there are doubts about how well matched central government initiatives are to local circumstances. For instance, the PIU states:

> Several local authority chief executives argued that education policy-making had become too centralised and insufficiently sensitive to variations in local circumstances. Some took the view that recent increases in funding for schools would, in their locality, have been better spent on dealing with factors outside school which contributed to poor educational attainment.[39]

Similar observations were made about the role of the Ministry of Agriculture, Fisheries and Food (MAFF). Good links between MAFF and other government activities are deemed to be of greater importance in an age where the emphasis is shifting from agricultural subsidies to sustainable regeneration of rural communities, which requires more integrated local and regional policy strategies. Very similar arguments can also be made in relation to health policy.[40]

The general thrust of the PIU's analysis of the fractured nature of regional governance and the inefficiencies it generates receives some endorsement in evidence given to the LGA's hearing on the regions. The LGA's witnesses emphasised the problems arising from the absence of key departments from GOs;[41] and the uneven capacity of GOs to engage as a genuine partner with

---

[36]   Examples of ABIs include: Health Action Zones, Employment Action Zones, Education Action Zones, Sure Start, Single Regeneration Budget and New Deal for Communities.

[37]   One effect of the proliferation of ABIs and lack of supervision in relation to them was revealed in a study conducted in Sheffield in 1997, which demonstrated, among other things, that projects could be funded several times through different ABIs in support of the same outputs (PIU 2000).

[38]   PIU, 2000: para 2.21. As a local authority chief executive said to the PIU: 'a lot of the lack of co-ordination is simply reflecting the separate silos at the centre' (quoted page 110).

[39]   PIU, 2000, para: 2.37.

[40]   See Ross and Tomaney, 2000.

[41]   For instance, as in the PIU report, the case of MAFF was highlighted by the LGA's witnesses: 'MAFF was seen as a centralised department which had in the past failed adequately to recognise regional variation in agricultural economy and practice' (LGA, 2000, para 45).

local and regional organisations.[42] The notion of a fragmented structure of regional governance, largely concerned with the delivery of policies designed in Whitehall and poorly matched to regional needs, is also a theme of the work of the North East Constitutional Convention, published prior to the PIU report and discussed further below.[43]

The PIU report makes two broad sets of proposals. Firstly, it makes a clear case for strengthening the role of GOs in the region as the primary local delivery mechanism of 'joined-up government'. Secondly, it proposes new mechanisms in Whitehall in order to achieve greater integration of central government policies which have a regional or local impact. In the case of the latter issue, the PIU proposed the creation of a unit with a strong interdepartmental identity, but which would be physically located within Department of Transport, Environment and the Regions (DETR) replacing existing weak monitoring. Day to day oversight of the new arrangements should be by an external minister and interdepartmental committee reporting to the deputy Prime Minister, who would have ultimate responsibility for the unit. The role of the unit, firstly, would be to manage GOs, providing a single reporting line for GO regional directors in contrast to the current situation of multiple reporting lines. Secondly, the PIU envisages that all existing spending departments would report any new initiatives with significant territorial implications to the Unit, in order to ensure that potential overlaps and conflicts are taken into account.

The Government announced the establishment of a new 'Regional Co-ordination Unit' (RCU), shortly after the publication of the PIU report. The RCU officially came into existence on 1st April 2000. Day to day responsibility for the RCU is in the hands of the Cabinet Officer Minister, Lord Falconer, who will report to the deputy Prime Minister, John Prescott.[44] Subsequently, the Government announced the appointment of Rob Smith, formerly of the Department for Education and Employment (DfEE), as the new Director General of the RCU.[45]

The PIU argues that its proposals for strengthened GOs have neutral implications for debates about elected regional government. It notes that even after the creation of elected assemblies, it will be necessary for central government to maintain a presence in the regions, although it also recognises that some of the activities it proposes for GOs could be controlled by assemblies. At a press conference at the launch of the report, John Prescott implied that strengthened GOs could form the basis of a 'regional civil service' under devolved regional government in England.[46]

---

[42] LGA, 2000, para 45.
[43] NECC, 1999; see also Tomaney 2000.
[44] DETR news release, 112, 16 February 2000.
[45] DETR news release, 438, 23 June 2000.
[46] *Journal* [Newcastle] 19 Feb 2000.

GOVERNMENT OFFICES IN THE REGIONS

At the centre of the PIU's study is an analysis of the roles and functions of the eight Government Offices (GOs) in the Regions. Although the GOs are headed by a 'senior regional director', hitherto they have had three separate reporting lines into the DETR, DTI, and DfEE — the three departments from which they drew their functions when they were established by the last Conservative government. Mechanisms were established within Whitehall to provide some central overview of their work in the form of a Government Office Management Board, a Government Office Central Unit and an Interdepartmental Support Unit.[47] Although GOs were intended to provide a greater integration of government activity, one longstanding criticism of GOs is that their structure prevented this in practice.[48] For instance, although they have some discretion to move funds *within* a programme, GOs have no power to vire funds *between* programmes. In addition, the PIU report also noted a lack of influence on central policymaking and incomplete and uneven coverage of policy domains contained within the GOs — for example, the absence of agriculture, education and health functions. A further issue identified by the report is the lack of co-terminous boundaries on the part of different government departments and agencies and the absence of regional structures on the part of others.[49] More recently, GOs have faced the problem that while they have responsibility for administering some ABIs, especially those connected with urban regeneration, others are administered centrally.[50] All this, it is argued, makes 'joined-up' government difficult.

As a result, the PIU report recommends that GOs establish closer links with other departments' regional (and HQ) staffs, especially in the fields of education, health, social care, crime, and agriculture, including widening the departmental presence within GOs. For instance, the report calls for MAFF's responsibilities for policy formulation and implementation on rural development and EU structural funds' issues to be integrated into the GO framework, including placing MAFF staff in GOs.[51] Government Offices are seen as providing a focus for co-ordinating central Government activity at the regional and local levels. This role is distinguished from that of RDAs, which are seen as providing 'regional leadership' or an 'independent voice of the

[47]   These activities will be replaced by the new RCU.

[48]   Mawson and Spencer, 1997.

[49]   The Government's White Paper, *Modernising Government* (Cm 4310), published in March 1999 argued that wherever possible at the regional level, boundaries of public bodies should coincide with Government Office regional boundaries.

[50]   According to the PIU, GOs were not consulted on the siting of the first round of Education Action Zones and Sure Start zones (para 2.32).

[51]   *Ibid.* Para 3.140. This broad approach is echoed in a separate PIU study on rural affairs, PIU (1999) *Rural Economies*.

region.'[52] The PIU report suggests that GOs and RDAs should establish concordats setting out their anticipated relationship and calls for an increase in the flexibility available to GOs (and RDAs) as part of the 2000 Spending Review.

All in all, the proposed changes to GOs have the potential to strengthen their position as repositories of administrative authority in the regions. However, some observers see in these developments the potential for centralisation, rather than devolution — stronger Government Offices become a means of stretching the tentacles of central government further into the regions.[53] These worries are heightened for some by perceived threats to local democracy resulting from the Government's proposals to remove local authority control over activities such as education and social services. This pattern of centralisation on the one hand, and decentralisation on the other, has been identified as a theme of the Government's approach to the governance of England.[54] A further dimension of this issue was highlighted by a report of the Select Committee on Environment, Transport and the Regions that noted a lack of clarity about the nature of the relationship between RDAs and Government Offices and the division of responsibility between the two.[55] The PIU report sought to define the division of labour in terms of GOs being responsible for the delivery of central government policy, while RDAs have responsibility for 'regional strategies'. While theoretically appealing, it remains to be seen whether such a neat distinction can be maintained in practice.

OTHER REGIONAL POLICY DEVELOPMENTS

In addition to the developments already outlined, there are parallel developments that, among other things, highlight the limits of the present arrangements. A good example is provided by an examination of the planning system and the relationship between RESs and Regional Planning Guidance (RPG). RPG sets out the land-use planning framework of a region and is prepared by the Regional Planning Conference (a forum of planning authorities), while the RES is concerned with economic development and social exclusion and is the responsibility of the RDA. The Select Committee on Environment, Transport and the Regions raised the question of which of

---

[52] *Ibid.* Para 3.16

[53] See for example, LGA, 2000. It is noteworthy that the Government rejected a suggestion by the Select Committee on Environment, Transport and the Regions that the RDA should chair the Programme Monitoring Committees that oversee the operation of the EU structural funds. The Government justified its decision in order 'to protect the Government Office's wide ranging financial accountability to Ministers and to overcome any perception of conflicts of interest'.

[54] *Economist*, 24 June 2000.

[55] House of Commons 1999.

these strategies takes precedence for planning purposes.[56] The Committee (and most of its witnesses) took the view that RPG should take precedence. The Government preferred not to a give a view on which took precedence, although the Committee regarded this as a recipe for conflict:

> Conflict was most likely to arise, we were told, as a result of the different priorities of the two strategies, particularly in relation to the relative weight given to regional competitiveness and to sustainability: for example where an RDA proposes the development of a greenfield site which is contrary to RPG. There were concerns that without formal mechanisms to resolve such conflicts, the RDA strategies could 'destabilise or undermine' RPG.[57]

The Committee also noted the RPG covers a 15-20 year period (compared with the 5-10 year period of RESs) and that, in most regions, RPG would only be completed after RESs. This raised the concern 'that RDA strategies start life within an outdated planning and transport policy context.'[58]

The Government also proposes to create a National Learning and Skills Council in order to improve the co-ordination and delivery of post-16 learning. The Government's plans for post-16 learning were outlined in a White Paper in 1999.[59] The National Learning and Skills Council will deliver its policies through 47 local Learning and Skills Councils (LSCs). These local organisations will have an important bearing on the ability of the RDAs to meet their objectives, particularly in relation to the delivery of their Skill Strategies and Action Plans. However, RDAs will have no direct control over the activities of LSCs. LSCs replace Training and Enterprise Councils (TECs), established by the last Conservative Government. These were individual private companies, with private sector-led boards, whilst the new local Learning and Skills Councils will be the local delivery arms of a national organisation. It is likely that they will engage in less direct delivery than the TECs and will be responsible for contracting with a plethora of organisations to deliver learning services. However, LSCs will have a stronger planning role in relation to training than was the case with TECs and the Further Education Funding Council — another important local actor. The other activities currently carried out by the TECs are to be passed to a range of other organisations, including the Employment Service, the Small Business Service, Connections, and the Learning and Skills Development Agency.[60] RDAs were consulted on the design of the boundaries of the LSCs, but both the White Paper and subsequent LSC 'prospectus',[61] make only

---

[56] House of Commons, 1999.
[57] House of Commons, 1997, para 16.
[58] House of Commons, 1997, para 21.
[59] Department of Education and Employment, 1999a.
[60] This organisation is currently the Further Education Development Agency but their remit is being broadened to encompass the development of other learning providers.
[61] Department for Education and Employment, 1999b.

minimal reference to how the relationship will work in practice. It is yet to be seen whether the new arrangements — which appear to contain the potential for both fragmentation and centralisation — can settle into a pattern of 'joined-up' government.

While RDAs have emerged as important new actors on the regional stage, key instruments of regional planning remain beyond their purview or control. Achieving 'joined-up government' of the type desired by the Government may prove to be a tall order in this context. However, for reasons discussed below, this is increasingly likely to presage a demand for more regional autonomy in the future.

CAMPAIGNS FOR ELECTED REGIONAL GOVERNMENT IN ENGLAND

In the context of the creation of new institutions of governance in the English regions, campaigns with a more civic orientation have begun to emerge. The longest standing of these is the Campaign for a North East Assembly (CNA). Founded in 1992, it campaigns for directly elected regional government.[62] Among its supporters are MPs, local government leaders, trade unionists and academic and cultural figures within the region. Among its initiatives was the 'Declaration for the North', in the aftermath of the Scottish and Welsh referendums, signed by many prominent regional figures which called on the Government to bring forward plans for elected assemblies.[63] The CNA has played an important role in raising the political profile of regional government in the North East. The media in the North East (especially the regional press) give considerable attention to the issue of devolution. These factors may help to explain why the North East consistently registers the highest levels of public support for regional government (see below).

In the aftermath of the 1997 election, the CNA played a part in establishing the North East Constitutional Convention (NECC). The Bishop of Durham, Rt. Rev. Michael Turnbull, chairs the NECC. Its steering committee draws in representatives of the main political parties, trade unions, voluntary and faith groups. The aim of the NECC is 'to agree a scheme for a directly-elected Assembly and gain the widest support for these proposals'. The background to the establishment of the NECC was twofold. On the one hand it was a concrete response to the Government's invocation to the regions to 'demonstrate demand' and put forward proposals. On the other hand, the creation of the NECC was influenced by the Scottish experience (relative to that of Wales) where the existence of the Scottish Constitutional Convention was judged to have helped to secure a firmer basis for an affirmative referendum vote. The NECC has produced two reports to date, although its work

---

[62] The CNA was founded as the Campaign for a Northern Assembly and changed its name in 2000.
[63] The Declaration was published in the *New Statesman*, 14th November 1997.

continues. As well as attempting to delimit the range of powers a regional assembly might possess, the work of the Convention also stresses the opportunities that a regional assembly would present in terms of achieving 'joined-up' government. In addition, it stresses that any new structure should offer the hope of a new 'democratic experience' and proposes new structures of democratic participation along these lines.[64]

Similar developments are beginning to occur in other regions. The Campaign for Yorkshire (CFY) was established in 1998 by a range of civic interests to promote the case for an elected assembly. It claims:

> Yorkshire and the Humber has distinctive characteristics which make it an ideal test bed for further reform. It has a strong popular identity. The region follows closely the historic boundaries of the three Ridings, and there is no serious debate about boundaries. It possesses strong existing regional partnerships including universities, voluntary and church associations. All this makes it realistic to regard Yorkshire and the Humber as the standard bearer for representative regional government.[65]

CFY also announced in mid-2000 that it proposed to found a Constitutional Convention, citing the North East experience as its inspiration. A Campaign for a West Midlands Assembly (CWMA) was established in 2000. Across the Pennines, the North West Constitutional Convention (NWCC) was established in 1999, largely under the leadership of the region's local authority association and chaired by The Bishop of Liverpool, the Rt. Rev. James Jones. NWCC launched a document, *New Way Forward — No Way Back*, which argued that decisions over billions of pounds of public spending are taken by non-accountable officials and civil servants in government bodies and quangos run by Whitehall. NWCC favours a 40-strong body exercising strategic responsibility over economic, environmental, social and cultural affairs, funded by a block grant. Launching the document, Bishop Jones invoked arguments about the need for 'joined-up government'.[66]

The proliferation of these regional campaigns has stimulated the development of a national umbrella organisation designed to link the separate regional campaigns. The NECC, CFY, CWMA, with the NWCC as an associate member, established the Campaign for the English Regions (CFER) in 1999. Its intention is to raise the profile of the regional campaigns at national level.[67] Its primary aim is:

---

[64] NECC, 1999; Tomaney 2000b. North East Constitutional Convention, 140-150 Pilgrim Street, Newcastle upon Tyne, NE1 6TH.

[65] This information was taken from the CFY website in July 2000 (see, http://www.cfy.org.uk/).

[66] *Times*, 7 July 2000.

[67] The present author is a founder member of the CNA, a signatory of the 'Declaration for the North, and is a member of the NECC steering Committee and is currently chair of the CFER.

...to secure a commitment in the manifesto of the Labour Party and the other main parties to allow referendums on directly elected and representative regional governments in England in the term of the next parliament.[68]

The main activities of the CFER to date have been aimed at Parliament, attempting to influence MPs and the national media about the case for regional government. 142 MPs (115 Labour, 20 Liberal Democrats and 5 others) signed an Early Day Motion in support of the establishment of the CFER. In addition to its parliamentary activities, the CFER has been active in stimulating developments in the South West of England by brokering meetings between groups interested in the regional question. A South West Constitutional Convention was established in Exeter in July 2000.

Overall, the level of civic pressure, although very modest to non-existent in some regions, has risen significantly in others, with questions of regional governance becoming issues for the media in some regions for the first time. The experience of the North East suggests that, over the longer run, this is likely to have an impact on public opinion, even if the initial coverage given to the issue is negative. However, other factors will also affect the development of regionalism in England.

ISSUES AND CONTROVERSIES

Further change in the regional arrangements in England is inevitable.[69]

The English regions have experienced a period of institutional change, which may amount to the consolidation of a tier of regional government — albeit one accountable to Parliament rather than directly to the people of the regions. These changes have certainly raised the profile of the regional issue, even in regions without strong pre-existing traditions of regionalism. At the same time, Labour's commitment (however vague) to the possible creation of elected assemblies has stimulated the growth of a self-conscious 'civic' regionalism in several parts of England. Whether all this activity points in the direction of a future 'England of regions', as a counterweight to Scottish and Welsh devolution, remains to be seen. A number of factors are likely to stimulate or hinder the forces of regionalism.

An issue that is gaining in salience in the English regional context, and one that has far-reaching political consequences, is the territorial distribution of public expenditure. The Treasury Select Committee, largely at the behest of MPs from the North East of England, set down a marker on this subject in 1997.[70] In the North East of England, in particular, political leaders and the media have argued the iniquity of the Barnett formula — which determines

[68] See the CFER website: http://www.cfer.org.uk/.
[69] LGA, 2000, 4.
[70] House of Commons, 1997b.

changes in government expenditure on Scotland, Wales and Northern Ireland — insofar as it has tended to contribute to higher public expenditure per head in Scotland, even though the North East has greater 'needs' (as reflected in poorer social and economic conditions).[71] Some fuel was poured on this fire when the North East RDA saw its planned budget for 2000/2001 fall by £700,000 to £148.6 million, while the budget for the RDA for the South East rose by 7 per cent to £79.7 million. This caused widespread consternation in the North East and much ammunition for pro-regional government arguments.[72] North East politicians have been foremost in making the case for a new needs assessment as a basis for greater equity in public expenditure. The resource issues are one of the most powerful forces driving the growth of English regionalism and are unlikely to disappear. Given the large and intractable regional economic disparities within England, debates about the territorial distribution of resources, if anything, seem likely to intensify.

Another factor that will have a bearing on the debate, is the position of local government. Local government has frequently been presented as uniformly hostile to the idea of regional government, because most discussion about elected assemblies rests on an assumption of a system of unitary local authorities as a pre-requisite for regional government. The report of the LGA's 'hearing on the regions' reveals the assumption of local authority opposition to be a simplification at best. The report (and its accompanying volumes of evidence) suggests there is substantial variation in the attitudes of existing local authorities toward regional assemblies.[73] Local authorities in northern regions are generally more sympathetic to regionalism, while those in the south are less supportive. At the same time, districts and unitary authorities are more sympathetic to regionalism, while shire counties are fearful of the consequences of regional government for them.

The report of the LGA's hearing, chaired by Lord (Ron) Dearing, attempts to pick its way through the conflicts and to shed some light on the debate from the local government perspective. Reviewing the Government's regional arrangements, the inquiry panel concludes that they represent decentralisation (regionalisation of administration) rather than devolution (a shift of power and control from the centre). Decentralisation, however, has encouraged greater 'partnership working' at the regional level. The report concludes that there is no single model appropriate for all English regions,

---

[71] The 'unfairness' of the Barnett Formula as regards the North East has been a large and regular theme of the regional press there for some time. This perception has been strengthened by recent commentary which has stressed the degree to which the North East is a manifest loser under the current funding regime (Barnett, 2000; MacLean, 2000; Midwinter, 2000; Robinson, 2000). However, it has also been picked up as an issue by the media elsewhere (see *Yorkshire Post*, 5th July 2000). The Birmingham Democracy Commission, chaired by Sir Adrian Cadbury, also argued for a new funding regime to accompany devolution (see *Financial Times*, 6.7.00).

[72] *Guardian*, 13 March 2000.

[73] LGA, 2000.

but arrangements will be most effective if they are designed locally. Moreover:

> ...the Government needs to recognise the diversity of the regions by reforming its own presence in the regions to allow for the growth of cross-cutting regional policies to be designed outside a Whitehall straitjacket.[74]

A further dimension of the way that future changes in local government may impact on debates about regional government lies in proposals to create directly elected mayors in large English cities. Tony Blair is on record as supporting elected mayors as a means of rejuvenating local politics. It is also alleged that he sees directly elected mayors as a solution to the English Question, although it is more difficult to find direct evidence, rather than press comment, to substantiate this claim. There are those who see strong city government, including elected mayors, as complementing regional assemblies.[75] However, others are more hostile to the idea of democratically elected regional assemblies and see mayors as an alternative. In this view, big city mayors would take on the role of regional leaders.[76] In the London case, the Government created a mayor and assembly model, although how applicable it will be as a model in an English regional context is unclear. One immediate effect of the controversies surrounding the London mayoral model was that public support for the idea of directly elected mayors for British cities dropped from 59 per cent in February to 22 per cent by mid-April 2000, according to an ICM survey.[77]

The Labour Party's position on regional government has been based on recognition of the uneven levels of support that exist for elected regional government in England. Underpinning the former are uneven degrees of regional identity. Evidence for this unevenness was demonstrated in a number of polls that were conducted during 1999 and 2000. The largest of these was conducted by MORI for *The Economist* (Figures 5.8 and 5.9). Excluding London, Figure 5.8 shows the highest level of net support for regional government to be in the North East, where there has been a long-standing debate about regional government.[78] The highest level of net opposition is found in the South East, the English heartland where regional identity has traditionally been weak. Figure 5.9 shows that in almost all

---

[74] LGA, 2000, 26.

[75] This argument has been made in relation to debates about an elected mayor for Newcastle. See Todd (2000).

[76] See Stoker 2000, Harding, 2000.

[77] *Guardian*, 19 April 2000. Opinion polls have tended to show around 60 per cent support for the idea of elected mayors.

[78] There is now a series of opinion polls conducted in the North East showing a majority in favour of elected regional government. A poll conducted by the BBC in November 1999 showed 55 per cent in favour.

regions those surveyed tended to regard a regional assembly as a better defender of their regional interests than central government.[79]

Figure 5.8. Support for 'elected regional assemblies'
Source: *The Economist*, 27 March 1999

	Support	Oppose	Net support
London	60	21	39
North East	51	29	22
West Midlands	46	37	9
South West	47	39	8
East Midlands	40	35	5
Eastern	43	42	1
Yorks/Humberside	42	42	0
North West	42	44	− 2
South East	37	47	−10
All	45	38	7

Figure 5.9. Regional assemblies would look after regional interests better than central government?

	Agree	Disagree	Net agree
North West	69	22	57
South West	72	17	55
North East	71	20	51
Yorks/Humberside	70	19	51
London	68	17	51
West Midlands	65	24	41
East Midlands	57	20	37
South East	60	29	31
Eastern	60	29	31
All	65	22	43

[79] A noteworthy feature of the poll, and one that, for instance, has influenced the stress placed by the NECC on democratic renewal in its work, is a mistrust of regional politicians to represent the regions. Whether this reflects a more general antipathy toward politicians, or a specific concern about the quality of regional political elites is not clear from the poll.

Paradoxically, given the Government's ambivalence about regionalism, the first years of the Labour administration have resulted in a new profile for the region within the public policy realm.[80] At the same time, in a variety of ways, it is possible to identify the beginnings of an assertion of the English regional interest in UK politics. A major stimulus for both developments has been the need to find counterweights in England to Scottish and Welsh devolution (although the new institutions within the English regions do not carry the authority of those created in Scotland and Wales). Despite the Government's activity, there is little sense of how its strategy fits together, either within its own terms, or as a solution to broader constitutional uncertainties that are thrown up by the English question.[81]

However, the new attention given to the regions has led to a rash of studies and documents, all of which have tried to define what might be the key issues as far as the governance of the English regions is concerned. These tend to acknowledge the existence of a tier of English government and, to one degree or another, tend to define the problem as one of how to render this more integrated ('joined-up'), transparent and democratic, and better equipped to resolve intra-regional disputes. The degree to which English regionalism finds itself in the ascendant (or descendant) in the coming period will remain a largely political question and will be tied to the uncertain outcomes of the next general election. Its resolution is likely to be affected by an interplay of forces including: the essential ambiguity at the heart of New Labour about the devolution project in general and English regionalism in particular; the extent to which the rising tide of English regionalism can be turned into a surge that seeps into regions beyond the disaffected north; and the degree to which the recently established regional arrangements serve to accommodate or further stimulate the growth of the new English regionalism.

BIBLIOGRAPHY

Barnett, J., 'How a temporary expedient became permanent', *New Economy*, 7 (2): 69-71, (2000)

Benneworth P., 'Reaching out, Regional Development Agencies and evolving regional Governance', *Regions: Newsletter of the Regional Studies Association*, 225: 22-40, (2000)

Bogdanor, V., *Devolution in the United Kingdom* (Oxford: OPUS, 1990)

Boudreau, J.A. and Keil, R., 'Seceding from Responsibility? Secession Movements in Los Angeles', *Paper to Annual Meeting of the Urban Affairs Association* (Los Angeles: 2000)

---

[80] It remains true, however, as the LGA (2000) notes that these institutions have a low level of visibility as far as the ordinary citizen is concerned.

[81] See Hazell, 2000.

The Constitution Unit, *Regional Government in England, Regional Chambers and Regional Development Agencies* (London: The School of Public Policy, University College London, 1996)

Danson, M., Lloyd, D., and Newlands, G. (1992) 'Regional Development Agencies in the United Kingdom', in Townroe, P. and Martin, R. (eds.) *Regional Development in the 1990s* (London: Jessica Kingsley, 1992)

Department for Education and Employment, *Learning to Succeed: A new framework for post-16 education,* Cm 4392 (London: The Stationery Office, 1999a)

Department for Education and Employment, *Learning and Skills Council Prospectus: Learning to Succeed* (London: DfEE, 1999b)

Department of the Environment, Transport and the Regions, *Regional Development Agencies for England*, Cm (London: The Stationery Office, 1997)

Harding, A., 'Is there a "missing middle" in English governance?', *Report for the New Local Government Network* (London: NLGN, 2000)

Harding, A., Wilks-Heeg, S. and Hutchins, M., 'Regional Development Agencies and English regionalisation: the question of accountability', *Environment and Planning C: Government and Policy*, 17 (6): 669-683 (1999)

Hazell, R., 'Regional government in England: three policies in search of a strategy', in Chen, S. and Wright, T. (eds.), *The English Question* (London: Fabian Society, 2000)

House of Commons, *The Barnett Formula*, Report of the Treasury Committee, HC 341 (London: The Stationery Office, 1997b)

House of Commons, *Regional Development Agencies*, Report of the Environment, Transport and Regional Affairs Committee, HC 415 (London: The Stationery Office, 1997c)

House of Commons, *The Relationship Between TECs and the Proposed Regional Development Agencies*, Report of the Education and Employment Committee, HC 265 (London: The Stationery Office, 1998)

House of Commons, *Regional Development Agencies*, Report of the Environment, Transport and Regional Affairs Committee, HC 232-1 (London: The Stationery Office, 1999)

Labour Party, *A Voice for England* (London: Labour Party, 1995)

Labour Party, *A New Voice for England's Regions* (London: Labour Party, 1996)

LGA, *Regional Variations: report for the LGA's hearing on regions* (London: Local Government Association, 2000)

Liberal Democrats, *Reforming Governance in the UK: Policies for Constitutional Reform,* Policy Paper 40 (London: Liberal Democrats, 2000)

MacLean, I., 'Can (or should) the Barnett formula survive?', *New Economy*, **7** (2): 76-80, (2000)

Mawson, J. and Spencer, K., 'The government offices for the English regions: Towards regional governance?' *Policy and Politics*, 25: (1) 71-84, (1997)

Midwinter, A., 'Why replacing Barnett would be a mistake', *New Economy*, **7** (2): 72-75, (2000)

Nathan, M., Roberts, P., Ward, M., and Garside, R., *Strategies for Success? A first Assessment of Regional Development Agencies Draft Regional Economic Strategies* (Manchester: Centre for Local Economic Strategies/National Council for Voluntary Organisations, 1999)

NECC, *Time for Change* (Newcastle upon Tyne: North East Constitutional Convention, (1999)

PIU, *Rural Economies*, A Performance and Innovation Unit Report, (London: The Stationery Office, 1979)

PIU, *Reaching Out: The Role of Central Government and the Regional and Local Level*, A Performance and Innovation Unit Report (London: The Stationery Office, 2000)

Regional Policy Commission, *Renewing the Regions. Strategies for Economic Development,* Report of the Regional Policy Commission ('The Millan Report'), (Sheffield: Sheffield Hallam University, 1996)

Robinson, P., 'Does the Government really have a regional policy', in Nathan, M. (ed.)., *The New Regionalism* (Manchester: Centre for Local Economic Strategies, 2000)

Robinson, P., 'Public spending in the regions', *New Economy*, 7 (2): 81-82, (2000b)

Robson, B., Peck, J. and Holden, A., *Regional Development Agencies and Local Regeneration* (York: Joseph Rowntree Foundation, 2000)

Ross, W. and Tomaney, J., 'Devolution and Health Policy in England', forthcoming in *Regional Studies,* (2000)

Stoker, G., 'Is regional government the answer to the English Question?', in Chen, S. and Wright, T. (eds.), *The English Question* (London: Fabian Society, 2000)

Todd, N., *The Democratic City: An elected mayor for Newcastle?* (Newcastle: TUPS, 2000)

Tomaney, J., 'New Labour and the English Question', *The Political Quarterly*, 70, 1: 74-82, (1999)

Tomaney, J., 'Democratically elected regional government in England: the work of the North East Constitutional Convention', *Regional Studies*, 34 (4): 383-389, (2000)

While, A., 'Accountability and regional governance', *Local Economy*, February, 329-345, (2000)

APPENDIX: GLOSSARY OF ACRONYMS

ABI — Area Based Initiative
AWM — Advantage West Midlands
CBI — Confederation of British Industry
CNA — Campaign for a North East Assembly
CFY — Campaign for Yorkshire
CWMA — Campaign for a West Midlands Assembly
CFER — Campaign for the English Regions
DETR — Department of the Environment, Transport and the Regions
DfEE — Department for Education and Employment
DTI — Department of Trade and Industry
EU — European Union
GO — Government Office for the Region
LGA — Local Government Association
LSC — Learning and Skills Council
MAFF — Ministry of Agriculture Fisheries and Food
NECC — North East Constitutional Convention
PIU — Performance and Innovation Unit
RCU — Regional Co-ordination Unit
RDA — Regional Development Agency
RES — Regional Economic Strategy
RPG — Regional Planning Guidance
TEC — Training and Enterprise Council
TUC — Trades Union Congress

6

Intergovernmental Relations: Whitehall Rules OK?

Robert Hazell

This chapter begins by describing the machinery established in Whitehall to handle relations with the devolved governments post-devolution. Much of it has been developed in an *ad hoc* and pragmatic way. In keeping with central government's low-key response, there was no attempt in advance of devolution to create the elaborate structures for consultation and co-ordination between the two tiers of government which are found in federations such as Australia and Canada.[1] The Cabinet Office had visited the Canadian Department of Intergovernmental Affairs in Ottawa, with its 150 staff, and deliberately decided not to create such a big co-ordinating department at the centre to handle intergovernmental relations in a devolved UK.

The Constitution Secretariat in the Cabinet Office has remained tiny by Canadian standards, with only a dozen staff. It has proceeded in a low key and gradualist way, issuing procedural guidance, arranging intergovernmental meetings with the devolved administrations mainly when UK ministers have wanted them,[2] and letting the structures evolve in response to need. In so doing, they were acting in accordance with ministers' strong preferences and with Whitehall's own instincts. And it has to be said that, in the first year of devolution, this pragmatic and gradualist approach has worked. There have been the inevitable teething troubles and occasional differences, but none of the fierce tensions and major disputes with political wrangling and court battles which can characterise intergovernmental relations in federal systems. Intergovernmental relations in the devolved UK have got off to a gentle and remarkably smooth start.

The opening three sections of the chapter describe the machinery which has gradually been put in place to handle intergovernmental relations post-devolution. The middle two sections describe the procedures which have been devised to ensure the smooth conduct of intergovernmental

[1] Described by R. Cornes, 'Intergovernmental Relations in a devolved UK: Making Devolution Work' in R. Hazell, (ed.), *Constitutional Futures: A History of the next Ten Years*, (Oxford University Press, 1999). See in particular the diagrams depicting the elaborate structures for IGR in Australia and Canada at Figs 9.1 (p 159) and 9.3 (p 164).

[2] The plenary meeting of the JMC held on 1 September 2000 was the first to be held largely at the behest of the devolved administrations.

relations. The closing sections give an account of intergovernmental relations in the first year of devolution, and conclude with an analysis of the main characteristics which have emerged so far.

THE CENTRAL MACHINERY OF
INTERGOVERNMENTAL RELATIONS

(1) The Joint Ministerial Committee

It is worth recording the origins of the Joint Ministerial Committee (JMC) as an example of the Government's minimalist and gradualist approach. It was not mentioned in the 1997 White Papers on devolution to Scotland and Wales; nor did the Government acknowledge the need for such a body in its evidence to the Scottish Affairs Committee's enquiry into Multi-Level Democracy.[3] It was eventually conceded late one evening in the House of Lords, during the Committee stage of the Scotland Bill. Baroness Ramsay, the junior government minister on duty, volunteered in response to amendments pressing for effective liaison machinery that:

> It is envisaged that this would be achieved through the establishment of a Joint Ministerial Committee of which the UK Government and the devolved administrations would be members. The Joint Ministerial Committee will be an entirely consultative body, supported by a committee of officials and a joint secretariat. Further details of the standing arrangements will be announced later.[4]

From this modest start, the JMC has grown to become the central piece of political machinery in underpinning the devolution settlement. It is the subject of the first Supplementary Agreement annexed to the *Memorandum of Understanding* between the UK Government and the devolved administrations which was published in October 1999 'setting out the principles which will underlie relations between them.'[5] The *Memorandum of Understanding* makes clear that the JMC is at the summit of the machinery for intergovernmental relations, which normally should continue to be conducted between officials or bilaterally between ministers, without invoking the more formal machinery:

> The UK Government and the devolved administrations believe that most contact between them should be carried out on a bilateral or multi-lateral basis, between departments which deal on a day-to-day basis with the issues at stake. Nevertheless, some central co-ordination of the overall relationship is needed. Therefore the administrations agree to participate in a Joint Ministerial Committee (JMC) consisting of ministers of the UK Government, Scottish

---

[3] Second Report of Session 1997-98, HC 460-1
[4] HL deb., 28 July 1998 col. 1488
[5] Cm 4444, October 1999, p1.

ministers, members of the Cabinet of the National Assembly for Wales and ministers in the Northern Ireland Executive Committee.[6]

The Supplementary Agreement sets out the terms of reference of the JMC:

- To consider reserved matters which impinge on devolved areas, and *vice versa*;
- To consider common issues of concern across all devolved areas;
- To keep the arrangements for liaison under review, and
- To consider disputes between the administrations.

The Supplementary Agreement then goes on to provide that the JMC will meet in two formats, 'plenary' and 'functional':

> Plenary meetings of the JMC will be held at least once a year. They will consist of the Prime Minister (or his representative), who will take the chair, and the deputy Prime Minister, the Scottish First Minister and one of his ministerial colleagues, the Welsh First Secretary and another Assembly Secretary, the Northern Ireland First Minister and deputy First Minister, and the Secretaries of State for Scotland, Wales and Northern Ireland ...The Joint Ministerial Committee may also meet in other 'functional' formats: for example, a meeting of the Agriculture Ministers of the UK Government and the devolved administrations, a meeting of Environment Ministers of the UK Government and the devolved administrations, and so on ... Irrespective of their location, the meetings will be chaired by the responsible UK Minister.[7]

The Supplementary Agreement provides that in functional format meetings of the JMC will be held at the request of the UK Government or any of the devolved administrations. In practice, in the first year of devolution, the first six meetings of the JMC were all held at the initiative of the UK Government (see the list in Figure 6.5 at page 165 below).[8] The other main function of the JMC is to resolve disputes:

> Where a dispute cannot be resolved bilaterally or through the good offices of the relevant territorial Secretary of State the matter may formally be referred to the JMC Secretariat... Where this appears likely, the JMC Secretariat should be consulted at an early stage in order to ensure a consistent interpretation of the devolution settlements, and to provide advice on handling of any differences of view.[9]

The JMC Secretariat comprises staff from the Cabinet Office and the devolved administrations, located in their respective capitals. The lead role falls to the Cabinet Office. The agreement provides for co-location if the

[6] *Ibid.* p7 para 22.
[7] *Ibid.* p 9 paras A 1.3-1.4.
[8] See note 2.
[9] *Ibid.* p10 para A 1.7.

volume of work increases, and for secondment of staff from the devolved administrations (a civil servant from the Scottish Executive, Donald Henderson, is currently on secondment to the Cabinet Office and is a member of the JMC Secretariat). The agreement also provides for a committee of officials from the UK Government and the devolved administrations to shadow the JMC and prepare for its meetings, to be chaired by the Cabinet Secretary. The first such meeting chaired by Sir Richard Wilson was held in November 1999, a month after publication of the *Memorandum of Understanding*.

(2) The Territorial Secretaries of State

Having emphasised the small size of the Constitution Secretariat in the Cabinet Office, with only four staff working on devolution in 1999–2000, it is worth mentioning, by contrast, the relatively large numbers of staff who continue to service the Secretaries of State for Scotland, Wales and Northern Ireland. 70 staff work for John Reid as Secretary of State for Scotland, and 40 staff work for Paul Murphy as Secretary of State for Wales.[10] The continuing role of the Secretaries of State was described in the *Memorandum of Understanding* as follows:

> The Secretaries of State for Scotland, Wales, and Northern Ireland also have responsibilities within the UK Government for promoting the devolution settlement, for ensuring effective working relations between the Government and the devolved administrations, and for helping to resolve any disputes which may arise.[11]

Little is known about why it requires such a large staff for what is essentially a liaison role: neither Secretary of State has any programme budget of his own. Both maintain quite large teams to monitor legislation: in the Scotland Office, teams of lawyers checking that proposed legislation is within the powers of the Scottish Parliament; in the Wales Office, checking that primary legislation at Westminster meets Welsh needs.[12]

In January 2000, the liaison role was described in more detail in two Devolution Guidance Notes issued by the Cabinet Office (see Figure 6.1). The Secretary of State enlarged on this during the year, when appearing before the Welsh Grand Committee and the Welsh Affairs Select Committee (see chapter 3, page 59). When presenting his annual report to the latter committee on 27 June 2000, Paul Murphy emphasised strongly the legislative role,

---

[10] In response to a Parliamentary Question from Dafydd Wigley MP in summer 2000 it was disclosed that the staff of the Wales Office in London had risen from 27.5 to 42.4 full-time equivalents over the past year.

[11] *Ibid.* p1.

[12] 'We've had one lawyer and ten policy staff covering three Bills with significant Welsh clauses and at least three more with Welsh relevance': spokesman for Wales Office quoted in *Wales on Sunday*, 13 August 2000.

Figure 6.1. Roles of the Secretaries of State for Scotland and Wales

The Secretary of State for Scotland

DGN 3 describes the role of the Secretary of State for Scotland in the following terms:

3. The Secretary of State for Scotland will continue to represent Scottish interests in reserved matters within the UK Government, advising colleagues about any distinctive Scottish interests that arise for reasons other than the impact on devolved matters. He will support colleagues in presenting UK Government policies in Scotland. The Secretary of State for Scotland will remain a member of most of the Cabinet committees of which he was a member before 1 July [1999], and will expect to be consulted by colleagues on the Scottish aspects of their proposals.

4. The Secretary of State for Scotland will also wish to promote the devolution settlement provided by the Scotland Act 1998, by encouraging close working relations between the UK Departments and the Scottish Executive, and between the UK and Scottish Parliaments. This does not mean that he will act as a conduit for the necessary communication between the UK Government and the Scottish Executive. Normally Departments should deal with the Scottish Executive direct. But the Secretary of State will want to keep himself informed about sensitive issues which involve both reserved and devolved matters, and more generally

The Secretary of State for Wales

DGN 4 describes the role of the Secretary of State for Wales in different terms which reflect the different nature of the devolution settlement in Wales:

2. The new role of the Secretary of State for Wales is:

• to act as guardian of the devolution settlement in Wales

• to ensure that the interests of Wales are fully taken into account by the UK Government in making decisions which will have effect in Wales

• to represent the UK Government in Wales...

Guardian of the devolution settlement

3. This does not mean that the Secretary of State is a channel of communication between the UK Government and the Assembly. Normally Departments should deal with the Assembly direct. The Secretary of State and his Department will:

• give advice on the handling of business in the light of devolution

• act as honest broker should there be any dispute between the Assembly and Whitehall or Westminster

• explain the nature and consequences of devolution to the Assembly on behalf of the UK Government ...

Voice of Wales in the Cabinet

5. The Secretary of State for Wales will speak for Wales in the UK Cabinet and will ensure that decisions are taken with full regard to any matters where Wales has

particular interests or concerns. He will not be a mouthpiece for the Assembly but he will need to know the views of the Assembly Cabinet before deciding his own line. This is particularly important in relation to proposals for primary legislation that affect Wales ...

8. None of this affects the Secretary of State's duty under the Government of Wales Act 1998 to consult the Assembly on the Government's legislative programme. This clearly means consultation with Assembly Members and will be carried out in a formal and public way ...

9. It will be the responsibility of the Secretary of State to steer through Parliament any clauses in legislation relating solely to Wales ...

describing how his Parliamentary Under-Secretary, David Hanson, had been safeguarding Welsh interests on three different Standing Committees at once. He also stressed the importance of Wales continuing to have a voice in Cabinet: he and David Hanson sit on 23 Cabinet Committees, and between them had attended 102 Cabinet Committee meetings since October 1999. He declined to be drawn on a possible merger of the three Secretaries of State; but a senior civil servant was subsequently reported as suggesting that Dover House, the home of the Scotland Office on the other side of Whitehall from the Wales Office in Gwydyr House, had been earmarked as the likely home for what he labelled an Office of the Regions.[13]

The other piece of central machinery worth mentioning is the Prime Minister's Office in No. 10. His Chief of Staff, Jonathan Powell, has been heavily involved in all the negotiations over Northern Ireland. The deputy Chief of Staff, Pat McFadden, is a Scot who was Special Adviser to Donald Dewar when he was shadow Scottish Secretary before he joined Blair's office in 1994. He has maintained close links with the Scottish Labour Party and has continued to be Blair's fixer in Scotland. He was succeeded as the constitutional affairs expert in the No. 10 Policy Unit by another Scot, Jim Gallagher (an official on loan from the Scottish Executive) when he became deputy Chief of Staff.

(3) The Network of British–Irish Committees

A third and special strand of intergovernmental committees derives from the Belfast Agreement of April 1998.[14] This created an interlocking network of committees designed to underpin the new devolved institutions in Belfast by linking them North–South, east-west and across the British Isles. Details of the three committees are set out in Strand Two and Strand Three of the Belfast Agreement. Strand Two provides for a North/South Ministerial Council, to bring together ministers from the Northern Ireland Executive and

---

[13] *Western Mail* 28 June 2000.
[14] *The Belfast Agreement: An Agreement reached at the Multi-Party Talks on Northern Ireland*, Cm 3883, April 1998.

the Irish Government, to develop consultation, co-operation and action on matters of mutual interest, including through implementation on an all-island and cross-border basis. To kick start the process, Strand Two requires the Council to identify at least six matters for co-operation, either through existing bodies or through the creation of new implementation bodies. Figure 6.2 sets out the possible areas for co-operation:

Figure 6.2. Areas for North/South co-operation identified in the Belfast Agreement

1. Agriculture — animal and plant health

2. Education — teacher qualifications and exchanges

3. Transport — strategic transport planning

4. Environment — environmental protection, pollution, water quality, and waste management

5. Waterways — inland waterways

6. Social Security/Social Welfare — entitlements of cross-border workers and fraud control

7. Tourism — promotion, marketing, research, and product development

8. Relevant EU Programmes such as SPPR, INTERREG, Leader II and their successors

9. Inland Fisheries

10. Aquaculture and marine matters

11. Health: accident and emergency services and other cross-related border issues

---

Strand Two provides for the Council to meet in plenary format twice a year, with Northern Ireland led by the First Minister and deputy First Minister and the Irish Government led by the Taoiseach; and in specific sectoral formats on a regular and frequent basis with each side represented by the appropriate minister. Recognising that this North–South co-operation was viewed with deep suspicion by the Unionists, as a series of further steps towards the republican goal of a united Ireland, the Agreement tries to prevent any boycotts or backsliding by making participation mandatory, for individual ministers and for the government as a whole:

> Participation in the Council is to be one of the essential responsibilities attaching to relevant posts in the two Administrations. It is understood that the North/South Ministerial Council and the Northern Ireland Assembly are mutually interdependent, and that one cannot successfully function without the other. [15]

---

[15] Belfast Agreement, Strand Two paras 3 and 13.

The British–Irish Council (BIC) was a late entry in the Belfast Agreement, inserted at the request of David Trimble to counter-balance the North–South co-operation which was so unpalatable to his Unionist supporters. It seeks to buttress the links between Northern Ireland and the rest of the Union. Strand Three provides that its membership will comprise:

> ...representatives of the British and Irish Governments, devolved institutions in Northern Ireland, Scotland, and Wales, when established, and if appropriate, elsewhere in the United Kingdom, together with representatives of the Isle of Man and the Channel Islands.[16]

The reference to 'devolved institutions ... elsewhere in the United Kingdom' leaves open the possibility of regional assemblies in England being included at a later date.

Because the BIC was inserted at the last moment, the Belfast Agreement is pretty vague about what it will actually do. Strand Three states its purpose in the broadest terms, as being 'to promote the harmonious and mutually beneficial development of the totality of relationships among the peoples of these islands.' Hence the colloquial title of 'Council of the Isles'. The remaining provisions about the BIC are an abbreviated carbon copy of the provisions in Strand Two for the North/South Ministerial Council. Thus the BIC will meet at summit level, twice per year; in specific sectoral formats on a regular basis, with each side represented by the appropriate minister; and in an appropriate format to consider cross-sectoral issues. In terms of subject matter:

> Suitable issues for early discussion in the BIC could include transport links, agricultural issues, environmental issues, cultural issues, health issues, education issues and approaches to EU issues.[17]

The Secretariat for the BIC will be provided by the British and Irish Governments. In a 1998 commentary, the Constitution Unit forecast that the two sovereign governments would dominate the agenda, and that the British–Irish Council would be unlikely to develop along the lines of the more evenly balanced Nordic Council, which was the model which had originally inspired David Trimble.[18]

The third intergovernmental body established under the Belfast Agreement trod more familiar ground. Strand Three provided for the establishment of a standing British–Irish Intergovernmental Conference, to subsume the Anglo–Irish Intergovernmental Council and Intergovernmental Conference established under the 1985 Sunningdale Agreement. The conference will

---

[16] Belfast Agreement, Strand Three para 2.

[17] *Ibid.* para 5.

[18] *The British–Irish Council: Nordic Lessons for the Council of the Isles*, Constitution Unit, University College London, November 1998.

meet as required at summit level (Prime Minister and Taoiseach), and more regularly to discuss Northern Ireland matters, in meetings to be co-chaired by the Irish Minister for Foreign Affairs and the Secretary of State for Northern Ireland. The conference will deal with non-devolved matters: security, rights, justice, prisons and policing in Northern Ireland, until these matters are devolved to the Northern Ireland administration, when they would fall to the North/South Ministerial Council.

PROCEDURES

(1) The Memorandum of Understanding and Concordats

The opening sections of this chapter have set out the different elements of the machinery put in place for the conduct of intergovernmental relations in a devolved UK. The next two sections describe the procedures which have been laid down for the smooth conduct of intergovernmental relations, and the more detailed guidance subsequently issued by the Cabinet Office to Whitehall departments. The main procedures were promulgated in the *Memorandum of Understanding* and the four main Concordats between the UK Government and the devolved administrations which were eventually published in October 1999.[19]

The Concordats had been a long time coming. They were first promised during the passage of the devolution legislation, and the original intention had been to publish them in draft in autumn 1998. But vigorous disagreements broke out in Whitehall about how prescriptive the Concordats should be when they were circulated to departments, so they were not finalised within Whitehall until spring 1999. The difficulty then arose that the Concordats were meant to be agreements with the devolved administrations, which would shortly come into existence in summer 1999. The decision was therefore taken not to pre-empt the new administrations (this would have been a gift to the nationalists in the May 1999 elections to the devolved assemblies), but to delay publication until after the administrations had come into being and could negotiate and signify their own consent.

The four overarching Concordats published with the *Memorandum of Understanding* cover:

- Co-ordination of EU Policy Issues;
- Financial Assistance to Industry
- International Relations, and
- Statistics.

---

[19] Cm 4444, October 1999.

Reflecting the importance of EU and international relations to both the UK Government and the devolved administrations, the two Concordats on these topics are longer and more detailed than the ones on Financial Assistance and Statistics. (Their effectiveness is considered below in the section on EU negotiations.) Most of the principles laid down in the *Memorandum* and the Concordats are simply principles of good administration and negotiation: no surprises, proper consultation, respect and understanding for each other's positions, clear definitions of roles and responsibilities. These are reflected in the early headings of the *Memorandum*: 'Communication and Consultation; Co-operation; Exchange of Information, Statistics and Research; Confidentiality; Correspondence'. Under each heading is a sensible set of provisions to ensure good communication and co-operation.[20]

One issue worth highlighting is the agreement about legislation, both at Westminster and by the devolved assemblies. The *Memorandum* recognises that the UK Parliament retains the authority to legislate on any issue, whether devolved or not:

> It is ultimately for Parliament to decide what use to make of that power. However, the UK Government will proceed in accordance with the convention that the UK Parliament would not normally legislate with regard to devolved matters except with the agreement of the devolved legislature. The devolved administrations will be responsible for seeking such agreement ...[21]

This convention, known as the Sewel Convention, has already been used in the first year of devolution, as at least 10 of the bills introduced at Westminster have trespassed — by consent — onto the powers devolved to Scotland. The Scottish Parliament has its hands full with its own legislative programme, and where it is content with the policy it has been happy for Westminster to make the legislative change.[22]

The *Memorandum* is also sensitive about the separate autonomy of parliament and the devolved assemblies, while pledging the best endeavours of the governments to keep their respective legislatures within bounds:

> The United Kingdom Parliament retains the absolute right to debate, enquire into or make representations about devolved matters. It is ultimately for Parliament to

[20]   Johanne Poirier, in 'The Functions of Post-Devolution Concordats in a Comparative Perspective', *Public Law* (forthcoming) identifies five broad functions of intergovernmental agreements: substantive policy co-ordination, procedural co-operation, para-constitutional engineering, regulating by contract and agreements as soft law. She agrees that procedural co-operation is the primary function of the Concordats published so far.

[21]   *Ibid.* p 5 para 13.

[22]   Bills in the 1999–2000 session to which the full Sewel Convention procedure applied are Welfare Reform and Pensions; Sea Fishing Grants (Charges); Representation of the People; Sexual Offences (Amendment); Race Relations (Amendment); Care Standards; Insolvency; Political Parties, Elections and Referendums; Regulation of Investigatory Powers; Government Resources and Accounts. A further 12 bills were passed using the pre-commencement enactment formula, because they had been passed before devolution, or were in progress at Westminster at the time of devolution.

decide what use to make of that power, but the UK Government will encourage the UK Parliament to bear in mind the primary responsibility of the devolved legislatures and administrations in these fields and to recognise that it is a consequence of Parliament's decision to devolve certain matters that Parliament will in future be more restricted in its field of operation.

The devolved legislatures will be entitled to debate non-devolved matters, but the devolved executives will encourage each devolved legislature to bear in mind the responsibility of the UK Parliament in these matters.'[23]

As for legislation by the devolved legislatures, the devolved administrations are required to notify legislative measures to the relevant Whitehall departments and Law Officers both when they are proposed and when they are adopted, in case the UK Government wishes to intervene. The *Memorandum* makes clear that if the consultative procedures it sets out are followed, formal intervention should be a matter of last resort:

> The devolution legislation contains various powers for the Secretary of State to intervene in devolved matters. It also contains powers for the Law Officers to refer questions of *vires* to the Judicial Committee of the Privy Council. Although the UK Government is prepared to use these powers if necessary, it sees them very much as a matter of last resort. The UK Government and the administration concerned will therefore aim to resolve any difficulties through discussion ... If formal intervention should become necessary, the UK Government will, whenever practicable, inform the devolved administration of its intentions in sufficient time to enable that administration to make any representations it wishes, or take any remedial action.[24]

Avoidance of litigation is one of the major concerns running through the *Memorandum of Understanding* and the Concordats, which betray some of the apprehensions inside the British Government as it prepared for such a big step into the unknown. The documents repeat again and again their intention not to create legal relations. The second sentence of the Explanatory Note says 'It is not intended that these agreements should be legally binding', and the *Memorandum of Understanding* emphasises:

> This memorandum is a statement of political intent, and should not be interpreted as a binding agreement. It does not create legal obligations between the parties. It is intended to be binding in honour only... Concordats are not intended to be legally binding, but to serve as working documents.[25]

For the avoidance of any doubt, the message is repeated in each of the Concordats, so that the Concordat on Co-ordination of EU Policy Issues adds:

---

[23] *Memorandum of Understanding* paras 14-15.

[24] *Ibid.* para 26.

[25] *Ibid.* p 3 paras 2 and 3.

This concordat is not intended to constitute a legally enforceable contract or to create any rights or obligations which are legally enforceable. It is intended to be binding in honour only.[26]

The Concordat on Financial Assistance to Industry states: 'This concordat does not create any legal relations between the signatories nor any legal right to be consulted.'[27]

Another respect which betrays the sense of a step into the unknown is that all of the documents provide for regular review, starting at the end of the first year. The *Memorandum of Understanding* concludes with a provision that it will be reviewed at a meeting of the JMC at least annually, and the Concordats contain similar provision for regular (mostly annual) review.[28] But in other respects, the Concordats suggest a continuation of business as usual. Thus, the Concordat on Financial Assistance to Industry recognises that the devolved administrations have inherited a set of common guidelines from the UK Government. And the Concordat on Statistics provides that the existing arrangements for cost-sharing will continue, and that the Office for National Statistics will continue to provide the Scottish and Welsh administrations with a range of professional, technical and personnel services, including all arrangements for staff recruitment and transfer.

The *Memorandum* indicates that the four overarching Concordats appended to it are only the first instalment, and that in due course they will be supplemented by bilateral concordats negotiated between individual Whitehall departments and their counterparts in Scotland and Wales. In the first year of devolution, there has been a steady outpouring of bilateral concordats. By June 2000, the Scottish Executive listed 18 concordats which it had concluded with 12 Whitehall departments and two UK-wide agencies:

Figure 6.3. Bilateral Concordats concluded by Scottish Executive in 1999–2000

- Cabinet Office
- Department of Environment, Transport and the Regions
- Department for Education and Employment
- Ministry of Agriculture, Fisheries and Food (MAFF: main concordat)
- MAFF (specific concordat on Fisheries)
- MAFF (specific concordat on State Veterinary Service and Animal Disease Compensation)
- General Registers Office (link to external website)

---

[26] *Ibid.* p 14 para B1.2.

[27] *Ibid.* p 24 para C4.

[28] *Ibid.* p 25 para C9, p 29 para D1.8, p 31 para D2.8, p 39 para E5. The Concordat on Statistics has slightly greater confidence in the future, providing for formal review after one year, and thereafter every five years.

- Department of Trade and Industry (DTI)
- HM Treasury and DTI (specific concordat on public procurement and related international obligations)
- Health and Safety Executive
- Department of Culture, Media and Sport
- Ministry of Defence
- Lord Chancellor's Department
- European Structural Funds (cross-departmental, but DTI lead)
- HM Treasury
- Department of Health
- Home Office
- Department of Social Security.

Half this number of bilateral concordats have been concluded with the Cabinet of the National Assembly for Wales: it has agreed bilateral concordats with the Treasury, Cabinet Office, Department of Health, Department of Social Security, Ministry of Defence, Lord Chancellor's Department, DTI, DETR and DCMS.[29] Because of the suspension of devolution in Northern Ireland, no concordats had been concluded with the Northern Ireland Executive by 31 July 2000.

(2) Cabinet Office Devolution Guidance Notes

From September 1999, the Cabinet Office started to issue a series of Devolution Guidance Notes (DGNs) to supplement the guidance already available to officials in the Concordats. From January 2000, these were published on the Cabinet Office website. By June 2000, the series had grown to 13 DGNs, but only eight had been published at that stage. The list of topics covered is as follows:

Figure 6.4. Devolution Guidance Notes: subject areas[30]

DGN1   Common Working Arrangements
DGN2   Handling Correspondence under Devolution
DGN3   Role of the Secretary of State for Scotland
DGN4   Role of the Secretary of State for Wales
DGN5   Role of the Secretary of State for Northern Ireland
DGN6   Circulation of Inter-Ministerial and Interdepartmental Correspondence
DGN7   Court Proceedings regarding Devolution Issues under the Scotland Act 1998 and the Government of Wales Act 1998
DGN8   Post Devolution Primary Legislation affecting Northern Ireland

---

[29] Listed at www.wales.gov.uk/cabinet/concordats/index_.ehtm.
[30] Still awaiting publication were DGNs 5, 7, 8, 9 and 11. The remainder can be viewed at www.cabinet-office.gov.uk/constitution.

DGN9   Post Devolution Primary Legislation affecting Wales
DGN10   Post Devolution Primary Legislation affecting Scotland
DGN11   Ministerial Accountability after Devolution
DGN12   Attendance of UK Ministers and Officials at Committees of the
        Devolved Legislatures
DGN13   Handling of Parliamentary Business in the House of Lords

The content of the early DGNs is unexceptionable. They are intended to rein-force the messages in the *Memorandum of Understanding* and Concordats, and emphasise again that the principal channel of communication should be through the bilateral links between the relevant departments of each adminis-tration. Extracts from DGN3 and DGN4 have already been quoted in an earlier section of this chapter which describes the continuing role of the Secretaries of State. Of the remainder which have been published, DGNs 10 and 13 are of particular interest, for the light they shed on the procedures Whitehall has put in place to guard against preparing legislation which tres-passes on devolved matters.

DGN10 instructs departments that any submission to the Cabinet's Future Legislation Committee seeking inclusion of a bill in the future legislative programme should state clearly that the bill either does not apply to Scotland, or has provisions which apply to Scotland, but that the responsible minister expects that the Scottish Executive and Parliament will agree to such provi-sions. By the time proposals reach Legislation Committee for final discus-sion of handling issues before the bill is introduced, devolution-related issues must have been substantively resolved, and papers for the Committee are required to contain a statement to that effect. Where the bill trespasses significantly on devolved matters in Scotland (as for example did the Food Standards Bill), the aim should be to confirm at Second Reading that the Scottish Parliament has consented. Where the trespass is less significant the aim should be to obtain consent by the time the trespassing clauses are debated in committee.

DGN13 contains some worked examples of how this will operate in the House of Lords, with forms of words for different occasions. One example is for a bill on welfare reform. Social security is a reserved matter, but the bill contains minor consequential provisions on family law in Scotland (a devolved matter):

> During the second reading debate it is argued that, under the Sewel Convention, the bill requires the consent of the Scottish Parliament and that this has not been given. The Minister replies: 'The Bill is for a reserved purpose and makes only incidental or consequential changes to Scots law on devolved matters. The Scottish Executive is aware of the bill and of our view that this legislation does not require the consent of the Scottish Parliament'.[31]

---

[31] Cabinet Office Devolution Guidance Note 13, 'Handling of Parliamentary Business in the House of Lords', para 2.6.

Another example given is of a case where consent is required but is not forthcoming:

> HMG introduces a bill to set up an Education Standards Agency. The bill makes provisions of major significance on devolved matters in Scotland and Northern Ireland. Before second reading, HMG is informed of the opposition of the Scottish Parliament or Northern Ireland Assembly. HMG should normally tell the House that it will either withdraw and reintroduce the bill or table amendments to remove from the bill any coverage in Scotland/Northern Ireland. If it proceeds regardless, the Scottish Parliament/Northern Ireland Assembly may subsequently repeal the Act as it applies to Scotland/Northern Ireland.[32]

INTERGOVERNMENTAL MEETINGS

(1) The Joint Ministerial Committee

The first year of devolution has seen half a dozen meetings of the new Joint Ministerial Committee (JMC). It was Gordon Brown who first spotted its potential, and who chaired the first two meetings of the JMC on Poverty and the Knowledge Economy, before the Prime Minister took up the reins and chaired the next three meetings of the JMC to promote his new initiative in Health (see the list of meetings in Figure 6.5 below). Brown spotted early on that the new JMC would enable him to maintain a strong personal profile in Scotland while pursuing his drive for more integrated policies on social policy and the economy.

Donald Dewar made the first announcement on 29 November, announcing:

> ...policy initiatives across a range of social justice policy priorities spanning devolved and reserved areas ...We are determined to see the devolution settlement deliver results on the key action areas of social justice, child poverty and pensioner poverty ...[33]

This allowed Brown to follow through with an announcement during a visit to Edinburgh on 1 December, that three Joint Action Committees were to be established under the umbrella of the JMC to cover pensioner poverty, child poverty, and the knowledge economy, and to spell out how joint action was needed between the two levels of government to tackle the problems of poverty and unemployment:

> On child poverty, the UK Government decides on child benefit, child tax arrangements and levels of income support, while the Scottish executive decide on education, health and social services. On pensioners, the UK Government decides on pensions and taxation while the Scottish Executive has responsibility

[32] *Ibid.* para 2.10.
[33] Scottish Executive Press Release, 'Dewar confirms Expansion of JMC Structure', 29 November 1999.

for housing, health and social services. On the knowledge economy, education and industrial support are devolved matters but the tax arrangements governing e-commerce rest with the UK Government.'[34]

In the event, the first JMC on 9 December tackled both pensioner and child poverty. 'Brown's Poverty Summit' was addressed by officials from the Treasury on Brown's plans for an integrated child tax credit, and by Alistair Darling, the UK Social Security Secretary. The First and deputy First Minister came from Northern Ireland, representing an administration just one week old; but Donald Dewar was unexpectedly absent, dealing with a staffing crisis, and Alun Michael, First Secretary of Wales, had a prior engagement to open a by-pass in Carmarthen.

Similar difficulties dogged Brown's second JMC on the knowledge economy, held in Edinburgh on 11 February. The Welsh team pulled out because of the political crisis over Alun Michael's resignation; but two ministers from Northern Ireland attended despite the suspension hours later of the Northern Ireland Executive. But for Brown the meeting generated big headlines in Scotland, being the first JMC held outside London. Brown repeated Government targets for schools on the internet, and computer learning centres, and defended devolution for breaking down over-centralisation and allowing for greater innovation in policy-making: '...in the new devolved framework, the whole of Britain can learn and benefit from the distinct initiatives and energies of each of its parts.'[35]

The meeting also provided photocalls for Donald Dewar and Scottish Secretary John Reid, which did not go unnoticed by SNP leader, Alex Salmond. He commented:

> The Scottish Executive are in hock to new Labour in London ...London Labour's latest tactic is to bind the Scottish Executive into Westminster's agenda, through Joint Ministerial Committees.[36]

Gordon Brown chose Edinburgh again as the site for the follow-up meetings of the JMC on the Knowledge Economy and on Poverty, which he chaired back-to-back on 26 May. On this occasion, Brown gave a lengthy press conference after the meeting. Discussion had focused on the employment opportunities created by the knowledge economy, and how the different administrations could ensure greater equality of access to them. The JMC on Poverty discussed pensioner poverty and the Children's Fund.

It is too early to judge the value of these meetings. They clearly have a political value, in photocall opportunities for ministers, and enabling Gordon Brown to maintain a profile in Scotland. On the substantive issues, the

---

[34] Treasury News Release, 'Joint Action to tackle Poverty and improve the Economy', 1 December 1999.

[35] Treasury News Release, 'Equipping Britain for the Future', 11 February 2000.

[36] BBC News Online, 'Power sharing comes to Edinburgh', 11 February 2000.

Figure 6.5. Calendar of intergovernmental meetings in the first year of devolution

(Meetings of the North–South Ministerial Council are listed in Figure 6.8 below)

1 Oct. 1999	Publication of *Memorandum of Understanding* and first four Concordats
24 Nov. 1999	First meeting of JMC(O) chaired by Sir Richard Wilson
9 Dec. 1999	Gordon Brown chairs first JMC on Poverty
13 Dec. 1999	Inaugural plenary meeting of North/South Ministerial Council in Armagh
17 Dec. 1999	Inaugural meetings of British–Irish Council and British–Irish Intergovernmental Conference in London
21 Jan. 2000	Publication of first six Devolution Guidance Notes by Cabinet Office
11 Feb. 2000	Gordon Brown chairs JMC on the Knowledge Economy in Edinburgh
7 April 2000	Prime Ministers chairs JMC on Health in Cardiff
26 May 2000	Gordon Brown chairs second JMC on Knowledge Economy and on Poverty in Edinburgh
5 June 2000	Prime Minister chairs second JMC on Health in London
16 June 2000	Prime Minister chairs third JMC on Health in Glasgow
1 Sept. 2000	Prime Minister chairs first Plenary JMC in London
31 Oct. 2000	Second meeting of British–Irish Council in Dublin

Treasury, DTI and DSS are all doing further work; but there is no systematic follow up by JMC(O). The value may in part be substantive, in facilitating co-operation through sharing responsibility for a problem, and pooling competencies; in part procedural, through maintaining networks and pooling experience.

The Prime Minister decided on Cardiff for his first meeting of the JMC on Health, which he convened as part of his personal initiative to improve the health service, following the announcement in the March budget of a huge increase in funding for the NHS. The first JMC on Health on 7 April was attended by First Ministers Donald Dewar and Rhodri Morgan, accompanied by their Health Ministers, Susan Deacon and Jane Hutt; by Alan Milburn, UK Health Secretary, and by Andrew Smith, Chief Secretary to the Treasury; and by the three territorial Secretaries of State. In a detailed joint statement, the ministers pledged to work together on five new initiatives: winter pressures; performance measures and management; tele-medicine; sharing best practice via the internet; and delivering services with a clear patient focus.[37]

---

[37] 10 Downing Street Press Notice, 'Joint Statement by the Joint Ministerial Committee on Health', 7 April 2000.

At the next JMC on Health on 5 June, Northern Ireland was back in the devolution fold, and the Prime Minister welcomed David Trimble and Bairbre de Brun, Minister for Health and Social Services. The meeting heard about Northern Ireland's experience in closer joint working between health and social services in combating bed-blocking and delayed discharges; heard from Alan Milburn on his plans to drive up performance in the NHS in England; and discussed a range of initiatives to combat winter pressures, on which they agreed to share information and best practice.[38] The third JMC on Health was held only 10 days later in Glasgow, on 16 June. It received two reports from Scotland and one from Wales. The Scottish Health Minister, Susan Deacon, presented papers on partnership, drawing on the Scottish experience of engaging local communities in service changes; and on preventative policies for cancer and heart disease, both big causes of premature death in Scotland. Welsh Assembly Secretary for Health, Jane Hutt, presented a paper on telemedicine, and the meeting heard about the National Plan for the NHS in England.[39]

After an understandable initial suspicion on the part of the devolved administrations that they were being brought together to be lectured by the UK Government on how to use the extra funding for the NHS, the JMCs on Health seem to have settled down into a genuine forum for the exchange of information and best practice. For the ministers attending from Scotland, Wales and Northern Ireland they provide opportunities to present and share innovation and research in a way which did not exist pre-devolution, and to show the local press how they are leading the way.[40] When questioned about the effectiveness of the JMC meetings, Paul Murphy expressed it this way:

> ... before devolution I rather fancy that ministers in the Welsh Office would not have known a great deal about the way the Northern Ireland health service works, for example, and vice versa. In a strangely ironic sort of way, it has taken devolution to happen to enable us to understand each other's problems in a much more effective way.[41]

Learning from each other's experience and the positive work done in the 'functional' JMCs on Health, the Knowledge Economy and Poverty were themes emphasised in the first plenary meeting of the JMC held on 1 September 2000. The Prime Minister and First Ministers and their deputies heard a presentation from Donald Dewar and Jim Wallace on Scotland's experience as a trial run for the Human Rights Act (over 800 challenges in the criminal courts, but less than 3 per cent successful). The Committee instituted a

[38] 10 Downing Street Press Notice, 'Joint Measures to Combat NHS Winter Pressures', 5 June 2000.

[39] 10 Downing Street Press Notice, 'Joint Ministerial Committee on Health', 16 June 2000.

[40] National Assembly for Wales Press Release, 'Wales leads the way in Telemedicine', 15 June 2000.

[41] Oral evidence to Welsh Affairs Committee, 27 June 2000.

formal review of the *Memorandum of Understanding* and Concordats, and signalled a particular interest in the difficulties of legislative co-ordination:

> The Committee recognised the importance of management of the relationship between the respective UK and devolved legislative programmes. Much had gone right; however increased effort is needed to ensure that legitimate interest in each other's programmes is fully built into the process of preparing legislation, not treated as an optional extra. To that end, the meeting stressed the importance of early sharing of information between administrations and consultation on policy options ...[42]

The formal meetings of the JMC are just the visible tip of the iceberg. There are countless other bilateral and multilateral meetings to bring together ministers from the UK Government and the devolved administrations — some on a regular basis, some to resolve an immediate issue. The press notices issued after meetings of the JMC give some indication of these other ministerial groups, by mentioning that: 'Less formal meetings of Ministers also take place to discuss issues of common interest and concern, e.g. on agriculture, housing, the environment.'[43]

The Agriculture Ministers meet on a monthly basis, and these meetings could have brought under the JMC umbrella (and one day might be); but so far MAFF has chosen not to do so.

(2) The British–Irish Committees

Figure 6.5 above shows how, interwoven in the cycle of meetings of the Joint Ministerial Committee, there have also been meetings of the three British–Irish intergovernmental bodies. There was a flurry of such meetings in December 1999 to underpin the new Northern Ireland Executive which had been formed on 2 December, with inaugural meetings of the British–Irish Council and the British–Irish Intergovernmental Conference held in London on 17 December. These were preceded by the inaugural meeting of the North/South Ministerial Council, held in Armagh on 13 December. Subsequent meetings of the North/South Ministerial Council were held in sectoral format in Newry on 24 January, and in Dublin on 3 February, just a week before the Executive was suspended (see Figure 6.8).

The inaugural summit meeting of the British–Irish Council (BIC) was held in Lancaster House and attended by 24 delegates: three from the British Government, four from Ireland, five from Northern Ireland, three each from Scotland and Wales, and two each from the Isle of Man, Jersey, and Guernsey. Chairing the meeting, Tony Blair said it was an extraordinary and historic occasion, with the inauguration of the last two political institutions established under the Belfast Agreement; but although it was mainly a

---

[42] Press Notice issued by 10 Downing Street following the 1 September meeting.
[43] *Ibid.*

symbolic occasion, ministers were also keen to show it had substance. They approved an initial list of issues for early discussion and nominated a lead administration for each:

Figure 6.6. British–Irish Council: lead administrations on initial topics

Topic	Lead administration
Drugs	Irish Government
Social inclusion	Scottish Executive and Welsh Cabinet
Environment	British Government
Transport	Northern Ireland Executive
Knowledge economy	Jersey

The Council agreed to hold its next summit in Dublin in June 2000, with the main focus to be on the issue of drugs. In the event, because of the suspension of the Northern Ireland Executive in February, that meeting did not take place. It was eventually rescheduled for 31 October. The first meeting of the Council also agreed an indicative list of other suitable topics, set out in Figure 6.7, including some areas which were already being taken forward bilaterally.

Figure 6.7. British–Irish Council: indicative list of possible future topics[44]

- Agricultural issues such as plant quarantine; rural development and rural depopulation; the development of renewable raw materials and energy crops; salmon fisheries; sea fisheries and aquaculture
- Health issues
- Regional issues, including links between cities, towns and local districts
- Interparliamentary links
- Energy issues
- Cultural issues
- Tourism
- Sporting activity
- Education issues
- Approaches to EU issues
- Minority and lesser-used languages
- Prison and probation issues.

[44] Communique 'Inaugural summit of the British–Irish Council' 17 December 1999, available at www.nics.gov.uk/press/ofmdfm.

The Northern Ireland political leaders were clearly sensitive to the charge that:

>...the Council was little more than a powerless talking shop designed to give David Trimble, Northern Ireland's First Minister, cover against opponents within his own party.[45]

David Trimble acknowledged that Scottish politicians had initially been opposed to the Council, but asserted (correctly) that they were now very keen on it. His deputy, Seamus Mallon, added that the two Councils should not be seen as separate sops to the two communities in Northern Ireland, with '...the North/South Ministerial Council the nationalist one, and the British–Irish Council the unionist one.'[46]

But that is inevitably how the North/South Ministerial Council is viewed, particularly by die-hard Unionists, and its first meeting on 13 December was boycotted by the two Democratic Unionist members of the Northern Ireland Executive (as they have boycotted all other institutions established under the Belfast Agreement, including the Northern Ireland Executive and the British–Irish Council).

The inaugural meeting of the North/South Ministerial Council was another historic occasion, captured in the opening lines of *The Guardian*'s report:

>In a highly symbolic encounter, the entire cabinet of the Irish Republic met Ulster's new coalition cabinet of Protestants and Catholics for the first time today in the ancient cathedral city of Armagh in the heart of British-ruled Northern Ireland.[47]

The 15 Irish ministers and the 10 ministers from Northern Ireland agreed to establish six cross-border implementation bodies to harmonise North–South policy on inland waterways, the promotion of the Irish and Ulster Scots languages, food safety, aquaculture and marine matters, trade and business development, and special EU programmes. They also agreed to work together in six further 'areas of co-operation': transport, agriculture, education, health, the environment and tourism.[48]

After the inaugural summit, the North/South Ministerial Council held just two working meetings in sectoral format before the suspension of the Northern Ireland Executive in February 2000. Both were overshadowed by the impasse over arms decommissioning. But after the re-establishment of the devolved institutions on 30 May, there was a flurry of sectoral meetings, with nine being held in the space of three weeks in June/July (see the list in

---

[45]   James Landale in *The Times*, 'Council draws Isles into new partnership', 18 December 1999.

[46]   BBC News Online, 'Council of substance and symbolism', 17 December 1999.

[47]   Mark Tran, 'North–South Ministerial Council meets for first time' *The Guardian* 13 December 1999.

[48]   BBC News Online, 'Historic Day for North–South Council', 13 December 1999.

Figure 6.8. Meetings of the North/South Ministerial Council

13 Dec. 1999	Inaugural plenary meeting in Armagh
24 Jan. 2000	Trade and Business Development in Newry
3 Feb. 2000	Education in Dublin
4 Feb. 2000	Food Safety and Health
16 June 2000	Special EU programmes in Dublin
21 June 2000	Inland Waterways in Belfast
21 June 2000	Language Matters in Belfast
26 June 2000	Agriculture in Dublin
28 June 2000	Environmental Matters in Belfast
30 June 2000	Second meeting of Trade and Business Development in Dublin
3 July 2000	Second meeting on Education in Cultra, Co Down
4 July 2000	Second meeting on Health and Food Safety
5 July 2000	Meeting on Aquaculture and Marine Matters in Dublin
26 Sept. 2000	Second plenary meeting in Dublin.

Details of all these meetings — the Ministers attending, and the business discussed — can be found in press releases issued by the Northern Ireland Executive and/or the Irish Government

Figure 6.8). Council meetings were held to supervise the work of establishing all six North/South implementation bodies which had been launched on 2 December, and to receive initial reports from their interim chief executives. The six North/South implementation bodies are the Special EU Programmes Body, the Trade and Business Development Body, the Food Safety Promotion Board, Waterways Ireland, the Foyle, Carlingford and Irish Lights Commission, and the Language Body for the Irish language and Ulster Scots. A further three Council meetings were held to discuss 'areas of co-operation' in education, health and the environment.

The location of the meetings alternates between north and south. Initially a quarterly cycle of meetings is being established, with the next round of meetings being set for September/October. The Irish Government is generally represented by a single minister, but the Northern Ireland Executive always fields two: they are carefully paired to represent the two communities, even if the portfolio of the pairing minister is marginal to the subject being discussed. How comfortable unionist ministers will feel about this growing co-operation with the Republic remains to be seen. The North/South Ministerial Council is fulfilling the expectation laid upon it in Strand Two of the Belfast Agreement, to meet in specific sectoral formats 'on a regular and frequent basis'. It has held a dozen meetings in the first year, and at the present rate is likely to hold twice that in the second year. In this respect the North/South Ministerial Council is going to eclipse by a long way the British–Irish Council; but that too was intended to meet in sectoral format on a regular basis. The unionists had hoped that the latter would be a counterbalance to all this North–South activity; but in the first year of devolution the

British–Irish Council will have met just once, at its inaugural plenary meeting in December 1999.

EU POLICY AND INTERNATIONAL RELATIONS

It was evident from early on that EU and international relations were going to be a major source of tension in the devolution settlement.[49] The main source of difficulty is the overlapping of responsibilities; many of the subject areas devolved are in fields like agriculture, economic development, industry, transport, and the environment, which are all important policy areas for legislation and regulation by the EU. But in the Council of Ministers and other EU negotiating fora, it is the UK which represents the interests of Scotland, Wales, and Northern Ireland, and not the devolved governments. The Scottish Office recognised the difficulties which might arise, and in the run-up to devolution sent a team to Brussels to see how other sub-national governments manage to influence EU policy. Their officials played a significant part in the drafting of the subsequent Concordat on Co-ordination of EU Policy Issues, which ensures that the devolved administrations are properly consulted on all devolved matters, and can make an input into the agreed UK negotiating line.

The formal position is summarised in the *Memorandum of Understanding* as follows:

> As a matter of law, international relations and relations with the EU remain the responsibility of the UK Government and the UK Parliament. However, the UK Government recognises that the devolved administrations will have an interest in international and European policy making in relation to devolved matters, notably where implementing action by the devolved administrations may be required ...The UK Government will involve the devolved administrations as fully as possible in discussions about the formulation of the UK's policy position on all EU and international issues which touch on devolved matters. This must, obviously, be subject to mutual respect for the confidentiality of those discussions and adherence to the resultant UK line, without which it would be impossible to maintain such close working relationships.[50]

An additional difficulty which is constantly emphasised by the European Secretariat in the Cabinet Office, is that EU negotiations are ongoing, flexible, pursued in many different times and places, and require rapid responses and quick decisions to enable UK officials and ministers to develop an effective UK line and negotiating position. This is reflected in the Concordat,

[49] For two early warnings from The Constitution Unit see G. Leicester: *Scotland's Parliament*, ch. 6, Constitution Unit 1996; and R. Cornes, 'Intergovernmental Relations' in *Constitutional Futures*, ed. R. Hazell, Oxford University Press 1999.

[50] Cm 4444, October 1999, paras 17, 19.

which spells out clearly the conflicting objectives which need to be reconciled:

> ... the co-ordination mechanisms should achieve three key objectives:
>
> • They should provide for full and continuing involvement of ministers and officials of the Scottish Executive in the processes of policy formulation, negotiation and implementation, for issues which touch on devolved matters;
> • They should ensure that the UK can negotiate effectively, in pursuit of a single UK policy line, but with the flexibility that fast-moving negotiations require, and
> • They should ensure EU obligations are implemented with consistency of effect and where appropriate of timing.[51]

So, the formal position is that the devolved administrations can make an input into EU policy, but only through the UK Government, and the UK Government will only allow that input so long as they respect confidentiality and support the UK line. In practice, rapid consultation is achieved by the lead Whitehall departments writing to their Scottish and Welsh counterparts at the same time as they consult with the rest of Whitehall. So, for example, MAFF will write to the Agriculture Ministers in the devolved administrations at the same time as it consults with DETR and DTI. The Cabinet Office say that so far this has worked: the UK has been able to develop its negotiating position in as effective and timely a way as it did pre-devolution.[52] And the formal machinery provided for in the *Memorandum of Understanding* has not so far been needed. The JMC, chaired by the Foreign Secretary, which was envisaged as 'one of the principal mechanisms for consultation on UK positions on EU issues which affect devolved matters'[53] has not been brought into play. Nor has its official counterpart, JMC(EU)(O), chaired by the Head of the European Secretariat. So far as Whitehall is concerned, things have gone reasonably smoothly.

But for the devolved administrations, it may not be sufficient to be consulted and make an input into the UK negotiating line. Their politicians want to see that input. They want to see Scotland or Wales influencing the outcome, and the most visible way of seeing that influence is when Scottish or Welsh ministers are included in the UK delegation. This is where there may be the greatest mismatch between expectation and reality. The Concordat allows others into the UK delegation, but only if they have a significant interest, and so long as they support the UK team:

---

[51] Concordat on Co-ordination of EU Policy Issues — Scotland, Cm 4444, October 1999, para B1.4. The Welsh Concordat is expressed in the same terms: para B2.4.

[52] Constitution Unit seminar, 27 June 2000.

[53] *Memorandum of Understanding*, Supplementary Agreement on the Joint Committee, para A1.9.

Ministers and officials of the devolved administrations should have a role to play in relevant Council meetings, and other negotiations with EU partners.

Decisions on Ministerial attendance at Council meetings will be taken on a case-by-case basis by the lead UK Minister. In reaching decisions on the composition of the UK team, the lead Minister will take into account that the devolved administrations should have a role to play in meetings of the Council of Ministers at which substantive discussion is expected of matters likely to have a significant impact on their devolved responsibilities.

...the role of Ministers and officials from the devolved administrations will be to support and advance the single UK negotiating line which they will have played a part in developing. The emphasis in negotiations has to be on working as a UK team; and the UK lead Minister will retain overall responsibility for the negotiations and determine how each member of the team can best contribute to securing the agreed policy position. In appropriate cases, the leader of the delegation could agree to Ministers from the devolved administrations speaking for the UK in Council ...[54]

By the end of June 2000, the score card of attendance was that Scottish ministers had attended nine Council meetings, Wales one, and Northern Ireland one.[55] Scottish ministers have attended meetings of the Agriculture, Education, Environment, and Fisheries Councils; sometimes in the face of considerable Whitehall reluctance (in one instance attendance was eventually conceded as a 'familiarisation exercise'). But in one respect this is nothing new: Scottish ministers used to attend EU meetings before devolution, especially of the Agriculture, Fisheries and Environment Councils; as more rarely did Welsh ministers. What has changed is the greater pressure to attend, exemplified in Rhodri Morgan's stated ambition to increase the attendance of Assembly Secretaries at meetings of the Council of Ministers.[56]

Another respect in which expectations outrun reality is in relation to the offices opened by the devolved institutions in Brussels. The National Assembly for Wales has opened its own office there, housed in the offices of the Wales European Centre. Its Head, Des Clifford, a grade 7 civil servant, is grandly referred to in the National Assembly and the Welsh press as 'Wales' ambassador in Europe'. Yet he heads a staff of just two, compared with the six and a half Scots, and the over 150 staff in the offices of UKREP, the UK's permanent representation in Brussels. He can at most provide a listening post: Wales is not going to gain a stronger voice in Europe this way.

Have the devolved administrations gained any greater influence in Europe? In the first year of devolution, the answer from Whitehall is probably not; but candid civil servants would add that Scotland and Wales never

---

[54] Concordat on Co-ordination of EU Policy Issues — Scotland, paras B3.12-14.

[55] See note 52.

[56] In the National Assembly debate on the annual report of the Committee on European Affairs, 27 June 2000 at p 50.

had that much influence anyway. And it is early days, with the new administrations still playing themselves in. The real test will come when they are led
by governments of a different political persuasion from Westminster; or
when the political faultlines open up over EMU, with the Europhile administrations in Scotland, Wales, and Northern Ireland[57] being much keener on
entry than the Europhobes of middle England. But even then, it is hard to see
how much additional leverage they might acquire. They can lobby in Europe,
and they can push for more Euro-friendly policies at home, but at the end of it
all the member state remains the UK, and they have no alternative voice in
the Council of Ministers, save in and through the UK delegation. And if they
push too hard or too publicly, they risk losing even that: the ground rules laid
down in the *Memorandum of Understanding* and the Concordat state clearly
that the UK Government will only allow their input so long as they respect
confidentiality and support the UK line.

Nor can they expect any significant change in the ground rules, even if
devolution leads in time to a more level playing field within the UK. This is
because the rules are based as much upon the constitutional fundamentals
and practice of the European Community as the devolution settlement within
the UK. Even in Belgium, now the most decentralised state in the European
Union, the subnational communities can only appear in the Council of Ministers so long as they speak with one voice:

> The Belgian Regions and Communities ... do not have right to act in their own
> right in the EU. The EU does not allow that. They can only act through the
> member state of which they are part: Belgium.

> ... the regions and communities can only act as such in the EU if they act *jointly*,
> that is, if their actions in the EU commit and bind Belgium in its entirety. That is
> indeed the condition clearly formulated in Art 146 TEC [Art 203 of the Consoli-
> dated Treaty of the European Community]. That article — which has been amend-
> ed in this sense at the insistence of Germany and Belgium — allows the member
> states to be represented in the Council of Ministers by members of a government
> other than the national government. But this is on condition that these representa-
> tives are empowered to commit their entire country, not just parts of it.'[58]

The rules were put to the test for Scotland during the first year over exports of
British beef. The French refused to allow imports of British beef after the EU
had lifted the ban, but the French Government indicated that it had no objec-
tion to grass-fed Scottish beef. For Scottish farmers and the Scottish Executive, the temptation must have been strong, but UK cohesion held and the
Scots faithfully supported the UK line. Wales has experienced difficulties of
a different kind. Some Whitehall departments are reluctant to share

---

[57] Seamus Mallon is in favour of joining EMU (as are most nationalists); but David Trimble is
opposed, and is similarly representative of unionist opinion on the issue.
[58] Bart Kerremans, 'Determining a European policy in a Multi-level Setting: The Case of
Specialised Co-ordination in Belgium', *Regional and Federal Studies*, vol. 10 spring 2000 no 1 at p 38.

information with Welsh officials for fear that it will be made public in the National Assembly: because the Assembly is a body corporate, they fear that information sent to Assembly Secretaries cannot be withheld from their colleagues in the Assembly. Rhodri Morgan has responded with an assurance that information supplied in confidence will be treated in confidence, even though he is leading the way towards greater openness by publishing Cabinet minutes within six weeks.[59] A more fundamental difficulty in Wales is lack of capacity: many parts of Whitehall complain of difficulties in dealing with Wales, of delays in obtaining responses, and delays in the Assembly in making and implementing legislation.

These delays have not yet resulted in infraction proceedings: another small success for the handling of EU matters in the first year of devolution. Should they ever do so the UK as the member state has primary responsibility for ensuring compliance with EU law, and liability for any breaches. But it has been made clear throughout the *Memorandum of Understanding* that any penalties will be passed on:

> The devolved administrations are responsible for implementing international, ECHR, and EU obligations which concern devolved matters. In law, UK ministers have powers to intervene in order to ensure the implementation of these obligations. If the devolved administrations wish, it is open to them to ask the UK Government to extend UK legislation to cover their EU obligations. The devolved administrations are directly accountable through the domestic courts, in the same way as the UK Government is, for shortcomings in their implementation or application of EC law. It is agreed by all four administrations that, to the extent that financial penalties are imposed on the UK as a result of any failure of implementation or enforcement, or any damages or costs arise as a result, responsibility for meeting them will be borne by the administration(s) responsible for the failure.[60]

FINANCE

Finance has been predicted to be the greatest likely source of tension in the devolution settlement.[61] In the first year of devolution, this has not proved to be the case, save for the big argument in Wales over who should supply the additional match funding for their new European Objective One structural fund programmes. The main reason for the lack of tension over finance is that the previous funding regime for allocating public expenditure to Scotland, Wales, and Northern Ireland has continued to apply. The devolved

---

[59] First Secretary's statement on Freedom of Information, 21 March 2000; followed by memo to all Assembly staff from the Permanent Secretary 28 March 2000, which urged them to reassure colleagues in Whitehall departments of their continuing commitment to respecting information provided in confidence. See also Assembly Standing Orders 17.2(iii) and 17.5(iii).

[60] Cm 4444, October 1999, para 20.

[61] Hazell, R., (ed.), *Constitutional Futures*, chs. 2 and 9, (Oxford University Press, 1999)

administrations have complete freedom to determine their own spending priorities within their assigned totals; and since for historical reasons the assigned totals are relatively generous (with the possible exception of Wales), they have little reason to rock the boat. When complaints have been voiced, they have come from the regions of England: in particular from the north-east, and from northern MPs at Westminster, who feel particularly disadvantaged in relation to the more generous levels of spending in Scotland just across the border.

The Treasury had early warning of the difficulties which might arise when, in late 1997, the Treasury Select Committee conducted an inquiry into the Barnett Formula — the population-based formula used to make annual adjustments to the blocks of public spending allocated to Scotland, Wales, and Northern Ireland.[62] The Treasury's territorial analysis of identifiable public expenditure suggested that in 1995–96, expenditure in Scotland was 19 per cent and expenditure in Wales 12 per cent above the UK average, while expenditure in England was 4 per cent below the UK average. The inquiry revealed widespread misunderstanding about how the Barnett Formula works, and about its results.[63] The Committee concluded its report with a call for a fresh needs assessment, to show whether the Barnett Formula remained the appropriate method of allocating annual expenditure increases to the four nations of the Union.

In the run-up to devolution, the Barnett Formula came under much closer scrutiny than it had ever enjoyed since it was first devised in 1978. The Treasury decided on a policy of full disclosure and transparency, and on 31 March 1999 they published *Funding the Scottish Parliament, National Assembly for Wales and Northern Ireland Assembly: A Statement of Funding Policy*.[64] This restates the principles by which the annual changes in the Scottish, Welsh, and Northern Irish blocks are determined, and then sets out in great detail the different heads of expenditure in the UK Government departments which provide the baseline for those changes. The *Statement of Funding Policy* begins by stating that devolution creates a requirement to define clearly the new financial relationships to be established within the UK, and goes on to say that:

> ...the way in which the budget of each of the devolved administrations is determined should be clear, unambiguous and capable of examination and analysis by each of the devolved administrations and the UK Parliament.

---

[62] Treasury Committee, *The Barnett Formula*, HC 341, December 1997.

[63] Subsequent evidence submitted by the Treasury to the committee in February 1998 showed the following differentials in 1995–96 in *per capita* spending between the three blocks and England: Scotland 32 per cent higher than equivalent spending in England; Wales 25 per cent higher; Northern Ireland 32 per cent higher. Treasury Committee, *The Barnett Formula: The Government's Response*, Appendix 2, para 9, HC 619, 10 March 1998.

[64] Obtainable from peu@hm-treasury.gov.uk, or viewable at www.hm-treasury.gov.uk

The *Statement of Funding Policy* was agreed, not with the devolved administrations (which did not yet exist), but between the Chief Secretary to the
Treasury and the Secretaries of State for Scotland, Wales, and Northern
Ireland. It is the Secretaries of State who still receive the funding voted by
Parliament, and they in turn make grants to the devolved administrations
under the devolution legislation. Provision for the costs of their own Offices
has to be found from within the moneys voted by Parliament. Once it is
passed on, the devolved administrations have the freedom to make their own
spending decisions within the overall totals.

This framework proved adequate for the major public spending allocations in Scotland, but not in Wales. In Scotland, throughout the debate about
changing the policy on tuition fees, one thing was crystal clear: any additional spending on higher education had to be found from within the Scottish
block. Despite the potential consequences for England, the UK Government
did not invoke the caveat in the *Statement on Funding Policy* that:

> …where decisions are taken by the devolved administrations which have
> financial implications for departments or agencies of the UK Government, … the
> body whose decision leads to the additional cost will meet that cost.[65]

For their part, the Scottish Executive accepted that they had to find compen-
sating savings from within their assigned budget to fund their more generous
policy.

But in Wales, the National Assembly did not accept that the additional
money to match the £1.3 billion European Objective 1 funding should come
out of their own budget: they looked to the Treasury to supply the additional
funding. The full story is told in chapter 3 on Wales (see pages 45–47). The
Treasury initially maintained that the Assembly would have to find PES
cover and match funding for EU receipts from within its assigned budget.
But when he announced the conclusions of his Comprehensive Spending
Review on 18 July 2000, the Chancellor had dramatic news for Wales: a 5.4
per cent real terms increase over the next three years, leading to an assigned
budget some £2 billion higher in 2003–04 than in 2000–01. The 5.4 per cent
increase was 1 per cent greater than the settlement for Scotland; and it was
achieved by breaking the Barnett formula. Although most of the increase in
Wales' assigned budget derived from applying the formula to the big spending increases announced for England, significant extra sums were awarded to
Wales outside the Barnett formula (£272 million over the next three years) to
provide the PES cover for the European funds.[66]

[65] HM Treasury, *Statement on Funding Policy*, para 2.2.viii.

[66] Institute of Welsh Affairs, *Unravelling the Knot; An Update*, July 2000; Constitution Unit,
Wales Monitoring report, August 2000, pp 5–8, viewed at www.ucl.ac.uk.constitution-unit; Adrian
Kay, 'Objective 1 in Wales: Rechar Redux?', *Regional Studies* vol. 34.6 pp 581-5.

Wales is the only devolved administration where calls are heard for a review of the Barnett formula. Although significantly poorer than Scotland, in terms of GDP per capita, Wales enjoys levels of public expenditure which are lower than in Scotland. Wales derives less visible benefit from the current system; but the Barnett formula is not and never was a needs-based formula. But in the political battles, the Scottish voice is louder; and the Scottish Finance Minister Jack McConnell has made clear that the Scots have no reason to rock the Barnett cradle.[67]

Lord Barnett himself has conceded that the formula he devised in 1978 was not strictly rational, but was intended simply as a stopgap until a more needs-based system came into operation. He accepts 'the overwhelming case for a change from the formula', and cites:

> ...just one example of terrible unfairness. In the north-east, GDP per head was 13 percentage points below Scotland in 1997, but government expenditure per head was not higher — it was 19 percentage points lower.[68]

The north-east is the one region of England where, in newspapers like the Newcastle *Journal*, comparisons are regularly made with spending levels in Scotland. But so far the only political party to respond to the calls for change is the Liberal Democrats. In July 2000 Charles Kennedy announced that the Liberal Democrats would re-evaluate the spending needs of the three nations and the nine regions of England by establishing a Finance Commission for the Nations and Regions, which would be charged with devising a new revenue distribution formula.[69]

Labour is unlikely to follow suit until pressure builds up all round for change: including in Scotland. That will not happen until the Barnett formula becomes the 'Barnett squeeze', as the gradual convergence between spending levels which is a by-product of the formula starts to take effect.[70] But that will take many years. Until then, the *realpolitik* was clearly spelled out in Peter Robinson's editorial to the Public Spending issue of *New Economy* in July 2000:

> ...in a country with asymmetric devolution, the parts with a credible threat of causing trouble (Scotland) have a bargaining advantage over those without (the English regions) ... Current Labour ministers in London and Edinburgh are not keen on changes that might favour the northern English regions, perhaps at the expense of Scotland, because disgruntled Scots have somewhere to go politically. Their

[67] Jack McConnell MSP, 'Funding Devolution: wby Barnett remains better than the alternatives', *New Economy* June 2000 p 65.

[68] Lord Barnett, 'The Barnett formula; how a temporary expedient became permanent', *New Economy*, June 2000 p 69.

[69] www.libdems.org.uk, news headline of 14 July 2000.

[70] Jack McConnell MSP, *op cit.*, p 66. For the reasons why convergence did not take place in the 1980s and 1990s, see the writings of Prof David Heald of Aberdeen, the leading expert on the Barnett formula.

counterparts south of the border lack the same option. This crude political logic currently outweighs the argument for a reasoned assessment of the case for change.[71]

CONCLUSIONS

In conclusion, how can we characterise the emerging nature of intergovernmental relations in the UK after the first year of devolution? The first thing to say is that so far they have been remarkably smooth. The work involved in drafting the *Memorandum of Understanding* and the Concordats has paid off: all sides have a shared understanding of the ground rules, and seem to agree on the guidance. The rules have been extensively quoted in this chapter because they are one of the main achievements of the first year: the creation of a body of soft law to set against the hard law found in the devolution Acts, to guide officials in their day-to-day dealings with each other across the new divide.

Officials say they rarely refer to the Concordats: 'if we refer to them we have failed.' But it is clear they have absorbed their ethos and procedures: in particular, the determination to avoid disputes going to court. Officials generally follow the graduated set of responses in which differences are first negotiated bilaterally between officials, then between individual ministers, then using the good offices of the Secretary of State, and only then going to the Joint Ministerial Committee as the political forum of last resort. It has helped that, in many cases, officials are simply continuing previous relations which they had with the Welsh Office and the Scottish Office. The greatest difficulties are reported where they are dealing with a 'new' function or new set of people in Scotland or Wales.

It could have been an awful lot worse. Stories circulate of parts of Whitehall saying 'Devolution — what's that?'; of UK ministers being appalled at having to meet with Welsh Assembly Secretaries; of a Secretary of State being bemused when his officials transferred to the devolved administration. None of this erupted in angry headlines, with the devolved governments railing at UK ministers or Whitehall.[72] Intergovernmental relations had a low political salience in the first year of devolution. It was helped in this by two things: ministers in the devolved governments had their hands full getting their own show on the road; and the new Labour administrations in Edinburgh and Cardiff still owed a strong sense of loyalty to Labour in London. Intergovernmental relations will only really be tested when they have to be conducted across a deeper political divide.

---

[71] *New Economy* July 2000 p 63.

[72] One exception was the disappointment expressed by Peter Law, Secretary for Local Government and Housing in the Welsh Assembly, at the UK Government's failure to grant the Assembly sufficient powers in clause 6 of the Local Government Bill. Statement to Assembly 4 July 2000 at pp 19-20.

The second characteristic of intergovernmental relations so far, is that the UK Government is the dominant partner. This should not come as a surprise, when the devolved assemblies operate under the sovereignty of the Westminster Parliament, and Westminster provides them with all their finance. But it is underlined in small ways in the machinery of intergovernmental relations. All meetings of the Joint Ministerial Committee are chaired by UK ministers, irrespective of their location, even when convened to resolve differences between the UK Government and one of the devolved administrations.[73] That is not the case in federations, where there is a rotating chair or intergovernmental meetings are co-chaired. And in the first year, all meetings of the JMC have been convened by the UK Government, in pursuance of its agenda, despite provision for meetings to be convened at the request of the devolved administrations.[74] The devolved administrations have so far shown no signs of solidarity with each other, of ganging up together against the UK Government in the way that states do against federal governments. This may again reflect how busy they have been just getting devolution going on their own patch. But it may also be a reflection of the underlying asymmetry in the devolution settlement, in which Scotland does not view Wales as an equal, and Northern Ireland is a special case. The real test of solidarity will come when the Welsh Assembly bids for legislative powers on a par with those in Scotland and Northern Ireland (see chapter 3): will the Scots and Northern Irish administrations support their case, or stand idly by?

Third, although hugely dominant, the UK Government has not pushed the devolved administrations around. It has not exercised its formal override powers. Even on Scottish student tuition fees, where the knock-on implications were considerable, the UK Government eventually bit its lip and stood back, recognising that the survival of the Lib-Lab coalition in Scotland depended on salvaging a workable formula from the Cubie report. And over beef on the bone, where the Chief Medical Officers in Wales and Scotland were more cautious about lifting the ban than was the CMO in London, the UK Government waited until they were ready. London could have put pressure on Edinburgh and Cardiff, but the prevailing view was that if devolution was going to work the UK Government must show an example in being flexible.[75] Even the Treasury's initial hard-line refusal to meet the demands from Wales for additional PES cover to match the EU Objective 1 programme funds ended in a major compromise, with significant additional funds being found for Wales outside the Barnett formula.

---

[73] *Memorandum of Understanding*, Cm 4444, October 1999 paras A1.4-5.

[74] *Ibid.* para A1.8. The plenary meeting of the JMC on 1 September was the first to be convened largely at the request of the devolved administrations.

[75] Michael White, 'The changing view from the windows of Whitehall', *Public Service Magazine*, July 2000.

Fourth, intergovernmental relations are likely to be a relatively closed process. This is underscored in the *Memorandum of Understanding*, which provides for confidentiality in the exchange of information: for the government providing the information to state what restrictions it wishes to apply, and for the receiving government to observe them. All this is subject to the forthcoming Freedom of Information Act, but the FOI Bill contains exemption provisions which will protect the exchange of information between the UK and devolved governments; as almost certainly will the proposed FOI regime in Scotland.[76] If Wales tries to develop a policy of greater openness they are likely to find that the flow of information from Whitehall dries up.

This is nothing new. Intergovernmental relations tend to be a closed process in federations as well. Federal and state parliaments both complain that they are sidelined when their respective governments negotiate with each other. Will parliamentary oversight be any more effective in the UK? Westminster has shown little interest in the intergovernmental meetings held so far, even within the Scottish, Welsh, and Northern Ireland Select and Grand Committees which might be expected to monitor such matters.[77] The devolved assemblies might be expected to take a greater interest, but they have no arrangements for reporting back after meetings of the JMC, no committees specifically to monitor intergovernmental relations[78], and no 'scrutiny reserve' procedure like that developed at Westminster to keep a check on UK negotiations in Brussels.

Finally, it is still early days. In the first year of devolution we have seen some of the structures fall into place, but by no means all. The politicians are still experimenting. The JMC has been the exclusive preserve of the Prime Minister and Chancellor of the Exchequer. Will other UK ministers be allowed to follow suit; or will their regular meetings with their devolved counterparts take place outside the JMC framework? And how will the JMC mesh with the British–Irish committees? The likelihood is that the JMC will become the efficient part of the machinery of intergovernmental relations, and the British–Irish Council the dignified part, wheeled out for state occasions; but because of the interruption to devolution in Northern Ireland the BIC has not yet been tested in any other than summit form.

[76] Clause 26 of the FOI Bill (Bill 5, introduced November 1999) exempts information whose disclosure would prejudice relations between the UK Government and the devolved administrations. The Scottish Executive's consultation document, *An Open Scotland*, SE/1999/51, November 1999, does not contain a full list of proposed exemptions, but comments: 'given the interplay between the UK Government and the Scottish Executive on matters of mutual interest, it is important that due account is taken of the UK Government's proposals ...' (para 4.13).

[77] Exceptions are a passing reference in the Scottish Affairs Committee report on Poverty in Scotland, HC 59, 12 July 2000, para 216 (JMC on Poverty should produce clear statement of its agenda and objectives); Question 6 in the Welsh Grand Committee, 20 June 2000 (about the 5 June JMC on Health); Question 12 in the Welsh Affairs Select Committee on 27 June 2000 (how often does the JMC meet, and how effective is it).

[78] In Australia the State parliaments of Western Australia and Victoria have both established such committees.

Another unknown quantity is the future of the territorial Secretaries of State. The Constitution Unit has said that if the separate offices endure, then devolution will have failed.[79] That is the logic of devolution; but the politics may dictate otherwise. The Secretaries of State may remain in being for symbolic reasons, or political balance, or patronage long after there has ceased to be a real job to do. But if, one by one, they do disappear, that will be a significant shift in intergovernmental relations. The devolved administrations will then deal with a stronger centre in Whitehall, focused on the Cabinet Office, rather than the multiple centres in play at the moment.

The final and biggest factor which will shape intergovernmental relations is the devolution settlement itself. Will it retain its underlying asymmetry, which helps Whitehall to divide and rule? How will Scotland and Northern Ireland respond when Wales bids for equivalent legislative powers? And will England remain for ever content to be excluded?

BIBLIOGRAPHY

The Belfast Agreement: An Agreement reached at the Multi-Party Talks on Northern Ireland, Cm 3883, April 1998.

Cabinet Office, *Devolution Guidance Notes 1-13*, www.cabinet-office.gov.uk/constitution

The Constitution Unit, *The British–Irish Council: Nordic Lessons for the Council of the Isles* (The Constitution Unit, University College London, 1998).

The Constitution Unit, *Wales Monitoring Report*, August 2000 (London: The Constitution Unit, University College London, 2000).

Cornes, R., 'Intergovernmental Relations in a devolved UK: Making Devolution work', in Hazell, R., (ed.), *Constitutional Futures: A History of the next Ten Years* (Oxford University Press, 1999).

Institute of Welsh Affairs, *Unravelling the Knot: An Update* (IWA, 2000).

Kay, A., 'Objective 1 in Wales: Rechar Redux?', *Regional Studies,* vol. 34

Kerremans, B., 'Determining a European Policy in a Multi-level Setting: The Case of Specialised Co-ordination in Belgium', *Regional and Federal Studies*, vol. 10 (Spring 2000).

Leicester, G., *Scotland's Parliament* (London: The Constitution Unit, 1996).

Lord Chancellor, *Memorandum of Understanding and Supplementary Agreements between the UK Government, Scottish Ministers and the Cabinet of the National Assembly for Wales*, Cm 4444, October 1999.

Poirier, J., 'The Functions of Post-Devolution Concordats in a Comparative Perspective', in *Public Law* (forthcoming).

Treasury Committee, *The Barnett Formula*, HC 341, December 1997.

---

[79] R Hazell (ed.): *Constitutional Futures*: Oxford University Press, 1999, p 137.

7

Devolution and Westminster

Tentative Steps towards a more Federal Parliament

Meg Russell and Robert Hazell[1]

In the first two years of the new Labour Government all the focus and energy was channelled into getting the devolved institutions up and running. Very little thought was given to how the centre itself would need to adapt. But since devolution went live in the summer of 1999, we have started to see the beginnings of adjustments in all three branches of central government: in the executive, the courts, and the legislature. This chapter focuses on Westminster, recording the main changes which have taken place so far, and the debates which have begun about further changes in the future.

The first year of devolution has seen Westminster making tentative first steps towards becoming a more federal parliament. In the Lords, this would mean representing the nations and regions of the UK, as second chambers represent the states or the provinces in federal systems. In the Commons, it means Westminster adapting its role as a Union parliament: a parliament which recognises and accommodates the territorial diversity of the UK by operating in different territorial modes. As well as being the parliament for the UK, Westminster has retained, post-devolution, the three sets of special fora in the Commons which enable it to operate as the parliament for Scotland, Wales, and Northern Ireland. Although these fora have lost business to the devolved assemblies, Westminster continues to be a three-in-one parliament through its networks of Scottish, Welsh, and Northern Ireland committees. The significant development during the year was the emergence of a debate about whether Westminster should become a four-in-one parliament: whether Westminster should start to develop special fora which would also enable it to operate as the parliament for England.

In terms of actual change, the period witnessed no more than gradualist, even minimalist, reform. The Government had no detailed plans alongside devolution to indicate how Westminster would need to adapt, yet many

---

[1] Particular thanks are due to Roger Masterman for his research support in the preparation of this chapter.

adaptations were going to be necessary. As Chair of the Procedure Committee, Nicholas Winterton, put it:

> Implementing devolution without changing the procedures of the House is like
> giving a person one's wallet but keeping a string of elastic attached to it: he has the
> wallet in his hand, but if he wants to use it to make a purchase that one disapproves
> of, one tug and the two are locked in conflict.[2]

Devolution changed many aspects of Westminster business, removing whole
tranches of Scottish policy, in particular, from the scope of the UK Parliament. As a result, it has potentially profound implications for the role of MPs
representing constituencies in the devolved areas. However, in the Commons
it has fallen largely to the initiative of parliamentarians to predict the changes
which would be necessary, and to put them onto the parliamentary agenda.
This has been achieved, in part, by inquiries held by two Select Committees.
Many changes have been reactive, driven by tensions in the chamber and
committees. Yet many tensions remain and may grow, particularly around
the question of Scottish MPs' involvement in 'English' business.

This chapter describes the actual and potential responses to devolution in
both parliamentary chambers. Much attention has been given, not least by
MPs, to the impact upon the work of the House of Commons. But in parallel
there has been an investigation — as part of the work of the Royal Commission on Reform of the House of Lords — into the role which the upper chamber could play in a quasi-federal Britain. The two sets of developments have
progressed wholly independently, with no real steer and no attempt at
co-ordination on the part of government or the parliamentary authorities.
Likewise, the changes within the House of Commons have happened piecemeal, with no clear coherence or sense of direction.

The chapter therefore looks at developments in both chambers. The main
part of the chapter is about the House of Commons, where we report on
procedural changes that have occurred, as well as proposals for further
reform and issues emerging from these debates. The focus is primarily on the
impact of Scottish and Welsh devolution, as debates were often limited to
these areas due to the uncertain future of arrangements in Northern Ireland
throughout the period. The second part of the chapter focuses on the House of
Lords, dealing largely with proposals made by the Royal Commission and
critiques of them.

THE HOUSE OF COMMONS

In real terms, the most immediate impact of devolution has been felt in the
Commons, where representation is geographically based, rather than in the
House of Lords. Nonetheless, progress has been slow. A survey conducted

---

[2] HC Deb, 21 October 1999, col. 630.

Figure 7.1. Key devolution events at Westminster to July 2000

30 July 1998	House of Commons Procedure Committee starts an investigation into 'The Procedural Consequences of Devolution', and calls for evidence
2 Dec. 1998	House of Commons Scottish Affairs Committee reports on 'Multi-layer Democracy'
December 1998	White Paper published on House of Lords reform, and announcement that a Royal Commission will be established to consider reform options
13 Jan. 1999	Procedure Committee's first report is published, comprising a memorandum from government Leader of the House, Margaret Beckett
10 Feb. 1999	Margaret Beckett makes a proposal to the Modernisation Committee that a new Standing Committee on English Regional Affairs should be established
13 April 1999	Modernisation Committee proposes establishment of 'Westminster Hall', with parallel plenary sessions to House of Commons chamber
14 April 1999	Procedure Committee second report, on Grand Committees
6 May 1999	Elections in Scotland and Wales
11 May 1999	House of Commons opposition day debate on impact of devolution on Westminster
19 May 1999	Procedure Committee publishes final report
1 July 1999	Power transferred to devolved institutions
7 July 1999	First Welsh questions post devolution – Speaker intervenes
12 July 1999	Speaker's statement setting down limitations on parliamentary questions
15 July 1999	William Hague speech to Centre for Policy Studies, calling for 'English votes on English laws'
1 Oct. 1999	Memorandum of Understanding between the Scottish, Welsh and UK institutions, including assemblies, is published
19 Oct. 1999	Government response to Procedure Committee report published
21 Oct. 1999	Commons debate on Procedure Committee report
25 Oct. 1999	Motion agreed governing parliamentary questions
20 Jan. 2000	Royal Commission on Reform of the House of Lords reports
11 April 2000	Standing Committee on Regional Affairs moved, debated and agreed

by the Constitution Unit shortly before the 2000 summer recess, a year after devolution went live, found that only 59 per cent of MPs felt that devolution had yet had a significant impact on Westminster. However, MPs appreciated that there is more change to come — 86 per cent of members agreed that devolution would have a significant impact in the future.

There have been two major investigations by House of Commons committees to anticipate changes necessary to respond to the new territorial politics. An early attempt was made by the Scottish Affairs Committee to alert government and parliament to some of the consequences of devolution in their 1997–98 inquiry into *Multi-Layer Democracy*.[3] This was a careful investigation which sought to anticipate the impact on Scotland of introducing a new layer of elected government. The committee considered how relationships might develop between MPs and MSPs, and the institutions in London and Edinburgh, although its main focus was not parliament itself.

In 1998, the Procedure Committee took up the baton and turned the focus on Westminster, with the launch of its inquiry into the *Procedural Consequences of Devolution*.[4] This was a strangely introverted exercise, in which the Committee took evidence almost exclusively from their fellow MPs.[5] The Government's initial memorandum and subsequent response to the Committee was minimalist, making the Committee's report appear radical by comparison.[6] The Procedure Committee reported six weeks before devolution went live on 1 July 1999. However the Commons did not debate its report until 21 October.

The Procedure Committee sought to investigate a wide range of issues, and many of its recommendations were sensible anticipatory adjustments. These are discussed throughout the chapter. Among the issues it considered were:

- The scope of legislation to be debated at Westminster, and new procedures for its scrutiny;
- Questions to ministers and rules of debate;
- The work of the territorial Select Committees and Grand Committees, and
- The relationships between MPs and members of devolved assemblies.

Each of these is discussed in more detail below.

---

[3] *The Operation of Multi-Layer Democracy*, Scottish Affairs Committee Second Report of Session 1997-98, HC 460-I, 2 December 1998.

[4] The Committee's report, *The Procedural Consequences of Devolution* (HC 185) was published on 19 May 1999.

[5] Of the 39 written memoranda received by the Committee, only four came from outside the House. Eight out of the nine sessions of oral evidence were devoted to hearing from their fellow MPs, in particular from the three territorial Select Committees on Scottish, Welsh and Northern Ireland Affairs.

[6] The Government's memorandum was published in *Procedural Consequences of Devolution: Interim Report*, Procedure Committee, HC 148, 13 January 1999. Their response to the committee's recommendations was published as *First Special Report*, Procedure Committee, HC 814, 19 October 1999.

At the start of its report, the Committee set down some general principles. Paragraph 1 stated that:

> We agree with the Government and the great majority of our witnesses that there should be an 'evolutionary' approach; our recommendations are intended to assist the House in the first stage of this evolution since some issues need to be resolved at a fairly early stage, even though the arrangements made may well have to be adapted in the light of experience. We do not attempt a definitive account of all the changes which might be needed; in the light of this the Committee intends a full review of the procedural consequences of devolution in due course.[7]

Further principles were set out in paragraph 5, which stated that:

> [I]n passing the legislation which underlies devolution, parliament has agreed that certain powers and responsibilities should pass from it to the devolved legislatures; parliamentary procedure or custom should not be called in aid to undermine that decision.

Also:

> [T]here should be as few procedural barriers as possible to co-operation between Members of Parliament and Members of other legislatures, where such co-operation is desired.

The Committee correctly anticipated that it would not be possible to deal with all the issues arising from devolution immediately and that it would be necessary to keep matters under review. In the main, the chamber has adhered to the principles it set down, with slow progress being made to adapt. The issues facing the House of Commons can be broadly broken down into two categories. Firstly, how matters relating to Scotland, Wales, and Northern Ireland should be dealt with at Westminster post-devolution. Secondly, the impact that devolution should have on the way in which English matters (or non-devolved matters across England and Wales) should be treated. These issues are addressed in the two sections that follow.

Scottish, Welsh, and Northern Irish Matters

Legislation
The most obvious impact which devolution has had on Westminster is the disappearance of many matters relating to the devolved areas from its legislative work. All matters previously the responsibility of the Scottish Office, and thus governed by Scottish Bills, are now the responsibility of the Scottish Parliament. In Wales, primary legislative power has not been devolved, but delegated powers previously given to the Secretary of State now reside with the Assembly. Thus much primary legislation governing Scotland and secondary legislation governing Wales disappeared from the work of

---

[7] *The Procedural Consequences of Devolution*, Procedure Committee Fourth Report of Session 1998-99, HC 185, 19 May 1999.

Westminster. This might be expected to have an impact on the overall work-load of parliament, although there is no sign of that yet; but it does seem likely to have an impact on the workload of MPs from the devolved areas, particularly Scotland.

The doctrine of parliamentary sovereignty was respected in the devolution legislation, meaning that, in principle, the Westminster parliament continues to have the right to legislate on any devolved matter. How to manage the boundaries between Westminster and the Scottish Parliament, in particular, has thus been the subject of some debate.

The matter was considered during the Procedure Committee's inquiry. In its memorandum to the committee, the Government stated that:

> None of the devolution legislation affects the House's ability to pass legislation on any matter. For all public Bills, the Government would expect that a convention would be adopted that Westminster would not normally legislate with regard to devolved matters without the consent of the devolved body. The Government is likely to oppose any Private Member's Bill which seeks to alter the law on devolved subjects in Scotland or Northern Ireland. It will remain a question of judgement for individual Members whether to introduce legislation on an issue which parliament has already decided should be devolved, unless it is clear that the proposal has the support of the devolved body concerned.[8]

These principles were supported by the Procedure Committee, which concluded that they would best be put into practice through convention. In October 1999, the *Memorandum of Understanding* between the Scottish, Welsh and UK institutions set down the guidelines for Westminster:

> The United Kingdom Parliament retains authority to legislate on any issue, whether devolved or not. It is ultimately for Parliament to decide what use to make of that power. However, the UK Government will proceed in accordance with the convention that the UK Parliament would not normally legislate with regard to devolved matters except with the agreement of the devolved legislature. The devolved administrations will be responsible for seeking such agreement as may be required for this purpose on an approach from the UK Government.[9]

The principle that Westminster will not legislate on Scottish devolved matters without the consent of the Scottish Parliament has become known as the 'Sewel Convention', following the contribution of Scottish Office minister, Lord Sewel, in the debate on the Scotland Bill.[10]

---

[8] *Procedural Consequences of Devolution: Interim Report*, Procedure Committee First Report of Session 1998-99, HC 148, 13 January 1999, para. 15.

[9] *Memorandum of Understanding and Supplementary Agreements*, Cm 4444, para. 13.

[10] Lord Sewel stated that 'we envisage that there could be instances where it would be more convenient for legislation on devolved matters to be passed by the United Kingdom Parliament. However, as happened in Northern Ireland earlier in the century, we would expect a convention to be established that Westminster would not normally legislate with regard to devolved matters in Scotland without the consent of the Scottish parliament'. (HL Deb, 21 July 1998, col. 791).

Speaking to the Scottish Parliament, First Minister Donald Dewar explained that this meant:

> The usual rule will be that legislation about devolved subjects in Scotland will be enacted by the Scottish Parliament. From time to time, however, it may be appropriate for a Westminster Act to include provisions about such matters. That might be the case, for example, where the two Administrations agree that there should be one regime of regulation with application on a UK-wide or GB-wide basis...I remind members that the Scottish Parliament will be able to amend or repeal legislation made at Westminster in so far as its provisions fall within this parliament's competence. That is the case for existing legislation, for this session's Bills at Westminster that affect Scotland and for future acts of the UK Parliament.

Although this facility exists in principle, it might have been assumed that it would be used rarely, if ever, in practice. In fact it was used for four Bills in the 1998–9 session, and another 10 Bills in the 1999–2000 session. These Bills are listed in Figure 7.2.

Figure 7.2. Westminster legislation 1999–2000 dealing with devolved Scottish matters

Bills tabled under Sewel convention in 1999/2000 session
Care Standards Bill
Government Resources and Accounts Bill
Insolvency Bill
Political Parties, Elections and Referendums Bill
Race Relations (Amendment) Bill
Regulation of Investigatory Powers Bill
Representation of the People Bill
Sea Fishing Grants (Charges) Bill
Sexual Offences (Amendment) Bill
Welfare Reform and Pensions Bill

Unfinished Bills from 1998/9 Session
Electronic Communications Bill
Financial Services and Markets Bill
Food Standards Bill
Limited Liability Partnerships Bill

In each case, the consent of the Scottish Parliament was sought and given for Westminster to proceed with the Bill. Consent was given shortly after devolution, on 23 June 1999, to proceed with the four Bills which had not yet completed their passage at Westminster but covered Scottish devolved matters. Throughout 1999/2000, this practice continued, despite the Scottish Parliament's capacity to legislate for itself. In one case, this was partly driven by necessity. The Sexual Offences (Amendment) Bill, which sought to equalise the age of consent for heterosexual and homosexual sex, was first introduced in the House of Commons in the 1998–9 session. This Bill was required to enact an international commitment, as the UK Government had been found to be in breach of the European Convention on Human Rights for maintaining an age differential. However, the Bill did not complete its legislative passage due to the House of Lords' opposition to reducing the gay age of consent to 16. The Bill was reintroduced in the new session, with a government pledge to use the Parliament Acts if necessary to override the Lords' objections. However, the terms of the Acts require that an identical Bill be reintroduced in the second session, meaning that government plans would have been prevented if the Bill had been amended to exclude Scotland. In the event, leaving this legislation to Westminster probably suited the Scottish Executive very well, given the difficulties they faced when seeking to lift the restrictions of Section 28 in Scotland (see chapter 2).

The extent of this form of co-operation is, however, somewhat surprising. It seems likely that such arrangements will become less common as devolution beds down and statute law in Scotland and the remainder of the UK diverges. It is certainly difficult to imagine such extensive co-operation should the Scottish Executive come to be dominated in future by parties in opposition at Westminster.

As far as Wales is concerned, the relationship is very different. The Welsh White Paper stated:

> Parliament will continue to be the principal law maker for Wales. The Assembly will need to establish a close partnership with Members of Parliament representing Welsh constituencies. They will continue to be involved in considering new legislation that applies to Wales, and to represent their constituents on all matters.[11]

It will be interesting to study the degree to which Welsh MPs develop distinct roles, representing the interests of government and opposition in the Assembly in debate over primary legislation affecting Wales. There have been moves from the Assembly to facilitate input into primary legislation affecting Wales, including a call for an inquiry by the Welsh Affairs Committee into the matter. The Welsh Cabinet have discussed how best to influence Westminster legislation and have agreed that it would be best to seek a 'Welsh slot' in the UK legislative programme each year.

There have been some tensions in the first year over the extent to which Westminster delegates powers to the Assembly, and no consistency in how Welsh matters are delineated. In some cases, such as the Learning and Skills Bill and Care Standards Bill, debated during the 1999–2000 session, there

---

[11] *A Voice For Wales: The Government's Proposals for a Welsh Assembly*, Cm 3718, July 1997, para. 3.37.

have been explicit Welsh sections, but there has been little consistency between Bills.[12]

One area of work which no longer falls under Westminster's responsibilities is the scrutiny of delegated legislation for Scotland or for Wales: this is now done by the devolved assemblies. A change to standing orders was agreed on 25 October 1999, with the result that statutory instruments made in Scotland and Wales would no longer be scrutinised by the Joint Committee on Statutory Instruments at Westminster. The change potentially lightens slightly the workload of that committee (though set against the general rise in statutory instruments this seems likely to be marginal). Of greater significance may be the new procedures for scrutiny, and possible amendment, of delegated legislation in Scotland and Wales: these raise the possibility that, in time, Parliament may seek greater control over statutory orders and instruments laid at Westminster, which cannot currently be amended.

Restricting the Scope of Questions and Debate
The restrictions upon business at Westminster post-devolution extend well beyond legislative scrutiny. A good deal of energy has been expended on discussing the appropriate rules for questions and debate on Scottish and Welsh matters. The situation was explained in the *Memorandum of Understanding*, as follows:

> The United Kingdom Parliament retains the absolute right to debate, enquire into or make representations about devolved matters. It is ultimately for Parliament to decide what use to make of that power, but the UK Government will encourage the UK Parliament to bear in mind the primary responsibility of devolved legislatures and administrations in these fields.
>
> The devolved legislatures will be entitled to debate non-devolved matters, but the devolved executives will encourage each devolved legislature to bear in mind the responsibility of the UK Parliament in these matters.[13]

One of the first of the Procedure Committee's recommendations to be accepted was that question time to the Secretary of State for Scotland should be cut back. It was generally agreed that, despite their considerable reduction in competencies, the territorial Secretaries of State must remain accountable through question times. Ultimately, the reduction agreed was minimal, with Scottish questions continuing to be held every four weeks, but restricted to 30, rather than 40 minutes duration. There was no change to the timing of Welsh question time.

The issue of what could properly be debated on these occasions proved more difficult to address. The Procedure Committee proposed a motion

---

[12] See *Monitoring the National Assembly for Wales May to August 2000*, Institute for Welsh Affairs (also available at http://www.ucl.ac.uk/constitution-unit/) for further details.

[13] *Memorandum of Understanding and Supplementary Agreements*, Cm 4444, paras. 14-15.

setting out the boundaries, but this was not put to the House before devolution went live. The first territorial question time post-devolution was thus rather bumpy, attracting some media attention. The first question to Welsh Office ministers was as follows:

> Mr. Michael Fabricant (Lichfield): If he will make a statement on the state of tourism in Wales, with particular reference to raising standards of bed-and-breakfast accommodation.

> The Parliamentary Under-Secretary of State for Wales (Mr. Peter Hain): I had responsibility for this matter until 1 July. In difficult circumstances, the industry in Wales has performed well. We have allocated an additional £1 million to the Wales tourist board. Quality standards in the bed-and-breakfast sector—

> Madam Speaker: Order. The Minister said that he had responsibility until 1 July. It is 7 July. Is it not a devolved matter?

> Mr. Hain: I understand that, Madam Speaker. I was just explaining that it is a devolved matter, but I was talking about what had gone on until 1 July.

> Madam Speaker: Yes, but if it is a devolved matter, we must pass on.

> Mr. Hain: It is indeed, from 1 July.

> Madam Speaker: Thank you.[14]

This exchange and those subsequent to it concerned a number of members, who went on to raise points of order about their rights to question the Secretary of State regarding his responsibilities and relationships with the Assembly.[15] In order to clarify matters, the Speaker made a statement the following week:

> Following questions to the Secretary of State for Wales on 7 July, Members raised with me points of order relating to the matters on which the Secretary of State can be questioned following the transfer of powers on 1 July. This issue also applies to questions to the Secretary of State for Scotland. I should emphasise that I do not wish the rules relating to questions to become unduly restrictive; but a fundamental rule relating to questions is that they must relate to matters for which Ministers in this House are responsible.
>
> I also note that the Procedure Committee, whose report on the procedural consequences of devolution has still to be debated, recently concluded that the rules for questions must recognise the fact of devolution and limit the range of permissible questions to Ministers at Westminster.
>
> Where matters have been clearly devolved to the Scottish Parliament or to the Welsh Assembly, questions on the details of policy or expenditure would not be in order. Where Secretaries of State have a residual, limited or shared role, questions should relate to that role.

---

14 HC Deb, 7 July 1999, col. 1013.
15 HC Deb, 7 July 1999, cols. 1045-6.

Examples of such limited areas of responsibility are: information that the United Kingdom Government are empowered to require of the devolved Executive; matters that are included in UK legislation relating to Scotland; all primary legislation relating to Wales; matters subject to substantive liaison arrangements between UK Government and the devolved Executives; operation of any remaining administrative powers.

In the case of reserved matters that are the responsibility of other Government Departments, questions should be tabled to the relevant Secretary of State. If questions are inappropriately directed to the Secretaries of State for Scotland or Wales, I would expect Ministers to transfer them to the responsible Department in the usual way.[16]

After these interventions, the House settled down relatively smoothly into its new pattern of questions, with no similar difficulties experienced at the first Scottish question time later in July. The Speaker has been more tolerant in her approach, and members, with the help of the Table Office, have managed to phrase their questions in such a way that they do not cross the line. There is early evidence that the number of written questions to the territorial departments has, unsurprisingly, dropped sharply following devolution. During the 1998/9 session the number of written questions to the Scottish Office was 1,216, whereas by the end of July in the 1999/2000 session the number was only 335. In Wales, the equivalent figures were 1,002 for 1998/9, dropping to 471 in 1999/2000.

On 25 October 1999, after the Procedure Committee's report had been debated by the House, a motion based on its proposal over questions was agreed. This left the scope of questions to the territorial ministers rather ill defined, but has as yet caused few difficulties. The motion agreed was as follows:

That, subject always to the discretion of the Chair, and in addition to the established rules of order on the form and content of questions, questions may not be tabled on matters for which responsibility has been devolved by legislation to the Scottish Parliament or the National Assembly for Wales unless the question:

(a) seeks information which the UK Government is empowered to require of the devolved executive, or
(b) relates to matters which:
(i) are included in legislative proposals introduced or to be introduced in the UK Parliament,
(ii) are concerned with the operation of a concordat or other instrument of liaison between the UK Government and the devolved executive, or
(iii) UK Government ministers have taken an official interest in, or
(c) presses for action by UK ministers in areas in which they retain administrative powers.

---

[16] HC Deb, 12 July 1999, cols. 21–2.

Ministers have used their answers to steer the House away from straying onto devolved matters where this is inappropriate. However, the rules for general debate have not been so tightly drawn, with the Speaker taking a more relaxed attitude if devolved matters are raised in debates. In July 1999, the then Scottish National Party (SNP) deputy Leader, John Swinney, raised a point of order in an attempt to restrict a debate from dealing with matters devolved in Scotland:

> ...the title of this afternoon's Opposition day debate on health care provision in the United Kingdom...Is it appropriate for a debate on health care provision in the United Kingdom to take place in the House of Commons, bearing in mind the fact that the Scotland Act 1998 has come into effect and legislative competence on health policy has been transferred from Westminster to Edinburgh, or is this another example of the Conservative party's inability to come to terms with constitutional change?

Dr Swinney was frustrated by Madam Speaker's reply that:

> No question of order arises. Let me tell the hon. Gentleman that the devolution statutes have, of course, altered ministerial responsibility, and they therefore affect questions and Adjournment debates to which such responsibility is directly linked, but debates on abstract motions, such as the one to which the hon. Gentleman refers...are not limited in the same way.[17]

It is somewhat ironic that the SNP is raising such issues at Westminster, when it is also testing the margins of procedure in the Scottish Parliament by pressing debates there on reserved matters as they apply to Scotland (see chapter 2). This is another area where tensions are liable to rise in the future, especially if and when the two administrations are controlled by opposing political groups. As the Scottish Affairs Committee inquiry noted:

> ...in a climate where the Scottish Parliament, like its analogues in Spain, debates reserved matters, and where the European Parliament regularly debates matters which are strictly outwith its remit, [restricting debate at Westminster] might prove neither acceptable nor enforceable.[18]

The Territorial Committees

One way in which Britain's territorial politics were already evident in the House of Commons, prior to devolution, was through the system of territorial committees.[19] For several years, there have been, for each of Scotland and Wales, three distinct forms of committee. First, the Select Committees,

---

[17] HC Deb, 20 July 1999, col. 967.

[18] *The Operation of Multi-Layer Democracy*, Scottish Affairs Committee Second Report of Session 1997-98, HC 460-I, 2 December 1998, para. 82.

[19] For a description of the territorial committee arrangements see J.A.G. Griffith and M. Ryle, *Parliament: Functions, Practice and Procedures*, London: Sweet and Maxwell, 1989; V. Bogdanor, *Devolution in the United Kingdom*, Oxford: Opus, 1999, pp.115-7 and 161-2. For further discussion see also R. Hazell, 'Westminster: Squeezed from Above and Below', in R. Hazell (ed.), *Constitutional Futures*, Oxford: Oxford University Press, 1999.

which scrutinise the work of the Secretary of State and territorial department. Second, the Standing Committees, which were constituted to take the committee stage of Bills certified by the Speaker as relating exclusively to the territory and had a party balance reflecting that of the House of Commons.[20] The Grand Committees comprised all MPs representing constituencies in the territory concerned, and had various powers including taking second and third readings of non-controversial Bills relating exclusively to the territory, questioning ministers, taking statements and holding general debates.

Following devolution and the subsequent reduction in Scottish and Welsh business at Westminster, there were inevitable questions about the need for such a plethora of Scottish and Welsh committees. The Standing Committees were constituted only on an *ad hoc* basis, but the status of the Select Committees, and especially the Grand Committees (which were originally a kind of substitute for devolution), was brought into some doubt.

These matters formed a central part of the Procedure Committee's inquiry, and a range of views were expressed. The Government's memorandum to the Committee proposed that the Grand Committees should remain, and could have a role in debating reserved matters as applied to each territory. However, whilst the Procedure Committee was sitting, the House agreed on an experimental basis to set up a parallel plenary chamber known as Westminster Hall (although it actually sits in the Grand Committee Room off Westminster Hall) to allow more time for adjournment debates and discussion of committee reports.[21] The Procedure Committee was concerned that it would be inequitable to retain the Scottish, Welsh, and Northern Irish Grand Committees to debate territorial matters if a similar forum was not available for English members. However, it felt that an English Grand Committee, with over 500 members, was impracticable. As a consequence, the committee proposed that the Grand Committees should be suspended for the duration of the Westminster Hall experiment, on the basis that 'Westminster Hall could provide a forum for debate on territorial matters.'[22]

The Government's response to the Procedure Committee's report however stated that it had concerns about suspending the Grand Committees, although it acknowledged that their role would need to change. In the debate on the report, Leader of the House, Margaret Beckett, indicated that it was too early to make a decision on the future of the Committees and was backed by the shadow Leader, Sir George Young, who proposed that their status be

---

[20] The committees generally comprised members only from the territory concerned. However during the periods when the Conservatives had few members in Scotland and Wales, English Conservative members were included on the committees to balance party strengths.

[21] The experiment is modeled on the Main Committee in Australia, and stems from the report of the Modernisation Committee: *Sittings of the House in Westminster Hall*, HC 194, April 1999.

[22] *Procedural Consequences of Devolution: Second Interim Report*, Procedure Committee, HC 376, 15 April 1999.

reviewed after a year. Suggested new roles for the Grand Committees included a greater focus on reserved matters as related to the territories, and potentially forging links with the Scottish Parliament and Welsh Assembly. Others, including the SNP, have alleged that the territorial committees — particularly the Scottish Grand Committee — have been retained unnecessarily in order to provide a role for Scottish and Welsh MPs left aimless following devolution.

There was rather more agreement over the need to retain the territorial Select Committees, which the Procedure Committee proposed were needed to scrutinise the (albeit reduced) work of the Secretary of State and also 'on occasion' the policies of other departments as relating to each territory. It was suggested that the Select Committees should take on a liaison role with the Assemblies and Parliament.[23] This chimed with the earlier proposals of the Scottish Affairs Committee, which envisaged new roles for itself post-devolution when it carried out its investigation into 'multi-layer democracy'. It emphasised the opportunities for building relationships with the new Scottish institutions, including possible future joint sittings with MSPs, and scrutiny of reserved matters as applied to Scotland. The committee even proposed possible development of a new Scottish committee 'which would scrutinise legislation for possible implications for Scotland', stating that: 'we do not think that other departmental Select Committees, containing in some cases none or at most one or two Scottish MPs, would be able adequately to carry out these functions.'[24]

Another idea, proposed by a working group of the Study of Parliament Group, when it gave evidence to the Procedure Committee on Westminster and the Welsh Assembly, was for a broader territorial committee which would encompass the roles of Grand, Select and Standing Committees. This could carry out inquiries, scrutinise draft Bills in terms of their effect on Wales (maybe facilitating amendments from the Assembly), and would liaise with the new Welsh institutions. Such a committee might either comprise MPs alone, or might even include AMs amongst its membership.

Either this proposal or that of the Procedure Committee would have resulted in just one permanent committee carrying out the various duties appropriate to each territory (with the possible addition of a standing committee as and when the need arose). This would have been a more coherent result than that which we are currently left with, where the lines of responsibility between the Select and Grand Committees are now blurred, with each searching for a new role. There is also a great lack of clarity about

---

[23] This proposal was agreed by an amendment to the committees' standing orders, on 25 October 1999. This incorporated 'relations with the Scottish Parliament' and 'relations with the National Assembly for Wales' into the responsibilities of the Scottish and Welsh Affairs committees, respectively.

[24] *The Operation of Multi-Layer Democracy*, Scottish Affairs Committee Second Report of Session 1997-98, HC 460-I, 2 December 1998, para. 86.

the appropriate forum for debating the Scottish and Welsh impacts of government policy in reserved areas. As Liberal Democrat constitutional affairs spokesman, Robert Maclennan, pointed out in the debate on the Procedure Committee report, the territorial committees cannot take on the role of debating reserved matters without creating overlap or conflict with the work of the departmental Select Committees. The Scottish Affairs Committee proposed that these departmental committees are currently inadequate due to their lack of Scottish representation (the current membership of Select Committees is shown in Figure 7.5, below). In Wales, the pressure to take a territorial perspective is likely to be greater, due to the greater scope for seeking to bring a Welsh perspective to future Westminster Bills. There are thus tensions between two possible approaches, each of which would see a greater segmentation by territory of Westminster's work. One would see a broadening of the role of the Scottish, Welsh, and Northern Irish committees, to take on more reserved matters and possible scrutiny of all-UK Bills, whilst the departmental committees become *de facto* English committees. The other is for all Select Committees to take a more overtly territorial role, with a spread of representation from England, Scotland, Wales, and Northern Ireland as appropriate. This would see Westminster adopting a more conventional federal structure, as applies in some overseas states.[25]

In terms of the actual operation of the committees in the first year of devolution, the Welsh Grand Committee met five times, the Scottish Grand four times, and the Northern Ireland Grand three times, during the 1999–2000 parliamentary session to July. The topics of discussion have been as varied as they were before devolution (see Figure 7.3). The Grand Committees have little effective power and have continued in their role as general talking shops.

The Role of MPs
The changes in Scotland and Wales, and latterly Northern Ireland, raise big questions about the role of MPs who represent constituencies in those areas. As discussed above, there are many new restrictions upon members' ability to engage in parliamentary business with relation to the territories, although in Wales there are also new opportunities. But the difficulty relating to members' role does not end there, as the arrival of a new cohort of politicians in the parliament and Assemblies creates possible conflict about local work as well.

Any impact in this area is likely to be felt slowly, not least because of the large number of Westminster members holding 'dual mandates' as members of the devolved assemblies. In Scotland, 15 MPs were elected as MSPs, 14 of them for their Westminster constituency and one for a list seat, and three

---

[25] See for example, the descriptions of the German federal Bundesrat in M. Russell, *Reforming the House of Lords: Lessons from Overseas*, Oxford University Press, 2000.

Figure 7.3. Work of the Grand Committees, 1999–2000 session (to July)

Scottish Grand Committee	Welsh Grand Committee	Northern Ireland Grand Committee

Statements:
Poverty in Scotland
Budget Implications
National Textile Strategy
Government Jobs (Dundee)
International Development
  (Scottish Contribution)
	Statements:
	Welsh GDP
	Radioactivity (Irish Sea)
	Sheepmeat Regime
	Comprehensive Spending
	  Review	

Debates:
New Deal and Youth
  Employment
Effect of the High Pound
Pensioner Poverty
Size of the Scottish
  Parliament
Employment Policy
	Debates:
	Government's Legislative
	  Programme and
	  Pre-Budget Report
	The Budget Statement and
	  its Implications for Wales
	Health Expenditure
	Welsh Economy
	Social Exclusion in Wales
		Debates:
		State of Northern
		  Ireland
		Agriculture
		Terrorist Related
		  Deaths
		Devolution in
		  Northern Ireland

	Legislation:
	Local Government Bill
		Legislation:
		Draft Appropriation
		  (Northern Ireland)
		  Order 2000

MSPs are members of the House of Lords. In Wales, seven AMs elected were also MPs, and one was a peer.[26] Ten of the 18 Northern Ireland MPs now also hold seats in the Assembly, and one Assembly member sits in the House of Lords. In total 31 MPs and five peers are now members of the devolved assemblies, with all three Speakers in the assemblies holding seats in the House of Lords. The number of members holding dual mandates in Scotland and Wales will fall sharply at the next general election, when most of them have announced they will stand down from Westminster. But in the first years of devolution, their presence will have helped a little to ease potential problems of liaison between the devolved assemblies and Westminster.

On the matter of local work, there is every possibility of turf wars between MPs and MSPs or AMs representing the same constituency or the regional list for the area. Potential problems lie ahead as members from competing parties — or even the same party — seek kudos through work with local businesses or other organisations or their local parties. The problem is particularly acute with respect to 'constituency casework' — the social work

---

[26] Following the resignation of Alun Michael as a list AM, all the remaining six represent the same constituency in both bodies.

function for individuals which has recently taken up a growing part of MPs' time.[27]

It is too early to be sure how these relationships are working out in practice, but the problem was put succinctly by the Scottish Affairs Committee in 1998:

> Even if the role of local government remains unchanged, the proliferation of elected representatives may confuse constituents. Even now, they often write to MPs rather than to local councillors and the interpolation of an additional layer (in addition to the already-existing MEPs) may serve to result in an increase in inappropriately-addressed requests.[28]

As early as May 1999, the possible conflict between MSPs and MPs over constituency work relating to Westminster's responsibilities was raised with the House of Commons Speaker:

> Mr. Brian H. Donohoe (Cunninghame, South): On a point of order, Madam Speaker. I have written to you in connection with the matter that I am about to raise. It concerns the role of Members of the Scottish Parliament in matters that are reserved in this House. Is it possible for you to have an early meeting with your counterpart in the Scottish Parliament to resolve what will become — if not nipped in the bud — a possible problem?
>
> Madam Speaker: I am grateful to the hon. Gentleman for giving me notice of the point that he has raised and I appreciate his concern. However, I must make it clear to him and to the House that it is not for me to arbitrate on relationships between constituents and those who represent them in whichever legislature they may sit. That is a problem that will have to be resolved outside the House by good sense and mutual respect, not by me as Speaker of this House.[29]

The Government sought to regulate this relationship through a guidance note on 'Handling Correspondence under Devolution'.[30] This advised that devolved assembly members should be discouraged from corresponding with UK ministers about non-devolved issues. It suggested whilst correspondence of this kind must be dealt with courteously:

> [T]he final reply should make it clear to the member of the devolved assembly that it is the role of Westminster MPs to represent their constituents' interests in non-devolved matters. The reply should urge the member of the devolved assembly, in future, to advise his or her constituents to refer such matters to their Westminster MP.

---

[27] The British Candidate Study 1992 found that MPs spend on average almost 15 hours per week on casework (P. Norris and J. Lovenduski, *Political Recruitment*, Cambridge: Cambridge University Press, 1995).

[28] *The Operation of Multi-Layer Democracy*, Scottish Affairs Committee Second Report of Session 1997-98, HC 460-I, 2 December 1998, para. 77.

[29] HC Deb, 15 May 1999, cols. 641-2.

[30] Cabinet Office Devolution Guidance Note 2, September 1999.

One place to look for inspiration in how to prevent interference by MSPs and AMs at Westminster was the Scottish Parliament itself, where similar tensions had arisen between constituency MSPs and list members, who were potentially in competition over constituency casework (see chapter 2). The competition was exacerbated because Labour dominates amongst constituency MSPs, while the Liberal Democrats and opposition parties are more strongly represented amongst list MSPs. This matter was partially dealt with in the Parliament by list members being denied part of the staff allowance made to constituency members, on account of their supposedly lesser constituency workload. This gave rise to a proposal, put in an early day motion, that Scottish MPs should be subject to lower allowances than English MPs at Westminster.[31] The matter was raised in the Commons by a Conservative member:

> Mrs. Eleanor Laing (Epping Forest): Will the Leader of the House make time in the near future for a debate on an important matter relating to the way in which parliament spends taxpayers' money — namely, the subject matter of early-day motion 709 on allowances for hon. Members representing Scottish constituencies?

> The right hon. Lady may not as yet be aware that earlier this week the Scottish Parliament passed a motion that Members who sit for regional constituencies — those who have been elected on a list — should have a reduced allowance on the grounds that they do not have constituency responsibilities. Given that, after 1 July, Members of this House who sit for Scottish constituencies will have reduced constituency responsibilities because many of those responsibilities will be taken over by MSPs, surely the House ought to have an opportunity to debate whether Scottish Members of this House should continue to receive the same allowance as Members who still have full constituency responsibilities.

> Mrs. Beckett: I certainly cannot undertake to find time for such a debate in the near future. I strongly hold the view, as the hon. Lady will know, that there is not and should not be such a thing as two different kinds of Member of Parliament. I should be surprised if my hon. Friends who sit for Scottish and Welsh constituencies — of course, they are only hon. Friends; there are no Scottish or Welsh Members on the Conservative Benches — find their work loads reduced. The hon. Lady is asking me to comment on a decision made by the Scottish Parliament, for which I am happy to say that I do not have responsibility.[32]

The issue of what Scottish members do with their time at Westminster will be eased marginally by the proposed reduction in their numbers as a result of the

---

[31] EDM 709 read: 'That this House notes the decision of the Scottish Parliament to reduce the allowances of regional Members of the Scottish Parliament on the grounds that they do not have constituency responsibilities; further notes that honourable Members representing Scottish constituencies will also have fewer responsibilities after 1st July 1999; and consequently invites the Senior Salaries Review Board to consider whether it is appropriate for honourable Members representing Scottish constituencies to be paid an allowance similar to that of other honourable Members.'

[32] HC Deb, 10 June 1999, cols. 794-5.

Scotland Act. Section 86 of the Act requires that the Boundary Commission for Scotland applies the electoral quota for England in their next review of Scottish seats in 2005, which would result in a reduction in the number of Scottish MPs from 72 to around 58. The Government is firm about this reduction, although it has hinted that it might not insist upon the corresponding reduction to the size of the Scottish Parliament that is required by the Act.[33]

The Conservatives have been critical of the fact that the reduction in the number of Scottish MPs — which will see a cut in Labour numbers in the Commons — will not happen until after the next election. A Private Member's Bill introduced by Lord Mackay of Arbrecknish during the 1998–9 parliamentary session sought to bring forward this reduction to the next election.[34] It would also have decoupled the reduction in Scottish MPs at Westminster from the corresponding reduction in the number of MSPs (something which was strongly backed by the Scottish Affairs Committee inquiry and by many in Scotland). Although the Bill was passed by the House of Lords, it did not receive the support of the House of Commons.

No one has explicitly addressed the need to make a similar reduction in the number of Welsh MPs, even though Wales is equally over-represented (with 40 MPs when an equal quota would supply 33). However, the Liberal Democrats favour cutting the overall size of the House of Commons to approximately 450, partly in response to devolution, and the Conservatives have adopted a similar principle.[35]

Access to the Westminster precincts for members of the devolved assemblies (a privilege that is extended to MEPs) was a matter considered by the Procedure Committee. However, the Committee rather preciously, and to the frustration of the Government, deferred a decision on this matter until it was clear whether reciprocal arrangements would apply. A weightier issue, indirectly connected to devolution, faced Westminster at the end of the 1999–2000 session. The Disqualifications Bill would allow members of the Irish Parliament to serve as members of the House of Commons. The Government claimed it was a modest Bill, removing the last major inconsistency in the way UK electoral law applies to Commonwealth and Irish citizens. However, when the Bill was debated in the House of Lords the day before the summer recess, some peers objected, claiming it was being rushed

[33] Schedule 1 of the Scotland Act 1998 requires that the constituencies for Scottish Parliament members are 'the [Westminster] Parliamentary constituencies for Scotland'. Responding to a debate on the size of the Scottish Parliament in the Scottish Grand Committee on 12 June 2000, Secretary of State for Scotland John Reid said that if a good case could be made nearer the time for changing the Scotland Act, the Government would consider it. During the passage of the Scotland Act, the Liberal Democrats had argued against a consequential reduction in the size of the Scottish Parliament. It is said that Donald Dewar sympathised with them, but No 10 was against.

[34] The Scottish Parliamentary Constituencies Bill.

[35] See *Reforming Governance in the UK: Policies for Constitutional Reform*, Liberal Democrat Policy Paper 40, September 2000; *Believing in Britain*, Conservative Party, September 2000.

through as a sop to Sinn Féin. They claimed that while it was permissible to hold a dual mandate between Westminster and a devolved legislature or the European Parliament, it was wrong to allow dual membership in two sovereign parliaments.[36] At the time of writing the fate of the Bill is unknown.

English Matters and the 'English Question'

Whilst the immediate impact of devolution has been on Scottish, Welsh, and Northern Irish matters, probably the most controversial issue at Westminster as a result has been the adaptations which might need to be made to accommodate English (or English and Welsh) matters.

The controversy has centred primarily around the 'West Lothian question', first asked during the devolution debates in the 1970s by Tam Dalyell, then Labour member for that Scottish constituency. The question relates to English matters in a situation of asymmetrical devolution, and is proving of particular interest to the Conservatives. Conservative leader, William Hague, revived the question in a speech in February 1998, putting it thus:

> For how much longer will the English acquiesce to Scottish Members of the Westminster Parliament having a vote over health, education and other domestic matters in England, when English Members of Parliament (and, indeed, Scottish Members of Parliament) have no vote over similar matters in Scotland?[37]

The West Lothian question, now increasingly referred to as the 'English question' (or at least forming part of it), interests the Conservatives due to their poor representation in Scottish and Welsh seats in the House of Commons. Parliamentary representation following the 1997 general election is shown in Figure 7.4.

The Conservatives currently enjoy no representation in the House of Commons in either Scotland or Wales, and at the 1992 election won only 17 seats in the two nations combined.[38] Labour, in contrast, is more strongly represented in both than it is in England, or the UK as a whole.

The West Lothian question therefore has two aspects. The first problem is one of basic constitutional fairness: whether Scottish MPs should be able to vote on English matters whilst English MPs do not have the equivalent power. However, in a party-dominated parliament the question becomes first and foremost a political one: is it right that a Labour Government should be able to pass legislation for England using the votes of Scottish and/or Welsh MPs, if it does not enjoy a majority amongst English MPs? Given the size of the Labour majority in England now, this appears a somewhat abstract argument. However, the Labour Governments of 1964 and 1974 did not enjoy a

---

[36] HL deb 27 July 2000, cols 705-720.

[37] *Change and Tradition: Thinking Creatively About the Constitution*, speech to Centre for Policy Studies, 24 February 1998.

[38] House of Commons Factsheet No. 61, *General Election Results,* 9 April 1992.

Figure 7.4. Balance of the parties in the House of Commons, May 1997

	Lab	Con	LD	Other	Total
England	328	165	34	2	529
Scotland	56	0	10	6	72
Wales	34	0	2	4	40
Northern Ireland	0	0	0	18	18
Total	418	165	46	30	659

majority in England, and relied on support from MPs representing Scottish and Welsh constituencies.[39] Hence this could present a real challenge to a Labour Government in the future with a reduced Commons majority. In these circumstances, it is not surprising that the Conservatives are seeking to raise the profile of the issue, whilst the Government's attitude is perhaps best summed up by the Lord Chancellor, Lord Irvine, who remarked that '[n]ow that we have devolution up and running, I think the best thing to do about the West Lothian question is to stop asking it'.[40]

A range of options for resolving, or ameliorating, the English question have been put forward and it remains unclear which, if any, of them, will prove to be the cure. Four of these options are discussed below: an English Parliament, or proxy English Parliament, 'English votes on English laws', new English structures at Westminster, or further constitutional reform.

Westminster as an English Parliament
One option that has been floated, though with little success, is that of an English parliament to balance the parliament and assemblies in the other nations of the UK. When William Hague raised the English question in 1998, this is one of four options which he put on the table.[41] There is now a fully-fledged Campaign for an English Parliament which holds Wednesday vigils, waving St George's flags in Parliament Square. However, the proposal is problematic. Those who make it are, in effect, demanding a full-blown federation, in which the four historic nations would form the component parts. But England, with four-fifths of the population would be hugely dominant: even more dominant than Prussia in the old Germany. It would be seriously over-balanced, with the English Parliament as important

---

[39] Figures supplied by House of Commons Library.

[40] HL Deb, 25 June 1999, col. 1201. Labour members with Scottish roots tend to have particularly little sympathy for the West Lothian question, given that the Conservatives decided policy for Scotland for 18 years without ever having a majority of Scottish MPs.

[41] *Change and Tradition: Thinking Creatively About the Constitution*, speech to Centre for Policy Studies, 24 February 1998.

Figure 7.5. Membership of departmental Select Committees, July 2000

	England	Scotland	Wales	Northern Ireland	Total
Agriculture	10		1		11
Culture, Media and Sport	10	1			11
Defence	10	1			11
Education and Employment	17				17
Environment, Transport and Regional Affairs	15	1		1	17
Foreign Affairs	9	1	2		12
Health	11				11
Home Affairs	11				11
International Development	9	1	1		11
Northern Ireland Affairs	9			4	13
Scottish Affairs	2	9			11
Social Security	9	1	1		11
Trade and Industry	9	2			11
Treasury	12				12
Welsh Affairs	2		9		11
TOTAL	145	17	14	5	181

as the Westminster Parliament. And there appears to be no strong public demand. William Hague has since focused his attention on the need for 'English votes on English laws', as detailed below.[42]

Part of the solution may lie in Westminster gradually developing its role as a proxy for an English Parliament within the wider shell of the Union parliament. Pre-devolution, it was clear when Westminster was operating in Scottish, Welsh, or Northern Ireland mode; post-devolution it may need to become clearer when Westminster is operating in English mode. Over the next few years, there is likely to be greater recognition and formalisation of English business at Westminster through the work of the Select Committees, many of which are largely *de facto* English Committees. This can be seen in part by their membership and the subject matter of their inquiries and reports in the 1999–2000 session, as shown in Figures 7.5 and 7.6.

Figure 7.5 shows there are four Select Committees which are *de facto* English committees in terms of their membership: the Education and Employment, Health, Home Affairs, and Treasury Committees are

---

[42] *Strengthening the Union after Devolution*, speech to Centre for Policy Studies, 15 July 1999.

Figure 7.6. Inquiries by departmental Select Committees, 1999–2000 (to June)[43]

	UK	GB	England & Wales	England	Scotland /Wales/ NI only	Total
Agriculture	5	1	1	1		9
Culture, Media and Sport	8		1	1		10
Defence	23					23
Education and Employment	2	5		7		14
Envt., Transport and Regional Affairs	10	2	2	4		18
Foreign Affairs	9					9
Health				2		2
Home Affairs		1	2	2		5
International Development	10					10
Northern Ireland Affairs					5	5
Scottish Affairs					3	3
Social Security		5				5
Trade and Industry	11	1	1			13
Treasury	4					4
Welsh Affairs					7	7

composed exclusively of English MPs. Scottish, Welsh, and Northern Irish members are largely restricted to their own territorial committees, with only eight Scots, five Welsh, and one Northern Irish member represented outside these committees. English MPs are far better represented, even in proportionate terms, with 132 holding seats on the subject committees. The chance of an English MP sitting on one of the 12 subject committees (as opposed to the three territorial committees) is 1 in 4; for a Scottish or Welsh MP 1 in 8; for a Northern Ireland MP 1 in 20.

The extent to which the scope of committee inquiries is becoming limited post-devolution is as yet unclear. Figure 7.6 shows, for example, that the Agriculture Committee considered five of its nine inquiries to be UK-wide, although agriculture is a devolved matter in all three jurisdictions. Likewise, the committee shadowing the Department of Environment, Transport and the Regions — now a largely English department — carried out 10 UK-wide

---

[43] The information in this table was largely provided by committee clerks, in response to written enquiries.

Figure 7.7. Ministers in the House of Commons, July 2000

Department	Area in which ministers are constituency MP				
	England	Scotland	Wales	N. Ireland	Total
Prime Minister	1				1
Agriculture, Fisheries and Food	3				3
Cabinet Office	3				3
Culture, Media and Sport	4				4
Defence	2				2
Education and Employment	7				7
Environment, Transport and the Regions	7				7
Foreign Office	2	1	1		4
Health	5				5
Home Office	5				5
International Development	1	1			2
Law Officers	3				3
Northern Ireland Office	2	1			3
Scotland Office		3			3
Social Security	3	1			4
Trade and Industry	4	1	1		6
Treasury	4	1			5
Wales Office			2		2
Total	56	9	4		

inquiries in the year. It remains within the formal power of the Westminster committees to investigate devolved issues, but the extent to which they are doing so is unclear without further investigation. As devolution beds down, they may start to draw their boundaries more tightly; or to seek a better fit between the scope of their inquiries and their membership. It is noteworthy that the Agriculture Committee, which conducted mainly UK-wide inquiries, has no MPs from Scotland or Northern Ireland; and that the Treasury Committee, all of whose inquiries were UK-wide, consists solely of English MPs.

The extent to which policy-making is already becoming territorially segmented is further illustrated by Figure 7.7 which shows the areas of the UK from which Commons ministers are drawn. This shows that Scottish members are well represented in departments dealing with all-UK issues, but are now entirely absent from other departments. Likewise, Welsh ministers, of whom there are only two outside the Welsh Office, are restricted to departments in which Westminster retains competence over Wales. A new convention may have emerged leaving certain departments — for example Health, Education and Employment, and Agriculture, the preserve of English members alone. This further restricts the career opportunities and *raison d'être* of Scottish MPs.

'English Votes on English Laws'

The solution to the English question which the Government is reluctant to concede, but which is increasingly being pressed by the Conservative Party and others, is to restrict Scottish MPs' involvement in legislative matters which do not extend to Scotland. This might be achieved either formally through standing orders, or less formally by convention.

Cross-party support was given by the members of the Procedure Committee (nine Labour, three Conservative and two Liberal Democrat) to proposals which would have implemented one form of this arrangement. These proposals would have built on existing standing orders for Scottish business, so that:

> ...the provision allowing the Speaker to certify Bills as relating exclusively to Scotland be transferred to a new Standing Order and adapted so that the Speaker may certify that a Bill relates exclusively to one of the constituent parts of the UK.[44]

This would have enabled the Speaker to identify, for the first time, Bills relating exclusively to England, or England and Wales. The committee then went on to propose a new process for any Bills so identified. Under these arrangements, such Bills would start their Commons passage by being referred to a Second Reading Committee, made up entirely of members of the territory concerned. The Procedure Committee proposed that the existing standing order requiring any Standing Committee (including a Second Reading Committee) to reflect the party balance of the House of Commons be lifted. This would allow the Second Reading Committee to reflect the balance in the area/s concerned. Thus, in future, were the proposal adopted, a Conservative Government might have difficulty getting agreement to Bills relating to Scotland or Wales, whilst a future Labour Government might face difficulties with English Bills. However, these difficulties would not be insurmountable, as the Committee proposed that the whole House would ultimately continue to control the outcome of second reading, and indeed might choose not to refer a Bill to a territorial committee at all. For this, the Procedure

---

[44] *The Procedural Consequences of Devolution*, Procedure Committee Fourth Report of Session 1998-99, HC 185, 19 May 1999, para. 27.

Committee was criticised for ducking the important issue of whether non-English members can vote on exclusively English Bills.[45]

The half-hearted nature of the Committee's proposal allowed the Government to dismiss it easily, stating that '[i]f...it were possible to identify some Bills as relating exclusively to England, it is not clear what benefit this would have for the House'.[46] The Government stated that it would prefer to see such Bills referred to a Grand Committee, although an English Grand Committee would create practical difficulties, due to its size. The Conservatives welcomed the proposal when the Procedure Committee's report was debated, with Sir George Young suggesting that it might be supplemented by Scottish members applying a self-denying ordinance in votes on English and Welsh legislation.[47] However, the views of both the Government and Liberal Democrats were summed up by the Liberal Democrat constitutional affairs spokesman Robert Maclennan:

> The problems that arise in respect of England may be de minimis problems because, as the hon. Member for Glasgow, Cathcart (Mr. Maxton) advised the Committee, it is hard to put one's finger on a purely English piece of legislation. One senses that those who are trying to stir up this issue are doing so not because there is a major constitutional problem but for political reasons of their own.[48]

The Conservative Party has since developed this idea further, and appears set to make 'English votes on English laws' a manifesto issue.[49] Of the four options set out in a speech by William Hague in July 1999, this was the only one considered suitable as a solution to the English question.[50]

These ideas have been developed by the Commission to Strengthen Parliament, established by Hague under the chairmanship of Lord Norton of Louth, which reported in July 2000.[51] The Commission proposed that Bills certified by the Speaker as relating to one of the constituent parts of the UK would be referred to a Bill Grand Committee, comprising all members from the territory concerned (but with rights for others to attend and speak). The committee stage would be taken in a special standing committee, also restricted to members from the territory, and reflecting party strength there, with report

---

[45]   See, for example, Peter Riddell in *The Times*, 25 May 1999.

[46]   Government response to the Fourth Report from the Procedure Committee 1998-99 on the Procedural Consequences of Devolution, HC 185, para 8.

[47]   HC Deb, 21 October 1999, col. 614.

[48]   HC Deb, 21 October 2000, col. 624.

[49]   The commitment appeared in the party's draft manifesto *Believing in Britain*, published in September 2000.

[50]   *Strengthening the Union after Devolution*, speech to Centre for Policy Studies, 15 July 1999. The other three options were a strengthening of English local government, a reduction in the number of Scottish MPs or an English Parliament. The first were considered desirable but insufficient and the third was rejected.

[51]   *Strengthening Parliament*, Report of the Commission to Strengthen Parliament, Conservative Party, July 2000.

stage taken in the Grand Committee. Third reading would take place in the Commons chamber, but with a convention whereby MPs representing constituencies outside the territory would not take part in the debate or vote.

The only legislative initiative to achieve this goal was, somewhat surprisingly, made by a Labour MP. On 28 June 2000, English backbencher Frank Field proposed the House of Commons (Reserved Matters) Bill, under the 10 minute rule. This Bill would have barred by law Scottish or Northern Irish members of parliament from speaking or voting, except on reserved matters. It would also have precluded such members from becoming UK ministers, except in posts relating to reserved matters. Frank Field acknowledged that the main purpose of the Bill was to raise the issue and start a debate and it was defeated by 190 votes to 131.

The matter has, however, been raised by both Conservative and Labour members in relation to legislation discussed in the 1999–2000 session. For example, on 12 June 2000, David Lidington asked in relation to the Government's plan to bring forward legislation on fox hunting:

> When the Bill comes before the House in the next Session, will the Home Secretary confirm that it will apply to England and Wales only, and that any decisions in respect of Scotland will be devolved to the Edinburgh Parliament? If so, will he therefore urge all hon. Members representing Scottish constituencies at Westminster to refrain from taking part in debates and votes on the Bill? Will not this be the first important test of the principle that laws that affect England and Wales should be made by the representatives of England and Wales?[52]

Jack Straw replied:

> It is absurd for members of the Conservative Party; I thought that, above all, they supported the Union. The change that we introduced was to give a degree of devolution to Scotland in order to bind the Union. It is most interesting that Conservative Members now say that they want to break the Union.[53]

Towards the end of the session, another controversy arose over the Criminal Justice (Mode of Trial) Bill, which sought to limit defendants' right to jury trial. This Bill had met difficulties in the House of Lords and been reintroduced as a Commons Bill. Given that its terms applied to the criminal justice system in England and Wales only, Bob Marshall Andrews, MP — a Labour member opposed to the Bill — wrote to all Scottish members urging them to refrain from voting on it. This was reported in the Scottish press. In the event, however, the Bill was passed, on 25 July, by 282 votes to 199, with support of 34 Scottish Labour members. Eight Scottish members (all Liberal Democrat) voted against the Bill. The Scottish members' votes did not, therefore, materially affect the outcome.

[52] HC Deb, 12 June 2000, col. 642.
[53] HC Deb, 12 June 2000, col. 643.

These tensions are currently no real threat to the Labour Government. However, it is clear that they will rise in prominence if Labour's majority is cut at the next general election. If Labour becomes more dependent on the votes of its Scottish supporters, there will be increasing pressure in the next parliament for these members to refrain from voting on controversial matters which no longer relate to Scotland.

A New Forum for English MPs
One sign of the Government responding to pressure to resolve the English question was the establishment of a new Standing Committee on [English] Regional Affairs. This was a revival of a committee which was created in 1975 and last sat in 1978.[54] The proposal to revive it was first made, in February 1999, by Margaret Beckett, the Leader of the House, who said:

> We recognise the need to take account of the regional dimension, and are conscious of the view that the interests of the English regions have, to some extent, been over-looked in recent years. The aim of reviving a regional standing committee would be to provide a forum in which MPs could debate, in a more focused way, matters affecting a specific region or touching on regional affairs generally.[55]

The Modernisation Committee expressed little enthusiasm for the proposal, and it began to appear that the matter had been dropped. However, in April 2000, Margaret Beckett returned to the charge, inviting the House to update the relevant Standing Order 117 and revive the committee. She was unsympathetic to claims that the notion of the committee should be questioned, boldly asserting that:

> The Standing Order was decided in the context of previous moves to introduce devolution for Scotland and Wales. It means that the House has already debated and decided the issue of principle.[56]

Sir George Young, for the Conservatives, suggested a rather different origin:

> A year ago, the Modernisation Committee reflected on this proposition, which had been put to it by the Leader of the House. After discussion, the Government decided — rightly — not to pursue it, so we heard no more for nearly a year. The week before last, in a great hurry, the proposition was taken off its dusty shelf by the Government, following some adverse press coverage of the Government's lack of progress in setting up regional assemblies.[57]

[54] See J. A. G. Griffith and M. Ryle, *Parliament: Functions, Practice and Procedures*, London: Sweet and Maxwell, 1989, p. 361.
[55] Cabinet Office Press Release CAB 36/99, 'English Regions may get a voice at Westminster', 11 February 1999.
[56] HC Deb, 11 April 2000, col. 290.
[57] HC Deb, 11 April 2000 col. 295.

The reformulated committee would be charged with considering 'any matter relating to regional affairs in England which may be referred to it'. Unlike the old committee, which was open to all English members and thus potentially difficult for government to control, it would have 13 core members from English constituencies, whose party balance would reflect that of the whole house, rather than English members. Any other member representing an English constituency would be entitled to take part in proceedings, but not to propose motions or vote. In the debate, Margaret Beckett proposed that the committee would debate matters of interest to the Regional Development Agencies, including economic development, employment and regeneration, and it was suggested that the committee would allow for some parliamentary scrutiny of regional government. The Government appeared to anticipate that the committee would look in turn at issues concerning particular English regions, rather than at English territorial matters in general.

The proposals were intended to provide some symmetry with the Scottish, Welsh, and Northern Irish Grand Committees. But the new committee would fall well short of the proposals of the Procedure Committee and others, as it would have no legislative responsibilities. Its agenda would be dominated by the Government and not by its members, putting it in a weaker position than Select Committees. The Conservatives were dismissive of the proposals, considering them no substitute for separate treatment of English legislation. Sir George Young also raised concerns about the relationship between the new committee and the existing Select Committees, pointing out that many regional matters could be dealt with by the Select Committee on the Environment, Transport and Regional Affairs, whilst:

> ...if the House wanted to examine agriculture in the south-west, fishing in the north-west or the motor industry in the north-east, those subjects come under other Select Committees. The proposal for a Standing Committee on Regional Affairs risks short-circuiting the existing Select Committees.[58]

This confusion on the part of government about where English territorial matters should be discussed mirrors the same dilemmas, discussed above, in relation to committee treatment of Scottish, Welsh, and Northern Irish matters.

The Liberal Democrats proposed amendments to the new standing order which would have increased the membership of the committee to 24 and required its party balance to reflect representation in England, rather than the whole UK. The latter proposal was supported by the Conservatives but defeated by 190 votes to 130, with 29 Scottish and Welsh members voting (25 of them against the amendment).

Listening to the criticisms levelled during the debate, Margaret Beckett indicated that the Government will be open to review and amendment of the

---

[58] HC Deb, 11 April 2000, col. 296.

committee's arrangements over time, and there are possibilities that it could expand its role if pressure for English forums at Westminster grows. Although an English party balance would not have been particularly disadvantageous to Labour at present, the Government will have been mindful of the dangers in creating an English committee which in the future might take on more powers and have a party balance opposed to Labour in government.

The experimental arrangements in Westminster Hall (see page 195) are also part of the process of piecemeal adaptation. In its early months, this forum has debated some regional matters, though perhaps more driven by members' individual constituency interests than anything else.[59] One issue to watch is who attends these debates and whether Westminster Hall becomes another *de facto* English part of the Westminster system. If it does, it is hard to see a role in the short term for the new Standing Committee for Regional Affairs. Notably, no progress appeared to have been made in appointing core members of the committee by the summer recess, some four months after its principle was agreed.

Future Constitutional Reform

The Liberal Democrats have always contended that the solution to the English question lies in further constitutional reform. If Britain were to progress to 'devolution all round', with elected assemblies in the English regions, this would go some way towards redressing the imbalance. The emphasis put on the English question by the Conservative Party, who are opposed to English regional devolution, may ironically be pushing Labour in exactly that direction. As reported in chapter 5, Labour ended the year voicing stronger support for English regional assemblies than previously. Progress in this direction after the next general election might help ease the situation, if some English matters were devolved from Westminster to the English regions, and away from the reach of Scottish and Welsh MPs. English devolution would take the UK towards a more fully federal system, with the likelihood that more federal structures would develop in parliament.

But English devolution is unlikely to be the end of the story, since few are suggesting English regional assemblies with powers equivalent to the Scottish Parliament. Thus many English matters would continue to be discussed at Westminster when equivalent Scottish matters are devolved — leaving questions about the role of Scottish MPs. The scope therefore still exists for future Labour Governments to come under pressure on these issues if they do not enjoy majorities amongst English MPs.

One factor which exacerbates the problem is the current electoral system. This tends to give a disproportionate number of English seats to the

---

[59] The committee has discussed, for example, housing in Norfolk, NHS provision in Oxfordshire, the economy of the East Midlands and prospects for shipbuilding and related industries on the River Tyne.

Conservatives, and a disproportionate number of Scottish and Welsh seats to Labour. The current make up of the House of Commons was given in Figure 7.4 above. Figure 7.8 demonstrates how the results of the 1997 election might have looked under Lord Jenkins' proposed system of 'alternative vote plus',[60] or under a more proportional additional member system with 50 per cent of members elected in constituencies and 50 per cent on regional lists. The political aspect of the West Lothian question is illustrated by the fact that Labour currently holds 62 per cent of seats in England (on 44 per cent of the votes cast in the 1997 election), but 78 per cent of seats in Scotland (with 46 per cent of the votes), and a huge 85 per cent of seats in Wales (with 55 per cent of the votes). Clearly, the inclusion of Scottish and Welsh members in votes at Westminster introduces a large Labour advantage.

Figure 7.8. Projected results of 1997 general election under more proportional voting systems[61]

	AV+ with 15% 'top up'				Under 50/50 AMS			
	Lab	Con	LD	other	Lab	Con	LD	other
England	301	150	77	1	246	183	100	0
Scotland	48	5	9	10	34	12	10	16
Wales	29	5	3	3	23	8	5	4
Total	378	160	89	14	303	203	115	20

Under the Jenkins proposals, this situation would be eased, but only slightly. Labour would hold 57 per cent of seats in England, 67 per cent in Scotland and 72 per cent in Wales. Inclusion of Scottish and Welsh members in votes would thus still tip the balance towards Labour, which could translate into a crucial advantage for a Labour Government with a smaller Commons majority. Under a more proportional system, the bias begins to disappear. Labour would hold 47 per cent of seats in both England and Scotland, though still enjoying 57 per cent of seats in Wales: proportions which closely reflect Labour's share of the vote in each country. (Of course, these figures derive from only one election, where Labour did well across the board. In future elections, Labour may have different representation because it enjoys different territorial patterns of support: as it currently does in Wales).

Thus, continuation of the Government's programme of constitutional reform to introduce regional assemblies in England, and a genuinely proportional electoral system, could start to end the controversy over the English

[60] *Report of the Independent Commission on the Voting System*, CM-4090-I, October 1998.

[61] Figures for AV+ taken from *The Performance of the Commission's Schemes for a New Electoral System*, Report to the Independent Commission on the Voting System, P. Dunleavy and H. Margetts, September 1998. Figures for AMS taken from *Making Votes Count*, P. Dunleavy, H. Margetts, B. O'Duffy and S. Weir, Democratic Audit, 1997.

question. In Spain, with asymmetrical devolution all round, and a PR-elected parliament, the question does not arise. However, for the UK this is going to be at best a long-term solution, if any solution at all.

THE UPPER HOUSE

Whilst much energy has gone into debating how devolution will impact on the House of Commons, it is the upper house which most parliamentary systems use to represent territorial politics. In all federal states with two-chamber parliaments, and a growing number of unitary states, the upper house is used to represent the constituent units — be they regions, provinces or states. This is classically seen in the US, where the Senate comprises two representatives of each state, and in Australia where each state has 12 members in the Senate. In some cases, notably the German Bundesrat, the upper house takes particular responsibility for territorial matters, and is organised along strongly territorial lines.[62]

In a quasi-federal Britain, there are thus important potential roles for a reformed House of Lords. It is a chance of history that Lords reform is being actively debated at the same time as devolution; but as a result it provides a unique opportunity to think how Westminster might be re-designed to support and underpin the devolution settlement. The Constitution Unit and others have suggested that one role for the Lords' replacement would be to represent the nations and regions.[63] This could help to counteract the centrifugal political forces released by devolution, and to give the devolved governments and assemblies a stake in the institutions of the centre. How strong a stake would depend upon the form of representation in, and the role given to, the reformed upper house.

The Royal Commission and its Proposals

These were the issues which faced the Royal Commission on Reform of the House of Lords which was established by the Government in February 1999. It also had many other issues to consider, but it was specifically charged in its terms of reference to 'take particular account of the present nature of the constitutional settlement, including the newly devolved institutions'.[64]

---

[62] For fuller discussion of these issues see M. Russell, *Reforming the House of Lords: Lessons from Overseas*, Oxford University Press, 2000; M. Russell, 'The Territorial Role of the Upper House', *Journal of Legislative Studies*, to appear, 2001.

[63] R. Hazell (ed.), *Constitutional Futures*, Oxford University Press, 1999; M. Russell, *Reforming the House of Lords: Lessons from Overseas*, Oxford University Press, 2000; J. Osmond, 'Reforming the House of Lords and Changing Britain' (Fabian Pamphlet 587), London, Fabian Society, 1998; Cabinet Office, *Modernising Parliament — Reforming the House of Lords*, London, The Stationery Office, 1999 (Cm 4183).

[64] *Modernising Parliament — Reforming the House of Lords*. London: The Stationery Office (Cm 4183).

The Royal Commission, which was chaired by Lord Wakeham, was given only 10 months in which to report. This presented it with considerable difficulties. The Commission issued a consultation document and invited submissions, but its tight timetable meant that these were required by the end of April 1999. It thus had little time to consult with the 'newly devolved institutions', which only came into being three months later. Given their other preoccupations as they found their feet, it is hardly surprising that no evidence was received from the new governments or assemblies of Scotland, Wales or Northern Ireland. Evidence was received from five territorial parties,[65] but only Seamus Mallon from Northern Ireland and Dennis Canavan from Scotland gave evidence as individual representatives from the devolved assemblies. Of the 209 expert witnesses recorded by the Royal Commission (most of whom were invited to submit evidence), only 28 were organisations from Scotland, Wales, Northern Ireland or the English regions.

Despite the shortage of evidence, the Commission devoted a whole chapter of its report to 'Giving a Voice to the Nations and Regions'. It recommended that:

> The reformed second chamber should be so constructed that it could play a valuable role in relation to the nations and regions of the United Kingdom, whatever pattern of devolution and decentralisation might emerge in the future.[66]

This was a laudable, if ambitious, aim. The way that the Commission sought to achieve it was primarily through the composition of the chamber, recommending that '[a]t least a proportion of the members of the second chamber should provide a direct voice for the various nations and regions of the United Kingdom.'[67] These members (referred to in the report as 'regional members') would be elected, but only as a minority of the new second chamber. The majority of upper house members would continue to be appointed. The Commission could not agree on the proportion of elected regional members, and offered three models, ranging from 12 to 35 per cent of the whole (which would contain around 550 members in all):

- Model A: 65 regional members selected by a party list system linked to the votes cast for the House of Commons at each general election (there would thus be no direct votes for the upper house). Only one-third of the 12 nations and regions would select their regional members at each election, with members serving three House of Commons terms;
- Model B: 87 directly elected regional members. One third of the nations and regions would select members alongside each European election and

---

[65] The Alliance Party of Northern Ireland, Plaid Cymru, The Scottish Conservative and Unionist Party, The Scottish National Party, and The Welsh Liberal Democrats.

[66] *A House for the Future*, Royal Commission on the Reform of the House of Lords, Cm 4534, January 2000, London, The Stationery Office, Recommendation 25.

[67] *Ibid*, Recommendation 27.

members would serve 15 year terms. Elections would preferably use the 'partially open' list system of proportional representation;

- Model C: 195 regional members directly elected in a similar way for 15 year terms, but with each nation and region choosing one third of its members at each European election.

A majority of the Royal Commission favoured option B, which would result in a chamber where some 16 per cent of members were elected, and 84 per cent appointed. But under the Commission's proposals, appointments would in future fall to an Appointments Commission, which would be required to ensure that the nations and regions were fairly represented in the chamber as a whole, and that the balance of political members in the chamber reflected votes cast at a general election. The Appointments Commission would have to trawl outside the metropolitan-biased lists of the great and the good, and seek members from the nations and regions to ensure a proper regional balance.

The compositional bias (rather than any radical rethink about role and function) was the Commission's main response to link Lords reform to devolution. But this is problematic in a number of ways. In terms of composition, the inclusion of a minority of members elected from the nations and regions seems unlikely to quell demand. As the Royal Commission itself said:

> ...we were told at our public hearing in Newcastle, people in the regions would not regard someone selected *for* their region by a London-based Appointments Commission as being an adequate substitute for someone selected *by* their region.[68]

Experience from Canada shows that different parts of the country are liable to be frustrated, and lose faith in the upper house, if members are appointed on their behalf from the centre.

But most importantly, the Royal Commission did not propose mechanisms which would ensure that members of the upper house — either elected or appointed — would retain meaningful links with their territorial areas. The Commission rejected the German Bundesrat model, where members of the upper house are drawn from state governments. It also rejected other forms of indirect election — such as representation of the devolved assemblies — fearing that members elected in this way would become 'delegates of the bodies that elected them, voting according to instructions rather than conscience.'[69] However, the danger with directly elected members, or appointees, is that they will be purely creatures of their parties, rather than true representatives of their nations and regions.

---

[68] *Ibid,* para 11.31
[69] *Ibid*, para 6.17.

A possible solution would be to require members representing the nations and regions to make regular reports to their assemblies or parliaments — answering questions in the chamber or accounting to its committees. Such arrangements exist for members of the German Bundesrat, but are dependent on its indirectly elected membership. Mechanisms like this could start in Wales, Scotland, and Northern Ireland, spreading to England if regional assemblies are established. This would build in a degree of accountability, and formal links between the institutions; but it would depend on the co-operation of both the devolved institutions and the will of regional upper house members.

The only real concessions made by the Commission in terms of territorial *roles* were its suggestions of a Devolution Committee in the upper house, and the idea that committees of the second chamber might sometimes meet outside London.[70] The Commission also proposed establishment of a Constitutional Committee in the upper house, which would 'keep the constitution under review'.[71] The role of the Devolution Committee, which would be a sub-committee of the Constitutional Committee, would be limited to considering relations between the devolved institutions and the centre, and relations between the institutions themselves. It was not suggested that the committee would consider the territorial impacts of legislation, as does the committee of the regions in the Spanish upper house, for example. There was also no suggestion that upper house committees would be routinely constructed to reflect the territorial balance of the chamber, as required by the rules in the Bundesrat. Ironically, both of these suggestions have been raised in relation to reorganisation of the House of Commons, but not with respect to reform of the Lords.

Although a central element in the Wakeham report, the links with devolution have not featured strongly in subsequent debates on Lords reform. In the five-hour debate in the Commons devoted to discussing the report, devolution was mentioned only once when the Plaid Cymru MP, Dafydd Wigley, asked the Government whether the opinions of the devolved assemblies would be sought in the preparations for stage two of the reforms.[72] Margaret Beckett's reply was that there had been no decision made as yet, but that the Government would of course listen to interested parties. During the equivalent debate in the Lords, which lasted for eight hours, devolution was mentioned rather more frequently. However, most references were simply to welcome the fact that the Wakeham Commission had discussed the issue, and only Lord Hurd and Lord Dahrendorf chose to expand on the subject.[73] In both debates, discussion centred around issues of selection of members of the

---

[70] *Ibid*, paras 6.22-26 and 6.27, respectively.
[71] *Ibid*, para 5.22.
[72] HC Deb, 19 June 2000, col. 49.
[73] HL Deb, 7 March 2000, col. 911 *et seq.*

reformed house rather than *how* it can best provide a voice for the nations and regions.

Nor have the links with devolution featured much in the Government's response to Wakeham. The Government is consulting with the other political parties at Westminster, to try to establish a Joint Parliamentary Committee as the next step in the long march to Lords reform. As Dafydd Wigley brought out, it has not sought to consult with the devolved governments or assemblies to seek their views on how a reformed second chamber can best build links with the devolved institutions.

The Current House of Lords

In contrast to the Commons, the House of Lords' make up is currently not based in any way on territory. There has thus been little debate about changes to the role of the chamber since it does not, for example face a 'West Lothian question'. Discussion has been limited to what matters are appropriate for debate, with ministers taking a strict line on not being drawn into discussion of devolved matters.[74] Given the more relaxed procedures of the House of Lords there has been no parallel Speaker's statement to that made in the Commons regarding questions to ministers.

One development which will be interesting to watch will be the new Constitutional Committee agreed by the House in response to the proposals of the Wakeham Commission.[75] The Committee will be required to: '...examine the constitutional implications of all public Bills ... and ... keep under review the operation of the constitution.'[76]

The establishment of the committee was agreed shortly before the 2000 summer recess and its members have not yet been appointed. The extent to which it will concern itself with devolution-related issues is yet to be seen. The committee's role in monitoring relations between the Westminster and Scottish parliaments was raised in debate by Baroness Carnegy of Lour:

> My Lords, I have a question for the noble Lord about the proposed constitutional committee. Can he tell the House into what degree of detail it is intended that the committee will go when it considers public Bills? From time to time, UK Bills on matters reserved to Westminster have implications for the Scots Parliament, of which the latter turns out not to be aware — or, alternatively, such Bills should have implications for the Scots Parliament but do not because the Government have tried to avoid getting into a matter that has in fact been devolved but which would be necessary for the implementation of the UK Bill.

There was no direct response given to this question, and very little about the committee's terms have yet been agreed. Yet this again illustrates the

---

[74] See, for example, Baroness Ramsay's answer to a written question at HL Deb 24 July 2000, col. WA2.

[75] HL Deb, 17 July 2000, cols. 584-96.

[76] Liaison Committee: Third Report, HL 81, 26 June 2000, para. 2.

potential overlap of responsibility between different Westminster committees with regard to the policy impact of reserved matters on Scotland. The House of Lords has been slower than the Commons at adapting in response to devolution. But this committee could mark the beginning of the upper chamber's development in this area.

CONCLUSION

The first year of devolution at Westminster has resulted in piecemeal adaptations and a degree of confusion about future direction. Parliamentarians are feeling their way towards new structures, procedures and roles to reflect the new quasi-federal structure of the UK. But asymmetrical devolution is proving difficult to accommodate in many ways, particularly given the lack of leadership from government or the parliamentary authorities.

A number of issues are outstanding after devolution's first year. A major one is procedure for English business, and the role of Scottish and Welsh MPs in this. The Conservatives are set to keep the pressure up on the issue, and will hope to build public support for changes after the general election if Labour's majority is cut. This is a peculiarly UK problem, not mirrored in federal states with more symmetrical arrangements. It will require imaginative responses, and seems unlikely to go away.

A subject of some confusion over the first year was how Westminster deals with reserved matters as apply to Scotland, Wales, and Northern Ireland. As everyone becomes more aware of territorial aspects, we may see turf wars between departmental and territorial committees, and between the Commons and the Lords, as to who deals with these matters. We may also see pressure both for better representation of devolved areas on certain departmental committees, and a search for more business for the territorial committees. This may help redress the problem of what Scottish MPs do post-devolution, but the resulting squeeze on the more numerous English representatives could lead to tensions. The only explicitly English forum proposed — the Standing Committee on Regional Affairs — has not been particularly well received and lacks both powers and a clear purpose. By September, six months after it was proposed, it seemed unlikely to get off the ground.

Little has yet been agreed in terms of fora to oversee territorial issues in general. When the Study of Parliament Group's working group on Westminster and the Welsh Assembly gave evidence to the Procedure Committee, they favoured a Devolution Committee for the Commons which would keep the arrangements throughout the UK under review. If such a committee were established with a partially internal focus, it might have taken some leadership responsibility for managing developments at Westminster. In the event, the Procedure Committee did not take up this recommendation, but instead

proposed that there should be some kind of 'Constitutional Affairs Committee' established in the Commons. This was a long-term goal, which has not
been acted on as yet. The Procedure Committee agreed to carry out a full
review of the procedural consequences of devolution 'in due course' — a
proposal which was gratefully received by government. Some of these issues
may therefore be revisited later.

These debates, however, flag up one of the most serious concerns about
the way devolution is handled at Westminster, which is the lack of clarity
about the respective roles of the upper and lower house. The Procedure
Committee discussed both a possible Devolution Committee and Constitutional Committee for the Commons. Yet both of these were also proposed by
the Royal Commission for the House of Lords, with a Constitutional
Committee now due to be established. The Royal Commission properly
recognised that there is an important potential role for the upper house in
representing the nations and regions post-devolution, as occurs in many
overseas states. This would give the upper chamber a distinct focus from the
House of Commons, where members' territorial concern is traditionally their
constituency. As the Government's White Paper on House of Lords reform
noted, an important principle is that: '[t]he role of the second chamber should
continue to complement rather than duplicate the role of the Commons.'[77]

However, whilst the political parties are in discussion about the implementation of the Royal Commission's report, the House of Commons is adapting
gradually to new territorial roles based on the nations and regions. There is a
lack of co-ordination between the two chambers, and an apparent danger that
both will compete over the territorial role, especially if Lords reform is
delayed.

In addition to the direct impacts of devolution on Westminster discussed in
the body of the chapter, over time indirect impacts are liable to be seen. As
described in chapters 2 and 3, the Scottish Parliament and Welsh Assembly
have sought to establish themselves with very different cultures, procedures
and working hours to their Westminster parent. Many MPs look enviously at
the facilities and working conditions enjoyed by MSPs and AMs, and this
seems likely to feed through to pressures for reform at Westminster. In 2000,
there was a lively campaign on MPs' working hours, and a report from the
Modernisation Committee sought to meet some of these concerns (including
proposals for delaying votes in a way used by the Scottish Parliament).[78] This
is in part therefore another of devolution's effects.

A final impact on Westminster will be the change in public perceptions
which results from devolution. An ICM poll in January 2000 found that 51

[77] *Modernising Parliament — Reforming the House of Lords.* London: The Stationery Office (Cm
4183), p. 36.
[78] *Programming of Legislation and Timing of Votes,* Modernisation Committee Second Report
1999–2000 session, HC 589, 5 July 2000.

per cent of Scots already felt that the Scottish Parliament was 'the most important [institution] in deciding Scotland's future', compared to just 31 per cent believing Westminster was the most important (and 13 per cent identifying the European Parliament). A MORI poll in April found that 37 per cent felt the Scottish Parliament would have the most influence over their lives in 20 years' time, compared to 33 per cent who felt the European Parliament held this role and only 17 per cent identifying Westminster as most important. One of the ultimate effects of devolution may be that Westminster is increasingly eclipsed by the new institutions.

BIBLIOGRAPHY

Bogdanor, V., *Devolution in the United Kingdom* (Oxford: Opus, 1999).

Conservative Party, *Strengthening Parliament*, The Report of the Commission to Strengthen Parliament (July 2000).

Hazell, R., 'Westminster: Squeezed from Above and Below', in Hazell, R., (ed.), *Constitutional Futures* (Oxford: Oxford University Press, 1999).

House of Commons, *The Operation of Multi-Layer Democracy*, Scottish Affairs Committee Second Report of Session 1997-98, HC 460-I (2 December 1998).

House of Commons, *The Procedural Consequences of Devolution*, Procedure Committee Fourth Report of Session 1998-99, HC 185 (19 May 1999).

House of Commons Library, *The Procedural Consequences of Devolution*, Research Paper 99/85 (20 October 1999).

Riddell, P., *Parliament Under Blair* (London: Politico's, 2000).

Royal Commission on the Reform of the House of Lords, *A House for the Future*, Cm 4534 (London: The Stationery Office, January 2000).

Russell, M., *Reforming the House of Lords: Lessons from Overseas* (Oxford University Press, 2000).

Russell, M., 'The Territorial Role of the Upper House', *Journal of Legislative Studies* (forthcoming), 2001.

Russell, M., and Hazell, R., *Commentary on the Wakeham Report on Reform of the House of Lords* (London: Constitution Unit, February 2000).

8

The People's Verdict

Public Attitudes to Devolution and the Union

John Curtice

INTRODUCTION

The success of devolution ultimately rests on public opinion. To work effectively, political institutions need to be accepted by those whom they attempt to govern. Enforcing decisions becomes very difficult unless the public accepts the right of their political institutions to make decisions even when they disagree with particular decisions that have been made. One of the first tasks of any new political institution, such as the new devolved institutions of the United Kingdom, is to acquire that legitimacy.

All of the new devolved institutions were apparently given a head start in that process. All three were established following affirmative votes in a referendum. But in two cases at least, the outcome was far from decisive. In Wales, half the electorate remained at home while only a narrow majority of those who did vote backed devolution. And while as many as 75 per cent voted in favour of the new arrangements in Northern Ireland, it appears that only just over half of Protestants did so. So, at least in these two territories, doubts about devolution were widespread.

But even in Scotland, the new Parliament faced the task of demonstrating that the confidence that Scots had put in her was not misplaced. And there was, of course, no better way of proving that than providing a period of stable, coherent, crisis free, and even uncontroversial governance. In short, in their early life at least, the legitimacy of the new institutions appeared to rest to a far greater degree on their perceived performance than is normally the case with a long established institution. The 1992–7 Conservative Government was widely perceived to have been an unsuccessful administration, yet no one drew the conclusion that, as a result, the UK government should no longer exist. But the same could not be assumed if perceptions of the early performance of the new institutions proved to be equally negative.

However, to be considered a success, devolution not only needs the new institutions themselves to be accepted by the public, it also has to influence attitudes towards the maintenance of the Union. By granting devolution, the Westminster government hopes to demonstrate that the hopes and aspirations of those living in the three territories can be fulfilled within the framework of the Union. As a result, remaining within the Union should be at least acceptable to both communities in Northern Ireland, while hopefully those in Scotland and Wales would embrace their continued membership with some enthusiasm.

Yet the results of the first devolved elections, at least, raised some questions about how far devolution would contribute to this aim. In both Scotland and Wales, nationalist parties became the official opposition, in the latter case after a record breakthrough by Plaid Cymru. In Northern Ireland, one of the two nationalist parties representing the Catholic community — the Social Democratic and Labour Party (SDLP) — denied the leading unionist party first place (on the first preference vote) for the first time in the province's history. In each case, the territory's constitutional future was a key issue in the election campaign for the first devolved elections, even though its determination did not lie within the competence of the body being elected. Hopes, expressed most often in Northern Ireland, but arguably of equal relevance to Scotland and Wales, that devolution would encourage a focus on 'bread and butter' politics were not wholly realised.

So there are at least two key tests that we need to set devolution in evaluating the first twelve months. First, do the new institutions themselves appear to be becoming accepted or is their ability to secure legitimacy in doubt? Second, by meeting the apparent demands within each of the three territories for more autonomy, is devolution succeeding in maintaining support for Union, or is it but the beginning of a slippery slope to independence? This chapter applies the two tests to each of the three devolved territories. There is, of course, no guarantee that, given their diverse circumstances and the different forms of devolution they enjoy, the answers to these two questions will prove to be the same in each case.

Of course, to apply these tests we need reliable and impartial evidence on public opinion in each of the devolved territories. For this we have to rely upon any opinion polls and social surveys that may have been conducted. Fortunately, in each of the three territories, such surveys have been conducted episodically, at least during the course of the first year. So, while the information available to us may be less complete and less systematic than desirable, it is sufficient to enable us to make an informed judgement as to how well devolution has been standing up to our two tests.

ATTITUDES TO THE NEW INSTITUTIONS IN SCOTLAND AND WALES

We have suggested that the new institutions might be more likely to secure public acceptance if they were seen to be working successfully in their early lives. In practice, however, not only were the new institutions in Scotland

Figure 8.1. Evaluations of First Minister/Secretary

Scotland

Evaluation	May 99	June 99	Jan. 00	Feb. 00 (1)	Feb. 00 (2)
	%	%	%	%	%
Favourable	50	63	51	47	44
Unfavourable	24	17	21	44	29

May 99, June 99, Jan. 00: Is Donald Dewar doing a good/bad job for Scotland? Favourable are those saying good job, unfavourable those saying bad job.

Feb. 00 (1): Satisfied/Dissatisfied with job Donald Dewar is doing as First Minister? Favourable includes those very/quite satisfied; unfavourable includes those not very/not at all satisfied

Feb. 00 (2): Rating of performance as leader on five-point scale from very good to very poor. Favourable comprises those saying very/quite good; unfavourable consists of those saying very/quite poor.

Sources: May, June 99, Feb. 00 (1): ICM/*Scotsman*. Jan. 00: ICM/*Scotland on Sunday*. Feb 00 (2): System Three/*The Herald*.

Wales

Evaluation	Jan. 00	Feb. 00	June 00
	%	%	%
Favourable	41	24	69
Unfavourable	36	56	16

Jan. 00: How good a job is Alun Michael doing as First Secretary? Favourable are those saying good, unfavourable those saying poor.

Feb. 00: Satisfied/Dissatisfied with job Alun Michael doing as First Secretary? Favourable includes those very/quite satisfied; unfavourable includes those not very/not at all satisfied

June 00: As Jan. 00 but asked of Rhodri Morgan.

Sources: Jan., June 00: NOP/HTV Wales. Feb. 00: ICM/*Scotsman*

and Wales subjected to widespread media criticism of their performance, but their early work was met with less than public enthusiasm.

The most obvious butt of criticism was the Welsh First Secretary, Alun Michael (see figure 8.1 which brings together the results of a number of surveys that all asked, albeit in different ways, about the performance of the Welsh First Secretary and the Scottish First Minister during the course of the year). He entered office tarnished in many people's eyes by being a leader foisted on Wales by the Labour Party in London (see chapter 3). He certainly proved incapable of winning the affection of those he was elected to serve.

True, slightly more (41 per cent) told NOP in January that Mr Michael was doing a good job as First Secretary than said he was doing a poor one (36 per cent). But in the same poll, over half said that the opposition parties would be right to try and secure his removal, should he prove unable to secure matching funds for the country's Objective One status (see page 39). Only 28 per cent were opposed. Even amongst Labour supporters, only 39 per cent were opposed to his removal, while as many as 37 per cent were in favour. Meanwhile, over half (56 per cent) told an ICM poll in February that they were dissatisfied with his performance, while less than a quarter (24 per cent) were satisfied. Perhaps most damagingly of all, a Beaufort poll the same month discovered that more people backed the Plaid Cymru leader, Dafydd Wigley, as the best First Secretary for Wales, than Alun Michael.

Scotland's First Minister, Donald Dewar, fared rather better than Mr Michael. As many as 47 per cent told ICM in February that they were satisfied with his performance. Not only did this compare highly favourably with the figure of 24 per cent enjoyed by Mr Michael in Wales, but it also meant that those satisfied slightly outnumbered those who were dissatisfied (44 per cent). Even so, in the same month, System Three found that more people (50 per cent) thought that the SNP leader, Alex Salmond, was doing a good job than said the same of Mr Dewar (44 per cent), let alone his Liberal Democrat Deputy, Jim Wallace (36 per cent). And one year after the Parliament assumed its powers, just 24 per cent thought that the Scottish Executive had been a success.

But of course dissatisfaction with the running of the executive may not necessarily mean voters are unhappy with the performance of the new Parliament/Assembly as a whole. After all, voters do not necessarily think any less of the House of Commons simply because they have doubts about the performance of the current UK Government. Indeed, clear evidence comes from Wales that voters' evaluations of the new institutions are not simply the product of what they think of the performance of those currently in post. In May, by which time Rhodri Morgan had succeeded Alun Michael as First Secretary, no less than 69 per cent told NOP that he was doing a good job, 28 points higher than the equivalent rating for Alun Michael in January. Yet the proportion saying that the National Assembly was doing a good job was exactly the same (46 per cent) in May as it was January.

Yet, in practice, there does seem to have been rather a lukewarm response to the performance of the new institutions as a whole (see figure 8.2 which, like the previous table, brings together the results of a number of differently worded questions on the subject). The 46 per cent 'good' rating for the Welsh Assembly, referred to above, was one of its more favourable figures. ICM's February poll in the principality found that while 41 per cent thought the new Assembly was good for Wales in principle, just 36 per cent gave it the same rating in practice. Indeed, in the same poll, no less than 42 per cent said they

Figure 8.2. Evaluations of Parliament/Assembly

Scotland

Evaluation	June 99	Jan. 00	Feb. 00	Apr. 00	June 00
	%	%	%	%	%
Favourable	43	45	37	27	27
Unfavourable	21	15	16	31	57

June 99, Jan. 00: Has having own parliament been good/bad for Scotland? Favourable are those saying good, unfavourable those saying bad.

Feb. 00: Has the Scottish Parliament in practice been good/bad for Scotland? Favourable are those saying good, unfavourable those saying bad.

Apr. 00: Has the performance of the Scottish Parliament been good/bad? Answers on a five point scale from very good to very poor. Favourable consists of those saying quite/very good; unfavourable comprises those answering quite/very poor

June 00: Satisfaction with performance of the Scottish Parliament in the first year: Answers on a five point scale from very satisfied to very unsatisfied. Favourable consists of those saying very/fairly satisfied; unfavourable comprises those saying very/fairly dissatisfied.

Sources: June 99, Feb. 00: ICM/*Scotsman*. Jan. 00: ICM/*Scotland on Sunday*. Apr. 00: System Three/BBC. June 00: System Three/*The Herald*.

Wales

Evaluation	Jan. 00	Feb. 00	Mar. 00	May 00
	%	%	%	%
Favourable	46	36	46	46
Unfavourable	41	19	44	40

Jan., Mar., May 00: Overall, how good a job do you think the National Assembly is doing for Wales? Favourable are those saying good, unfavourable those saying poor.

Feb. 00: Has the National Assembly in practice been good/bad for Wales? Favourable are those saying good, unfavourable those saying bad.

Source: Jan., Mar., May 00: NOP/HTV Wales. Feb. 00: ICM/*Scotsman*

thought devolution had been a failure in Wales, while just 25 per cent rated it a success.

Meanwhile in Scotland just 43 per cent said to ICM in January that the new Parliament had been good for Scotland — over a third said they simply did not know. In February, 48 per cent thought that having the new Parliament was good for Scotland in principle, but just 37 per cent took that view when it came to its performance in practice. By April opinion was, if anything, even less favourable. Just 27 per cent told System Three that the performance of

Figure 8.3. Constitutional preferences in Scotland

	Sep.97	Feb.98	May98	Jan.99	Feb.99	Jan.00	Feb.00
	%	%	%	%	%	%	%
Independence	28	28	33	26	24	23	27
Devolution	38	48	48	53	54	54	46
No parliament	30	21	17	18	18	19	22

The detailed question wording was as follows:-

Sep. 97
How would you like Scotland run as a whole?

An independent Scotland which is separate from England & Wales but part of the European Union

Scotland remaining part of the UK but with its own devolved assembly and some taxation and spending powers

No change from the present system

Feb. 98 to Feb. 00
Thinking about the running of Scotland as a whole, which one of the following would you like to see?

Scotland being independent of England and Wales, but part of the EU

Scotland remaining part of the UK but with its own devolved parliament with some taxation and spending powers

Scotland remaining part of the UK but with no devolved parliament.

Source: ICM/*Scotsman* and *Scotland on Sunday*

the Parliament had been 'good', while in July, the same company ascertained that exactly the same proportion were 'satisfied' with the Parliament's performance.

Why were these judgements apparently so unenthusiastic? Not, it seems, because the new institutions were doing much harm. Rather it was because they did not seem to be doing much at all. By February, only 5 per cent of people in Scotland and 4 per cent in Wales thought that their new Parliament/assembly had achieved a lot. True, 64 per cent of people in Scotland thought the Parliament had achieved a little and only 27 per cent, nothing at all, but in Wales, even those who thought the Assembly had achieved a little (40 per cent), were outnumbered by those who thought it had made no difference at all (48 per cent). The picture appears to have been unchanged by the time the first year drew to a close. Asked by NOP in May whether the National Assembly for Wales had made any difference to the running of agriculture, the economy, health or education, between 60 per cent and 72 per cent either said it had made no difference, or that it was too soon to say. And in June, System Three found that no less than 78 per cent of Scots felt that the new Parliament had still not made any difference to people's lives — for either good or ill.

Yet despite this disappointment at the apparent failure of the new institutions to make more impact, these evaluations seem not to have undermined support for devolution in either Scotland or Wales. In Scotland, ICM polls conducted during the year found that only around one in five did not want any kind of parliament (see the last row in figure 8.3). In July, even in Wales, just 23 per cent said that the Assembly had failed and should be abolished. Meanwhile, a reading in March suggested that as many as 60 per cent of people in Wales would now vote to keep the Assembly in a referendum. In both territories, these readings are more favourable to devolution than those that had been obtained at the time of the September 1997 referendums, though they were largely unchanged from those that had been obtained in the run-up to the devolved elections in May 1999. In any event, it is clear that support for devolution is less dependent on the perceived performance of the new institutions than initially suggested.

Indeed, if anything, the desired remedy to the disappointments of the first year appears to be a wish for more devolution not less. In July, no less than 43 per cent of people in Wales said that the Assembly should be given law-making powers, whereas only 28 per cent felt that the Assembly should continue with its existing more limited range of powers. Meanwhile, in Scotland, in April, a System Three poll found that no less than 62 per cent of Scots wanted their Parliament to have more powers. Just 8 per cent wanted it to have fewer powers, while 22 per cent would opt for no change.

ATTITUDES IN NORTHERN IRELAND

But what of Northern Ireland? The picture here is different in one crucial respect. Devolution did not get off the ground until December 1999, was then suspended after only ten short weeks, and only re-commenced at the end of May (see chapter 4). In other words to date the voters of Northern Ireland have had little opportunity to judge the impact of devolution in practice.

In fact, such experience as they have had appears not to have been evaluated particularly unfavourably. A poll conducted in May, for the BBC programme *Hearts and Minds* by PricewaterhouseCoopers, found that 58 per cent reckoned that David Trimble had done a good job in his initial ten weeks as First Minister, while as many as 60 per cent thought the same of his Deputy, Seamus Mallon. Even the most controversial appointee, Martin McGuiness, the Education Minister, had slightly more (40 per cent) thinking he had done a good job than thinking he had done a poor one (37 per cent). Moreover, David Trimble had developed a rare cross-community appeal, with as many nationalists as unionists giving him a good rating.

Figure 8.4. Support for the Belfast Agreement

% voted/would vote Yes

	May 98	Autumn 99	May 00
Protestant/Unionist	54	49	43
Catholic/Nationalist	98	98	96

May 98 and Autumn 99 figures refer to Protestant/Catholic. May 00 figures refer to self-described Unionist/Nationalist. Those who did not vote/did not know how they would vote have been excluded.

Sources: May 98: Northern Ireland Referendum and Assembly Election Study 1998. Autumn 99: Northern Ireland Life and Times Survey 1999. May 00: PricewaterhouseCoopers/BBC.

Yet in contrast to Scotland and Wales, there was in fact an adverse trend in attitudes in Northern Ireland towards devolution during the year (see figure 8.4). Both the election results themselves and survey evidence had suggested that, while there was almost unanimous support for the Belfast Agreement amongst Catholics in the May 1998 referendum, even then only just over half of Protestants were in favour. The Northern Ireland Election Survey, for example, found that 54 per cent of Protestants backed the agreement. So, despite the high hopes that greeted the result of the May 1998 referendum, it was always the case that devolution began its life with Protestant support on a knife-edge.

Now, it appears that the balance within the Protestant community has shifted in favour of the anti-agreement camp. At the end of 1999, when the Northern Ireland Life and Times Survey asked people how they would vote now, slightly more Protestants said they would vote 'No' than said they would vote 'Yes'. Then in May the BBC *Hearts and Minds* poll reported that just 43 per cent of Unionists would vote in favour now, while as many as 57 per cent would vote against. True, at 96 per cent, support for the Agreement amongst the nationalist community remains overwhelming. But as the Agreement is intended to be an accommodation with which both communities in the province can live, this development meant that the year ended with an even bigger question mark over the legitimacy of the new institutions than there already was at its onset.

So support for the new institutions decreased in one of the two communities in Northern Ireland. But the reason does not evidently lie in adverse evaluations of its operation, albeit that its provisions contained a number of controversial and untested provisions such as those for the formation of the Executive (see page 84). Rather, it lies in the circumstances of its implementation, most notably in the continuing controversy about decommissioning. The Northern Ireland Referendum and Assembly Election Survey had revealed that, when they voted in the May 1998 referendum, a clear majority of both Protestants and Catholics believed that the Belfast Agreement included a provision that 'parties with links to paramilitary organisations that have not decommissioned their weapons are not allowed a place on the Northern Ireland Executive'. And certainly this was what a majority of both communities believed should be the case. According to the Northern Ireland Life and Times Survey, no less than 64 per cent of Protestants believed, at the end of 1999, that total decommissioning should take place before the Executive was put in place, while another 30 per cent thought that some decommissioning should happen. Meanwhile, although only 29 per cent of Catholics felt that total decommissioning was required, no less than 45 per cent believed that some was necessary — a combined total of 74 per cent. Little wonder that the absence of decommissioning made it so difficult for the Ulster Unionists to agree to form a government.

True, on the advent of the reformation of the Executive in May, many appear to have accepted, as did the Ulster Unionists, that decommissioning was not going to happen. By this time, the IRA had accepted external scrutiny of its arms dumps. Even so, according to the *Hearts and Minds* poll, while four out of five nationalists regarded the IRA's proposals as acceptable, no less than two-thirds of unionists felt they fell short of what was required as evidence of decommissioning. As a result, while 97 per cent of nationalists felt that David Trimble and his party should rejoin the Executive, unionists were evenly split with 50 per cent in favour and 50 per cent opposed.

SUPPORT FOR DEVOLUTION MAY NOT DEPEND ON PERFORMANCE

So, a clear lesson emerges from the first year of devolution in the United Kingdom. Support for the continued existence of the new structures does not appear to depend, as might have been thought, on the performance of the initial occupants of the new bodies. Although the initial experience of devolution appears to have been a mild disappointment for the people of Scotland and Wales, in both territories support for the principle of having their own parliament or assembly remained as high at the end of their first year of existence as it had been at the beginning. Where support did fall was amongst the unionist community of Northern Ireland. But this was because widespread doubts about the new devolution settlement, that still existed at the time of the May 1998 referendum, were strengthened by the continuing row about decommissioning. In short, the problem faced by the devolution settlement in Northern Ireland was not its perceived efficacy but rather its fairness.

At the time of the September 1997 referendums, devolution in Scotland and Wales had had its opponents, most notably the Conservative Party. But after their defeat, opponents accepted that devolution was here to stay, even though the outcome in Wales had been so narrow. Devolution might have been unwelcome but it was not a threat, and it even brought the Conservative Party itself some advantage. In contrast, in Northern Ireland, the Democratic Unionist Party maintained its opposition to the Belfast Agreement, while many inside the Ulster Unionist Party also voiced their worries about such issues as decommissioning. What then appears to be vital for the success of devolution is the development of an elite consensus in its favour. In the absence of that consensus, new political institutions have a much more diffi-cult task on their hands. That such a consensus still does not exist in Northern Ireland is, of course, a reflection of the long-standing intractability of the issues at stake.

THE NATIONALIST THREAT AND SUPPORT FOR THE UNION

The second key test for devolution is whether it has helped to bolster support for the maintenance of the United Kingdom. Is support for independence withering in Scotland and Wales, along with popular support for those parties that espouse independence? Has devolution helped to make staying within the United Kingdom acceptable to the nationalist community in Northern Ireland? And what has happened to people's emotional attachment to the Union as indicated by the incidence of British national identity?

At first glance it looks as though this will be the harder test for devolution to pass. After all, perhaps the biggest surprise that devolution has produced to date has been the success of Plaid Cymru, the Welsh nationalist party, in the first devolved elections. With 28 per cent of the constituency vote and over 30 per cent of the list vote, the party became the principal opposition to Labour in Wales for the first time ever. Meanwhile, in Scotland, the SNP also advanced on their 22 per cent vote in the 1997 Westminster election with 27 per cent in the list vote and nearly 29 per cent in the constituency vote. And of course, in both cases, the new proportional representation electoral system meant that nationalist performances in votes were also largely reflected in seats. As a result, both parties became significant parliamentary forces for the first time ever.

So, rather than putting the nationalist genie back in the bottle in Scotland and Wales, devolution appears to have given it a new lease of life, for it has enabled the nationalist parties to prosper in a way they rarely, if ever, have done before.

But nationalist success is not necessarily indicative of a rise in support for nationalism. Rather, it appears that devolution has created a forum in which the nationalist parties appear more attractive to voters than they do in a UK general election. Survey research, up to and during the first devolved elec-tions, ascertained that voters were more willing to vote for nationalist parties

Figure 8.5. Voting intentions in Wales

Assembly election

	Jan. 00	Mar. 00	May 00	July 00
	%	%	%	%
Conservative	13	14	14	15
Labour	45	43	41	40
Liberal Democrat	6	10	10	8
Plaid Cymru	33	31	32	34
Other	3	2	3	3

Westminster election

	Jan. 00	Mar. 00	May 00	July 00
	%	%	%	%
Conservative	21	20	23	25
Labour	56	50	47	51
Liberal Democrat	8	12	12	9
Plaid Cymru	13	16	15	13
Other	3	2	2	2

Source: NOP/HTV Wales

in elections to the new institutions than they would have been in elections held at the same time to the UK House of Commons. For example, the 1999 Scottish Parliamentary Election Study found that amongst those who voted in the first devolved elections, 7 per cent more people backed the SNP as their first preference party for the Scottish Parliament elections than said they would vote SNP in a May 1999 Westminster election. Meanwhile, in Wales, the Welsh Assembly Election Study ascertained that the equivalent figure for Plaid Cymru was no less than 17 per cent. In both cases, the principal loser from this nationalist devolution bonus was Labour.

This pattern has been maintained in the first year of devolution (see figure 8.5). In four NOP polls conducted between January and July, Plaid Cymru secured an average rating of no less than 33 per cent when people were asked how they would vote in a devolved election. In contrast, when exactly the same voters were asked how they would vote in a UK general election, just 14 per cent backed the nationalists. At 19 points, the gap between the two readings has, if anything, become even wider than it was at the time of the 1999 election.

Meanwhile, in Scotland, System Three ascertained people's voting intentions for both Westminster and the Scottish Parliament on a regular monthly basis throughout the first year of the Scottish Parliament (for full details, see figure 8.6). Over the year as a whole, the SNP obtained an average score of

Figure 8.6. Voting intentions in Scotland

Scottish Parliament election

Vote	Con 1st	Con 2nd	Lab 1st	Lab 2nd	LD 1st	LD 2nd	SNP 1st	SNP 2nd	Others 1st	Others 2nd
	%	%	%	%	%	%	%	%	%	%
1999										
May	10	10	44	36	13	17	28	30	5	8
June	11	10	43	34	12	13	28	31	6	11
July	12	10	41	34	12	14	30	31	5	11
August	12	11	40	29	11	17	31	29	6	13
September	11	8	35	32	12	15	35	32	7	12
October	10	9	39	36	10	13	35	31	6	11
November	9	10	44	33	11	14	30	30	6	13
December	8	9	43	37	9	12	34	33	6	10
2000										
January	11	9	42	34	10	14	31	31	6	12
February	12	11	37	32	9	13	36	33	6	11
March	14	11	33	29	11	15	37	34	6	11
April	14	13	34	30	10	14	35	31	8	13
May	13	11	40	31	10	13	30	33	8	13
June	12	11	33	27	12	16	36	35	6	12
July	11	11	37	33	10	12	35	30	6	14

Westminster election

	Con %	Lab %	LD %	SNP %	Others %
1999					
May	13	47	14	22	3
June	13	49	10	24	4
July	13	49	11	24	2
August	16	46	12	24	3
September	14	42	13	29	3
October	12	45	13	27	3
November	12	50	13	24	2
December	12	50	9	27	2
2000					
January	14	49	11	24	2
February	15	45	11	27	3
March	16	40	11	29	3
April	17	44	9	26	3
May	14	48	10	24	4
June	17	39	11	31	3
July	15	46	9	26	4

Source: System Three/*The Herald*

34 per cent on the constituency vote for the Scottish Parliament, but only 27 per cent for a UK general election. Here too then, although the difference is smaller than that in Wales, there is little sign of the gap in nationalist support narrowing.

Why has devolution opened up this apparently persistent gap? It appears that in creating separate institutions for Scotland and Wales, devolution has invited voters to ask which party would be most likely to use those institutions to promote the interests of Scotland and Wales. And in both countries, voters apparently have doubts about the ability of Labour to engage in that task. According to the Welsh Assembly Election Study, no less than 82 per cent of people in Wales trust Plaid Cymru to look after the interests of Wales very or fairly closely, while only 57 per cent take the same view of the Wales Labour Party. And while in Scotland the Scottish Parliamentary Election Study found that as many people (67 per cent) trust the Scottish Labour Party to look after the interests of Scotland as they would the SNP (68 per cent), Scots have doubts about the willingness of new Labour in London to do so (40 per cent). Certainly such perceptions were clearly associated with the willingness of voters to vote for the nationalists in the devolved elections when they would not do so for Westminster.[1]

Of the two nationalist parties, the SNP has made the greater advance in the first year of devolution. Plaid Cymru support averaged just three points more than their list vote performance in the 1999 elections, whereas SNP backing was up five points on 1999. Neither party was, however, clearly stronger at the end of the first year than they were at the beginning. But thanks to a slide in Labour support, the SNP found itself neck and neck in most of the Scottish polls conducted from February onwards. Evidently, the possibility that the SNP might emerge as the largest party after the next Scottish election cannot be discounted.

NATIONAL IDENTITY AND ATTITUDES TO THE UNION

So devolution hardly seems to have helped insulate the Union from demands for independence in Scotland or Wales. Rather, it appears to have given its advocates a platform they did not have before. But maybe it has nevertheless helped to strengthen the emotional ties to the Union. After all, if the nationalist parties are regarded as a useful battering ram to get the best deal for Scotland and Wales within the Union, their level of support is not necessarily incompatible with strengthening emotional bonds to the Union.

But, in practice, there is little evidence that devolution has done much to help bolster a sense of British national identity. In January, ICM found that

---

[1] See, for example, L. Paterson, A. Brown, D. McCrone, A. Park and P. Surridge, *New Scotland, New Politics* (Edinburgh: Edinburgh University Press, 2001)

Figure 8.7. National identity in Scotland

	Apr. 97	June 98	Apr. 99	Jan. 00
	%	%	%	%
British not Scottish	7	7	11	9
More British than Scottish	3	3	3	3
Equally British and Scots	22	26	26	27
More Scots than British	26	33	32	28
Scottish not British	37	26	25	32

Source: ICM/*Scotsman* and *Scotland on Sunday*

Figure 8.8. National identity in Northern Ireland

	Religion	
	Protestant	Catholic
1989	%	%
British	66	10
Irish	4	60
1996		
British	59	10
Irish	7	57
1998 (1)		
British	77	10
Irish	2	63
1998 (2)		
British	68	8
Irish	3	64
1999		
British	72	9
Irish	2	68

Sources: 1989, 1996: Northern Ireland Social Attitudes Survey. 1998 (1): Northern Ireland Referendum and Assembly Election Study 1998. 1998 (2), 1999: Northern Ireland Life and Times Survey.

just 12 per cent of Scots regarded themselves as either 'British not Scottish' or at least 'More British than Scottish' — little different from the readings obtained by the same company over the course of the previous three years (see figure 8.7). Meanwhile, those who regarded themselves as 'Scottish not British' were as numerous as 32 per cent, an increase of no less than seven points on ICM's previous reading just before the 1999 election. True the proportion who deny all sense of Britishness was still lower than that obtained by ICM in one poll in April 1997 but, even so, we certainly cannot conclude that devolution has so far done anything to strengthen emotional ties to the Union in Scotland.

Figure 8.9. Constitutional preferences in Northern Ireland			
		Religion	
	Protestant	Catholic	All
1989	%	%	%
Remain part of the UK	93	32	69
Reunify with rest of Ireland	3	56	24
1996			
Remain part of the UK	85	35	62
Reunify with rest of Ireland	8	47	20
1998 (1)			
Remain part of the UK	87	22	61
Reunify with rest of Ireland	4	47	21
1998 (2)			
Remain part of the UK	84	20	58
Reunify with rest of Ireland	3	48	21
1999			
Remain part of the UK	87	16	56
Reunify with rest of Ireland	3	46	21

Sources: 1989, 1996: Northern Ireland Social Attitudes Survey.
1998 (1): Northern Ireland Referendum and Assembly Election Study 1998.
1998 (2), 1999: Northern Ireland Life and Times Survey.

Unfortunately, questions about national identity were not asked in Wales during the first year of devolution, but the Northern Ireland Life and Times Survey maintained a long-running series on the subject (see figure 8.8). National identity remains a source of significant division between the two communities in Northern Ireland. Given a range of categories to choose between, no less than 72 per cent of Protestants describe themselves as British while a similar proportion of Catholics say they are Irish. Perhaps, more importantly, there is no sign of any growth in the willingness of Catholics to call themselves British. Just 9 per cent do so — a figure that has barely changed over the last ten years. In contrast, the proportion calling themselves Irish was, in fact, the highest ever. If anything, the Belfast Agreement has made Catholics more confident in declaring their non-British identity, rather than engendered any developing sense of Britishness.[2]

Equally, there is no sign at all that the Agreement has encouraged support for the maintenance of the Union within the province (see figure 8.9). Rather the opposite appears to be the case. According to the 1999 Northern Ireland Life and Times survey, just 56 per cent of people in Northern Ireland now think that the best thing for Northern Ireland's long-term future is to remain part of the United Kingdom. Not only is this the lowest figure ever, but it

---

[2] See page 111 for a discussion of how the Belfast Agreement has strengthened the religious/nationalist divide in the province.

Figure 8.10. Constitutional preferences in Wales

	May 99	Feb. 00
Independence	10	11
Assembly with tax powers	23	30
Assembly no tax powers	38	27
No Assembly	22	25

Thinking about the running of Wales as a whole, which one of the following would you most like to see?

Wales being independent of England and Scotland, but part of the EU

Wales remaining part of the UK but with its own devolved Assembly as at present

Wales remaining part of the UK but with its own devolved Parliament with tax varying powers

Wales remaining part of the UK but with no devolved Assembly or Parliament

Source: Feb 00: ICM/*Scotsman*. May 99: ICM/BBC

means support for the maintenance of the Union is now rather close to the psychologically important 50 per cent mark.

The source of the decline in support for remaining part of the United Kingdom is quite clear. The drop is confined entirely to Catholics. Just 16 per cent of Catholics now believe that Northern Ireland should remain part of the United Kingdom, less than half the proportion in 1996. This figure had already fallen sharply by 13 points to 22 per cent by the time of the 1998 Northern Ireland Election Study and it has subsequently slipped yet further. It appears that the role given to the Irish Republic in the government of the province by the Belfast Agreement has generated doubts about the long-term wisdom of the Union amongst those Catholics who previously gave it their backing. Certainly the BBC *Hearts and Minds* poll found that over half of Catholics (55 per cent) now do not believe that Northern Ireland will still be part of the UK in 2020.

Intriguingly, however, the decline in support for the Union amongst Catholics has not been accompanied by a rise in support for unification with the Irish Republic. Indeed, at 46 per cent, that figure is now also at an all-time low. It looks as though the moves towards the dual involvement of both the UK and the Irish Governments enshrined in the Belfast Agreement are now being reflected in the increasing rejection amongst Catholics of an 'either/or' stance on the issue of sovereignty in Northern Ireland. To that degree at least, the Belfast Agreement may be judged to have had some success.

There is also little sign that devolution has done much to assuage the demand for independence in Scotland or Wales, though at least here there is also little evidence that support for the Union has been undermined. In

February, ICM found that just 11 per cent of people in Wales wanted independence — little different from the one in ten who said they wanted it at the time of the 1999 election (see figure 8.10). Meanwhile, in Scotland, ICM recorded levels of 23 per cent in January — a record low — but 27 per cent in February, a figure little different from that found in most ICM polls over the last three years. Moreover, just one in four Scots expect their country to be independent in ten years, while only one in five think that it would mean that Scotland would be better off. As in Wales, the safest conclusion appears to be that devolution has so far at least had little impact on aspirations for independence.

So the record of devolution on our second test is not a particularly good one. The Belfast Agreement has apparently reduced the extent to which Catholics in Northern Ireland believe that the future of their province necessarily lies in remaining part of the United Kingdom. In Scotland and Wales, it has given new life to political parties that aspire to independence. True, support for Scottish and Welsh independence has not grown, while the demand for unification with the Irish Republic amongst Northern Irish Catholics has not risen either. But even so, it is difficult to conclude, from the evidence of the first year, that devolution has yet made much of a contribution to the maintenance of the Union.

CONCLUSION

Of course, it is still early days for devolution. Its full impact on public opinion in the devolved territories will not be apparent for some time. Even so, the first year was crucial. A bad start could have resulted in adverse public perceptions that might have taken a long time to change. And if, in its early life, we find that the trend of public opinion is adverse to the hopes of devolutionists, it certainly raises serious questions about how realistic those hopes were.

In practice, the new institutions did not have the best of starts. The early performance of the Scottish Parliament and Welsh Assembly may not have been the subject of harsh criticism, but it did lead to some disappointment. The new institutions simply did not seem to be achieving very much. Yet the lesson of the first twelve months appears to be that even if this perception persists, devolution will not be subjected to a lingering death. Rather, it looks as though Scotland and Wales will demand that their new institutions are equipped with extra powers to ensure that devolution does make a difference. Indeed, in February, no less than 68 per cent of Scots and 62 per cent of people in Wales told ICM that they thought further change to the devolution settlements would be needed. In Scotland and Wales at least, it appears that, while there is little debate about whether to have devolution, there is still considerable room for argument about what powers the new institutions should have. Moreover, it seems that, if necessary, voters will be prepared to use a nationalist vote as a way of gaining more powers even if they do not necessarily accept the nationalist dream of independence.

Amongst Protestants in Northern Ireland, however, the legitimacy of the new institutions remains in doubt. This is not because the institutions themselves are deemed ineffective, but rather due to the continuing concern that too many concessions were made in their formation, either to nationalists in general, or the IRA in particular. Unlike Scotland and Wales, the devolution settlement remains a source of political contention. Meanwhile, the Belfast Agreement appears to have reduced long-term Catholic support for remaining a part of the Union. In the face of these trends, the best hope for Northern Irish devolution in the next twelve months must be that the institutions manage to operate without significant hitch, while issues such as decommissioning recede into the political background. If that does happen, both opposing devolution and leaving the Union might seem a somewhat less attractive prospect by this time next year.

The final judgement on devolution in the court of public opinion has still to be rendered. But one clear conclusion emerges from the first twelve months. Any hopes there might have been that we have now seen the end of the long-running debates about the constitutional status of the three peripheral territories of the United Kingdom are unlikely to be fulfilled. Yet how the public reacts to those continuing debates remains to be seen.

9

The Governance of London

John Tomaney[1]

INTRODUCTION

The creation of a Mayor and Assembly for London (collectively known as the Greater London Authority [GLA]), represents a significant element of the Labour Government's package of constitutional innovations. The story of the establishment of the GLA is interesting in its own right, but its importance is enhanced by the frequency with which aspects of its structure are invoked as offering clues about the likely shape of English regional government should that come to pass. At the same time, because the GLA incorporates the innovation of a directly elected mayor, it is likely that it will also pre-figure future changes in local government, especially in some large cities in England and Wales.[2] The Local Government Act 2000 permits local authorities to propose local referendums on elected mayors. Much controversy surrounds the question of whether this innovation represents a form of devolution or the establishment of an upper tier of local government to replace the former Greater London Council (GLC) which was abolished by Margaret Thatcher's Conservative Government in 1986.[3] This issue is itself tied to the question of whether London is best understood as a region or as a city or, as some would have it, as a city-region.[4]

Prior to the London election of 6 May 2000, the phenomenon of the directly elected mayor did not exist in the United Kingdom. Debate about the merits, or otherwise, of this innovation however developed over the preceding period, especially during the 1990s. Michael Heseltine, as Secretary of State for the Environment in John Major's Government was strongly associated with arguments in favour of elected mayors, although the Major Government did not pursue the idea. The Commission for Local Democracy, which sat in the mid-1990s, advocated elected mayors.[5] The growth in interest in elected mayors is a response to a widely perceived crisis of legitimacy

[1] I would like to acknowledge the advice and assistance of Robert Hazell, Edward Wood, Helen Child and Michelle Mitchell in the preparation of this chapter.
[2] The Scottish Parliament has rejected the idea of elected mayors/provosts.
[3] See, for example, Bogdanor, 1999.
[4] See, for example, Harding, 2000.
[5] Commission for Local Democracy, 1995.

in local government, with levels of electoral turnout that are by far the lowest in the EU.

The arguments in favour of elected mayors were summarised by the New Local Government Network in its response to the Draft Local Government (Organisation and Standards) Bill. It is argued that elected mayors, as a new form of leadership, offer greater accountability, visibility and electoral competition to the local community. Opinion surveys demonstrate that the public supports elected mayors. The New Local Government Network believes these arguments are so powerful that elected mayors should be imposed on large cities in the UK.[6]

The inspiration for elected mayors is frequently held to be the United Sates where mayors have a high profile. More generally, levels of local electoral turnout are higher in other countries than in the UK, although this is not uniformly the case in the United States. US mayors, of course, come in various shapes and sizes. One widely used distinction is that between 'strong mayors' (with extensive powers) and 'weak mayors' (with a more limited range of powers).[7] This distinction probably does not capture the diversity of US local government systems. It also true that not all city mayors in the US are directly elected. Some city leaders in European countries have very high profile — and extensive — powers, but are not directly elected. It is difficult, therefore, to ascribe the precise role of elected mayors in ensuring vigorous local democracy. The striking difference between the UK and just about every other developed state is that local government elsewhere derives a significantly higher proportion of its revenue from local taxes. This may account for higher levels of citizen interest in local elections.[8]

A further feature of the GLA model is its 'slimline' character. The GLA will directly employ about 400 staff rather than 20,000 employed by the GLC in the early 1980s. The reduction in numbers reflected a conscious effort on the part of the Government to avoid the charge that it was creating a new 'tier of bureaucracy'. But it probably also reflects an alleged shift — as posited in

---

[6] House of Lords/House of Commons, 1999: Appendix 38.

[7] New York, under Rudolf Giuliani, is usually offered as an example of what can be achieved by an elected mayor. However, New York falls very much into the strong mayor category. A contrasting example is that of Los Angeles, currently governed by Richard Riordan, which does not possess the powers of the New York mayor. Notwithstanding the recent economic upturn in LA (much of it attributable to the impact of federal dollars), successive elected mayors have struggled to address the main problems facing LA, including social deprivation and violent crime in south central districts, police corruption and poor educational achievement. Amongst other things, this has led to a growing movement on the part of the prosperous San Fernando Valley to secede from the city (Boudreau and Keil, 2000). Correspondingly, this has led to a renewed interest in metropolitan regionalism in southern California.

[8] Hambleton (2000) compares local government in Baltimore (mayor/council), Christchurch (council/manager) and Oslo (cabinet/council). Recent election turnouts were 46 per cent, 52 per cent and 69 per cent respectively. The proportion of revenue derived from local taxes was 37 per cent, 37 per cent and 55 per cent respectively. Although not exhaustive, thus study is highly suggestive of some key, and as yet unresolved, issues in UK local government.

some of the political science literature — in the nature and art of government. In this perspective, government is about the exercise of influence in networks, rather than the exercise of authority in organisations.[9] These issues and the legacies left by previous efforts to restructure London government helped to determine the choice of model adopted by the Labour Government.

THE PROBLEM OF LONDON GOVERNMENT

Prior to the 1850s, London did not exist as an administrative entity, although the London Police Act 1829 established the Metropolitan Police District, covering an area within a 15-mile radius of Charing Cross. The first genuine metropolitan authority for London was the Metropolitan Board of Works, set up initially to improve the sewage system. Its activities gradually expanded until the London County Council, which was established by the Local Government Act 1888, replaced it. The London Government Act 1899 subsequently created 27 metropolitan boroughs within the LCC area, together with Westminster City Council. This pattern of government remained largely unaltered until the creation of the GLC in 1965. In the intervening period, the expansion of London continued apace, so that the urban area spilled over the boundaries of the LCC. A number of abortive attempts were made to reform London government during the early part of the 20th century.[10]

The GLC and 32 London boroughs were established in 1965 by the provisions of the London Government Act 1963.[11] Responsibility for education in inner London was given to a special committee of the council, the Inner London Education Authority (ILEA), which later became a directly elected body. The powers of the GLC included strategic planning, housing, fire and civil defence, and major roads. The GLC assumed responsibility for London Transport in 1970 (although this responsibility was removed from the GLC by the Conservative Government in 1984). The boroughs had responsibility for social services, housing, local roads, libraries, recreation and parks, and in the outer boroughs, education. This system never worked in a way that was entirely satisfactory. The emphasis in the 1963 reform had been on creating strong boroughs and this left the GLC with an ill-defined purpose.

---

[9] Rhodes provides one description of this supposed process: 'New Labour rejects the command bureaucracy model of Old Labour with its emphasis on hierarchy, authority and rules ... Distinctively, it advocates "joined-up government", or delivering public services by steering networks of organisations where the currency is not authority (bureaucracy) or price competition (markets) but trust. In the parlance of the chattering classes, it is the "third way" in action. It exemplifies the shift from the providing state to the minimal state of Thatcherism to the enabling state ... but the arrival of joined-up government signals a further switch from management to diplomacy.' (Rhodes, 2000: 163)

[10] Haywood, 1998; Inwood, 1998; Travers and Jones, 1997.

[11] An additional actor was the City of London, which can be regarded as an additional borough for the purpose of this discussion, albeit one with an idiosyncratic internal structure.

Figure 9.1. Chronology of main events in London

October 1997	GLA (Referendum) Bill.
March 1998	White Paper, *A Mayor and Assembly for London.*
7 May 1998	Referendum on GLA.
October 1999	Archer selected as Conservative Mayoral candidate.
November 1999	GLA Act receives Royal Assent.
	Archer resigns as Conservative Mayoral candidate.
	Dobson, Jackson and Livingstone allowed to contest Labour candidacy.
February 2000	Dobson beats Livingstone to Labour nomination. Livingstone condemns result as 'tainted'.
March 2000	Livingstone announces independent candicacy.
6 May 2000	Elections for Mayor and Assembly. Ken Livingstone elected Mayor of London.

The abolition of the GLC in 1986, however, was the product of a bitter political conflict between the left-wing Labour administration elected in 1981 — and led by Ken Livingstone — and the Conservative Government led by Margaret Thatcher. The abolition was preceded by conflicts over subsidies to London Transport, employment policy, the funding of voluntary groups, minority groups and cultural activities and housing and overt political campaigning by the GLC against the Government. All of this occurred in the context of reduced public expenditure on local government on the part of central government and tighter restrictions on local revenue raising. The GLC was abolished by the Local Government Act 1985. ILEA was abolished in 1990 and its functions transferred to the boroughs.

The governance of London in the aftermath of the abolition of the GLC became a byword for complexity (see figure 9.2). Travers and Jones (1997) undertook the most thoroughgoing study of the structure of London's governance in the aftermath of the GLC. The 32 London boroughs and the City of London formed the basis of London's government. Beyond this a range of appointed bodies and joint committees were responsible for an array of activities ranging from arts (for example, London Arts Board, funded by the then Department of National Heritage) to research (for example, the London Research Centre funded by the boroughs). Finally, a number of Whitehall departments retained direct responsibility for public provision, notably the then Department of Environment and Department of Transport, which included a Minister for Transport for London. In 1994, in common with the rest of England a Government Office for London (GOL) was created to co-ordinate central government activity in the region. A Cabinet sub-committee for London was created in 1992 in recognition of the direct role that central government played in London. Travers and Jones (1997) stressed the weaknesses within the new system of government, pointing to its fragmented character and the inefficiencies to which this gave rise.

Figure 9.2. The Governance of London after the Abolition of the GLC

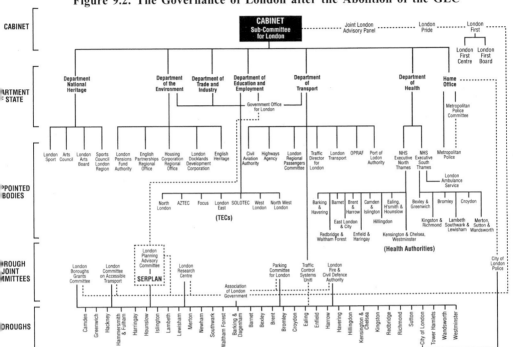

Source: Travers and Jones, 1997

The post-1986 structure left a set of legacies that any future reform would need to address. Inevitably, the relative stature of the London boroughs grew after the abolition of the GLC and ILEA. For instance the inner boroughs became local education authorities for the first time. The boroughs formed a single London-wide association (Association of London Government). Meanwhile inter-borough co-operation, typically through joint committees, became an important feature of London's government and, although it proved to be lasting, remained an obstacle to the integrated government of London.

Central government was disproportionately involved in the direct governance of London. For instance, unlike in other parts of England, the Home Secretary was the police authority for London. Many other activities were the responsibility either of quangos and other bodies controlled by central government, or of central government itself. This rendered government opaque and complex. Travers and Jones (1997) concluded that the muddle of Whitehall-appointed boards and agencies was difficult to understand and virtually impossible to hold to account.

The creation of the Cabinet sub-committee for London and GOL were tacit acknowledgements on the part of the Government of the weight of this criticism. The Government also played a role in promoting 'partnerships'.

After 1992 London witnessed a proliferation of partnerships. The most prominent of these was London First, a 'growth coalition', bringing together businesses, voluntary organisations and the voluntary sector.

The fragmented nature of London's governance led Travers and Jones to conclude:

> London is a city with much government but relatively little political power, particularly for matters that cross borough boundaries. While this contrast has been true in the past, the demands of a modern, advanced democracy make the failures of weak and fragmented government more important than before. Fragmentation of government — and the lack of effective political power that goes with such a system — is now worse than in the past. The recent creation of new London-wide committees and boards, the growth of new Whitehall involvement and the rapid development of partnerships together suggest there is a power vacuum.[12]

Travers and Jones were among those that proposed the creation of a strategic authority and/or Mayor in order to impose some order on the chaos of London governance. Labour had already taken up this idea in opposition. In 1996 Tony Blair floated the idea of an elected Mayor for London[13] and the idea was included in the Party's election manifesto.

LABOUR'S PROPOSALS

In the 1997 General Election, Labour's manifesto stated:

> London is the only western capital without an elected city government. Following a referendum to confirm popular demand, there will be a new deal for London, with a strategic authority and Mayor, each directly elected. Both will speak up for the needs of the city and plan for its future. They will not duplicate the work of the boroughs, but take responsibility for London-wide issues — economic regeneration, planning, policing, transport, and environmental protection. London-wide responsibility for its own government is urgently required. We will make it happen.

The new government acted swiftly to issue a Green Paper *New Leadership for London* in July 1997. This described London's 'democratic deficit' and how the existing structure of government prevented London's problems being adequately addressed. Among these problems were social exclusion, poor infrastructure, and worsening transport problems.

The Government introduced a Greater London Authority (Referendum) Bill in October 1997. Amendments by the Conservatives — in favour of a Mayor, but with an indirectly elected Assembly made up of borough leaders

---

[12] 1997: 25.
[13] Hambleton, 2000.

— and by the Liberal Democrats — in favour of an Assembly but not a Mayor — were rejected. The Greater London Authority (Referendum) Act 1998 restricted the referendum to approval or disapproval of the Government's policy for the creation of a directly elected Mayor and Assembly. The referendum took place on 7 May 1998, at the same time as the elections for the London borough councils. This produced a large majority in favour but on the basis of a comparatively low turnout.

Figure 9.3. Referendum on the Greater London Authority: 7 May 1998

Yes	72%
No	28%
Turnout	34.6%

Source: DETR

The Government published a White Paper, *A Mayor and Assembly for London*, in March 1998. It described the Greater London Authority (GLA) as embodying a directly elected Mayor 'to provide strong leadership' and an elected Assembly 'to hold the Mayor to account on London's behalf'.[14] The Assembly would also have a role in setting the budget for the GLA. The GLA would have a 'strategic', rather than service provider role, in relation to transport, economic development, the environment, planning, police, fire and civil defence, culture, and health.

THE GREATER LONDON AUTHORITY[15]

The Greater London Authority Act received Royal Assent on 11 November 1999. Most of the sections of the Act came into effect via commencement orders in the period December 1999 to July 2000. The GLA Act was significant for the constitutional innovations it incorporated and for the complexity of its passage through parliament, notably in terms of the large number of amendments tabled to the Bill. The bulk of these amendments were technical in character and were proposed by the Government, or accepted by the Government with little controversy. Major amendments proposed by the Conservatives or Liberal Democrats, designed to alter the fundamental structure of the GLA, were defeated. However, the Greater London Act in the end was over 400 pages long (bigger than the Scotland Act or the Government of Wales Act).

---

[14] DETR, 1998: 8-9.
[15] This section of the chapter is derived from a study of the GLA Act and associated Guidance Notes and relevant parliamentary debates. I am grateful for the advice of Edward Wood of the House of Commons Library in this regard.

The Act creates the GLA and three new 'statutory organisations' (or 'functional bodies'), namely Transport for London (TfL), the London Development Agency (LDA), and the London Fire and Emergency Planning Authority (LFEPA).[16] The Mayor will have responsibility for an additional body, namely the Metropolitan Police Authority, which the Act creates in order to oversee the Metropolitan Police. The Act defines the general purpose of the GLA as promoting the social, economic and environmental development of London and gives the Authority the power to do anything, which the Mayor considers will further that broad purpose. The Mayor must exercise these powers with a concern for the health of Londoners and the achievement of the sustainable development of the UK. This amounts to giving the GLA a 'power of general competence' and represents an innovation: typically, the powers of local government in the UK have been tightly defined by legislation. The powers of the GLA, by contrast, are defined by what it cannot do rather than by what it can, although the Secretary of State can give guidance concerning this general purpose[17] — one of a number of central government constraints upon the activities of the GLA. Also, the Authority must not duplicate any of the activities or expenditures of its 'statutory organisations', London health authorities or London boroughs. However, the Mayor does have the power to co-operate with any of these bodies to further the interests of London.

Most commentators, however, stress the degree to which the GLA model is recognisably a local government one,[18] albeit one which incorporates a number of innovations, including those listed above; a requirement to hold a 'People's Question Time' and 'State of London' debate and powers to require the attendance of witnesses as part of the Assembly's scrutiny functions. It contains the additional major innovation of the GLA in that it is to consist of a directly elected Mayor (the Mayor of London) and an elected Assembly (the London Assembly) which consists of 25 members, elected by proportional representation. The Mayor is elected by the supplementary vote (SV) system, while the Assembly is elected by the additional member system (AMS). 14 Assembly members are elected on a constituency basis (formed from groupings of London boroughs), while a further 11 are elected on a London-wide basis.

Most of the executive powers of the GLA are vested in the Mayor, with the Assembly having a scrutiny function. The Mayor, however, can delegate powers to a deputy Mayor (selected from Assembly members), GLA staff, and the agencies over which he or she has authority, or the boroughs. The

---

[16] The GLA will assume control of a number of London wide bodies — the London Ecology Committee, the London Research Centre (LRC) and the London Planning Advisory Committee (LPAC).

[17] This power will be extended to all local authorities in England and Wales by the Local Government Act 2000.

[18] Bogdanor, 1999; Harding, 2000.

Figure 9.4. Structure of the Greater London Authority

ELECTORATE

| Vote for mayor | Vote for constituency member | Vote for London member |

THE GREATER LONDON AUTHORITY

Executive
Mayor
- Proposes policy
- Proposes budget
- Co-ordinates partners
- Makes appointments to TfL, the LDA, the MPA, and LFEPA
- Speaks for London
- Appoints cabinet

Proposals

Scrutiny

Assembly
14 constituency members
11 London members
- Scutinises mayor
- Can arrange budget or proposals with 2/3 majority
- Must be consulted by mayor
- Conducts investigations into London issues
- Provides members for the LDA, the MPA and LFEPA
- Represents Londoners

Officers

| Transport for London (TfL) | London Development Agency (LDA) | Metropolitan Police Authority (MPA) | London Fire and Emergency Planning Authority (LFEPA) |

Source: Hambleton, 2000

Mayor may also contract out functions. In addition, the Mayor may also appoint a Cabinet to assist in his or her work, although the Act does not oblige him or her to do so. The Mayor's primary task is to publish strategies on a number of issues including transport, economic development and regeneration, spatial development, biodiversity, waste management, air quality, noise pollution, and culture. In preparing the strategies, the Mayor must consult with the Assembly, the GLA's functional bodies, the London boroughs, and any other individual or organisation deemed appropriate. But the mayor must also ensure that the strategies are consistent with such national policy and international obligations as the Secretary of State might bring to the Mayor's attention. The Mayor is held accountable through a monthly report to the Assembly, attendance at monthly meetings of the Assembly to answer questions, the publication of an annual progress report followed by a 'State of London' debate, and a twice-yearly 'People's

Question Time', held in conjunction with the Assembly. The Mayor may appoint two political advisers (whose posts need not be advertised) and ten policy advisers (whose posts must be advertised) for the duration of his or her term of office.

The Assembly must elect a Chair and deputy Chair from among its members. The Chair takes over some (but not all) of the main functions of the Mayor in his or her absence and that of the deputy Mayor. The Assembly's main task is to scrutinise the actions of the Mayor, although it can also make proposals for the Mayor's consideration. The Assembly also has the power to call for certain categories of persons and papers to inform its work. The Assembly has powers to establish committees, subject to the normal local government provisions concerning political balance. These committees, taken together with the powers of scrutiny just mentioned, have the potential to operate broadly in the manner of parliamentary select committees.

A primary task for the Mayor is to prepare a budget in support of the activities for which he or she is responsible. The Mayor must draw up the budget in consultation with the Assembly and the functional bodies and present a draft to a public meeting of the Assembly by 1 February each year. The Assembly may approve this draft, or amend it, both by simple majority vote, before returning it to the Mayor. The Mayor will then prepare a final draft budget and present it to a public meeting of the Assembly before the end of February. If the final draft does not include amendments from the Assembly, the Mayor must give reasons why. The Assembly must then approve the final budget by a simple majority, or amend it by a two-thirds majority.

The GLA will, in effect, inherit the funding streams for the existing functions incorporated into the bodies for which it will have responsibility, amounting to £3.6 billion in its first year. The Authority must calculate its own budget and those of its four functional bodies separately. These budgets are then consolidated, but a budget requirement of one constituent body should not be included in the budget calculation of another. The GLA will be a precepting authority, subject to normal local government rules, in respect of its policing, and fire and emergency planning functions, which will be funded by a precept on the London boroughs. However, the Home Secretary is allocated a reserve power to set a minimum level for the Metropolitan Police Authority's budget (see below). The GLA's principal funding will come through central government grants.

The GLA Act creates two new central government grants. The first of these is an annual general-purpose grant to pay for the majority of costs of Mayor and Assembly (with London council taxpayers covering the remainder). The Government anticipates that the Authority's running costs will be around £26 million (about 3 pence per week for each council tax payer, or less than 1 per cent of the GLA's planned spending). The second grant is an annual GLA Transport Grant, which draws together existing streams for funding transport in London. The Act makes clear that the grant is paid for the purposes of Transport for London (TfL), which includes both the services it runs itself and the support it will provide to the borough councils. The Act compels the Mayor to pay the GLA Transport Grant received from the Secretary of State directly to TfL and it is thus not available to the Mayor to spend on other purposes or for allocation to other functional bodies. The scope of the Mayor's activities in the transport field may also be constrained by the terms of the public private partnership (discussed below) that the Government has asserted as the mechanism for the modernisation of the London underground. Taken together, these stipulations place tight limits on the financial flexibility the Mayor will have.[19] The GLA will have access to some limited resources of its own in the form of the power to introduce road user charging and a levy on workplace parking, which are discussed below.

Transport

In relation to transport, London has been subject to a series of statutory measures over time and is governed by a range of institutions (see figure 9.2). The Act amends existing legislation in the light of the new institutions and brings together a range of existing separate functions into Transport for London (TfL). These include London Regional Transport (including London Underground and the regulation of bus services) together with the Docklands Light Railway, Croydon Tramlink, strategic roads, traffic regulation, water transport, and the licensing of taxis. During the passage of the Bill through parliament, the Mayor was given powers to plan commuter rail services. Specifically, the Mayor can order the Strategic Rail Authority to run additional rail services to make the best use of scarce track capacity. The Mayor must bring forward a transport strategy that will not be confined to those forms of transport for which the Mayor or TfL will be directly responsible. For instance the boroughs will remain responsible for 95 per cent of London's roads. Although the boroughs are required to put the transport strategy into effect in their areas they retain most of their existing powers. The Secretary of State will retain a power to direct the Mayor to change the strategy if it is inconsistent with national policy. The Mayor can assume the role of chair (or appoint another) and can appoint between eight and fifteen members of TfL. The Act gives the Mayor the power to introduce road user charging and a levy on parking places. Revenue from these sources can only

---

[19] The Act makes a novel stipulation in its provisions on the use of capital receipts insofar as it enables the redistribution of capital resources within the GLA and its functional bodies by means of internal grants. It also enables the redistribution of revenue finance within the GLA and its functional bodies by means of internal grants. Although the level of potential resources involved presumably would be modest, the intention of the provision is to enable the GLA to overcome the normal restriction that local authorities may not use their capital resources for non-capital expenditure. Thus, using these mechanisms, a body within the GLA that had a surplus of capital resources and a shortage of revenue funds, for example, would be able to trade with another GLA body that faced the opposite situation.

be used for improvements to public transport or traffic management. The Act also establishes a London Transport Users Committee to represent consumer interests.

A major feature of the Act is the power it gives to the Secretary of State to make provisions for a public private partnership (PPP) for the London Underground, which was announced in 1998. The proposed arrangement would see the Underground split between the infrastructure (tracks, signals, etc) — the modernisation of which will be funded through the PPP — and day to day operations. The latter (including the operation of trains and stations) would remain in the public sector, under the control of the Mayor. The full hand-over of control over TfL to the Mayor will only occur once the arrangements regarding the PPP have been put in place by the Secretary of State. The arguments surrounding the merits of PPPs (as opposed to bond financing) are beyond the scope of this chapter, but they emerged as an issue in the election and are discussed further below.[20] However, it is incontrovertible that the PPP places a restriction on the range of actions that the Mayor can take to promote the modernisation of the Tube. Overall the content of the Act, according to one commentary: '…provides no clear guide to how a clash between the central government and the mayor over the future of the tube would be resolved.'[21]

Economic Development

Regional Development Agencies (RDAs) were established in the eight English regions on 1st April 1999, but the London Development Agency (LDA) was not established until April 2000. Prior to the establishment of the LDA, key interests in London established the London Development Partnership, which operated, in effect, as a 'shadow' RDA. RDAs in the rest of England are Non-Departmental Public Bodies accountable to ministers, albeit with a duty to be responsive to regional views. In most respects, the LDA will resemble the other eight RDAs in England, in terms of its structures and sources of funding. However, the GLA Act gives the Mayor the power and duty to appoint the board of the LDA, in consultation with the Assembly. Four seats on the board of the LDA will be retained for elected members of the Assembly or boroughs. In most other respects, the powers of the Secretary of State are given over to the Mayor.

---

[20] Critics of the Government's approach, including the *Economist,* the *Financial Times,* the Institute for Public Policy Research and Ken Livingstone, describe the Government's approach as 'partial privatisation', a term which the Government rejects. A number of academic and media commentators have argued that a more efficient way to fund the modernisation of the Underground's infrastructure would be through a bond. This issue has gained in importance with the election of Ken Livingstone as Mayor (see below).

[21] *Economist,* 11 December 1999.

Policing

The GLA Act established a new Metropolitan Police Authority (MPA) comprising 23 members, including 12 members from the Assembly (including the deputy Mayor), four magistrates, and seven independents. The Mayor will appoint the members of the MPA and set its budget, although the Home Secretary will retain a reserve power to determine a minimum policing requirement and will appoint one of the independents. Hitherto, the Home Secretary was the police authority for London. At one level, the GLA Act brings London into line with the rest of the country. The main tasks of the MPA will be to secure best value in the delivery of policing services, to produce an annual policing plan (drafted by the Commissioner) in consultation with local communities, to set targets and to make representations to the Home Secretary in relation to the appointment and removal of senior officers. The appointment of the Metropolitan Police Commissioner will continue to be a Crown appointment, made on the advice of the Home Secretary, although the Act requires that he or she must have regard to any recommendations from the MPA and the Mayor before making that appointment.

Fire and Emergency Planning

The GLA Act replaced the London Fire and Civil Defence Authority, previously under the control of the boroughs, with the London Fire and Emergency Planning Authority (LFEPA), which is directly accountable to the Mayor. The LFEPA comprises 17 members, nine of which will be drawn from the Assembly and eight of which will be appointed by the boroughs. The main task of the LFEPA will be to provide fire services for London. The Mayor will appoint the board and set the LFEPA's budget.

Planning

The GLA Act proposes new arrangements for planning in London. The Mayor is given a role in the planning system, but one that does not appear to displace the role of the boroughs or that of the Secretary of State. The Mayor will not be a planning authority, nor will he or she be a superior authority hearing appeals against the refusal of planning permission. The boroughs will continue to be responsible for dealing with all planning applications, although the Mayor will be a statutory consultee for planning applications with potential strategic planning implications. The Mayor can comment upon planning applications and refuse them, but he or she cannot compel the acceptance of planning applications. The Act gives the Secretary of State the power to define the types of planning applications that must be notified to the Mayor by the boroughs. The White Paper estimated that these should be in the range of 100 to 300 applications per year, less than 0.5 per cent of all the applications submitted on average in London.

The Mayor's main task is to produce a Spatial Development Strategy (SDS), an innovation which will set out the Mayor's priorities for London and which will have statutory force within the planning system. The SDS replaces the regional planning guidance issued by the Secretary of State. The borough's Unitary Development Plans (UDPs) must conform to the SDS. The Secretary of State will continue to set the framework of national planning policy within which the SDS must be framed. The Act explicitly states that the Mayor must have regard to national policies and any planning guidance issued by the Secretary of State so far as it relates to areas adjacent to London.

Environment

The GLA Act allocates significant responsibilities in relation to the Environment to the Mayor. The Mayor will produce a four-yearly report on the state of London's environment, develop an air quality strategy, a waste management strategy, an ambient noise strategy and a biodiversity action plan. The 'state of the environment report' is likely to have a high profile and be the subject of wide public interest. These strategies must inform the Mayor's policies over the areas for which he or she has direct responsibility (notably transport) but should set the framework for London as a whole. The Assembly may also conduct investigations into environmental issues and scrutinise the Mayor's approach. The boroughs will continue to be key actors in the field of environmental policy and the role of the Mayor will be more in the way of setting broad frameworks designed to shape the delivery of policies by other agencies.

Culture

The final area in which the GLA Act assigns a role to the Mayor is in the area of culture, media, and sport. The Mayor's task will be to produce a strategy for the development of culture in London and to represent London's cultural interests at the regional, national, and international levels. The Mayor will be able to propose and endorse bids for major events such as the Olympics. The Act establishes a Cultural Strategy Group for London (CSGL) to advise the Mayor.[22] The Mayor will appoint the members of the CSGL and its chair. Although not specified in the Act, it is anticipated that the Mayor will play a role in making some appointments to publicly funded arts organisations and, in some cases, to control part of their funding. However, in the main the Mayor will rely on other agencies to implement the strategy for culture. The Act gives the Mayor a role in the promotion of tourism. The Mayor will also

[22] The CSGL replaces the London Heritage Forum comprising London Arts Board, the London Tourist Board, the South Eastern Museums Service, Sport England, English Heritage, the Royal Parks Agency, the Historic Palaces Agency, London and South Eastern Library Region, and the London Film Commission.

have responsibility for Trafalgar Square and Parliament Square, with the expectation that he or she will develop a strategy for their improvement.

Health

In the period before the election of the Greater London Assembly, a Kings Fund report called for health to be an integral and essential component of the GLA's policies.[23] During the passage of the Bill, an amendment was introduced which gave the GLA a duty to promote the health of Londoners and to take into account how its other policies may impact on health. The Mayor will not have any direct health responsibilities, which will continue to be provided by the NHS. However, as Harling notes, the Mayor and the Assembly have the potential to be an influence on London's health, by exercising the influence that comes through its democratic mandate.[24]

Assessment

Overall, the Mayor has extensive powers of patronage, but the Mayor's ability to implement his or her strategies will depend also on the actions of the boroughs and the Secretary of State, in areas like policing, transport, and planning. A high level of co-operation between different actors is required if the new arrangements are to improve the governance of London. At the same time, the system of governance embodied in the GLA Act throws up real possibilities for conflict. The risk of such conflict seems to be especially high in relation to transport and planning. In the case of transport, the issue of the PPP (or 'part privatisation') emerged as an issue during the election campaign. In addition, controversies over planning jurisdictions seem likely in the future, when questions arise as to whether a development application is of national or London-wide importance.

SELECTING THE CANDIDATES[25]

In both the Labour Party and the Conservative Party, the selection of candidates for the position of Mayor of London proved to be eventful. As early as March 1999, Trevor Phillips and Ken Livingstone declared their candidature

---

[23]   Davies and Kendall, 1999: 1; see also Harling 1999.

[24]   The successful Mayoral candidate, Ken Livingstone, in fact gave a prominent place in his manifesto to health issues. The Mayor's role may be one based on the exercise of influence, but Livingstone's manifesto promised to 'ensure that improving the health of Londoners is a central objective of all the Mayor and Assembly's policies'. Specifically, Livingstone proposed a Healthy London Commission and a Health Improvement Programme for London. In addition, he proposes to 'set up arrangements for the London Region of the NHS to report regularly to the Mayor and Assembly on progress in meeting targets for health improvement in London and make this information widely available through a new web-site'.

[25]   This section and the following one draw on the coverage of the election in the *Financial Times,* the *Guardian,* the *Independent,* the *Economist* and the *Evening Standard.*

for the Labour Party nomination. At the same time, Jeffrey Archer announced his candidature for the Conservative nomination, later to be joined by Steven Norris. In July 1999, Glenda Jackson resigned her position as Minister for Transport in London, in order to seek nomination as Labour's mayoral candidate. However, the first of the main parties to actually select their candidate was the Liberal Democrats, who selected Susan Kramer, a transport consultant, in August 1999. In October, Jeffrey Archer was selected to become the Conservative candidate, beating Steven Norris by a large margin. The Conservative Party leader, William Hague, enthusiastically endorsed Archer. Also in October, after much speculation, Frank Dobson left his job as Health Secretary and announced his candidature for the Labour nomination, with the implied backing of Tony Blair. Nick Raynsford, the Minister for London, who had announced his own candidacy only days before, withdrew from the race. Shortly afterwards, Trevor Phillips also withdrew announcing he would be Dobson's running mate and was selected as an Assembly candidate for the Labour Party's top-up list.

By this stage, for the Labour leadership, the issue was already that of stopping Ken Livingstone from becoming Mayor of London. A poll published in mid October 1999 showed that Livingstone would easily win the mayoral election, even if he did not win the Labour nomination and stood as an independent. At the end of October, Tony Blair gave a ringing public endorsement of Dobson for the first time. Leadership support for Dobson's candidacy proved controversial when the Data Protection Registrar launched an investigation into whether Frank Dobson broke the law in obtaining a list of London Labour party members to assist his campaign for the nomination.[26]

By mid-November, after much deliberation, the leadership allowed Ken Livingstone to compete with Frank Dobson and Glenda Jackson for the Labour nomination, but the process was protracted to the last. Contrary to expectations, the party announced that the selection process for the mayoral candidacy would not be on the basis of one vote cast by each Party member in London. Instead, the candidate was to be chosen by an electoral college similar to that used in Wales, and divided into three parts: London members, affiliated trade unions in the capital and London's Labour MPs, MEPs and candidates already adopted for the Greater London Assembly. This arrangement was widely seen as being designed to prevent Ken Livingstone from being elected by London party members as their candidate.[27] This impression was compounded by the announcement that individual unions would not be expected to conduct a ballot of their London membership. Moreover, prior to the ballot of Party members, all candidates were subject to an interview by

[26] Livingstone and Jackson were only given the list of London Party members in January 2000, some three months after senior Party officials gave it to Dobson. Livingstone and Jackson agreed jointly to compile a dossier of unfair practices on the part of Labour's Millbank HQ.

[27] For instance borough councillors, who were considered likely to support Livingstone, were not given a special status in the electoral college.

the London Party executive. Livingstone's interview proved prolonged. The interview was designed to elicit two commitments from him. First, it was designed to secure his commitment to the PPP for the London Underground, which he had criticised in the past. Secondly, Livingstone was asked to give a commitment that if he lost the selection battle, he would not stand against the Party as an independent. Livingstone agreed to the latter commitment.

On 20 November attention was distracted from events inside the Labour Party by the dramatic resignation of Jeffrey Archer as the Conservative Party mayoral candidate. Archer resigned following newspaper allegations that he had asked a friend to lie ahead of the libel case against the *Daily Star* that he had won 13 years previously. The Conservative Party was compelled to reopen its selection process. The Essex MP, Teresa Gorman, put her name forward as a candidate, but was barred from standing the following day by the Conservative selection committee. Steven Norris emerged as the new favourite for the Tory nomination. However initially the selection committee banned him from standing. After intense pressure from the Tory leadership, Norris was immediately reinstated to the competition for the Conservative nomination. Norris was finally selected as the Conservative mayoral candidate in January 2000.

On 20 February 2000, after strong support from Tony Blair and others,[28] Frank Dobson scored a narrow win over Ken Livingstone in the ballot for the Labour nomination. Dobson received 51.53 per cent of the vote to Livingstone's 48.47 per cent, after Jackson was eliminated in the first round. Livingstone described the vote as 'tainted', pointing to the fact that he had won a majority in the members and union section of the ballot and demanded that Dobson step down. Moreover, those unions that had conducted ballots of their members had tended to support Livingstone, whereas those that did not ballot tended to support Dobson. In the days following the result, Livingstone's independent candidacy was widely predicted, although it was not until two weeks later, on 6 March, that he announced his decision to run. Livingstone acknowledged that in doing so he had broken the commitment he had given to the London Labour executive not to run. Tony Blair described a Livingstone mayoralty as 'a disaster for London'. A poll the following day immediately gave Livingstone a 55 point lead over Dobson, suggesting Livingstone would win a first round victory under SV.

The Mayoral and Assembly Campaign

Livingstone's lead was eroded only partially during the campaign. Policy issues played a secondary role to personality issues in the campaign. Livingstone proved immune to sustained attacks on his character. The first charge

---

[28] For instance, both Blair and Gordon Brown attacked Livingstone (and supported Dobson) in articles in the London *Evening Standard.* (Blair, 1999, Brown, 2000).

was laid against him by the House of Commons standards committee in March 2000, which found him guilty of failing to declare £158,599 earned from regular commitments including speech making and journalism. Livingstone was forced to make an apology to the House of Commons. Subsequently, it emerged that the complainant in the matter was the former treasurer of Trevor Phillips' mayoral campaign. Further allegations of financial impropriety levelled against Livingstone were unfounded, while statements by Livingstone that were interpreted as attacks on the international financial system or support for the Seattle rioters had little impact on his poll standing.

By the end of March, Labour's private polling apparently indicated that the Party should prepare for the defeat of Frank Dobson. Ken Livingstone was expelled from the Labour Party on 3 April, for at least five years. On 12 April, Tony Blair made his first official appearance for the Dobson campaign, describing him as a man of 'integrity and courage', but promising to 'work with whoever is mayor'. However, opinion polls showed that Blair's support for Dobson was harming his candidature. An opinion poll on 13 April showed a 12 per cent fall in support for Livingstone, but this still left him 49 per cent of first preferences. Significantly, Steven Norris had overtaken Frank Dobson to move into second place. A poll later in April confirmed Norris' position in second place, although 34 points behind Livingstone. The Labour Party's traditional ally, *The Mirror*, called on its readers to vote for Norris.

While negative campaigning is not an entirely new feature of British politics, it is true to say that policy issues rarely obscured character attacks during the course of the mayoral campaign. To the extent that policy issues received public attention, they tended to focus on transport. In particular, Ken Livingstone strongly rejected the government's proposed PPP for the Underground, arguing that the modernisation scheme should be a matter for the electors of London rather than pre-empted by Act of Parliament. The Liberal Democrats were also strongly associated with opposition to the PPP. At the time of writing the issue of the PPP was unresolved and was likely to prove a source of tension between the Mayor and the Government into the autumn of 2000. A second policy issue that received a modest airing was congestion and parking charges. Frank Dobson accused Ken Livingstone of proposing a system of congestion charging that would cost the motorist £300 per month. This charge proved difficult to substantiate because Livingstone's manifesto made few quantifiable commitments. Dobson, however, committed himself to not introducing congestion charges for four years. All the party manifestos — with the possible exception of the Greens — eschewed detailed commitments in favour of broad statements of aspirations. Livingstone's manifesto, however, did have a green tinge and he himself called on his supporters to vote Green after Labour in the Mayoral and Assembly elections.[29]

Election Results

There were 11 candidates for Mayor. Of these, only four had any significant public profile: Livingstone, Norris, Dobson, and Kramer. Of those who 'also ran', only Darren Johnson of the Green Party achieved a public profile, reflected in his notable share of second preferences. Figure 9.5 shows the final result.

**Figure 9.5. London election May 5th 2000:
Candidates for Mayor of London**

Name	Party	1st. Pref	%	2nd. Pref	%	Final**
Ken Livingstone	Independent	667,877	39.0	178,809	12.6	776,427
Steve Norris	Conservative	464,424	27.1	188,041	13.2	564,137
Frank Dobson	Labour	223,884	13.1	228,095	16.0	
Susan Kramer	Liberal Democrats	203,452	11.9	404,815	28.5	
Ram Giddomal	Christian People's Alliance	42,060	2.4	56,489	4.0	
Darren Johnson	Green	38,121	2.2	192,764	13.6	
Michael Newland	British National Party	33,569	2.0	45,337	3.2	
Damian Hockney	UK Independence Party	16,234	1.0	43,672	3.1	
Geoffrey Ben-Nathan	Pro-Motorist Small Shop	9,956	0.6	23,021	1.6	
Ashwin Kumar Tanna	Independent	9,015	0.5	41,766	2.9	
Geoffrey Clements	Natural Law Party	5,470	0.3	18,185	1.3	

---

[29] It is fair to say that was very little media coverage of the Assembly election, beyond a few profiles of better known candidates such as Trevor Phillips. Such coverage as did occur within the print media was generally prefaced with a statement about how little interest and coverage the Assembly election had generated relative to the mayoral election.

Although Ken Livingstone's massive early opinion poll leads were not sustained in their entirety, the result on election day accorded him a crushing victory. Of equal significance to Livingstone's victory was Frank Dobson's relegation to third place. Dobson's performance undoubtedly reflected a desire on the part of voters to punish Labour for a perceived fix in the process of selecting its mayoral candidate. This aspect of the result was clearly revealed in polling. Steve Norris, as well as Livingstone, was able to benefit from the damaging charge that Dobson was 'Blair's poodle'. A final noteworthy feature of the result was the relatively impressive share of second preferences won by Darren Johnson. It is likely that Johnson (who was in fact elected to the Assembly) benefited from Livingstone's endorsement of his party, the Greens.

The main features of the Assembly election results are the poor performance of Labour in the constituency section and the relatively good performance of the Conservatives. It is likely that similar processes were at work in the Assembly election as in the mayoral contest. The other principal feature of the Assembly result was the high profile electoral breakthrough on the part of the Greens. This breakthrough is probably attributable to the combined effects of the proportional voting system, the genuine appeal of green policies in London and the endorsement of the Party given by Ken Livingstone. The Green result (along with the make-up of the Scottish Parliament and Welsh Assembly) provides further evidence of how PR appears to contribute to greater electoral diversity. A notable feature of the election, however, was that there was little ethnic minority representation in the assembly. In a city such as London, where at least one third of the population is non-white, this must be a cause for concern. In answering the question why this situation came about, attention might focus on party selection procedures.

An important feature of the GLA elections, although one which received relatively little media attention, was the comparatively low turnout at 34.7 per cent. The turnout was in line with average local government election turnouts and substantially lower than for the Welsh Assembly and Scottish Parliament. Given the extraordinary level of (national) media attention on the contest and the claim that elected mayors would lead to higher turnouts, this ought to be a cause of concern for the advocates of elected mayors.[30]

---

[30] The turnout was less than that predicted on the basis of opinion polling in advance of the election.

Figure 9.6. London election 2000: constituency results

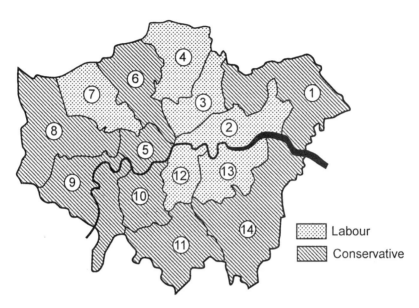

Name of constituency	Constituent boroughs
1. Havering & Redbridge	Havering and Redbridge
2. City & East	Barking & Dagenham, City of London, Newham and Tower Hamlets
3. North East	Hackney, Islington & Waltham Forest
4. Enfield & Haringey	Enfield and Haringey
5. West Central	Hammersmith & Fulham, Kensington & Chelsea and Westminster
6. Barnet & Camden	Barnet and Camden
7. Brent & Harrow	Brent and Harrow
8. Ealing & Hillingdon	Ealing and Hillingdon
9. South West	Hounslow, Kingston upon Thames and Richmond upon Thames
10. Merton & Wandsworth	Merton and Wandsworth
11. Croydon & Sutton	Croydon and Sutton
12. Lambeth & Southwark	Lambeth and Southwark
13. Greenwich & Lewisham	Greenwich and Lewisham
14. Bexley & Bromley	Bexley and Bromley

Figure 9.6. (cont.) London election 2000: parties/independents contesting the 11 London-wide list seats (top-up seats to provide proportionality).

Seat No.	Party/Independent name	Number of votes / Seats + 1
1	Liberal Democrats Against Tube Privatisation	245,552
2	Green Party	183,910
3	Liberal Democrats Against Tube Privatisation	122,777
4	Green Party	91,955
5	Liberal Democrats Against Tube Privatisation	81,851
6	Labour Party	71,839
7	Labour Party	62,859
8	Liberal Democrats Against Tube Privatisation	61,388
9	Green Party	61,303
10	Labour Party	55,874
11	Conservative Party	53,450

Source: DETR

Overall party standings in the Assembly:

• Labour: 9 seats (6 constituencies, 3 London-wide)
• Conservative: 9 seats (8 constituencies, 1 London-wide)
• Liberal Democrats: 4 seats (all London-wide)
• Greens: 3 seats (all London-wide)

THE LIVINGSTONE ADMINISTRATION

The major task confronting Mayor Livingstone between his election and the first summer recess was the appointment of an administration, comprising an advisory cabinet and the membership of the boards of 'functional bodies'. In May the Mayor announced his intention of assembling 'a broad based government for London' involving Labour, Liberal Democrat and Green Assembly members to create 'a uniquely inclusive administration.'[31] The Mayor's first appointment was that of Nicky Gavron, a Labour assembly member, as deputy Mayor. In forming his cabinet, the Mayor emphasised its

---

[31] All direct quotes in this section, unless otherwise stated, are taken from GLA news releases which are archived on the GLA website at http://www.london.gov.uk/.

advisory role and stressed that, under the terms of the Act, he would make all decisions. The Mayor announced his initial cabinet on 19 June.

Figure 9.7. London Mayor's Advisory Cabinet (June 2000)

Nicky Gavron (Deputy Mayor)	Spatial development and strategic planning
Toby Harris (Labour AM)	Police
Graham Tope (Lib Dem AM)	Human rights and equality
Val Shawcross (Labour AM)	Fire and emergency planning
Darren Johnson (Green AM)	Environment
Judith Mayhew	City and Business
Glenda Jackson MP	Homelessness
John McDonnell	Local Government
George Barlow	Economic development
Kumar Murshid	Regeneration
Lee Jasper	Race Relations
Diane Abbott MP	Women and Equality
Richard Stone	Community Relations
Sean Baine London	Voluntary Services Council
Caroline Gooding	Disability Rights

The membership of the 'functional bodies' was also announced in June. The membership of the boards provides some justification for the Mayor's claim that his administration would be characterised by inclusivity. As well as being politically balanced, the appointments show a strong concern with gender balance and ensuring representation for ethnic minorities. The latter issues take on a heightened importance given the poor representation of ethnic minorities in the Assembly. The main appointments (at June 2000) are listed below.

Figure 9.8. Assembly appointments (June 2000)

London Fire and Emergency Planning Authority (June 2000)

Assembly Members:
Valerie Shawcross (Chair), Trevor Phillips, Samantha Heath, Brian Coleman, Robert Neill, Eric Ollerenshaw, Jennifer Jones, Lynne Featherstone, Louise Bloom.

Borough representatives (nominated by the Association of London Government):
Janice Long (Brent), Roy Shaw (Camden), Philip Portwood (Ealing), Toby Simon (Enfield), Peter Forrest (Haringey), Anne Gallop (Sutton), Liaquat Ali (Waltham Forest), Maurice Heaster (Wandsworth)

London Development Agency (June 2000)

George Barlow (Chair — Former chair of Peabody Trust), Honor Chapman (Vice chair — Jones Lang La Salle), Len Duvall (Vice Chair — London Assembly Member), Tamara Ingram (Saatchi and Saatchi), Yvonne Thompson

(ASAP Communications Ltd), Mick Connolly, George Kessler, Michael Frye, Judith Mayhew (Corporation of London), Kumar Murshid (Mayoral advisor), Lord Paul, Andrew Pelling (Assembly member), Cllr Sally Powell, Mary Reilly.

Transport for London (June 2000)

Ken Livingstone (Chair — Mayor of London), Dave Wetzel (former GLC councillor), Professor Stephen Glaister (Imperial College), Kirsten Hearn (Consultant), Mike Hodgkindon (Chief Executive BAA plc), Ollie Jackson (TGWU London), Jimmy Knapp (General Secretary, RMT), Susan Kramer (former mayoral candidate), Professor Robert Lane (University of Westminster), Joyce Mamode (TGWU), Paul Moore (former GLC councillor), Steve Morris (former mayoral candidate and former Minister for Transport in London), David Quarmby (Chair, Docklands Light Railway), Tony West (Assistant General Secretary ASLEF).

The formal inauguration of the GLA took place on 3rd July 2000. Trevor Phillips was nominated as chair of the Assembly. In his acceptance speech, he promised that the Assembly would act as 'a critical and constructive scrutineer' of the Mayor. He warned the Mayor that if he used his platform for 'political ends', the Assembly would 'kick your ass'. Sally Hamwee (Liberal Democrat) was appointed deputy chair. Subsequently the Assembly announced the formation of a number of committees. Additional 'short term scrutinies' were announced to cover affordable housing and nuclear waste trains.

Figure 9.9. Assembly committees and chairs (July 2000)

Transport policy and spatial development	Chair: Lynne Featherstone (LibDem)
Transport Operations Scrutiny	Chair: John Biggs (Labour)
Environment	Chair: Samantha Heath (Labour)
Economic Development	Chair: Eric Ollerenshaw (Conservative)
Planning	Chair: Tony Arbour (Conservative)
Appointments	Chair: Len Duvall (Labour)
Budget	Chair: Sally Hamwee (Liberal Democrat)
Audit	Chair: Valerie Shawcross (Labour)
Standards	Chair: Jenny Jones (Green)

The Mayor's policy priorities were signalled by his appointment in July of an eighteen-person Housing Commission, chaired by Chris Holmes, the Director of Shelter, to report on London's housing needs and make policy recommendations. In addition, the Mayor welcomed the publication of a House of Commons Select Committee Report into the modernisation of the London Underground. The report appeared to cast doubt on the value of Public Private Partnerships as the mechanism for modernisation. Finally the Assembly announced an investigation into congestion charging in advance of the production of the Mayor's draft transport strategy. The lines of policy battle were beginning to become clearer, as the Mayor and Assembly members departed for their summer break.

ISSUES AND CONTROVERSIES

I noted at the outset some of the issues that surrounded the creation of the GLA. The GLA model reflected Labour's desire to restore London-wide government, but in a way which did not imply any threats to power for the boroughs. It reflects also some of the Government's priorities for local government in general, especially the appeal of elected mayors. The Mayor and Assembly model is very much influenced by the alleged impact of city mayors in the United States. But as the description of the Mayor's powers given earlier indicates, the London mayor model probably corresponds more closely to the 'weak mayor' model as it is understood in the US.

Much of the GLA's room for manoeuvre is constrained by the powers reserved by the Secretary of State. One aspect of the London settlement that, to date, has received comparatively little attention is the new role of the Government Office for London (GOL). The currently defined tasks of GOL include the implementation of the GLA, meeting the needs of central government after the establishment of the GLA and its agencies, the management and delivery of central government programmes in London, and management of DETR's relationship with London Transport. A close analysis of the activities of GOL over the coming period may indicate the likely future relationship between central government and regional assemblies, should they come to pass.

A further striking feature of the GLA, compared to local government systems in other EU states, as well as the US, is its limited financial autonomy. This is true not just in terms of the proportion of the GLA's revenue that will be raised locally, but also in relation to the way central government money is given to the GLA in the form of hypothecated grants. However, this does not necessarily mean that the Mayor will be unable to get to grips with the issues facing London:

> On paper these reserve powers severely limit the Mayor's freedom of manoeuvre. In practice, the Government may find them hard to exercise. For one thing, the Mayor will have huge visibility in the media. But the new Mayor will not only be famous, he will have unparalleled legitimacy. No one else in British public life will have been personally chosen by an electorate as large as 5 million people. Far from being constrained in his core areas of responsibility, the Mayor is more likely to be an important influence even on policies such as health and education, where he has very limited formal powers.[32]

[32] *Economist*, 11 December 1999: 34.

Nevertheless, the nature of the Mayor's powers means that the success of the statutorily required strategies will depend upon the actions of organisations outside the direct control of the Mayor. The implications of the GLA model for the actions of the Mayor have been described thus:

> [The] new Mayor will need to be more like a broker, inserting himself into the space that remains between the mighty national government on his doorstep and the bloody-minded boroughs that will go on running London's main services. With more influence than power, he will be expected to conduct the orchestra, not write the score.[33]

As noted earlier in this chapter, most commentators have stressed the degree to which the GLA is a recognisable local government model, albeit incorporating a number of innovations. It falls far short of a genuine devolution of political power from parliament. As such it remains unclear what impact the model will have on wider debates about devolution (as opposed to local government reform). It is worth noting, however, that Ken Livingstone in particular sought to raise the alleged unfairness of London's financial settlement in terms of public expenditure. Given the financial pressures that surround the GLA, it is likely that these claims pre-figure the shape of things to come in relation to future resource battles.

A notable feature of the Livingstone's administration, which has yet to make a policy impact, is its 'inclusive' character. The Mayor's appointment to his cabinet of representatives of Assembly members from Labour, Liberal Democrats and Greens and the failed Conservative Mayoral candidates Susan Kramer (Liberal Democrat) and Steve Norris (Conservative) to the board of Transport for London, bear testimony to his search for a cross party mode of governance for London. It will be interesting to see whether this 'non-ideological' approach to politics survives into the future, especially as the Mayor seeks to assert his policy priorities. Another aspect of the Mayor's search for 'inclusivity' has been the prominent role given to both women and people from ethnic minorities in the Mayor's administration.

The London mayoral election throws up interesting questions about the future shape of local politics. A striking feature of the election campaign itself, especially as far as the media coverage is concerned, was the degree to which it focused on the personality (and characters) of the Mayoral contenders, rather than focusing on substantive policy issues. Whether this signals the more general shape of local politics under elected mayors remains to be seen. The Local Government Act 2000 raises the prospect of elected mayors in other parts of England and Wales. In two cities (Birmingham and Liverpool), advisory commissions have recommended the creation of elected mayors as means of reinvigorating citizens' interest in local politics. The London experience, with a high level of media interest, accompanied by a

---

[33] *Economist*, 29 April 2000: 25.

low electoral turnout, offers mixed signals.[34] In addition, coming after recent episodes in Scotland and Wales, the story of the London mayoral election points also to the difficulty of centralised party management in an era of new forms of decentralised government. Mayoral elections may prove to be particularly unsusceptible to centralised forms of party management. Whatever the strengths and weaknesses of the GLA model, it suggests the emergence of a new landscape of government that will present novel challenges to the political class.

BIBLIOGRAPHY

Blair, T., 'The last thing we want is an extremist mayor', *Evening Standard,* 19 November 1999.

Boudreau, J.A. and Keil, R., 'Seceding from Responsibility: Secession movements in Los Angeles', *Paper for the Urban Affairs Association Annual Meeting*, Los Angeles, 3-6 May 2000.

Brown, G., 'Livingstone must not be London Mayor', *Evening Standard*, 19 January 2000.

Commission for Local Democracy, *Taking charge: the rebirth of local democracy. The final report of the CLD* (London: Municipal Books, 1995).

Davies A., and Kendell L., *Health and the London Mayor* (London: Kings Fund, 1999).

Hambleton, R., 'Modernising political management in local government', *Urban Studies*, 37 (5-6): 931-950, 2000.

Harding, A., *Is there a 'missing middle' in English governance?* A report for the New Local Government Network (London: NLGN, 2000).

Harling R., London's health: a role for the new mayor, editorial, *British Medical Journal*, 318: 478-9, 1999.

Haywood, I., 'London', *Cities*, 15 (5): 381-192, 1998.

House of Lords/House of Commons, Draft Local Government (Organisation and Standards) Bill — Appendices to the Minutes of Evidence — First Report (1999).

Inwood, S., *A History of London* (London: MacMillan, 1999).

Rhodes, R., 'New Labour's Civil Service: Summing-up Joining-up', *Political Quarterly*, 71 (2): 151-166, 2000.

Travers, T. and Jones, G., *The New Government of London*, Report for the Joseph Rowntree Foundation (York: York Publishing Services, 1997).

---

[34] One immediate effect of the controversies surrounding the London mayoral model though was that public support for the idea of directly elected mayors for British cities dropped from 59 per cent in February to 22 per cent by mid-April 2000, according to an ICM survey for the *Guardian* (*The Guardian*, April 19th, 2000).

10

Conclusion

The State and the Nations after One Year of Devolution

Robert Hazell

This concluding chapter draws together the threads from the preceding chapters and summarises the emerging characteristics of the devolution settlement after its first year. The main conclusions are that the settlement is very lopsided and asymmetrical, with the differences between the devolved administrations and assemblies far outweighing their similarities; the UK Government remains quietly dominant, with no serious challenge so far to its position or its policies; but the dynamics of devolution mean that the settlement will continue to evolve, with the English regions and the whole English Question presenting the biggest challenges in the years to come.

CONSTITUTIONAL ASYMMETRY

The emphasis in this book on developments in Scotland, Wales, and Northern Ireland could easily lead the reader to forget that in population terms they constitute only 15 per cent of the UK. Devolution has been conferred on a small minority of the UK's population, and for most citizens, in particular the 85 per cent who live in England whose lives remain unaffected, it has simply passed them by. This is the biggest respect in which the devolution settlement remains asymmetrical. We return to England and the English Question at the end of the chapter.

But even as between Scotland, Wales, and Northern Ireland the settlement is very different. The main differences in size, powers, and functions of the three assemblies were outlined in chapter 1. Asymmetry runs through every clause and schedule of the devolution legislation, from the fundamentals of powers and functions down to the niceties of nomenclature. Scotland has a parliament while Wales and Northern Ireland have only an Assembly (in the case of Wales, dignified as the National Assembly). Scotland and Northern Ireland have Ministers, while Wales has Assembly Secretaries. These are not accidental choices: the nomenclature for Wales was discussed and voted on in Cabinet Committee. They are deliberate differences chosen to emphasise the difference in style and substance between the three devolved assemblies, and in particular between each of the devolved assemblies and their parent body at Westminster. These are different institutions with different constitutions, and none of them is to be confused with the Prime Minister, Cabinet and Parliament in London.

Many of the differences between the three devolution Acts are due to the different circumstances and starting points in each country. Thus, the Northern Ireland Act has to be seen as part of the peace process, and so includes provisions on power-sharing and qualified majorities to ensure cross-community support for key votes in the Assembly which are absent in Scotland and Wales. But there are many other differences which are less easily explained. To take just two examples, the rules for government formation and government dissolution are different between the three Acts.

In Scotland, the process of government formation begins with the parliament nominating one of its members to be the First Minister, and The Queen makes the appointment. The Scottish Parliament then votes to approve the First Minister's nominees to serve as Scottish ministers, and these too are presented to The Queen for appointment. In Wales, the Act provides that the Assembly shall elect, not nominate, one of its number to be the Assembly First Secretary, and he or she then appoints the remaining members of the Executive Committee without reference to the Assembly or the Sovereign. In Northern Ireland, the position is very different. The First and deputy First Ministers have no authority as government leaders to nominate, appoint or dismiss other members of the ministry. Instead elections are held in the Assembly for ministerial positions using the d'Hondt system of proportional representation. As chapter 4 described, nominating officers for each party propose candidates, office by office; and once elected, a minister can only be dismissed by that nominating officer or a successor. This makes a huge difference in terms of collective responsibility and the power of the First Minister: it means that in Northern Ireland the First and deputy First Minister have no means of disciplining the government as a whole.

In terms of government dissolution, the big difference is between the constitutional position in Wales, where there is no provision for an early dissolution, and the Scotland and Northern Ireland Acts, which allow for a dissolution on a two thirds majority. Again this is more than a constitutional nicety: as chapter 3 records, Wales had a mini-constitutional crisis and a major political crisis when it seemed, in February 2000, that the Assembly could pass repeated votes of no confidence in Alun Michael, without succeeding in replacing him as First Secretary. In the event, the crisis was solved when Alun Michael resigned just before the vote, thus averting the risk of nugatory votes of no confidence and enabling Rhodri Morgan subsequently to be elected as his successor.

These are just two examples of basic constitutional differences. In a detailed comparison of the three devolution Acts, Professor Alan Ward lists the following discrepancies:

Little attempt was made to simplify or clarify this complexity, by standardising the provisions that could be standardised, for example, or actually setting out to produce a coherent constitution for the United Kingdom, rather than a set of improvisations. The powers devolved to the three countries are different in each Act and some provisions in one or two Acts are missing from the others for reasons that are hardly self-evident. The Scottish Act, for example, provides that The Queen, by Order in Council, may make payments to registered opposition parties. This could easily have been left to ordinary Scottish law, and there is no similar provision in the Northern Ireland or Wales Acts. The Welsh Act alone creates an office of Administrative Ombudsman. Only the Northern Ireland Act declares that the executive power in the province 'shall continue to be vested in Her Majesty.' Scottish ministers serve at the pleasure of The Queen, but not those in Northern Ireland or Wales. The Northern Ireland and Wales Acts provide that only the government may propose a spending measure, but not the Scotland Act ... Scotland has its own law officers, but not Northern Ireland or Wales.[1]

To what extent do these differences matter? Viewing the devolution legislation from an American perspective, Alan Ward clearly thinks that they matter a lot:

Devolution might even evolve into a UK federation, or home rule all round, which might do a great deal to cement the regions into the Union permanently. Unfortunately the devolution Acts are so different that they might almost have been written to discourage this. Indeed one's overall impression of Labour's constitutional design is its incoherence. Some would see this as evidence of the genius of a flexible constitution, not a problem at all, but they are wrong. The constitutional innovation of recent years has produced a UK constitution that is so complex that it must be incomprehensible to most citizens, and constitutional incoherence surely contributes to the democratic deficit in the UK.[2]

DOMINANCE OF THE UK GOVERNMENT

The second characteristic of devolution in the first year is that the UK Government has remained quietly dominant. The Westminster Parliament remains sovereign, and Westminster retains its ability to legislate even on matters which have been devolved. This is not simply a theoretical power: in the first year of devolution it has been exercised repeatedly, as chapter 7 records, in listing the dozen or so bills passed by Westminster which have trespassed on matters devolved to Scotland. But this is not so much Westminster asserting its dominance, as negotiating a legislative partnership with the new Scottish Parliament. The development of social, environmental or industrial policy will often require a sharing of powers, functions or budgets

---

[1] Alan Ward, 'Devolution: Labour's strange constitutional "design"' in J. Jowell and D. Oliver eds, *The Changing Constitution*, Oxford Univ Press 2000, p136.

[2] *Ibid* p135.

across the devolution divide;[3] coherent policy may best be achieved by a common legislative scheme enacted by a single legislature.

It remains to be seen whether the high number of trespassing bills in the first session reflected legislative schemes already in the pipeline, which it was inconvenient to divide, or whether Westminster will continue to pass significant amounts of legislation which trespass on devolved matters. There will certainly continue to be a steady trickle, because the Scottish Parliament will be busy with its own legislative programme, and there will always be issues (for example, where legislation is required to comply with an international obligation) where it may suit the Scots to allow Westminster to legislate for them. What will be important to monitor is in how many cases Westminster legislates with full-hearted Scottish consent, following the Sewel Convention; on how many bills Scottish consent is forced or grudging; and on how many bills the trespass by Westminster is by oversight rather than by design.[4]

Another important feature of devolution so far is the absence of public wrangling between the UK Government and the devolved administrations. If the Scots felt aggrieved by Westminster trampling on their patch, it has rarely been voiced. There have undoubtedly been difficulties and disputes, but they have seldom been aired in public. The main reason for this is probably observance by officials of the previous tradition of collective responsibility, which ensured that such disputes were dealt with discreetly and without disclosing too many chinks in the Whitehall curtain. Equally important were the ties of party solidarity, which linked the Labour politicians in London, Cardiff, and Edinburgh. It is also a tribute to the effectiveness of the graduated arrangements for handling disputes described in chapter 6. This has involved the Constitution Secretariat in the Cabinet Office playing an informal role in mediation and arbitration, sometimes drawing on the good offices of the Secretaries of State, and not yet wheeling out the formal dispute resolution machinery of the Joint Ministerial Committee (JMC).

Most disputes have been bilateral, and the parties have not wanted to wash their dirty linen before the other devolved administrations. As a result, the JMC has not yet been deployed as the forum of last resort in the political machinery for dispute resolution. Instead, it has been used by UK ministers to launch high profile policy initiatives in policy fields where the co-operation of the devolved governments is needed. In the hands of Gordon Brown and Tony Blair, the JMC has become more of a publicity vehicle than a piece of intergovernmental machinery.

---

[3] Lucy Hunter, *Managing Conflict after Devolution: A Toolkit for Civil Servants*, Constitution Unit, University College London and Governance of Scotland Forum, Edinburgh University (forthcoming).

[4] It is hoped to carry out some of this monitoring in a new Constitution Unit research project, funded by the ESRC, on how the law shapes the devolution settlement.

UK dominance is reflected in the fact that all meetings of the JMC were convened and chaired by UK ministers, to discuss items on the UK agenda. It was not until the first plenary meeting of the JMC, held on 1 September 2000, that the devolved administrations began to assert themselves: not least by requesting that the plenary be held.[5]

UK dominance is also reflected in the funding arrangements for devolution, where all the devolved governments are dependent on block funding from Whitehall (as very substantially is the new Mayor in London). And UK dominance is reflected in the Concordats, especially that on Co-ordination of EU Policy Issues. The EU Concordat makes it quite clear that the continuing flow of information and consultation by Whitehall is dependent on the devolved governments observing confidentiality and adhering to the resultant UK line.

NO SIGNIFICANT POLICY DIFFERENCES

Another way of assessing the impact of devolution is to ask what difference devolution has made in terms of policy. In the first year, there has been little to upset UK policy dominance. The JMC struggled to identify items of significance in recording the achievements of the first year for the Downing Street communiqué following its 1 September meeting:

> In Scotland, the Executive and Parliament have established a Scottish Drugs Enforcement Agency, created a new system of funding support for students in higher education, and set challenging targets on social justice;

> In Wales, the Assembly is introducing free bus travel for the elderly and disabled, has established uniquely open processes of government and decision making, and working with the Secretary of State for Wales, has brought in a unique innovation in strengthening the rights of children in care;

> In Northern Ireland, power-sharing is now working. The Assembly has begun legislating and overseeing the eleven NI Departments. A Civic Forum will be established later this year, and

> In England, the UK Government has put in place legislation to modernise local government and successfully established a new London-wide authority and Mayor. And the Regional Development Agencies are spear-heading economic development, competitiveness and regeneration.

Not surprisingly, the communiqué reports policy differences only in Scotland and Wales. (In Northern Ireland, the Executive has not been in being long enough to make a difference in policy terms). Of these, the most significant policy departure (which did cause the UK Government some

---

[5] *The Memorandum of Understanding* requires there to be such a meeting at least once a year, attended by the Prime Minister and all the First Ministers and their Deputies, plus the three territorial Secretaries of State.

discomfort) was the scrapping of higher education tuition fees in Scotland, and their replacement by a form of graduate tax, following the recommendations of the Cubie committee.

Ironically, the greatest policy controversy in Scotland during the year was over an issue where the Scottish government was not trying to depart from UK policy, but to maintain the same policy as the UK Government; or rather to effect a similar change. This was the repeal of Section 2A of the Local Government Act 1986 ('section 28' in England, restricting the 'promotion' of homosexuality in schools). By the end of July, the Scottish Executive had succeeded in changing the law, despite fierce opposition in Scotland; while the UK Government had failed in its attempt, because the amending legislation had twice been blocked in the House of Lords.

In Wales, the Assembly has made very little policy difference. Business Secretary, Andrew Davies, was quite candid about this in a debate on the lack of Assembly law making in March:

> At this stage of our development, we have originated little legislation of our own. Therefore, we are largely dependent on Whitehall and the European Union, in terms of the timetable for drafting Orders ... In our early months of operation, we have largely been constrained by forces outside our control.[6]

The greatest policy issue during the year in Wales was the long running battle to persuade the UK Government to provide additional funding to support the EU Objective One programme for West Wales and the Valleys. Some Welsh officials believe that the Treasury's eventual change of heart, announced in July with the conclusions of the Comprehensive Spending Review, would not have been won without the existence of the Assembly and the additional political leverage it gave to the opposition parties.

The concluding sections of chapter 3 underline the weakness of the Welsh Assembly and its inability to diverge significantly from the UK policy line. The main policy achievement, through Welsh clauses in the UK Care Standards Bill, was the creation of a Children's Commissioner for Wales. A lesser achievement was the extension in the Assembly's budget of free eye tests to ethnic minorities, the hearing impaired and those with single vision. Two other policy issues from the first year bring home the Assembly's underlying weakness. On GM foods, the Cabinet and the Assembly wanted to maintain a GM-free Wales, but received legal advice that they had no powers to enforce such a policy. On performance-related pay for teachers, the legal advice to the Executive suggested a similar lack of power, although closer inquiry suggested a possible alternative avenue. But the Education Secretary, Rosemary Butler, was content to follow the UK Government's policy for England, despite the reservations of the Assembly's Education Committee.

---

6 Assembly *Record*, 21 March 2000.

NOT A STABLE SETTLEMENT

The final conclusion to emerge from this analysis of the first year is that devolution has not reached a steady state. This is meant to be a stronger statement than the truism that the settlement will continue to evolve. In Northern Ireland, in Wales, even in Scotland, there is serious questioning about the adequacy of the settlement; while in the English regions, everything is still to play for.

The settlement in Northern Ireland is particularly precarious. Chapter 4 paints a stark picture of the fragility of the new institutions, and the many factors which could yet undermine them. Continuing battles over policing, flags and decommissioning, against a background of worsening paramilitary violence, could lead to the re-imposition of direct rule. But even without the troubles, it may be that the involuntary coalition which lies at the heart of the consociational model enshrined in the Belfast agreement is so unworkable that the Northern Ireland Executive has been set up to fail. That is the view of at least one expert commentator:

> Devolution can only work with power-sharing if there is a supply of understanding, goodwill, and self-restraint amongst parties in the province that is unprecedented ... they are being asked to make something work that on its face is unworkable.[7]

Chapter 4 contains similar gloomy predictions, including the warning of one adviser that 'the Executive itself will be an involuntary coalition with internal political tensions that could degenerate into continual attrition between and within unionist and nationalist blocs'. But it also contains the interesting observation that one way in which it might be made to work is by the Office of First and Deputy First Minister accruing more and more power, to overcome the centrifugal tendencies in the rest of the Executive. The chapter records how this is gradually starting to happen. If the trend continues the four-party coalition would become centralised into a working coalition of the UUP and SDLP, focused on the Office of First and Deputy First Minister — a 'government-within-a-government', which might not be very democratic, but could be one way of getting the executive to work.

In Wales, fundamental questions are also being asked about the institutional design. Few members of the National Assembly believe that it has sufficient powers to make a difference. The questioning goes right through to the top. During the first year of the Assembly's life, Ron Davies, its creator, then Lord Elis-Thomas, its Presiding Officer, and lastly Rhodri Morgan as the new Leader have all expressed doubts about the design and functioning

---

[7] Alan J. Ward, 'Devolution: Labour's strange constitutional 'design'', in J. Jowell and D. Oliver, eds, *The Changing Constitution* 4th edn, Oxford Univ Press, 2000, at p 134.

of the new body. Lord Elis-Thomas has been the most outspoken, arguing in a major speech:

> It is not based on any clear legislative principle ...We are not at the beginning of a new constitution for Wales. We are at the beginning of the end of the old constitution ...We have the least that could be established at the time. We shouldn't say that a political fix is a national constitution. It is time we looked for more.[8]

Ron Davies has always said that devolution is a process, not an event. Since stepping down as leader of the Wales Labour Party he has become more open about his wish for the Assembly to acquire legislative powers. Chapter 3 suggests that the first year of devolution saw the Assembly turn itself into a constitutional convention: the convention which, as Rhodri Morgan has observed, the Scots had before devolution, but the Welsh missed out on. The next step in the process is Rhodri Morgan's review, starting in autumn 2000, of the workings of the Assembly, in co-operation with the other political parties. One issue will be Lord Elis-Thomas' call for a much clearer separation of powers between the Executive and his own Office of the Presiding Officer, which is not formally separate but has become the defender of the Assembly in its role of checking and scrutinising the actions of the Executive. But this will have to be achieved within the confines of the Government of Wales Act. Rhodri Morgan made clear when announcing the review that: '...we act within that Act and I am not eager to discuss whether we should amend it...'[9] Any wider review of the statutory framework and of the Assembly's powers is unlikely to take place until the Assembly's second term.

The UK Government will expect the model of executive devolution to be properly tested and demonstrably found wanting before Wales comes back for more. The real test for Wales will come when the Assembly has developed a set of policies and proposals which require primary legislation from Westminster. The whole scheme of executive devolution is predicated on Westminster continuing to legislate for Wales: and on Whitehall taking account of Welsh interests each year when preparing the legislative programme, and giving the Welsh legislative time at Westminster. This was identified as the crucial stumbling block in the whole scheme, in speeches about the first year of the Assembly given in summer 2000 by two senior figures: the Presiding Officer Lord Elis-Thomas and Labour's Lord Prys Davies.[10] Only when the Assembly finds that it is not accorded sufficient

---

[8] *Wales — A New Constitution*, Welsh Governance Centre, Cardiff University, 2 March 2000.

[9] Assembly *Record* 12 July 2000.

[10] Lord Elis-Thomas, *National Assembly: A Year in Power?*, Institute of Welsh Politics, Aberystwyth, 8 July 2000; Lord Prys Davies, *The National Assembly: A year of laying the Foundations*, lecture to the Law Society at Llanelli National Eisteddfod, 9 August 2000. Both are cited extensively in the Institute of Welsh Affairs quarterly monitoring report, *Devolution Looks Ahead: May to August 2000*, published on the Constitution Unit website www.ucl.ac.uk/constitution-unit/.

legislative time or is not allowed sufficient headroom in Westminster legislation to develop its own distinctive policies, will Wales be able to mount a strong campaign that it needs to be given legislative powers.

The spark for such a campaign may emerge from Rhodri Morgan's review, due to report by about September 2001; but the fuse is likely to be slow burning, and linked to the electoral cycle. Ron Davies has been reported as thinking ahead to the Assembly's second term:

> The crucial time for Labour, he predicts, will be 2003, when the party will have to have a clear statement on how it sees the Assembly progressing. After that, he pinpoints a general election around 2005 as the appropriate time to seek a mandate from the people for substantial alterations needed to the current settlement.[11]

But Plaid Cymru's internal thinking suggests that it may not be until the third term that the Assembly is ready to assume legislative powers:

> We cannot lay claim or plan for legislative devolution until we have mastered executive devolution and pushed at its boundary. In ten years time, with a significant increase in staff, we may have accumulated enough legislative experience to be able to claim the expertise possessed by Scotland to successfully operate legislative devolution. At present we cannot make such claims.[12]

What links these two statements is the prediction that legislative devolution in Wales is no longer a matter of if, but when. And chapter 8 shows that they also link to public opinion in Wales, where 43 per cent of the people want the Assembly to be given law-making powers, against 28 per cent who feel that it should continue with its existing more limited range of powers.

The model Wales will aspire to is Scotland. The Scottish Parliament has substantial legislative powers; and the first year legislative programme in Edinburgh shows the parliament beginning to exercise them to the full. But even in Scotland, calls have been made for extra powers. The Scottish opinion polls, reported in chapter 8, show most Scots disappointed in the performance of their parliament; and a surprising 62 per cent concluding that the parliament needs extra powers to make a real difference to their lives. In coming to this conclusion, they are echoing some of the end-of-year writing on the performance of the Scottish Parliament in its first year. Thus, Professor Lindsay Paterson, writing under the headline 'The majority see the only route to further progress in a stronger parliament than we have', concludes his article:

> The utopian dreams which always underlaid the whole project for home rule are now turning not into disillusionment but to the demand for a parliament with substantial extra powers.'[13]

[11] Reported in the *Western Mail*, 15 August 2000.
[12] Jocelyn Davies AM, *Developing the Functions of the Assembly*, internal Plaid Cymru policy paper, April 2000.
[13] *The Scotsman*, 14 August 2000 p 12.

It remains to be seen whether, in the second year of devolution, the demand
for extra powers picks up any groundswell of support in the Scottish Parliament; and whether it starts to be linked (as it clearly is in Wales) to specific
issues where the devolution settlement does not deliver sufficient power. If it
is simply an expression of general frustration, then the grant of extra powers
may not be the answer; the difficulties may lie more in the internal workings
of the Scottish Executive or the parliament than in the extent of their formal
powers.

THE ENGLISH QUESTION

England remains the gaping hole in the devolution settlement. It is the space
where everything is still to play for. A recent report on the options for
regional government in England speaks of the chaos in the middle of English
governance, and concludes that the current organisational landscape is
unbalanced and unlikely to prove stable.[14] Chapter 5 explains the reasons
why. The final sections of this concluding chapter come back to the English
Question.

In constitutional terms, the English Question is best approached as a series
of questions about English representation in our new quasi-federal system:

- Should there be an English parliament to match the Scottish Parliament
  and the Welsh and Northern Ireland Assemblies?
- Should England instead be divided into eight or so regions, each with its
  own assembly, which in population terms would come much closer to the
  size of the devolved assemblies?
- Or, should Westminster be adapted to give greater voice to English
  concerns, without going as far as creating a separate English parliament?

An English Parliament?

An English parliament does not seem a realistic option. Those who demand
one are, in effect, demanding a full-blown federation, in which the four
historic nations would form the component parts. But England would be too
dominant. There is no successful federation in the world where one of the
parts is greater than around one-third of the whole. Nor would it meet the
demands for representation coming from the English regions: to them, an
English parliament looks like another form of London dominance.

The Campaign for an English Parliament is a political gesture, making a
political point as much as it is pressing for the establishment of a new political institution. The point is that with devolution the Scots, the Welsh, and the
Northern Irish will have a louder political voice, and the English risk losing

---

[14] Professor Alan Harding, *Is there a 'missing middle' in English Governance?*, New Local
Government Network 2000.

out. But the answer for the English may lie in adapting Westminster and Whitehall, in some of the ways discussed in chapters 6 and 7, and not in a separate English parliament.

Regional Assemblies or Elected Mayors

Regional assemblies are one of Labour's two unfulfilled pledges from their 1997 manifesto, which promised legislation to allow the people of England, region by region, to decide in a referendum whether they want directly elected regional government. Following the regional policy statement approved by the Labour Party conference in September 2000 (reproduced at page 122), similar pledges are likely in Labour's next manifesto.

Chapter 5 describes how 2000 also saw the launch of the Campaign for the English Regions, formed by the vanguard regional bodies of the North East, North West, the West Midlands and Yorkshire. The north-east is making the running, and in direct imitation of Scotland, three of the regions have established Constitutional Conventions. So far none has got beyond sloganising: there is nothing like the detailed planning about powers, functions and composition which went into the work of the Scottish Constitutional Convention. If they are serious, they will need to engage with the detail, and to persuade Labour to rethink the conditions it has proposed before any region can establish a directly elected regional assembly:

- A predominantly unitary structure in local government;
- Approval in a region-wide referendum, and
- No additional public expenditure.

Prof Alan Harding has shown how these requirements need to be revisited, since they are mutually incompatible, and are too easily seen as barriers to reform, rather than facilitators of it.[15] He has also proposed, as one of three possible alternatives, the model of city-regions. This is partly in response to the new challenge which has emerged to regional assemblies, in the form of directly elected Mayors. They are not necessarily incompatible, but there is an interesting tension between the two models. For at regional level there may not be room for two political leaders claiming to be the voice of the region, one as leader of the regional assembly and the other as the Mayor of the largest city.[16] Which model wins through may depend upon who occupies the political space first.

At present, the elected mayors look likely to get there first. The enabling provisions are in the Local Government Act 2000. The Government wants to see more, and other cities could opt for elected mayors from May 2001

---

[15] *Ibid* pp 26-27.
[16] Although in countries such as France and Spain they have high profile Mayors co-existing with a regional tier of government.

onwards. Regional assemblies are a long way further back. Elected mayors
as the leaders of the biggest local authority in the region may prove to be one
more voice that discovers little interest in moving on to a regional assembly,
once they realise that it would be a countervailing source of power over
which they would have less control. Elected mayors may prefer, with encouragement from government, to become the leaders of networks of regional
and sub-regional governance in which they would be amongst the biggest
players.

Westminster as a Proxy for an English Parliament

Chapter 7 describes how Westminster is gradually coming to terms with the
impact of devolution. The changes so far have been minimalist and piecemeal, with no leadership and no clear sense of parliament's new role. But in a
series of tentative and fumbling steps, Westminster is gradually developing
its role as a quasi-federal parliament. This includes operating as a proxy for
an English Parliament, within the wider shell of the Union Parliament.
Pre-devolution it was clear when Westminster was operating as the legislature for Scotland, Wales, and Northern Ireland; post-devolution it will also
need to become clearer when Westminster is operating in English mode.
Chapter 7 is the first attempt to map the extent of English business at Westminster, and over the next few years we will try to record more comprehensively how Westminster operates as an English parliament. English business
is transacted through the work of the Select Committees, many of which are
already *de facto* English Committees; through the proposal to revive the
Standing Committee on Regional Affairs (which will be open only to English
MPs); through Questions to ministers on English matters; and through Westminster Hall, which provides a further forum for English debates.

What is missing from this list, at present, is English legislation. The Procedure Committee, in its report on the Procedural Consequences of Devolution,
recommended a special procedure for English or England and Wales bills,
which the Government rejected.[17] In July 2000, the proposal was revived by
the Conservative Commission on Strengthening Parliament, chaired by
Professor Philip Norton (Lord Norton of Louth). In his draft manifesto,
William Hague has summarised the proposal as 'English votes on English
laws.'[18] In the coming years, we will seek to identify how much of the legislation passed by Westminster can be analysed as 'English' or 'England and
Wales', and so might be eligible for special procedures involving only
English MPs.

---

[17] Procedure Committee, *The Procedural Consequences of Devolution*, HC 185, 19 May 1999.
[18] Conservative Party, *Believing in Britain*, September 2000, p 23: 'We must have English votes on
English laws. Only English MPs should be able to take part in the decisive stages of legislation that
affect only England and only English and Welsh MPs on laws that affect only England and Wales.'

Another issue to watch is who attends these English debates. Will Scottish and Welsh Members stay away from debates on English matters which are of no interest to them? And will any follow the self-denying ordinance set by Tam Dalyell and decline to vote on such issues? If all the Scottish, Welsh, and Northern Ireland MPs were to follow Dalyell's example, William Hague's pledge of English votes on English laws would have been achieved, but by a new convention rather than making the change by law.

Chapter 7 also reminds us about the importance of second chambers in territorial representation. In a quasi-federal Britain, one obvious role for a reformed House of Lords would be to represent the nations and regions, as second chambers in federal systems represent the states and the provinces. The Wakeham Commission on Lords Reform came down against a full-blown federal solution, but recommended that a minority of the members of a reformed second chamber (ranging from 12 to 35 per cent) should be elected to represent the nations and regions. The proportion of elected members may be too small, but the principle — that the second chamber could play an important role in helping to bind together the newly devolved nations and regions with the centre — is surely right. Another strand to our research on devolution and Westminster will be to study whether the Lords, in developing their role as guardian of the constitution, also come to see themselves as guardians of the devolution settlement.

THE DYNAMICS OF DEVOLUTION

This chapter has come full circle back to Westminster, the creator of the devolved institutions, because we believe that devolution will have a profound impact on all the institutions of the British state. The devolved governments and assemblies are changing before our eyes as they grow into fully fledged institutions; the changes in Westminster and Whitehall are less visible and working their way through much more slowly, but they will be equally profound. Devolution will require changes in the organs of central government, and in the governing arrangements for England, as much as in the devolved nations themselves.

What is striking in this report on the first year of devolution is the absence of any strong sense or vision in the government of how the centre needs to change. The greatest challenge facing the political parties as they sit down to write their manifestos for the next election is to articulate a vision of how the UK is going to reshape itself in the light of devolution. That includes a vision for the parts devolution has not yet reached: in particular the largest part, the nation of England, and the central part, the institutions of central government in Westminster and Whitehall.

Index